MAKING A PLACE FOR OURSELVES

MAKING A PLACE FOR OURSELVES

The Black Hospital Movement 1920–1945

Vanessa Northington Gamble

New York Oxford
OXFORD UNIVERSITY PRESS
1995

Oxford University Press

Oxford New York Toronto
Delhi Bombay Calcutta Madras Karachi
Kuala Lumpur Singapore Hong Kong Tokyo
Nairobi Dar es Salaam Cape Town
Melbourne Auckland Madrid

and associated companies in
Berlin Ibadan

Published by Oxford University Press, Inc.
200 Madison Avenue, New York, New York 10016

Library of Congress Cataloging-in-Publication Data
Gamble, Vanessa Northington.
Making a place for ourselves : the Black hospital movement,
1920–1945 / Vanessa Northington Gamble.
p. cm.
Includes bibliographical references and index.
ISBN 0-19-507889-6
1. Afro-Americans—Hospitals—History—20th century. I. Title.
RA981.A45G363 1995
362.1'1'08996073—dc20
93-617

2 4 6 8 9 7 5 3 1

Printed in the United States of America
on acid-free paper

To the memory of my grandmother,
Reverend Cora Northington
and
to the memory of my mother,
Carrissa Northington Gamble.

They never let me know that the odds
were against me and always encouraged
me to make a place for myself.

I miss them.

Acknowledgments

The book is done. Now comes the difficult part: thanking all those individuals who assisted me in writing it. I wish that I had the space to thank all the people who provided assistance, but unfortunately I can only name a few or the length of these acknowledgments would match the text. To my friends and colleagues whose names do not appear below, please do not take offense. I assure you that your efforts are much appreciated.

Financial support for this project came from a faculty grant from the Graduate School of the University of Wisconsin and the Rockefeller Archives Center. The Publication Grant Program of the National Library of Medicine and the Travel to Collections Program of the National Endowment for the Humanities also provided financial assistance. Portions of Chapters 4 and 5 appeared earlier as "The Provident Hospital Project: An Experiment in Race Relations and Medical Education," *Bulletin of the History of Medicine* 65 (1991): 457–75 and are reproduced here with the permission of the Johns Hopkins University Press.

The tedious chore of tracking down sources for this book was greatly eased by the work of archivists and librarians from the Cleveland Health Sciences Library, the Duke University Library, the Fisk University Library, the Moorland-Spingarn Research Center of Howard University, the Library of Congress, the National Archives, the Rockefeller Archive Center, the Tuskegee University Library, the University of Chicago, the Francis A. Countway Library of the Harvard Medical School, and the Western Reserve Historical Library. I especially want to thank Glen Jenkins, Ellen Gartrell, Ann Allen

Shockley, Beth Howse, Esme Bhan, Tom Rosenbaum, Richard J. Wolfe, and Daniel T. Williams. I am also grateful to Dr. and Mrs. Ulysses G. Mason for sharing their time and memories with me.

My research benefited from the research of several graduate students: Diane Edwards, Judy Houck, Dawn Corley, and Jennifer Munger. Sarah K.A. Pfatteicher bore the brunt of the monotonous aspects of this project. She responded with her usual aplomb and good humor. In the course of writing this book, I also had to call upon the exceptional secretarial skills of Carolyn Hackler and Stephanie Sams.

Todd L. Savitt, Kenneth Kusmer, and Brenda Gayle Plummer read parts of the manuscript and made important suggestions. Some friends went beyond the call of duty, even though I know at times that I stretched the bonds of friendship. Harold Cook, Bonnie Ellen Blustein, Jennifer Gunn, and Ellen Fitzpatrick found time in their busy schedules to read every word of this manuscript. They also had to handle the periodic crises that developed as I tried to finish the book. Christine Ruggere, Jarvis McCarther, Linda Earle, Luis Hernandez, and Bernice Siegel always let me know that they were only a phone call away. They believed in me and this project even when I had my doubts. Jim Cord provided me with a refuge at a crucial time in the writing of this manuscript. It definitely did help to be near a beach.

This book began as a dissertation under the direction of Charles E. Rosenberg and Rosemary A. Stevens. I owe them an immeasurable debt. When I was a graduate student, they generously offered guidance and advice. I am glad to learn that the transition from student to faculty did not mean the loss of their support and wisdom. When I was looking for a job a few years ago, Rosemary advised me to go to a place where I would be nurtured as a junior scholar—I did not expect it to be in Wisconsin! Judith Walzer Leavitt made my decision to move to the Midwest easier than I had anticipated. She made it very clear that I and the issues that I care deeply about would have a home in the Department of the History of Medicine at the University of Wisconsin School of Medicine. She has been a mentor, but more important, she has become a friend. Now if only she could do something about the winters.

Finally, I would like to thank Joel E. Davidson whose love, support, and good humor sustained me during the last months of this project. Joel, you wanted to be a part of this book. You are.

Contents

Introduction, *xi*

ONE Roots of the Black Hospital Reform Movement, *3*

TWO At the Vanguard: The National Medical Association and the National Hospital Association, *35*

THREE "Where Shall We Work and Whom Are We to Serve?": The Battle for the Tuskegee Veterans Hospital, *70*

FOUR Black Hospitals and White Philanthropy, *105*

FIVE "Progressive Disappointment and Defeat": The Provident Hospital Project, *131*

SIX Cleveland—A Black Hospital at Last, *151*

Conclusion: The Black Hospital—A Vanishing Medical Institution, *182*

Manuscript Collections, *197*

Notes, *199*

Index, *245*

Introduction

As a child growing up in the late 1950s and early 1960s in predominantly black West Philadelphia, Mercy-Douglass Hospital, a black hospital, was very much a part of my life. I knew and visited people who received care there. I vividly remember seeing black physicians in their white coats taking care of patients, and I imagined that one day I too would work at Mercy-Douglass Hospital. Becoming a physician was a childhood dream, and I thought that one day I would be employed at the hospital where black doctors worked. For most of the twentieth century, before the strides made by the civil rights movement and the establishment of affirmative action programs, most black physicians trained and practiced and many black patients received care in black hospitals such as Mercy-Douglass. These hospitals were vital and important institutions within the African-American community. In 1919, some 118 black hospitals existed in the United States. In 1944, there were 124 in operation. By 1993 the number of historically black hospitals had declined to 8. Most black physicians now work and train in predominantly white institutions. I did fulfill my childhood dream of becoming a physician, but when it came time for me to do a residency I entered a program at a predominantly white medical center in New England. In fact, Mercy-Douglass Hospital had closed in 1973, a year before I began my medical education.[1]

When I went to medical school I did not attend either Meharry Medical College or Howard University School of Medicine, the two existing black medical schools. Nor, for that matter, did many of the other black medical students who matriculated in the 1970s and

1980s. Whereas in 1948 only 25 percent of the African-American students entering medical school enrolled in predominantly white institutions, by 1968 the figure was 47 percent, by 1983 it was 61 percent, and by 1990 it had grown to 84 percent. In contrast to earlier generations of black physicians, my cohorts and I, and the black medical students who followed us, are not as dependent on black medical institutions for our professional survival and advancement.[2]

The range of options available to us is much wider than that available to Dr. Lillian Atkins Moore in 1923. Moore, a senior medical student at the Woman's Medical College of Pennsylvania, applied for an internship at the college's hospital on the strength of apparently unimpeachable credentials. She had been a good student, winning the freshman anatomy prize, and had been elected secretary of her senior class. Despite her achievements, she was rejected for the internship solely because she was black, ironically by an institution that had been founded in response to the sexual discrimination that women encountered in medicine. Dr. Jessie W. Pryor, medical director at the hospital, freely admitted that race had been the deciding factor in the hospital's action. She informed Moore:

> I had been told that we could not possibly undertake to give you a service here. We are all your good friends and it is a most unpleasant thing to have to tell you that just because you are colored we can't arrange to take you comfortably into the hospital. I am quite sure that most of the interns who come to us next year will not give us as good work as you are capable of doing.

Dr. Pryor did offer to help her get an appointment—at one of the "colored" hospitals. Moore finally secured a position at Douglass Hospital, the precursor to Mercy-Douglass. Her predicament underscores the importance that black medical institutions once had to the careers of black health-care professionals.[3]

Although I never did work at Mercy-Douglass, the hospital had an impact on my life in another way. In December 1979, I wrote a graduate seminar paper on the founding of that hospital for Professor Rosemary A. Stevens at the University of Pennsylvania, thus beginning my work on the history of black hospitals. When I tell people about my work they frequently reply, "I never knew that there were black hospitals." The lack of awareness about these institutions was poignantly and graphically pointed out to me by a friend on the staff at Howard University Hospital. That institution is the successor to Freedmen's Hospital, which was established by the Freedmen's Bureau to take care of former slaves who had migrated to Washington, D.C. during and after the Civil War. While lecturing to a group of medical students about the history of their own institution, my friend discovered, to his dismay, that several of them assumed that the hospital had taken its name from a wealthy Jewish philanthropist!

Since a black hospital was very much a part of my life as I was growing up, I used to find this unfamiliarity with black hospitals puzzling. Three factors explain the lack of awareness among the general public. First, it is difficult for many people to reconcile their views of medicine as a value-free profession with the fact that issues of race and racism have played a significant role in the development of American medicine. Second, the fact that so few historically black hospitals remain has made them virtually invisible. Finally, scholars in the history of American medicine and African-American history have, until recently, paid scant attention to issues of race and American medicine. The work of Darlene Clark Hine, Todd L. Savitt, David McBride, and Edward H. Beardsley has done much to remedy the gap, but more research needs to be done.[4]

This book examines an important, but not widely chronicled, event at an intersection of African-American history and American medical history—the black hospital movement. Black physicians associated with the two leading black medical societies, the National Medical Association (NMA) and the National Hospital Association (NHA), initiated the movement in the 1920s in order to upgrade the medical and educational programs at black hospitals. These doctors recognized that their careers depended on access to hospitals, and feared that changes in medical care and hospital practice, including the growing importance of hospital accreditation and standardization, would lead to the elimination of black hospitals and, with it, the future of the black medical profession. The history of the black hospital movement shows how black physicians made a place for themselves within the profession of medicine between 1920 and 1945, a time when few of them had options beyond the separate, but never equal, black medical world. The medical societies, medical schools, and hospitals of this world may have been peripheral to mainstream American medicine, but, as the case of Dr. Moore demonstrates, the survival of the black medical profession was inextricably linked to their existence.

Between 1870 and 1920, the American hospital evolved from a benevolent institution that served lower-class patients and elite physicians to a medical workshop that served patients of all classes and a broader cross section of physicians. This modern hospital was to become central to medical education, medical care, and clinical investigation. Medical historians such as Rosemary A. Stevens, Charles E. Rosenberg, David Rosner, and Morris Vogel have examined this transformation, attributing this change to factors internal to medicine (such as the rise of scientific medicine and reforms in medical education) as well as factors external to it (such as urbanization and industrialization). These studies go beyond earlier histories of hospitals that focused on the evolution of one institution or that viewed hospitals solely as value-neutral medical establishments. The historians stress that hospitals, in addition to being medical institutions, are social institutions that reflect and reinforce the beliefs and values of the wider society. Another important contribution to the social history of medicine is Virginia Drachman's study of New England Hospital for Women and Children, in which she analyzes the forces that have influenced the development of women physicians and their hospitals. However, none of this recent scholarship examines, in any detail, the dilemmas faced by black physicians, nurses, and patients.[5]

In this study we shall see how the changes associated with the rise of the modern hospital affected African-American physicians and how they responded to these changes at a time when racial discrimination severely restricted their options. We will learn much about the hopes, fears, and aspirations of these physicians and about their views of medical practice. We shall see that black medical leaders adopted the ethos of scientific medicine, although they recognized that its adoption would lead to the closing of the prototypical black community hospital—small, proprietary, and without training programs. However, they hoped that their activities would increase the number of first-class hospitals—large, modern facilities with approved training programs.

The campaign to improve the status of black hospitals was led by men, and consequently, the focus of this book is on the experiences of black male physicians and not on those of their female colleagues. The contributions of women were important in establishing and maintaining black hospitals. Women led fund-raising campaigns for the institutions, made significant donations, worked as physicians and nurses, ran hospital nurse-training programs and, in some cases, even established hospitals. Women were willing workers for the movement, but because of sexual discrimination, no women became visible leaders and spokespersons in the organizations associated with the hospital reform movement. Thus, I, a black woman physician, find myself in the peculiar situation of writing a history in which the voices of women are for the most not heard.[6]

This book concentrates on the activities of the hospital reformers in the historically black hospitals, that is, facilities that had a traditional mandate to serve black people. Those hospitals have been of two broad types: segregated and black-controlled. Segregated black hospitals were facilities established by whites to serve African Americans exclusively, operating predominantly, but not invariably, in the

South. The civil rights legislation of the 1960s abolished—at least in legal terms—these racially exclusive institutions. Black-controlled facilities were founded by black physicians, fraternal organizations, and churches, generally not as exclusively black enterprises, but as interracial ones that would not discriminate. There is also a third type of black hospital, which I call "demographically determined," established neither to serve African Americans nor founded by them, but evolving from white hospitals progressively into black institutions because of a rise in black populations surrounding the hospitals. The foremost example is Harlem Hospital, which opened its doors in 1887, long before the black migration uptown began. When blacks began to move into Harlem in large numbers, the hospital's admissions reflected the change in community composition. The hospital reformers did not concentrate on this third category because most of those hospitals, during the time of the black hospital movement, barred black physicians or only admitted a few. Reformers directed their efforts instead toward those institutions to which they had access.

The black hospital reformers recognized that the support and financial assistance of the white community were crucial for the success of their venture, and their activities often brought them into contact with white philanthropies, governmental agencies, and professional medical and hospital organizations. Thus, this examination of the black hospital movement also illuminates the attitudes of those white Americans towards black physicians, nurses, patients, and their hospitals. This study provides insight into the rationale behind white support of black institutions and the justifications used to exclude African-American health professionals from majority institutions, and also makes plain that there were consequences to white financial support of African-American institutions.

Any understanding of the black hospital movement is, of course, rooted in an analysis of the internal dynamics of the African-American community itself, both locally and nationally. The ability of particular communities to support a hospital was often tied to factors specific to that community such as the size of the black population, the existence of a large black middle class, the number of black health-care professionals, the extent of support from other black institutions, and the degree of racism in hospital care that was thought to exist.

The reform movement also became entangled in contemporary racial politics that were not geographically bound. Physicians associated with the movement viewed the improvement of separate black medical institutions as the key to their professional survival. Asserting that their programs represented a practical response to the racial realities of American life, the black hospital movement, as they saw it, was a self-help endeavor. As one physician put it, "If they don't make a place for us, we should make a place for ourselves." Integration, these physicians argued, was a slow process, and the advancement—and health—of the race could not afford to wait for integration's eventual development. But, the black community—lay and medical—did not unanimously support such separatist thinking. Integrationists rejected the establishment of separate black institutions by either black or white Americans, regarding the call for separate black hospitals not as self-help but as self-imposed segregation. They pushed for the integration of hospital facilities and argued that the "place" for black physicians should not be in Jim-Crow institutions. The demarcation, however, between separatists and integrationists over the role and necessity of black hospitals was not always well defined. Organizations such as the National Medical Association and the National Hospital Association, which were at the vanguard of separatism, simultaneously called for the integration of municipal hospitals. Different strategies were therefore employed for different situations. In addition, specific individuals at different times took both separatist and integrationist stances. Because of this lack of clarity, I think that it is more useful to think of the two views not as iron-clad political ideologies, but as fluid, if divergent, strategies for black advancement. Conflicts, divisions, and negotiations within the black community over these competing strategies cannot be minimized, because they were major factors influencing not only the establishment of hospitals but of other black institutions as well.[7]

Tensions between integrationism and separatism as strategies for professional advancement also affected women physicians. They too struggled with the question of the role of separate institutions. Thus, at first glance, it may be tempting to borrow the model that women's historians have advanced to analyze the situation of women physicians and apply it to African-American physicians. However, issues of race created unique problems. For example, Virginia G. Drachman points out that at the end of the nineteenth century opportunities for women to train in previously all-male institutions began to expand. But her assessment applies, for the most part, only to white women. During the very same period, black women and men encountered increasing obstacles in their attempts to enter mainstream medicine. The turn of the century brought the solidification of Jim Crow laws in the South and escalating racial tensions in the North. Furthermore, legalized segregation not only limited the professional options of African Americans, but restricted the medical care available to them. And there is a broader issue here, too. While sexism and racism were both sanctioned by law and by custom, and while the two intersected in ways that often reinforced both, there were crucial differences between those forms of oppression. The strategies and responses of black men and women to racism were by no means identical to those of white women to sexism. Historical models developed to analyze one cannot be mechanically transferred to the other.[8]

This book analyzes the black hospital movement at both the national and local levels, and focuses on the movement in three communities—Tuskegee, Alabama; Chicago, Illinois; and Cleveland, Ohio. When I first began work on this book I soon discovered that most of the records of black hospitals had been lost or destroyed; therefore, their availability played a major role in choosing the communities included for examination. But, there were substantive reasons for their selection as well. Histories of black hospitals within the three communities illustrate more general themes and issues, and an examination of the black hospital movement in them should not be seen as three free-standing case studies. Although local conditions and forces influenced the direction of the hospital movement in each of the communities, broader factors were also at work. In Tuskegee we learn about the attitudes and policies of the federal government toward black hospitals and the black medical profession. In Chicago we can explore the programs of white philanthropists, how they came to clash with a segment of the black population, and how these conflicts shaped approaches to black medical education. In Cleveland we will be able to see the impact of the integration of a municipal hospital on the black hospital movement.

Chapter One discusses the origins of black hospitals and the roots of the hospital reform movement. Chapter Two describes the work and strategies of the National Medical Association and the National Hospital Association to improve black hospitals. As we shall see, the controversy in Harlem over whether a black hospital should be built demonstrates that not all black physicians supported the activities of these medical societies. Chapter Three explores the factors underlying the decision of the federal government to establish a national black veterans hospital in Tuskegee, Alabama, and analyzes the successful struggle of the black community to place black physicians and nurses at the facility. Chapter Four studies the activities of three foundations—the Duke Endowment, the Julius Rosenwald Fund, and the General Education Board—with regard to black hospital reform. Chapters Five and Six return to an examination of the black hospital movement in specific communities, Chicago and Cleveland, respectively. The Chicago study traces a novel approach to black hospital reform: the partnership of a black hospital, Provident Hospital, with a white university, the University of Chicago. The Cleveland chapter analyzes several attempts to establish a black hospital. Ironically, success occurred only after the city's municipal hospital opened its doors to black physicians and nurses. The book's conclusion assesses the impact of the black hospital movement, and discusses the status of the contemporary black hospital, using the historical perspective developed throughout the book.

This is a history of black hospitals. But it is also a history of race and the American hospital. Many historians of medicine erroneously perceive research in black medical history as standing apart from general American medical history, and my work is rather narrowly regarded as a study of black physicians and their hospitals. Yes, this book is about black physicians and their hospitals, but it is about more than just that. It uses the black hospital as a prism to understand how issues of race and racism affected the development of the American hospital system. The reader will also find out a great deal about the attitudes and beliefs of white Americans. By concentrating on the situation of African Americans, I am not contending that other groups did not suffer from discrimination. By choosing this focus and omitting explicit reference to other ethnic groups, I do not intend to engage in what one historian has criticized as "victimizing one-upsmanship." Rather, I hope that readers will find in my work an approach that may prove useful in the much-needed study of other ethnic groups. By focusing on issues of race and racism I intend not only to provide a fuller picture of the spectrum of American medicine than has been portrayed thus far, but to raise questions and challenge general assumptions about the history of American medicine. Race has been, and continues to be, a fundamental issue in American medicine, as it is in other American institutions. Historians, no matter what their field, must not be allowed to forget this.[9]

MAKING A PLACE FOR OURSELVES

ONE

Roots of the Black Hospital Reform Movement

❧

In a 1900 address, Dr. Daniel Hale Williams, the founder of Chicago's Provident Hospital and Nurse Training School, the nation's first black-controlled hospital, urged other African Americans to build their own hospitals. The existing racial discrimination against black physicians, nurses, and patients had prompted his call. In his 23 January 1900 speech before the Phillis Wheatley Club of Nashville, Tennessee, Williams contended,

> In view of this cruel ostracism, affecting so vitally the race, our duty seems plain. Institute Hospitals and Training Schools. Let us no longer sit idly and inanely deploring existing conditions. Let us not waste time trying to effect changes or modifications in the institutions unfriendly to us, but rather let us seek to promote the doctrine of helping and stimulating our race.

During the last decade of the nineteenth century and the first two decades of the twentieth century, various segments of the black community did indeed take Williams's advice and create hospitals for themselves. Members of the white community also opened black hospitals. The number of these institutions grew rapidly. In 1912, 63 existed; seven years later, 118 black hospitals were in operation. Racial discrimination, white self-interest, black professional concerns, divergent strategies for black social advancement, and changes in hospital care and medical practice all played major roles in the development of these institutions. Any understanding of the character and goals of the later black hospital reform movement must be rooted in an analysis of the evolution of black hospitals.[1]

The early-nineteenth-century American hospital differed markedly from its mid-twentieth-century successor. The nineteenth-century institution was peripheral to the provision of medical care, medical education, and medical research. It operated primarily as a traditional welfare institution that cared for a variety of indigent and dependent persons, including (but by no means restricted to) the sick. Hospitals offered limited therapeutics and functioned, in part, to maintain the social order by isolating the socially marginal and by serving as loci for moral as well as medical care. Poverty and dependence were the main criteria for admission. Municipal hospitals, such as New York City's Bellevue and Philadelphia's General, began their institutional lives as medical departments in almshouses. The social elite in many cities also established voluntary or not-for-profit hospitals as charities to keep the "worthy poor" out of the almshouse and to protect them from the stigma and demoralizing influence of the almshouse. Principles of Christian stewardship regarding upper-class obligations to the poor encouraged the development of many voluntary hospitals and even governed their day-to-day operations. For example, the certification of one's worthiness by a lay trustee, not a physician's diagnosis, was the primary prerequisite to admission. The home served as the primary site of medical care for persons with resources and roots in the community. Hospital care offered no therapeutic advantages over domestic care; indeed, most people tried to avoid hospitals because of their identification as charitable institutions and because they feared contracting hospital-originated infections and fevers.[2]

In the early nineteenth century, hospitals also played an insignificant role in the professional development of the average practitioner. Medical education did not require clinical training in hospitals, and contemporary medical practice did not demand that physicians serve internships or residencies or hold hospital appointments. The average physician could complete his or her medical education and have a successful practice without setting foot in a hospital. Hospital appointments were part of the career paths of a small group of elite, urban physicians, rather than of the general medical profession. Furthermore, it was the values and interests of lay trustees that dominated hospital decision-making, rather than those of the physician.

Early in the nineteenth century, communities, especially in the South, organized institutions to provide medical care to sick black people. The creation of slave hospitals represented one response. Those rudimentary facilities usually contained only a few beds and were located in buildings separate from the main slave quarters. They provided an efficient means to care for sick slaves because all medicines could be housed in one location. The facilities also isolated slaves with contagious diseases. A Tennessee physician urged in 1853,

> Every plantation should be provided with a hospital. . . . By bringing all the sick into the same house, the convenience of the physician is subserved, the time of the nurses economized, and better attendance secured. There should always be two rooms, so that the sexes may be kept separate, and there should be a water closet attached to each room. These rooms require to be close and warm. . . .
>
> The hospital should be located near the dwelling of the owner or overseer, surrounded by shade trees, kept neat and clean, and conducted in a manner to cheer and enliven the drooping spirits of the sick. Single beds should be used, with good mattresses, and made as comfortable as possible.

Such hospitals, however, only existed on the larger plantations. Slaveowners, their families, and their overseers usually staffed them. Physicians were only called in for the most serious cases. The hospitals were also frequently tended by slave women whose tasks included nursing, cleaning, and cooking.[3]

A few free-standing hospitals and infirmaries for African Americans, free and bond, also existed in the antebellum South. Those infirmaries, many of which had been established by physicians, operated away from the plantations and provided, for a fee, medical attention, board, and lodging. Georgia Infirmary, established in 1832 in Savannah, "for the relief and protection of aged and afflicted Africans," was the first hospital established by whites for the care of blacks. It had an endowment to provide care for free Africans, but owners were financially responsible for the care of their slaves. Twenty years later in the same city, three white physicians established an infirmary "for the reception of negroes requiring medical and surgical treatment." The infirmary accepted maternity cases, but not patients with contagious diseases. An advertisement for the infirmary described it as a "well-appointed establishment" with competent nurses, comfortable beds, well-ventilated wards, extensive pleasure grounds, and good food. Another institution, Mississippi State Hospital in Natchez, cared only for slaves and charged their owners a dollar a day for its services.[4]

These hospitals were not common. Few institutions in antebellum America existed specifically for the care of African Americans, and most medical facilities in the South excluded them. Contemporary racial customs and mores also restricted black access to hospital care in the North. Hospitals either denied African Americans admission or accommodated them, almost universally, in segregated wards often placed in undesirable locations such as unheated attics or damp basements. At Philadelphia's Pennsylvania Hospital, for example, attending physicians were unwilling to visit certain wards, particularly the black and venereal corridors. Syphilis and gonorrhea were considered to be contagious—at a time when most diseases were not thought to be—and were associated with immorality. Many whites believed that African Americans possessed intrinsic racial characteristics such as excessive sexual desire, immorality, and over-indulgence which resulted in high rates of venereal disease. A similar contempt, it appears, existed in the care of patients with black skin and those, no matter their color, with venereal disease.[5]

Emancipation left open the question as to who would assume the responsibility for the medical care of the former slaves. One mechanism was the Freedmen's Bureau, established in 1865, which temporarily filled the void by setting up hospitals in the Southern and border states. However, its medical department suffered from a lack of funding and from organizational weaknesses. Because of low pay, the Bureau could not attract physicians with superior qualifications, and turnover was high. Financial constraints also forced it to use abandoned houses and old army hospitals, rather than be able to build new facilities. Many of the facilities were not permanent, but frequently opened, closed, and relocated. The Freedmen's Bureau hospitals provided at least some medical care to the large number of dependent freedpeople who migrated from the plantations to urban areas. But the Freedmen's Bureau's efforts were grossly inadequate to meet the medical needs of five million former slaves. At its peak in September 1867, the Bureau operated forty-five hospitals with a capacity of 5,292 beds. Furthermore, the Freedmen's Bureau had been created to aid the former slaves only until local governments could do so. By October 1868, only eleven of its hospitals remained, even though most local governments had not made provisions to care for the freedpeople. Public and private hospitals in many communities continued to exclude black patients. By 1872, all of the hospitals established by the Freedmen's Bureau had closed except the one in Washington, D.C., which was allowed to remain open because the Bureau thought that the disproportionately large number of freedpeople who had fled to the city would unduly burden local institutions. A special congressional mandate allowed the facility to continue as Freedmen's Hospital, first under the auspices of the War Department, and later, under the Department of the Interior.[6]

During and following Reconstruction, the white community gradually began to supply hospital care to African Americans, usually in separate, and not equal, facilities. Historian Howard N. Rabinowitz has argued that the establishment of these segregated facilities represented an improvement over previous conditions in which African Americans had been totally excluded. African Americans now had at least some access to hospitals. Several factors spurred the establishment of these white-sponsored hospitals. Some founders expressed a genuine, if paternalistic, interest in supplying health care to black people and in offering training opportunities to black health professionals. However, white self-interest was also at work. The germ theory of disease, popularized by the end of the nineteenth century, recognized that "germs have no color line." Medical and public health journals at the turn of the century portrayed African Americans as carriers of disease who posed a threat to white people, because "bacteria have a disconcerting fashion of ignoring segregation edicts." Despite Jim Crow, the argument went, white people remained at risk from diseases of black people. An editorial in the *Atlanta Constitution* warned that residential segregation would not protect white people

> because from that segregated district negro nurses would still emerge from diseased homes, to come into our homes and hold our children in their arms; negro cooks would still bring bacilli from the segregated district into the homes of the poor and rich white Atlantan; negro chauffeurs, negro butlers, negro laborers would come from within the pale and scatter disease.

The health of black people and that of white people were inextricably linked, so, if not for humanitarian reasons then at least for self-protection, whites needed to pay attention to the medical problems of African Americans. The white community also established black hospitals in order to escape the embarrassment of entirely neglecting the black sick, but without having to take care of them in white institutions. Regardless of motive, the goal behind the establishment of these hospitals was the same—to maintain and create a segregated hospital system.[7]

Segregated hospitals existed predominantly, but not invariably, in the South. They included Dixie Hospital and Nurse Training School, Hampton Institute, Virginia, established in 1891; MacVicar, Spelman Seminary, Atlanta, Georgia, established in 1896; St. Agnes, St. Augustine School, Raleigh, North Carolina, established in 1896; Kansas City (Missouri) General Hospital, No. 2 (Kansas City Colored), established in 1908; and St. Louis (Missouri) City Hospital, No. 2, established in 1919. Dixie Hospital and MacVicar Hospital were founded as adjuncts to two white-run educational institutions for African Americans, Hampton Institute and Spelman Seminary, respectively. The existence of nurse training schools at these institutions and the need to provide the nursing students with clinical experience provided the impetus for their establishment. As in other segregated black hospitals, Dixie Hospital and MacVicar Hospital did not allow black physicians to practice.[8]

In contrast, St. Agnes Hospital did provide access to black physicians. The hospital's founder was Sara Hunter, a white Episcopal churchwoman and wife of the principal of St. Augustine School, a black junior college. She saw providing black physicians a place in which to hospitalize their patients as part of her mission to improve the health of black people. However, black physicians had to work under the supervision of white ones: at least until 1925, all the chiefs of various services were white. Hunter had raised funds for the hospital from other members of the women's auxiliary of the Episcopal Church. On 18 October 1896, the hospital opened on the grounds of the school in a small building that had previously been a physician's residence. According to staff physician Mary Glenton, the hospital contained:

> No water in the house, except one faucet in the kitchen.
>
> No hot water, but what could be heated on the ward stoves. . . .
>
> Two small steamers for sterilizers . . . formed the operating room equipment. . . .
>
> No screens in windows or doors, and flying things innumerable, with wings small and great. . . .
>
> No plumbing anywhere—only earth closets.
>
> No Diet kitchen—the trays kept on a shelf in the kitchen.
>
> No gas for cooking nor for lighting; simply oil lamps.
>
> Not always enough food for patients; nor the proper kind for nurses and staff.

This makeshift facility was not atypical of small hospitals and infirmaries—black and white—in the late nineteenth century. The hospital, despite its rudimentary facilities, did provide a place for black physicians, nurses, and patients. It was the only hospital in the vicinity open to black patients, and many had to travel great distances to make use of its services. In 1898 two black women graduated from its nurse training school.[9]

Local governments also established separate hospitals to care for their black citizens. The push for such a facility in Kansas City, Missouri, came from the black community. In 1903, black physicians, led by Dr. Thomas C. Unthank, initiated efforts to establish a municipal hospital for African Americans because the existing one had very limited and inadequate accommodations for black patients, who often found themselves housed in the basement. The hospital also had no black staff. Unthank, an 1898 graduate of Howard University School of Medicine, had ample experience in the hospital field, having previously been involved in the founding of two small black private hospitals on both sides of the state line: in 1898 he established Douglass Hospital in Kansas City, Kansas, and in 1903 he opened Lange Hospital in Kansas City, Missouri. Unthank, in addition to his private practice, worked in Kansas City, Missouri, as an assistant city physician assigned to the city's African-American population. In this position he developed ties to City Hall that would later prove invaluable.[10]

In 1908, the city did establish a black hospital after it constructed a new municipal hospital and transferred most of the white patients to the new facility. Dr. J. Park Neal, first superintendent of the new hospital, reported that

> upon taking charge of the . . . Hospital, there were one hundred and twenty-six patients in the old hospital wards. On October 8, 1908, sixty-eight of these patients, all white, were transferred to eight wards of the new hospital. All the colored patients and those white patients suffering from tuberculosis and contagious diseases were left in the old hospital buildings for the care of all classes of colored patients and for tuberculosis and contagious diseases.

Again, we see the stigma attached to caring for black patients and those with contagious diseases. The old hospital was renamed Kansas City General Hospital, No. 2, or Kansas City Colored Hospital. The facilities at the two hospitals were by no means equal. The older hospital, built in 1873, lacked diagnostic facilities and clinical laboratories, and the funds spent on patients at the two facilities also demonstrated inequities. In 1908, costs per patient day were estimated to be $1.86 for whites and $.86 for blacks. From the city's point of view, the black hospital was not intended to provide clinical care equal to that of the white hospital, but to supply separate care.[11]

Moreover, Kansas City General Hospital, No. 2 did not initially meet the goals that the black physicians had set for professional development. Although it did provide care to indigent black patients, during its first three years of operation it had no black physicians and nurses on staff. However, in 1911 the hospital administration appointed four black physicians, including Unthank, to staff positions, selected its first black intern, and opened a training school for nurses. The hospital gradually came under black administration, but remained municipally financed and controlled. In 1914, the hospital became the first municipal hospital to be managed by African Americans when Dr. William J. Thompkins became superintendent and Mrs. Mary K. Hampton-Brown was named superintendent of nurses.

By 1924, black people had assumed responsibility for all departments of the hospital even though the city was not completely convinced of the competence of African Americans to run the facility. White physicians from Kansas City General Hospital, No. 1 continued to serve as supervisors and consultants.[12]

During its early years, Thomas C. Unthank played a major role in the direction of the hospital. In a 1924 study of black nurse training schools commissioned by the Rockefeller Foundation, Ethel Johns, an Englishwoman, described the physician's remarkable political acumen. She wrote:

> He is reported to be a "political boss" of the more benevolent Tammany type, but honest and sincere upon the whole. The feeling at the white hospital is "that without him nothing could have been done at No. 2" . . . He undoubtedly possesses executive capacity and the ability "to get things out of the City Hall."

The gradual evolution of Kansas City General Hospital, No. 2 to an institution under black administration depended, in large measure, on Unthank's political connections.[13]

A segregated municipal hospital was also organized in St. Louis. As in Kansas City, black citizens protested the fact that the existing hospital barred black physicians and housed black patients in the rear sections of two floors. African Americans contended that as taxpayers they should have wider access to publicly financed facilities. In 1919, the city purchased and renovated the vacated hospital of Barnes Medical College to serve as St. Louis City Hospital, No. 2. Several years later, Dr. W. Montague Cobb, editor of the *Journal of the National Medical Association* and a prominent medical civil rights activist, argued that the establishment of the two segregated municipal hospitals in Missouri represented the "old-clothes-to-Sam" pattern of hospital development. That is, the "transfer of . . . secondhand products of modern American culture to Negro hands as the brown population increases in an urban community." Both hospitals had been created out of vacated and outmoded facilities.[14]

During the last decade of the nineteenth century and the first two decades of the twentieth century, black physicians, educational institutions, churches, and fraternal organizations also established hospitals. The creation of these facilities demonstrates the strength and resilience of the black community. African Americans were not passive victims in the face of oppression; rather, they developed mechanisms to take care of themselves. Confronted with the racism in American medicine, black people responded by establishing their own institutions. It should also be noted that black-created hospitals arose within the context of the solidification of Jim-Crow laws in the South and increased racial tensions in the North. Historians have shown that an emphasis on black self-reliance and the development of black institutions are frequently found during periods of black discouragement and increased racist oppression. However, black-controlled hospitals should not be viewed solely as reactions to a segregated, exclusionary society, but also as growing out of the African-American community's longstanding tradition of providing for its members. The first black-controlled hospitals included Provident Hospital and Nurse Training School, Chicago, established in 1891; Tuskegee Institute and Nurse Training School, Tuskegee Institute, Alabama, established in 1892; Frederick Douglass Memorial Hospital and Training School, Philadelphia, established in 1895; and Home Infirmary, Clarksville, Tennessee, established in 1906.[15]

The motives behind the establishment of these black-controlled hospitals varied. Leaders of the National Medical Association (NMA) contended that physicians needed access to hospitals to keep abreast of professional developments in scientific medicine. The late nineteenth century saw the establishment of the germ theory of disease, breakthroughs in therapeutics and diagnostics, the development of technologies such as the x-ray, and the growth of surgery as a specialty because of the advent of asepsis, anesthesia, and new surgical techniques. These advances led to increases in the prestige, power, and reputations of physicians, and hospitals became essential components of this new scientific medicine, as sites of clinical practice and medical education for all physicians, not just for the urban elite physician. In hospitals, physicians could exchange professional knowledge and have access to expensive hospital-based technologies. In other words, as Charles E. Rosenberg has argued, "the hospital had been medicalized" and "the medical profession had been hospitalized."[16]

The transformation of the hospital paralleled a rapid growth in the number of black physicians from about 900 in 1890 to about 3500 in 1920. Regardless of their credentials, most found it difficult to obtain hospital admitting privileges. Not all well-qualified white physicians found it easy to obtain hospital connections in this period either, and if white physicians had difficulty, it is clear that the situation for black physicians was all the more bleak.[17]

Black physicians also began hospitals to help themselves economically. They needed the facilities in order to survive professionally and to establish their legitimacy in the community. They also had to compete with white physicians, if not for white patients, then at least for the small pool of paying black patients. Physicians of both races cared for black patients, but white physicians had an advantage in that they could promise continuity of professional attendance upon hospitalization, which their black colleagues could not because they lacked admitting privileges at most facilities. Black physicians had to relinquish care of their hospitalized patients to white physicians, even in some white-run black hospitals, a practice that undermined confidence in black physicians and contributed to a perception that they were inferior to their white peers. In the case of paying patients, it also adversely affected the black physicians' pockets. W.E.B. DuBois in his classic study, *The Philadelphia Negro*, accurately described this professional dilemma:

> At first thought it would seem natural for Negroes to patronize Negro merchants, lawyers, and physicians, from a sense of pride and as a protest against race feeling among whites. When, however, we come to think further, we can see many hindrances. If a child is sick, the father wants a good physician; he knows plenty of good white physicians; he knows nothing of the skill of the black doctor, for the black doctor has had no opportunity to exercise his skill. Consequently for many years the colored physicians had to sit idly by and see the 40,000 Negroes healed principally by white practitioners.

Thus, black physicians maintained that the creation of black-controlled hospitals was necessary for their financial and professional well-being.[18]

The black community also organized hospitals in order to train black women to be nurses. The late nineteenth century saw a transformation in the role of of nursing, as well as that of hospitals. In the earlier part of the century, nursing was a menial occupation associated with lower-class, poorly educated women; in fact, many hospital nurses were actually convalescing patients. The professionalization of nursing began in 1873 with the establishment of the first training schools for nurses, founded originally to provide respectable work for middle-class women and to improve the moral climate of hospitals by the introduction of middle-class women to the wards. By 1900, there were 432 training schools, most controlled and run by hospitals. Nursing curricula emphasized efficiency and discipline. Pupil nurses provided hospitals with a source of cheap labor. As was true with medical schools, most programs shut their doors to black women, but consequently, black communities established hospitals and nurse training schools to provide their daughters with a career.[19]

The continued exclusion and segregation of black patients also forced the African-American community to act. In Newport News, Virginia, for example, black patients were housed in the city jail until the 1914 establishment of a black hospital, Whittaker Memorial Hospital. Other hospitals worked to maintain the color line and even consciously developed mechanisms to do it efficiently. In 1907, one hospital administrator advocated the following creative scheme:

> the negro department must always be as far from the white and executive as possible. . . . The equipments in all departments are practically the same; however, the linen, gowns and every individual article of the different departments must be kept as separate as if in a different part of the city. Say, for instance, at a glance you can note where each article belongs, as all are marked in large letters—cream and white blankets for private rooms and white wards; slate-colored blankets for colored wards, and red blankets for ambulance service.

Some founders of black hospitals contended that their hospitals were necessary to provide black patients with much-needed services but also to assure that they were treated with respect and dignity. Black-controlled hospitals, they argued, could offer black patients "a high type of service along with the courtesy which was lacking in the majority of hospitals where colored patients were admitted." For many middle-class black people, these hospitals also represented a less onerous option since, despite their resources, these patients were usually placed in municipal hospitals or in the same inferior facilities as poor African Americans in voluntary hospitals. At the time, race more than class determined the nature and quality of hospital care.[20]

Organizers of black hospitals also claimed that only black physicians possessed the skills required to treat black patients optimally and that black hospitals could provide black patients with the best possible care. Mixed hospitals, with their segregated wards and mistreatment of black people, did not have the "heart" of black-controlled hospitals. Furthermore, they argued that the patients preferred to be treated in black hospitals. "Just as the German Hospital is the choice above others for the Germans," the 1898 annual report of Philadelphia's Douglass Hospital noted, "so is the Douglass Hospital especially preferred by a large class of our colored citizens." One reason, it was argued, that black patients favored black-operated facilities was that in majority institutions they were "apt to be subjected to experimental work." Many African Americans feared that if they entered a white hospital that they would be used as subjects for medical experimentation and demonstration. Such sentiments were not based on unwarranted paranoia. Slaves had been used as experimental subjects by antebellum physicians. Although slavery had ended, black people knew that, given the nation's racial and political climate, they still might not be able to refuse to participate in such practices.[21]

Discrimination and mistrust of the larger society had in fact prompted the formation of other ethnic and religious hospitals.

Catholics and Jews founded denominational hospitals because they feared religious conversion and had encountered religious intolerance at Protestant institutions. The desire of Jewish patients to keep kosher and to speak Yiddish when hospitalized and the wishes of Catholic patients to receive the sacraments had been major factors in the establishment of sectarian hospitals. As Charles E. Rosenberg has argued, "Not the peculiar technology of medical diagnosis and therapeutics, but rather the need for good and familiar food, for warmth, cleanliness, and dignity justified the founding of such ethnic and religious hospitals." In creating their own hospitals, African Americans were following a precedent set by other ethnic groups to maintain institutions that answered their particular needs.[22]

The establishment of these black-controlled hospitals represented, in part, the institutionalization of Booker T. Washington's political ideology. His accommodationist philosophy, popular at the turn of the century, emphasized self-help, racial solidarity, and economic development as more productive strategies for racial advancement than politics, agitation, and the demand for immediate integration. Washington also stressed social uplift of the race as the key to racial equality. With the acquisition of wealth and morality, the philosophy went, African Americans would gain the respect of white people and consequently be accorded their rights as citizens. The creation of hospitals would contribute to racial uplift by improving the health status of black people, by demonstrating that black people could take care of themselves, and by contributing to the development of a black professional class.[23]

As was true of hospitals in general, most of the black medical institutions, established as for-profit facilities that would enable their owners to care for patients and to perform surgery, were small and did not offer training programs. Given their size, equipment, resources, and the training of their owners, it is doubtful whether such institutions provided patients with superior medical care. Examples of these private black hospitals included Home Infirmary in Clarksville, Tennessee, and Fair Haven Infirmary in Atlanta. Dr. Robert T. Burt opened the Home Infirmary in 1906, serving as both sole owner and surgeon-in-chief. Most patients entered the infirmary to have surgery: in 1911, surgical cases represented two-thirds of the case load. In 1909, a group of black physicians opened Atlanta's Fair Haven Infirmary, a twelve-bed facility even featuring an operating room in which physicians performed major surgery, including abdominal cases. White physicians also utilized the infirmary to hospitalize their black patients.[24]

The establishment and development of the early black-controlled hospitals, however, were not without controversy within the black community, especially in the North. Tensions emerged over the role and mission of the institutions. An examination of the evolution of Provident Hospital in Chicago and Douglass Hospital in Philadelphia will demonstrate some of the obstacles faced by two of the first black-controlled hospitals. It also shows how some of the problems that these institutions encountered remained unsolved and would later plague the black hospital reformers.

The racially exclusionist policies of Chicago nursing schools had provided the primary impetus for the establishment of Provident Hospital and Training School in 1891. After a young black woman, Emma Reynolds, was refused admission to all of Chicago's nursing schools solely because of her race, her brother, the Reverend Louis H. Reynolds, turned to the prominent black surgeon Dr. Daniel Hale Williams (1856–1931) for help. A committee of physicians, ministers, and community leaders failed to find a place for Reynolds at any one of the city's nurse training schools. The experience spurred Williams to organize a biracial association of medical and civic leaders to establish an interracial hospital and nurse training school in Chicago.[25]

Williams successfully solicited funds and supplies from both black and white citizens. His venture was helped immensely by black clubwomen who embarked on fund-raising activities of their own. Fannie Barrier Williams (no relation to Dr. Williams), a noted clubwoman and journalist, became the official solicitor for the campaign, raising more than $2000 from black and white donors. Another clubwoman, Mrs. Cora Scott Pond, coordinated a fund-raising event that raised over $1300 for the endeavor. Individual donors from the black community also contributed supplies to the hospital, including a parlor stove, a clothes wringer, chiffon lace for nurses' caps, books, and portraits. The donation of such gifts to hospitals was common practice at the turn of the century. Nanahyoke Sockum Curtis, a nurse and wife of Dr. Austin M. Curtis, who would later become Provident's first intern, successfully enlisted the support of meat-packing industrialist Philip D. Armour in the campaign to open the hospital. Other prominent white businessmen, including Cyrus H. McCormick, Herman Kohlsaat, and George M. Pullman, also gave funds. Self-interest undoubtedly played a role in the charitable actions of these men, since the maintenance of a healthy black work force required that black employees have access to medical facilities. In June 1891, only five months after the creation of the hospital association, a fourteen-bed hospital opened in a two-story frame house.[26]

Daniel Hale Williams's enterprise did not escape censure. Some members of the black community accused him of perpetuating segregation. One minister went so far as to curse the building and pray that it would burn to the ground. Williams was able to overcome such criticism because of the wide biracial support that the hospital received. Furthermore, the founder perceived the hospital not as an exclusively black enterprise, but as an interracial one that would not practice racial discrimination with regard to staff privileges, nurse training school applicants, and the admission of patients. Williams did not want black physicians to be separated from medicine's mainstream, nor did he want Provident Hospital to be used as an apology for the continued racism at other Chicago hospitals. At the time, the only other hospital to accept black patients was Cook County Hospital on the west side of the city, far from the black South Side.[27]

Williams's personal biography is crucial to understanding how he came to establish Provident Hospital. He had been born in Hollidaysburg, Pennsylvania, in 1856. His father, Daniel Jr., was a barber and well-to-do landowner. His mother, Sarah, was a housewife. After his father's death, the family moved to Rockford, Illinois. At the age of seventeen Williams settled in nearby Janesville, Wisconsin, where, while he attended school, he worked as a barber just as his late father had done. In 1878 he graduated from Haire's Classical Academy. Shortly thereafter he decided that he wanted to become a physician and he apprenticed himself to a prominent white Janesville physician, Dr. Henry Palmer, who had previously served as Wisconsin Surgeon General for ten years.

Williams's medical education continued at the Chicago Medical College, a predominantly white school, from which he was graduated in 1883. At a time when postgraduate training was not the norm for the average practitioner and practically inaccessible for black physicians, Williams completed an internship at Mercy Hospital, a Catholic hospital associated with his alma mater. His qualifications thus equalled those of elite physicians of either race and exceeded those of many other doctors in late nineteenth-century America. Williams went on to enjoy wide contact and much prestige within the city's white medical community. His connections with this group surely made him aware of the increasing importance of hospitals to physicians' careers, and he later obtained appointments at the South Side Dispensary and the Protestant Orphan Asylum. In 1889 he became the first black physician named to the Illinois State Board of Health, while also maintaining a lucrative interracial private practice. Williams's career was anomalous. It was probably aided by the physician's fair skin—he was light enough to pass for white. Other black physicians found themselves barred from Chicago medical institutions, and therefore the establishment of Provident Hospital would certainly benefit their careers.

Although Williams had access to the white medical world and called for Provident Hospital to be interracial, he was not isolated from the black medical world. He was one of the founders of the National Medical Association, established in Atlanta in 1895. He was offered the presidency of that organization, but declined, serving instead as its first vice president. After the establishment of Provident Hospital, Williams conducted surgical clinics at Meharry Medical College and at various black hospitals throughout the South. He acknowledged that racism, especially in the South, seriously limited the opportunities afforded black nurses and physicians and adversely affected the health care received by black patients. He urged that the black community establish its own hospitals and nurse training schools because "a people who do not make provision for their sick and suffering are not worthy of civilization."[28]

Provident Hospital in its first years reflected Williams's interracial vision. He used his connections to enlist white medical leaders such as Frank Billings and Christian Fenger to serve as consultants and trustees at Provident. The medical staff, although biracial, had a racial division of labor: white physicians served primarily as consulting staff and black physicians as attending and resident staff. Dr. Austin Maurice Curtis, later the first black physician appointed to the staff of Cook County Hospital, was Provident's first intern. However, during the hospital's first twenty-one years most interns were white. The patient census also reflected biracial patronage. In its first year, the small hospital admitted 189 patients, thirty-four (18 percent) of them white.[29]

Provident Hospital flourished. In 1893, two years after its opening, Daniel Hale Williams performed one of the first successful open-heart surgeries there. Five years later, the hospital moved into a new 65-bed facility, the construction of which had been financed by white benefactors including Kohlsaat and Armour. By 1912, the hospital had no debts, an endowment of $50,000 (of which $45,000 had been donated by blacks), and a plant valued at $125,000.[30]

In spite of Williams's original intentions, Provident Hospital gradually evolved into a black institution. By 1915, some 93 percent of the patients were black. By 1916, all of the nurses (except the supervisor) and almost all of the staff physicians were black. This evolution reflected the deterioration of race relations in Chicago, as a rise in white hostility and institutional racism had greeted the growing number of black migrants from the South. In response, black leaders created separate institutions, organizations, and businesses to serve Chicago's burgeoning black population, which was predominantly confined, because of residential segregation, to the city's South Side. The 1920 census estimated that 109,458 African Americans lived in Chicago—an increase of almost 150 percent over 1910. The well-established Provident Hospital, emerging as an important center of this "black metropolis," was accordingly expected by the black community to meet its needs and aspirations.[31]

A change in the leadership at Provident Hospital had also contributed to its development as a black institution. Daniel Hale Williams resigned as medical director in 1894 when he became surgeon-in-chief at Freedmen's Hospital in Washington, D.C. He returned to the staff of Provident Hospital four years later; however, during his absence, a professional and personal rival, Dr. George Cleveland Hall, had become medical director. In addition, Hall's allies had gained control of the hospital's board of trustees. The longstanding feud between Williams and Hall may well have stemmed initially from Williams's unsuccessful attempt to block Hall's staff appointment to Provident. Hall graduated in 1888 from the sectarian Bennett Eclectic Medical College, a proprietary school nominally affiliated with Chicago's Loyola University. Williams did not view Provident Hospital as an egalitarian institution open to all black physicians regardless of their credentials. He wanted the hospital to be a first-class, competitive institution, and insisted that all staff members meet the highest professional standards. He did not consider Hall, a graduate of an inferior sectarian school, to be a qualified candidate. Nonetheless, Hall's allies in the black community and on the Provident board secured him an appointment in spite of Williams's objections.[32]

The antagonism between Hall and Williams extended beyond the walls of Provident Hospital and reflected divisions within the black community at large. The historian Allan Spear views the feud between the two physicians as a manifestation of the power struggle between two factions within the black community—the old elite and the new leadership class. Williams represented the former, which had dominated black community life in Chicago until the first decade of the twentieth century. This group espoused integration and had economic and professional ties in the white community. After 1900, a new leadership class, of which Hall was a prominent member, rose to power. Advocating black self-help and solidarity, this group relied on its economic and professional ties in the black community. Unlike Williams, Hall maintained close association with several black community organizations, including the National Negro Business League, the Wabash Avenue YMCA, and the NAACP. His conception of Provident Hospital differed significantly from that of its founder. Hall viewed the institution, not as a model of interracial cooperation, but as "the Colored people's hospital . . . an establishment in which, more and more each year, the Colored folks are taking personal pride."[33]

Williams remained on staff until 1912, when he resigned bitterly. Accounts of the reasons behind his departure vary. One centers on the passage by the board of trustees of a Hall-sponsored resolution requiring all staff physicians to limit their practice to Provident. Such a measure would have undoubtedly been aimed at Williams, who had been appointed associate attending surgeon at the predominantly white St. Luke's Hospital. In this version, Williams chose to resign from Provident rather than limit his practice and isolate himself from his white colleagues. In another account, he resigned after the board of trustees of the hospital refused to meet his demands that Hall be removed from the hospital staff and its board. Whatever the reason, after his resignation Provident's founder never again took an active role in its activities. The year after he broke ties with Provident Hospital, he gained additional status in the world of elite white physicians as the only African American out of the 1059 physicians named charter members of the American College of Surgeons.[34]

Tensions over the role and direction of the black hospital also emerged in Philadelphia at the Frederick Douglass Memorial Hospital and Training School. Unlike the situation in Chicago, the resolution was not the departure of the hospital's founder, but the establishment of a new hospital. The history of Douglass Hospital was inextricably bound to the career of its founder, Dr. Nathan Francis Mossell (1856–1946). Mossell's medical and racial philosophies, personality, and drive dominated hospital policy during his thirty-eight-year tenure as medical director. Much of his racial philosophy, which prompted him to found Douglass Hospital, can be traced to his parents. Aaron and Eliza Bowers Mossell were free blacks who migrated to Canada from Baltimore because of racism and the paucity of educational opportunities in the South for their children. Their third child, Nathan, was born on 27 July 1856 in Hamilton, Ontario. Nine years later, when Aaron Mossell lost the brickyard he had established in Hamilton, the family moved to Lockport, New York. In this small town, not far from Rochester, the elder Mossell worked as a day laborer until he reestablished himself in business. As his business flourished, with even whites in his employ, Aaron Mossell became a respected and prosperous member of the Lockport community. This, however, did not shield his family from racism. Lockport maintained a separate school for black children. Mossell refused to allow his children to attend it, but pressured the school board to abolish its segregated school system. Nathan Mossell later remembered his childhood as being "conditioned by an environment which propelled me toward a manly approach to life. The only man for whom I ever worked was father. I had no opportunity to become a white man's 'boy'."[35]

In 1871, 15-year-old Nathan Mossell left Lockport to join his older brother, Charles, at Lincoln University, a black institution in southeastern Pennsylvania. There he enrolled in the college preparatory department. Three years later he matriculated in the undergraduate program at Lincoln, from which he graduated with honors in 1879.

Mossell had decided to become a physician during his last year at Lincoln. In the fall of 1879, he called on Dr. James Tyson, Dean of the University of Pennsylvania School of Medicine, to request admission to the school. No African American had previously enrolled in the medical school, and Tyson, a Quaker, favored Mossell's admission. He noted that both Harvard and Yale had admitted black students, without major problems, and that Pennsylvania should be "equally liberal." Subsequently, Dean Tyson obtained the necessary faculty approval for Mossell's admission.[36]

Nathan Mossell began his medical education on 15 October 1879. His welcome to the University of Pennsylvania was not exactly warm. When he walked into a lecture hall students stomped their feet and hissed, "Put the damn nigger out." In the following weeks students sent letters protesting his admission. The opposition was not merely verbal. On one occasion, while Mossell walked along the Schuylkill River, just east of the campus, some students attempted to push him into it. Despite his cruel introduction to medical school, Mossell stayed and graduated with honors in 1882. At his graduation, he received a standing ovation from his classmates. Mossell wrote, much later, that the racism that he had encountered had not disturbed him because he considered himself "better prepared than most of the students. In those days one needed only a high school diploma to study medicine. Out of a class of 140-odd, about thirty of us had Bachelor of Arts degrees." Mossell's claim of indifference may be questioned; however, his courage and determination cannot be doubted.[37]

As was the case with Daniel Hale Williams, Mossell took a career path that was not the norm for the average practitioner, black or white. Following graduation, he actively pursued postgraduate education. Mossell worked for two years at the out-patient surgical clinic at the Hospital of the University of Pennsylvania. He took a postgraduate course at the Philadelphia Polyclinic. In 1889, he spent four months in London studying surgery at the prestigious Guy's Hospital and at St. Thomas Hospital. Mossell's career received a further boost in 1888 with his election as the first black member of the Philadelphia County Medical Society. Nominated by J. Britton Massey, a Southerner and a specialist in electrotherapy, his endorsers also included the distinguished surgeon, D. Hayes Agnew, and his former sponsor at the University of Pennsylvania, James Tyson. Initially there was resistance to Mossell's admission because some members questioned whether a black man could have the requisite credentials. Opposition subsided after Dean Tyson pointed out that "Dr. Mossell graduated with an average higher than three-fourths of his class." Despite his ties to the city's white medical establishment, there were limits to Mossell's ability to break racial barriers. He could not secure admitting privileges at any Philadelphia hospital, which surely must have disturbed a man of his training and professional aspirations.[38]

In addition to his medical activities, Mossell participated in many professional, political, and civic organizations devoted to racial equality and the social and economic advancement of African Americans. He was instrumental in the founding of the National Medical Association and in 1907 served as its eighth president. In 1900, Mossell helped establish the Philadelphia Academy of Medical and Allied Sciences, a constituent chapter of the National Medical Association. Outside of the medical world, he led a protest in Philadelphia against the dramatization of Thomas Dixon's racist novel, *The Clansman.* The novel, the basis of the film *The Birth of a Nation*, praised the Ku Klux Klan and belittled African Americans. The following year, Mossell was one of the organizers of the meeting that launched the Niagara Movement, the forerunner of the National Association for the Advancement of Colored People.

On the evening of 25 June 1895, Dr. Mossell convened a meeting of black Philadelphians to discuss the feasibility of establishing a nurse training school. The group demonstrated the unusual strength and diversity of Philadelphia's black middle-class community and included ministers, business owners, and teachers. Significantly, Mossell was the only physician at the meeting. As was true of the organizers of Provident Hospital, this group of prominent African Americans considered it their obligation to establish a nurse training school because young black women who wished to study nursing faced bleak prospects, alleging that only one Philadelphia school, the Training School of Philadelphia Hospital, admitted them. The training school organizers maintained that nursing education offered black women an opportunity to develop a profession and that the development of such a class of women would greatly contribute to racial uplift. Nursing education would discourage "idleness and profligacy" in young black women and would provide them with a career that would be "useful and [a] benefit to themselves, to the sick, and to the community." The organizers also realized that a training school could not operate independently, but that a hospital was a necessary adjunct. A hospital would also provide much-needed facilities for the city's black physicians. They pledged $1000 to build a hospital and a nurse training school. Mossell later reminisced:

> With all, we wish it had not been necessary to establish the Douglass Hospital. We deprecate the present trend in the dominant public mind

> to create in many sections of the country hospitals and medical schools, especially for colored people—it means extravagance, inefficiency, duplication of effort, and is undemocratic in that it establishes caste.

However, the needs of the black community and the racism at the other hospitals and training schools in Philadelphia forced them to act.[39]

Plans for the hospital progressed. A board of managers was elected and, not surprisingly, Dr. Mossell was chosen to be medical director of the yet unnamed institution. A relative of Mossell's wife Gertrude, Jacob C. White, Jr., was named to head the board. Most of the board's members were African Americans. As the historian Roger Lane has noted, the board's racial composition represented a break with the usual tradition of having rich white supporters chairing the city's black philanthropies. This was not the case at Douglass, which would not be white-dominated. Whites were a minority on the board and served in no position higher than treasurer. Philadelphia attorney and president of the board of education Samuel B. Huey took that office. At the 5 August 1895 meeting, the board of managers named the institution in memory of Frederick Douglass, the abolitionist and human rights champion who had died a few months earlier.[40]

Although the hospital was to be black-controlled, the organizers did not perceive the hospital as an exclusively black institution. Mossell and the board insisted that the hospital "not be an apology for the discriminatory practices of the other public agencies." It would not discriminate with regard to staff privileges, training school applicants, or the treatment of patients. Whites provided assistance in planning the hospital, served on the board of managers, and donated funds.[41]

The proposed hospital prompted some opposition from both the white and black communities. White opponents complained that the hospital represented an unnecessary addition to the already large number of charitable institutions in Philadelphia. At the forefront of black criticism was *The Weekly Tribune*, a black-operated newspaper whose editors viewed the establishment of Douglass Hospital as a concession to race prejudice. They wrote that it was "the quintessence of foolhardiness to continually prate about breaking down color barriers and then go on rearing them ourselves." Furthermore, they portrayed a rosier picture of the status of black patients and nurses than the supporters of the hospital had advanced. Critics claimed that none of the city's hospitals barred black patients and that black women, in the past, had graduated from the nurse training programs at Women's Medical College, the Hospital of the University of Pennsylvania, and Philadelphia Hospital. They also questioned whether the black community had the financial resources to support a hospital and pointed out that a number of black-run enterprises had failed because of a lack of funds. "We are not so enthused over the opening of the so-called Colored Hospital," a 7 September 1895 *Weekly Tribune* editorial noted.

> Because it should be borne in mind that a hospital is a very expensive institution to manage successfully. As a people, are we in a position to support such an undertaking? Or do the projectors intend to depend more upon the philanthropy of our white friends.

As had been the case in Chicago, the strength and breadth of support, including that of the African Methodist Episcopal Preachers' Meeting and the Baptist Minister's Union, enabled the hospital organizers to overcome such opposition.[42]

The Frederick Douglass Memorial Hospital and Training School opened on 31 October 1895, only four months after the first organizational meeting. The fifteen-bed facility occupied a three-story leased building in South Philadelphia. The basement of the remodelled house served as the dispensary, the first floor as offices, and the second and third floors as patient wards. In addition, a small room on the second floor was outfitted to serve as an operating room—evidence that Mossell recognized the increasing importance of surgery to a hospital's function.

The nurse training school opened a few months after the hospital. During its first year of operation, the Douglass Hospital received fifty-eight applications and admitted six young African-American women. The training school's impact stretched beyond the black population of Philadelphia. The first two women who graduated from the program (on 22 May 1897) were Hattie E. Mosely of Iowa and Mary E. Wilson of Virginia. By 1904, fifteen women, all black, had graduated from the school. The graduates secured a variety of positions: Mary E. Wilson, class of 1897, became the head of a private sanitarium in Philadelphia; Carrie B. Earley, class of 1899, later became head nurse and matron at Douglass. She was succeeded by Marie J. Narcisse of the class of 1904. Graduates were also employed by such institutions as the Home for Aged and Infirmed Colored Persons in Philadelphia and the Home for Colored Persons in Atlantic City. Most of its graduates, as did the majority of those from white training schools, sought and obtained private employment. Both white and black families hired them.[43]

The hospital also succeeded in offering professional opportunities to black physicians. Of the twenty professionals, including the pharmacist and head nurse, comprising the original medical staff at Douglass, twelve were African Americans. The medical staff was organized into consulting and attending staffs. The roster of attending physicians was mostly black, while that of consulting physicians was exclusively white. The consulting physicians and surgeons, including prominent members of the Philadelphia medical establishment such as James Tyson, Roland G. Curtin, Thomas S.K. Morton, and John B. Deaver, provided a reassuring legitimacy to the young institution. It is not clear whether their involvement with the hospital went much beyond this. For instance, it is not documented whether they ever admitted patients to the hospital. By 1900, the hospital created associate staff positions to include black physicians who had suffered from "caste disabilities" in the suburbs and neighboring cities such as Wilmington, Delaware; Chester, Pennsylvania; and Atlantic City, New Jersey.[44]

Douglass Hospital also offered postgraduate training to black medical school graduates. During the hospital's first ten years, many of its residents had trained at Mossell's alma mater, the University of Pennsylvania. By 1904, seventeen black physicians, all men, had completed residencies at Douglass. After residency, some stayed on at the hospital. J.Q. McDougald became assistant gynecologist; R.W. Bailey, assistant pathologist, and Arthyr T. Boyer, assistant ophthalmologist. Some obtained positions at black hospitals in other cities with large black populations. Samuel P. Stafford became chief of staff at Provident Hospital, St. Louis, and J.E. Dibble became attending surgeon at Douglass Hospital, Kansas City, Kansas. Graduates also entered private practice, mostly in the Philadelphia area.

Despite these successes, Douglass Hospital had financial difficulties. The majority of its patients were poor African Americans who could not afford to pay the hospital's five-dollar-per-week fee. They either paid a reduced fee or were treated free of charge. In order to increase revenues, the hospital used a strategy employed by many contemporary hospitals; it attempted to increase the number of paying patients. But this tactic ultimately failed because Douglass could not greatly expand the number of paying patients because of space limitations.[45]

The hospital also tried to solicit funds and support from the white and black communities. However, the appeals to the two groups differed. The campaign to the white community stressed its relative wealth and its Christian obligation to those less fortunate. "We appeal to our white friends," one solicitation implored

> because God, who has so arranged it in His economy that the wealth of the land is theirs, and the meagre salaries of the employed will not permit a contribution large enough to help other than modestly an institution, even though it tends to their own vital interest.

Campaigns to African Americans stressed the hospital's importance to racial uplift. "It is your Institution, the only one in its kind in the State," they were reminded. "You cannot afford to sit idly by and wink only as opportunities pass; help this work, help educate your girls and your young men."[46]

Gertrude Mossell, Nathan Mossell's wife, headed the hospital's fund-raising activities, once again indicating the importance of black women to the development of the race's hospitals. During the hospital's first year, a sum of over $5000 was raised, of which $4300 came from members of the black community. Some contributions were as small as 25 cents. In 1896, Zion Wesley African Methodist Episcopal Church endowed the hospital's first bed for charity patients. Members of the black community responded not only with funds, but by donating needed items such as food, linens, and magazines, and by organizing charitable activities—balls, poetry readings, recitals at the Academy of Music, and classical music concerts. One especially publicized event was the February 1896 grand ball and concert featuring the famous soprano Sisseretta Jones ("Black Patti").[47]

As the hospital grew, the percentage of contributions coming from the black community decreased, and the need for supplemental funds became apparent. In 1896, the year in which the hospital was incorporated, representatives of the State Board of Charities visited Douglass Hospital and approved the institution to receive funds from the state legislature. Subsequently, the legislature appropriated $10,000 for the hospital's maintenance, but for unclear reasons, this appropriation initially was delayed. Mossell himself attributed the problem to "misguided" black politicians who resented his political independence. Mossell, however, was able to muster some political support of his own and defeat his critics. Between 1896 and 1904, Douglass Hospital received funds from the state ranging from $5000 to $10,000 per year.[48]

Despite its fund-raising activities, by 1904 the hospital had accumulated an $18,000 deficit. However, its financial situation did not stop Douglass from making plans to enlarge. Expansion had become a necessity because the hospital had quickly outgrown its original facilities. In 1896, the hospital treated 61 inpatients; in 1904 it treated 242. Similar growth had taken place in the outpatient department: from 987 patients treated in 1896 to 1,997 in 1902. Mossell also insisted that the new hospital be equipped with pathology and bacteriology laboratories in order to keep in step with contemporary developments in medicine. In 1904, Douglass purchased two houses for $8000 to use as a new facility. Plans called for a 75-bed hospital with more accommodations for private patients and a larger operating room.

The hopeful expectations produced by the proposed expansion temporarily masked a growing controversy at the hospital that centered on its internal control. A headline in the 21 January 1905 *Weekly Tribune* announcing, "Dr. N.F. Mossell, Chief of Staff Asked to Resign His Place," gave some indication of the depths of the problem. Although the board of managers later denied this report, the headline did indeed herald the development of sharp and divisive tensions at Douglass Hospital.[49]

The conflicts ostensibly revolved around the hospital's operating room practices. Its policy, printed in each annual report, was that

> In order to facilitate Nurse Training and to extend the usefulness of the Institution, we permit all physicians to place their patients in the Hospital and attend them while there—except in operative cases—the Hospital reserves the right to use discretion as to the operator.

At the time, hospitals, especially those affiliated with university medical schools, commonly used such closed-staff arrangements as a way of controlling surgery. Mossell, it seems, was trying to duplicate procedures employed at elite hospitals. However, the criteria used for staff privileges were often unclear and appointments were frequently made on the basis of "favoritism over skill." The use of a closed-staff policy at Douglass Hospital led several members of the medical staff to question whether the goal of the institution was to provide professional opportunities for black physicians in general or for Nathan Mossell exclusively. During the hospital's first year, thirty-one inpatient operations were performed, two-thirds of them by Mossell. It is not clear whether Mossell continued to perform such a large percentage of the surgery, but it *is* evident that some black members of the medical staff perceived that he did. Mossell's critics alleged that his domination of the operating room limited their clinical experience and threatened their professional advancement. They became dissatisfied with the professional opportunities offered by Douglass Hospital, and Nathan Mossell became the target of their discontent. This controversy needs to be understood on two levels. On the one hand, some physicians clearly chafed under Mossell's undisputed medical control of the hospital. But a deeper tension existed as well. As we shall see later, Mossell saw himself and his hospital as representatives of new professional standards.[50]

Factions developed within the hospital and soon extended beyond its walls. The black press closely followed the staff problems and took sides. The *Weekly Tribune* had originally opposed the establishment of Douglass Hospital, but conceded by January 1903 that it was an essential community institution. The newspaper, however, supported Mossell's critics by portraying the medical director as an autocrat who ran a private hospital—not a hospital that benefited the general black community. Furthermore, it alleged that his continued presence threatened the hospital's existence. A 21 January 1905 article in the newspaper argued that

> The public at large are fast losing confidence in the Douglass Hospital because they plainly see the methods of its head are faulty. Hence public condemnation follows in its wake, making unpopular an institution which should be the joy of every charitably inclined and patriotic citizen.

In contrast, *The Courant*, another black publication, blamed the problems at Douglass on the managers, who it contended had "failed to perform their duty, and are a set of hedgers, unworthy to conduct either a hospital or any other public charity."[51]

Nathan Mossell attributed the hospital's problems to professional jealousies. In a 1908 paper, "The Modern Hospital: Its Construction, Organization, and Management," which he presented at the annual meeting of the National Medical Association, Mossell reflected on the tensions at the hospital. Mossell asserted:

> the ideal arrangement . . . would seem to be a combination between all the reputable physicians located in the town and all the leading citizens in the management of the enterprise, but experience has shown that local jealousies first between the physicians and finally extending to the private patients and sympathizers of those who are disgruntled are sure to greatly hamper the work of the institution, if not disrupt it.[52]

As the months went by, conditions at Douglass continued to deteriorate. In October 1905, fifteen of the twenty-four practicing black physicians in Philadelphia petitioned the board of managers for a reorganization of the medical staff. Shortly afterwards, the board of managers voted to remove Mossell as medical director and replace him with Dr. Edwin C. Howard, a graduate of Harvard Medical School. The coup had been led by board member Dr. Eugene Theodore Hinson, an 1898 graduate of the University of Pennsylvania School of Medicine. Howard, however, held the position only briefly: later in the month, the board met again and nullified his election. Dr. Mossell had contended that the election was invalid because the newly elected members of the board had not been informed of the pivotal meeting. He was able to elicit support for his position from the majority of the board and was reinstated as medical director. This action so enraged Howard's supporters that they threatened court action, but the threat proved to be empty and a suit did not follow.[53]

The power struggle at Douglass Hospital resulted in the establishment of a second black hospital in Philadelphia. On 5 December

1905, a group of black physicians and lay people, believing that Douglass Hospital had become a "privately managed, narrow, unprogressive institution," met at Dr. Howard's office to make plans for a new hospital. The group proceeded with their plans, and on 12 February 1906 (Lincoln's Birthday), Mercy Hospital and Nurse Training School opened only four blocks from Douglass Hospital.[54]

Although Douglass had been founded to provide clinical opportunities to black medical professionals, Nathan Mossell did not visualize the hospital as a democratic institution. In a 1906 article, "An Institution That's Doing a Great Job," he wrote that the hospital had "never for a moment considered it wise or desirable to have every colored physician's name associated with the hospital simply because he is colored." Mossell's operating room policy was designed to limit access. His actions must therefore be viewed from the perspective of his professional aspirations and goals. Wanting to be accepted as a skillful surgeon and Douglass Hospital to be seen as a first-class hospital, he had to limit access to those he deemed to be qualified, no matter how ill-defined and arbitrary his criteria. This undemocratic process was commonplace in American hospitals and also led to tensions among physicians at other institutions. Ironically, the procedure that Mossell supported had been used to exclude black physicians from majority hospitals. Perhaps he wanted to demonstrate that black physicians could meet the growing demands of scientific medical practice and satisfy the standards established by elite, technologically sophisticated white hospitals. Mossell's critics did not control the hospital board as had George Cleveland Hall's supporters in Chicago, and therefore they could not force the hospital's founder from his sinecure. Frustrated at Douglass and barred from other hospitals, Mossell's opponents had no other choice but to organize another black hospital in Philadelphia.[55]

Between 1912 and 1919, the number of black hospitals and nurse training schools, white and black controlled, increased from approximately 63 to 118. About 80 percent of these facilities operated in the South. This regional concentration can be attributed to two factors. First, the black population lived primarily in the South. Most black physicians went to school and practiced in the region. Second, the establishment of black hospitals in the North often met with stiff opposition from segments of the African-American community who argued that the less restrictive racial climate of the North did not require it. Opponents conceded that the stringent racial situation in the South necessitated the establishment of black-controlled institutions in that region.[56]

Supporters of black hospitals responded that racism did indeed exist in the North and that the region also needed black-controlled institutions. The National Medical Association made its position clear in a 1909 editorial in the *Journal of the National Association*, lamenting that

> It is needless for our brethren in the North to longer hide behind the mantle of inactivity and continue to say that these things are needless—they inject the race question—they draw the color line. Not so. The race question is already drawn, and with such a heavy, dark stroke as to not be recognized.

Leaders of the NMA pointed out that even in the North hospitals barred patients or admitted them to segregated and inferior wards and excluded black physicians from their staffs. Black hospitals, they maintained, should not be limited to the South.[57]

The inability of many black physicians to obtain membership in the American Medical Association (AMA) worked to bar them from hospital appointments. Many hospitals' criteria for staff positions included membership in the AMA or its local affiliate. In order to join, a physician had just to be accepted by a local affiliate. However, many local medical societies, especially in the South, excluded black physicians until the 1950s. Those black physicians fortunate enough to gain admitting privileges often had to work under the supervision of white physicians, causing one Georgia physician to complain angrily, "These white surgeons don't want Negroes to learn. And even when he is operating on my own patient he works in an incision the size of a rathole and I can't even see what he is doing." Black medical leaders feared that their lack of hospital opportunities would relegate them to second-class citizenship within medicine.[58]

Some historians have interpreted the plight of black physicians as due to their race. On one level this certainly is true: it would be absurd to attempt to write a "color-blind" history of black physicians. But to say that "race did get in the way of success," obscures a crucial point. It was not the color of a physician's skin that blocked his or her path. It was white reaction to skin color: the *racism* of the society in which they lived, including the racism that permeated the medical profession. This racism was not limited to the prejudiced attitudes of isolated individuals. It was institutionalized in the structure of American medical practice. And, sadly, this institutionalized racism actually intensified as medicine became more scientific and as new standards for medical practice developed in the first decades of the twentieth century.[59]

The transformation of the hospital and the rise of scientific medicine led to efforts to standardize and improve hospitals. Previously, hospitals had reflected community needs and values more than national medical standards. Indeed, there had been no formal criteria governing the provision of hospital care and the management of hospitals. The American College of Surgeons, founded in 1912, attempted to remedy this problem by establishing national yardsticks for the evaluation of hospitals. The College hoped that adherence to its guidelines would upgrade or eliminate inferior hospitals. In 1919, it issued its first set of rules that specified minimum standards for staff, equipment, facilities, and basic operating procedures. These guidelines had to be met before a hospital could be placed on the American College of Surgeons' list of approved hospitals.[60]

In 1910, the Carnegie Foundation for the Advancement of Teaching had released Abraham Flexner's highly critical study of American medical education. Several historians have explored the many significant reforms in American medical education during the years surrounding the publication of the Flexner Report. One key change that they have identified was a new emphasis on clinical training in hospitals as an integral component of medical education. The American Medical Association's Council on Medical Education had recommended in 1905 that medical school graduates complete an internship as part of their basic medical education. By 1914, an estimated 80 percent of medical school graduates served an internship; five medical colleges required an internship as a prerequisite for a medical degree; and one state board, the Pennsylvania board, required it as a prerequisite for licensure. The reforms in medical education also led to efforts to improve the quality of postgraduate training. In 1919, the Council on Medical Education started issuing "The Essentials of an Approved Internship," a list of minimal criteria that approved internships had to meet in order to warrant approval. In addition to the internship, specialty training and other forms of hospital-based medical training began to expand.[61]

Black physicians, however, continued to find it difficult to obtain postgraduate training. In a 1917 *Woman's Medical Journal* article, Dr. Isabella Vanderwall candidly discussed her inability to obtain an internship. This black physician, a 1915 graduate of New York Medical College for Women, was rejected by four hospitals, including the one affiliated with her medical school, not because she was unqualified—she had graduated first in her class—but because she was black. Vanderwall's story reveals much about racial discrimination in medicine and the pain and frustration it brought. It also makes plain the young physician's determination and perseverance in the face of racism. She wrote:

> I had almost given up hope of securing an internship when one day, I saw a notice on the college bulletin board saying the Hospital for Women and Children in Syracuse, New York, wanted an interne. Here

> I thought was another chance. So I wrote, sent in my application, and was accepted without parley. . . . So to Syracuse I went with bag and baggage enough to last me for a year. I found the hospital; I found the superintendent. She asked me what I wanted. I told her I was Dr. Vanderwall, the new interne. She simply stared and said not a word. Finally when she came to her senses, she said to me: "You can't come here; we can't have you here! You are colored! You will have to go back." Go back! . . . No, indeed, not I! So for three days I stayed in Syracuse, trotting hither and thither, seeing this authority and the other official. Everywhere I met the same answer: "No, we cannot have you. We do not doubt your ability, but you are colored, therefore we will not have you." So they sent me home without any interneship.

Vanderwall contended that the inability of black physicians to obtain internships threatened their future in medicine. She, herself, was able to practice, having obtained her licenses in New York and New Jersey before the laws on compulsory internship went into effect.[62]

The expected track for black physicians wanting to obtain an internship was to pursue it at one of the black hospitals. However, not all black hospitals admitted them. Dr. Roscoe C. Giles, the first black graduate of Cornell University School of Medicine, recalled that "excuses, alibis, and subterfuges" were used to deny him a position at several New York City hospitals, including Lincoln Hospital. Lincoln Hospital, a municipally operated hospital, had begun its institutional life in 1842 as the Home for Worthy, Aged, Indigent Colored People. The work of the institution increasingly included medical care, and in 1882 it changed its name to the Colored Home and Hospital. In 1898, the hospital moved from Manhattan's East Side to the then semi-rural and predominantly white South Bronx, and in 1912 it changed its name again to Lincoln Hospital and Home. The hospital's relocation resulted in a change in its patient population. The chronic care and nursing home wards remained exclusively white. The hospital wards became progressively white. The hospital, however, did not fully abandon its commitment to African Americans. Black patients were not barred from admission to the facility. In addition, it continued to operate the training school for black nurses it had begun in 1898. Although the hospital trained black nurses and offered them employment, it denied such opportunities to black physicians. Commenting on their status at the black division of Atlanta's Grady Hospital, another institution that admitted black patients and nurses, one black physician lamented, "We envy the nurses, they at least get a chance—we have none." The situations at Lincoln and Grady hospitals make clear, once again, that not all institutions considered to be black hospitals, usually those operated by whites, supported the advancement of black physicians. Dr. Giles, who in 1938 became the first black physician certified by the American Board of Surgery, finally did obtain an internship—at Provident Hospital.[63]

The changes in medical education that took place during the first two decades of the twentieth century mandated that medical schools provide clinical training to all students. The University of Pennsylvania School of Medicine, Dr. Nathan Mossell's alma mater, attempted in 1916 to forge a relationship with Douglass Hospital. The university wanted to use the hospital's wards to train black medical students in obstetrics. The affiliation with Douglass Hospital was to be for black students only. It is clear that racial and sexual taboos about black men touching white women were at work here, since the arrangement was not suggested for any other clinical clerkship. Mossell adamantly refused the proposition, stating that it would be acceptable only if the medical school would send both black and white students. Mossell's confrontation with the University of Pennsylvania was dramatized later in the 1947 play, "Within Our Gates," written by Sylvia James to honor the physician and his work. In her account, James used the character Dr. Browning to represent Dr. William Pepper, III, who was the actual dean of the medical school. The play read in part:

BROWNING (Dr. Browning of the U. of Pa.):
It's an unpleasant duty that brings me here. . . . You know that we have a few colored students at Penn . . .

MOSSELL Yes, I know I helped to get some of them in.

BROWNING That's right . . . you did. Well, they seem to be doing all right. . . . I'm sure they'll make fine doctors. These boys have to serve their internship some place, Dr. Mossell . . . there's been increasing pressure on us to bar them from interning at our hospital.

MOSSELL I'm sorry . . . I don't get that. Why?

BROWNING Well . . . some of the white patients object to being treated by colored doctors . . . our white boys are resentful at having to work so closely with them. It's bad . . . I don't like it . . . but there it is.

MOSSELL I see. And I suppose you're going to ask me to permit them to come here.

BROWNING That's right. Douglass is the only adequately equipped colored hospital in the state.

MOSSELL Dr. Browning . . . we don't claim here at Douglass that we are a *colored* hospital. True, most of our staff are colored, most of our patients too. But this hospital was organized to protest against racial segregation,

> not to encourage it. We have no intention of aiding any Jim Crow tendencies. And we won't become a dumping ground for other schools, who are as well equipped as we to train their own students.

The discriminatory practices of hospitals in Philadelphia had forced the creation of Douglass Hospital. Mossell argued that it had been established to protest segregation, not to foster it. If Mossell had accepted the offer from the University of Pennsylvania, it would have undermined his intention that the hospital be interracial. Furthermore, he would have been an accomplice in the creation of a segregated program for black medical students. Such an act would have been contrary to his views on racial equality.[64]

The hospital's stance was not without consequences. The Chamber of Commerce and the State Board of Charities withdrew their endorsements because the hospital had not cooperated with the university. These actions decreased the hospital's chances of raising money. In 1919, the state legislature attached a rider to Douglass Hospital's appropriation: the institution would not receive its $22,000 appropriation unless Mossell were removed as medical director. The hospital remained firm and, for two years, it went without state funding. Mossell alleged that its rival institution, Mercy Hospital, did not have its financial stability jeopardized because it had gone along with the university's plan. He believed that the physicians at Mercy had "sold their birthright of freedom for a mess of pottage, i.e. white recognition and support." State funding to Douglass was finally reinstated after a battle waged by Edwin Vare, a Philadelphia political leader, resulted in the removal of the rider. Although Douglass had been financially damaged, Mossell had proved his point: "Douglass Hospital [would] not accept subordinate management [nor be] forced, therefore, to help the larger and more powerful institution carry out schemes of race segregation." It was one thing for the black community to establish institutions as a response to racism. It was another for the white community to attempt to use those institutions to serve and perpetuate segregation.[65]

By 1920, ambiguities and conflicts remained over the role and mission of black hospitals, as illustrated in the controversy at Douglass Hospital and the subsequent establishment of Mercy Hospital. Were these hospitals to be democratic institutions that offered opportunities to all black physicians? Or were they to be elitist institutions that excluded physicians who did not meet particular, and sometimes arbitrary, standards? Certainly, the medical profession as a whole grappled with this tension between breadth of opportunity and the desire to raise standards. But the stakes were even higher for black physicians. Unless they secured appointment to a black facility, they usually had no hospital affiliation, and hence no firm anchor to the institutional foundation of modern medicine.

Other questions remained. Were black hospitals necessary or were they concessions to segregation? In the case of white-controlled institutions, were they to be open to black physicians at all? Whose expectations and interests should they meet? The conflict between Douglass Hospital and the University of Pennsylvania illustrates some of the dilemmas faced by black hospitals. Douglass Hospital had been established to provide black physicians and nurses with educational and professional opportunities. However, when a white institution attempted to use the hospital for that purpose, charges of Jim Crowism surfaced.

By 1920, black hospitals faced additional challenges. Their agendas would be greatly influenced by the changes that had taken place in medical practice and hospital care. Regardless of sponsorship or individual history, most black hospitals were ill-equipped small facilities lacking clinical training programs. Consequently, they were inadequately prepared to survive contemporary changes in scientific medicine, hospital technology, hospital standardization, and hospital accreditation. Of course, many other American hospitals faced a similar predicament, but the stakes were extraordinarily high for black institutions. In many communities they provided the only place in which black patients could be treated and black health care professionals could receive training and opportunities to practice. Compelled by community and professional needs, their options limited by racism, and haunted by unsolved questions about the role of black hospitals, black medical leaders went to work to improve their hospitals.

TWO

At the Vanguard: The National Medical Association and the National Hospital Association

❧

During the summer of 1923, the African-American community focused much attention on efforts to make sure that black physicians and nurses would be allowed to work at the recently opened Tuskegee (Alabama) Veterans Bureau Hospital, No. 91. This hospital had been built to care for black ex-soldiers but had no black professional personnel. The National Medical Association (NMA) was one of the organizations actively involved in the campaign to open up the hospital to black staff. Its involvement in this battle (described in more detail in Chapter Three) put the broader issue of black physicians' access to quality hospitals at the forefront of the Association's agenda. At its annual meeting, held in St. Louis in August of 1923, the NMA established the National Hospital Association (NHA) to ensure proper standards of education and efficiency in black hospitals. The founding of the NHA, which was to operate under the direction of the NMA, launched the black hospital movement.

Growing concerns about the effects of standardization programs of the American Medical Association and the American College of Surgeons played a major role in the formation of the new organization. "This [standardization] movement, however wise, strikes a death blow at us as a profession," warned Dr. H.M. Green, president of the NMA in 1922 and the first president of the National Hospital Association. Black medical leaders feared that the increasing importance of accreditation and standardization would lead to the elimination of black hospitals and with it the demise of the black medical profession. This threat to the black medical profession provided the major impetus for the black hospital movement. Fears were based on recent bitter experience: in 1900, ten black medical schools existed; by 1923, only two, Meharry Medical College and Howard University School of Medicine, remained. Leaders of the NMA and NHA did not want black hospitals to suffer a similar fate. They wanted to improve the status of black hospitals from within before housecleaning by outside (and possibly unfriendly) forces swept these institutions away. The physicians realized that their own programs might eliminate many of the prototypical black hospitals, which were (like most white hospitals) small, proprietary, and without training programs, however they hoped that their programs would increase the number of "class A" hospitals—large, modern facilities with approved postgraduate training programs—and ensure the survival of smaller hospitals that had met standardization criteria.[1]

Throughout the 1920s and 1930s, the NMA and NHA worked to upgrade the medical and educational programs at black hospitals. To accomplish their goals, the medical associations created their own standardization criteria, sponsored professional conferences, produced literature about proper hospital administration, and lobbied foundations and major health-care organizations to take more active roles in the reform of black hospitals. The NMA and NHA based their strategy to promote and protect their professional interests on the necessity of separate black hospitals, asserting that their programs represented a practical response to the racial realities of American life. They believed that integration was a slow process and that the advancement—and health—of the race could not afford to wait for its eventual development. However, not all black physicians supported this strategy. Opponents argued that the integration of facilities was the best tactic to improve the professional status of black physicians and the health of black patients.

The activities of the NHA and NMA continued a pattern that black physicians had established for their professional survival. Denied access to many of the institutions essential for their professional development, they moved to establish parallel institutions: not just hospitals, but also medical journals, medical schools, and professional organizations. In 1892, one year after his graduation from Meharry Medical College, Dr. Miles V. Lynk began publishing *The Medical and Surgical Observer*, the nation's first black medical journal. The publication lasted but one year because of financial difficulties. However, Lynk continued his work on behalf of the black medical profession, establishing the University of West Tennessee College of Medicine and Surgery in Jackson, Tennessee, in 1900. This endeavor was also burdened with financial problems. When Abraham Flexner visited the school, which had moved to Memphis in 1907, he found "meager equipment for chemistry, pharmacy, and microscopy. Otherwise, the rooms are bare." The medical school closed in 1923.[2]

In 1895, Lynk, as one of the founders of the NMA, became involved in a more longlasting endeavor. Black physicians created the organization only after they had waged a long and unsuccessful effort to integrate the American Medical Association. The first meeting of the medical society was held at the Cotton States and International Exposition in Atlanta, the event where, a month later, Booker T. Washington would make his famous Atlanta Compromise speech in which he elaborated his philosophy of racial advancement. The goals of the NMA fit closely with Washington's views on racial solidarity and self-help. The NMA's charter called for it

> 1. To effect a strong organization among Negro physicians, dentists, and pharmacists . . . in order that they may have a voice in matters of public health and medical legislation in general, and in as such matters may affect the Negro race in particular; and to develop a profound race consciousness.
> 2. To stimulate professional development by contact, by reading, and discussion of papers, by reports of cases and by demonstrations.
> 3. To encourage its members to give particular study to the cases under their observation and treatment, to subscribe to medical publications, and to buy and study the latest works pertaining to their professions.
> 4. To interest itself in everything that affects the professional development and standing of the medical and nursing professions.
> 5. To better the health and living conditions of the Negro people by educating them in matters of public health and hygiene.

In order to assist its members, the NMA sponsored an annual convention at which scientific papers were presented, clinical demonstrations held, and participants informed of the latest developments in medical practice and medical education. In 1909, the NMA began publication of the *Journal of the National Medical Association*. Meanwhile, black physicians had also formed local medical societies. The first of these organizations was the Medico-Chirurgical Society of the District of Columbia, founded in 1884. By 1914, forty local societies had been established, including the Lone Star State Association in Texas in 1886, the Palmetto State Medical Association in South Carolina in 1896, the Old North State Medical, Dental and Pharmaceutical Association in North Carolina in 1897, and the Philadelphia Academy of Medicine and Allied Sciences in Philadelphia in 1900.[3]

The NMA's work in the hospital field began in 1910 when its Committee on Medical Education conducted an informal survey of the quality of care at eight black hospitals. The committee observed that most black physicians did not understand the importance of hospitals for their work and urged them to establish more facilities. However, the NMA's activities in the hospital area were insignificant until 1923, when the NHA was established.[4]

At the NHA's initial meeting, thirty-three black hospitals became members. Any hospital that admitted black patients was eligible for membership, but throughout its history only black-controlled hospitals joined. No white-operated hospital or segregated black hospital, that is, a white-run institution for African Americans, joined. One of the first tasks of the new organization was the election of officers: Dr. H.M. Green of Knoxville, as president; Dr. Joseph H. Ward, of Indianapolis, as vice-president; Dr. John A. Kenney of Tuskegee Institute, Alabama, as secretary; and Miss Petra Pinn, a nurse from West Palm Beach, as treasurer.[5]

The NHA set an ambitious agenda. It hoped to

1. bring these institutions into one compact body for the good of all;
2. standardize black hospitals;
3. standardize the curricula for the training of black nurses;
4. encourage the establishment of hospitals in areas with sufficient black populations to support them;
5. create internship opportunities for black medical students;
6. conduct an educational and statistical survey of black hospitals.

The NHA also planned to establish a clearinghouse and information service for black hospitals. Its goals did not include programs to finance or construct hospitals. Unfortunately, its efforts to achieve those laudable and well-intentioned objectives were hampered by a weak organizational structure. The NHA never had a full-time executive director or a permanent office, and was managed by unsalaried physicians who could devote only limited time to the NHA's affairs.[6]

Nonetheless, a group of physicians associated with the National Hospital Association and the National Medical Association led the way in spearheading the black hospital movement. The men who played the most significant roles in the campaign included Dr. Peter Marshall Murray, Dr. Midian O. Bousfield, Dr. H.M. Green, and Dr. John A. Kenney. Their prominence as heads of black medical institutions and, in some cases, their connections with white medical and philanthropic organizations, gave them platforms to articulate the concerns of black physicians about their hospitals. While the movement was of course not limited to these four physicians, they were the most visible and vocal advocates of black hospital reform.

In March 1935, Dr. W.T. Sanger, president of the white Medical College of Virginia, wrote Dr. Robert A. Lambert, a medical adviser of the Rockefeller Foundation, about the credentials of Dr. Peter Marshall Murray (1888–1969), who had been suggested by black physicians as a possible lecturer at a postgraduate clinic. Lambert's response gives some indication of the high regard in which Murray was held by the staff of influential medical and philanthropic organizations. Lambert replied that he had known Murray for years and that he considered him "one of the most influential Negro medical leaders" and that he was an "experienced clinician and surgeon, and a person of broad interests and sympathy." Murray, born in Houma, Louisiana, graduated from Howard University Medical School in 1914 and completed his internship at Freedmen's Hospital. After his internship, he worked as an instructor in surgery at his alma mater. Black institutions had thus been crucial to his professional development. Murray moved to New York City in 1920, where he did postgraduate work at several hospitals, including New York Postgraduate Hospital and New York University. However, he maintained his ties with Howard University. In 1924, he began a twenty-four-year tenure on its board of trustees.[7] During his first fifteen years in New York City, Murray performed most of his operations at Wiley Wilson's Sanitarium, a small proprietary black hospital. In 1927, Murray became one of the first black physicians named to the staff of Harlem Hospital. Three years later he became the first black physician certified in gynecology by the new American Board of Obstetrics and Gynecology. This was not the last time that Murray was to be a pioneer. In 1949, he was the first African American elected to the American Medical Association's House of Delegates, and in 1954 he became the first black president of the Medical Society of the County of New York.

Murray, elected president of the NMA in 1932, was one of the most visible advocates of black hospital reform. He acknowledged that white support was essential for the reform movement. In a February 1930 address before the Annual Congress on Medical Education, Medical Licensure, and Hospitals, he observed that the state of the professional development of the black physicians mandated the "assistance of the broadminded, sympathetic white profession." Murray urged his white colleagues to provide black physicians with the help that they needed. In his role as a spokesperson for black hospital reform, he also visited black medical societies and served as a consultant for white foundations such as the Julius Rosenwald Fund and the Duke Endowment.[8]

Dr. Midian O. Bousfield (1885–1948) served as president of the NMA two years after Murray's term. Bousfield had even stronger ties to the white philanthropic community: in 1935, he became director of the Negro Health Division of the Julius Rosenwald Fund, a division established to coordinate the philanthropy's activities in black medical care. It supported projects to train black medical and nursing personnel and to encourage the study of black health care. Bousfield provided the Rosenwald Fund with a direct link to black medical leaders and, in turn, gave the black hospital reformers a voice in a major philanthropic organization.[9]

Bousfield, a 1909 graduate of Northwestern University Medical School, interned at Freedmen's Hospital. After completing his training, he lived in Brazil for a short time before returning to Chicago, where he had to work temporarily as a barber and as a porter to earn enough funds to set up his medical practice. Prior to his appointment at the Rosenwald Fund, he served as an executive and medical director of Supreme Liberty Life Insurance Company, one of the nation's most prosperous black businesses. As a proponent of black hospital reform, Bousfield also spoke to white medical associations. In 1933, he became the first black person to address the American Public Health Association in its sixty-year history. He used the platform to articulate candidly views that might make his white audience uncomfortable, but which he believed were important to improve the health status of African Americans. He stressed that white support was indispensable to any effort to improve black health care. However, he urged that African-American leaders and organizations be consulted before the initiation of any health programs in their community. He argued that respect for the African-American community and its goals should be an essential element of such programs. Bousfield further instructed the members of the public health organization that when making speeches to black audiences they should "make no reference to the race question. Leave out former experiences with colored people, forgo any expression of your own lack of prejudice and omit the 'darky' story in dialect."[10]

Murray and Bousfield often worked with H. (Henry) M. Green (1876–1939), president of the NHA for eleven years, to push for the cause of black hospitals. Green had graduated from Knoxville Medical College, a proprietary black medical school. After graduation, he returned to his alma mater as a teacher and administrator. When Abraham Flexner visited the school in January 1909 he found that it had no laboratory facilities and was housed in a floor above an undertaker's business. In his report on medical education he scathingly wrote that the school's catalogue was "a tissue of misrepresentation from cover to cover." The school closed in 1910, the same year the

Flexner Report was published. In addition to his education at Knoxville Medical College, Green took some postgraduate courses at Northwestern University School of Medicine in Chicago. Upon his return to Knoxville, he established a large private practice and became chief of the medical staff at Wallace Memorial Hospital, a small black hospital. He also worked as an assistant health officer for the Department of Public Health, the first African American to hold such a post in the South.[11]

Green, perhaps spurred by his personal experience with the possible consequences of standardization and accreditation, emerged as a tireless crusader for the black hospital movement. While maintaining his practice and public health position, he ran the National Hospital Association. Green traveled extensively, at his own expense, to promote hospital reform and to investigate conditions at black hospitals. He also published numerous articles on the topic, including a widely distributed pamphlet, "A More or Less Critical Review of the Hospital Situation Among Negroes in the United States." Green, in this publication, described the desperate situation of black hospitals and the adverse consequences it had on black doctors, nurses, and patients, and urged financial contributions, especially from white Americans, to assist the institutions. "The hospital situation among negroes," Green concluded, "stands as a challenge to American justice, American intelligence, and American Christianity."[12]

Another graduate of a defunct black medical college, Dr. John A. Kenney (1874–1950) also took an active role in the black hospital movement. Kenney, the son of former slaves, graduated in 1901 from Leonard Medical College in Raleigh, North Carolina. The school, affiliated with Shaw University, would close in 1918. After Kenney completed his internship at Freedmen's Hospital, Booker T. Washington hired him to be the resident physician at Tuskegee Institute. He worked at the institute for twenty-two years, later serving as Washington's personal physician and as medical director and chief surgeon at the school's John A. Andrew Hospital. In 1912, Kenney started the John A. Andrew Clinics, a postgraduate training program for black physicians. Six years later he moved to Newark, New Jersey, where the limited access that black physicians and nurses had to hospitals in the Garden State led him to open a thirty-bed proprietary institution, Kenney Memorial Hospital, in 1927. In 1935, he donated the hospital to the Booker T. Washington Community Hospital Association, a nonprofit organization. At the time of the ownership transfer, the hospital was renamed Community Hospital. For a number of years Kenney served as secretary of the NHA, but his most influential role was as editor-in-chief of the *Journal of the National Medical Association*, a position he held for thirty-two years, from 1916 to 1948. In this capacity he wrote numerous editorials describing the plight of black physicians and their hospitals. In a 1930 volume of the journal dedicated to black hospitals, Kenney advocated, in an obvious allusion to the contemporary arts revival, a "Negro Hospital Renaissance." As was fitting for a man who had worked with Booker T. Washington for so many years, Kenney saw the establishment of black hospitals as a model of black self-help, representing "a good example of civic interest and good citizenship" by demonstrating that African Americans could solve their own problems, just like other segments of the society.[13]

Leaders of the NMA and NHA urged black physicians to become active in black hospital reform. They reminded their members that their lack of access to quality hospitals adversely affected their pockets, and that participation in the hospital movement would protect their economic interests. "Without access to well-equipped hospitals we are gradually losing our professional grip among our people. . . . We are losing our practice and it is not all due to the economic depression," warned Dr. L.A. West, NMA president in 1930 and a member of the first executive committee of the NHA. Another threat to the economic status of black physicians was the growth of medical specialization and the development of specialty boards. Specialty training and practice involved extended periods of hospital work. Black medical leaders cautioned that black medical practice could be limited to the economically less secure and less lucrative field of general practice. They also feared black physicians would be, as Chicago surgeon U.G. Dailey stated in 1929, "destined to treat only the minor ailments and to get the dregs of practice, with consequent inadequate return upon [their] educational investment."[14]

Concerns about the inability of black medical graduates to obtain internships in approved programs also persisted. In 1923, approximately 202 black hospitals existed. Only six had internship programs and not one had a residency program. Of the approximately 169 black hospitals that operated in 1929, the American Medical Association approved only fourteen for internship training and two for residencies; the American College of Surgeons approved seventeen for general accreditation. However, two of the approved hospitals, Grady Hospital in Atlanta, and St. Philip Hospital in Richmond, admitted black patients but barred black interns and physicians. In 1929, only seventy internship slots were available to the approximately 125 black medical students who graduated each year. By 1932, the number of internships available to black students had increased to 103—93 in fourteen black hospitals and ten in predominantly white hospitals. At the same time, however, a surplus of positions existed for white graduates: 6044 internships at 682 hospitals for 4814 graduates.[15]

The quality of some of the approved programs in black hospitals was suspect. Formal approvals from the accrediting agencies did not always indicate that the hospitals had met the minimum standards of the organizations. Representatives of the American Medical Association's Council on Medical Education and Hospitals freely admitted that a number of these programs would not have been approved except for the need to supply at least some internship opportunities for black physicians. The Council's approval reflected the accepted practice of educating and treating African Americans in separate, and not necessarily equal, facilities. Leaders of the NMA and NHA viewed improving the quality of internship programs in black hospitals, rather than increasing the quantity, as one of the more pressing goals of their hospital movement.[16]

The black hospital reformers also sought to improve black nurse training schools before accreditation criteria closed them. Many of these schools mercilessly exploited their students, as did many of their white counterparts. The young women worked long hours and received either no funds or a very minimal allowance for their toil, which usually included not only caring for patients but also domestic chores such as cleaning and laundering. The institutions often operated for profit and made money off the student nurses' backs. The women were hired out as private duty nurses, and any income from their services went into the pockets of the school's owners. The training schools promised the students supervised instruction in nursing, but the curriculum at many of them was mediocre, and at some nonexistent.[17]

In 1925, the Rockefeller Foundation commissioned Ethel Johns, a white Englishwoman, to conduct a study of black nurse training schools. In her final report she detailed the wretched conditions at the schools. Johns acknowledged that time constraints prohibited her from observing the teaching at many of the schools that she visited, however, she harshly criticized those she did see. She wrote:

> Teaching equipment is inferior as a general rule. In the twenty-two schools visited only seven had adequate facilities and of these only one had really first class equipment. Only five hospitals provide nurse instructors and of these only one is fully qualified to teach. Statements regarding the hours of teaching must be taken with a large grain of salt. Several times I was informed that the regular teaching program was actually in progress and a few minutes afterwards shown a classroom which obviously was not in frequent use.

NHA president H.M. Green acknowledged the dismal state of many of the black nurse training schools and described many as "simply boarding houses for sick Negroes with a few ignorant colored girls giving their time in an effort to get an education." He pledged the NHA's assistance to halt such practices. However, Miss Hulda Lyttle, superintendent of nurses at Meharry Medical College's George W. Hubbard Memorial Hospital, told Johns that she did not believe that the NHA had a sincere interest in nursing education and complained about the attitudes of black physicians toward black nurses. "They do all they can to keep us down," she observed. "All they are out to do is to save the lives of . . . hospitals." Miss Lyttle's assessment was on the mark. In spite of Green's professions, the NHA devoted most of its energy to promoting the interests of physicians.[18]

The leaders of the black hospital movement saw their activities for improvement of professional opportunities as part of the broader racial uplift movement. The historian Carter G. Woodson, in his 1934 monograph *The Negro Professional Man and the Community*, described physicians as the most important professional group in the African-American community. He noted that they had assumed civic, economic, and political leadership positions. In addition, they had become missionaries of health and had begun to develop public health programs. Woodson considered their work essential for the social uplift of the race. The black hospital reformers echoed this theme in their speeches and writings. The statements of Dr. Algernon B. Jackson, a professor of public health at Howard University, typified their sentiments in a 1923 article entitled, "Public Health and the Negro":

> the successful operation of hospitals among our people is doing much to bring about a higher degree of racial consciousness, racial respect and good will, all of which breed a confidence and faith in the profession which is destined to lead our race to a higher level, socially and economically.

Thus the black hospital movement reflected not only an attempt to protect and promote black professional interests, but a well-intentioned effort to improve the social status of the race.[19]

The health needs of the black population also prompted the physicians to act. They considered the limited number of hospital beds available to black patients to be a pressing problem and worked to increase the quality and quantity of hospital beds. Although Northern hospitals continued their practices of excluding or segregating black patients, the problem of black hospitalization was even more acute in the South with its larger black population and its more restrictive racial codes and customs. African Americans who lived in Southern rural counties especially encountered difficulties obtaining hospital services because these areas usually lacked accommodations for black patients in white institutions and did not have the black doctors needed to staff or establish black ones.

The color line in hospital care was so rigid that even medical emergencies did not bend it. Hospital segregation often led to tragic, and, at times, fatal consequences. Dr. George Moore, a black physician, learned firsthand the extent to which racial discrimination was an accepted and deadly component of contemporary medical practice. In 1927, his son, also named George, died from injuries suffered in an automobile accident after he was denied medical care because of his skin color. After his son's untimely death, Dr. Moore wrote poignantly about the tragedy:

> About 8:00 A.M. November 4, 1927, my boy met with an automobile accident on the highway between Athens and Decatur, Alabama. A Mr. Gordon . . . rushed my son, in his car, to Athens, Alabama, and Decatur, Alabama, in vain search for hospital accommodation. He was not only refused medical aid for his disability, fractured–dislocation of the third cervical vertebra with compression of the spinal cord, but was absolutely refused admittance to any hospital available in that territory on the ground that there were no hospital facilities for Colored patients, regardless of the severity of the disability.
>
> An ambulance of the hearse ambulance type was finally secured after a wait of several hours and he was rushed to Huntsville, Alabama, a distance of thirty some odd miles from Decatur, Alabama, where he was admitted to McCormick Memorial Hospital where he received every attention and was rendered service far beyond the ordinary. He died the following evening at 9:00 P.M. November 5, 1927, from pneumonia, induced and aggravated by unnecessary exposure, lack of adequate medical care and treatment and particularly on account of the inability of Mr. Gordon to secure for him hospitalization at a time favorable for recovery.
>
> It is obvious that Mr. Gordon was unable, in spite of his incessant pleading in behalf of my boy, to persuade the hospital authorities, other than at Huntsville, Alabama, to treat or regard him as a human being. He therefore died as a martyr to the traditional and sectional psychology so prevalent in many sections of our country.[20]

Louise Allyn, a white resident of Athens, Alabama, offered another perspective on the accident:

> The young man, in company with others on his way by auto, to attend a football game, when for some reason their car, which was going at a high rate of speed, left the gravel highway on a curve, outside of Athens and overturned, injuring Mr. Moore, seriously.
>
> The only ambulance in Athens belonged to the undertaker who had two funerals scheduled for that afternoon. He made strenuous efforts to adjust his business so as to take the young man to Huntsville hospital twenty-five miles distant, it being the nearest one which has a col-

> ored ward. Athens has no hospital of any sort and Decatur which has a small hospital for white people is fourteen miles from Athens.
>
> Our Athens people are exceedingly kind and friendly each race toward the other race and everything was done which could be done for Mr. Moore at the doctor's office where he was taken. As usual in cases of accident there seemed need of haste and possibly there was some confusion in making the necessary arrangements but everything was done which anyone knew to do.

Allyn's description of the accident inadvertently makes plain the value placed on a black life in Southern society at the time. Apparently, as evidenced by the ambulance delay, it was more urgent to tend to the dead than to a dying black man. Furthermore, it is clear that when Allyn stated that "everything was done which anyone knew to do" she meant that "everything was done which anyone knew to do *for a black person*." A white person would have surely received treatment at the nearest hospital. Allyn ended her sympathetic account by concluding that "the whole tragic occurrence proves that hospitals are sorely needed for Negroes, in this vicinity."[21]

The circumstances surrounding the death of the young Mr. Moore were not isolated. Hospitals could, and routinely did, refuse medical care to black patients even in emergency situations. One widely publicized incident was the November 1931 death of Juliette Derricotte, Dean of Women at Fisk University. Miss Derricotte also died after she was refused hospital care after an automobile accident in Dalton, Georgia. She received treatment at the office of a white physician, but was then moved to the private home of a black woman who had no medical or nursing training. Apparently the residence, which witnesses claim was filthy, was where black patients were treated in Dalton because the local hospital, George W. Hamilton Hospital, would not admit them. Juliette Derricotte remained at the private home for several hours, and died after she was transported fifty miles to the black ward of a Chattanooga hospital. One friend remarked that her death was due to a hospital system that was "rotten and wicked and unspeakably cruel . . . because it would harm any poor ignorant, wicked, unfortunate victim of an accident if he happened to be a Negro."[22]

George White, the father of Walter White, assistant secretary of the National Association for the Advancement of Colored People, also died in 1931. His death too was probably hastened as a result of his treatment following an accident. Crossing a street in Atlanta, Mr. White was hit by a car, and then taken to Grady City Hospital where, because of his fair skin, he was admitted to the white ward of the facility. The "error" was discovered when Mr. White's son-in-law showed up at the hospital. Walter White, in his autobiography, described the scene at the hospital when Mr. White's true racial identity was uncovered. He wrote,

> "Do you know who this man is?" [my brother-in-law] was asked.
>
> "He is my father-in-law," my brother-in-law, whose skin is brown, replied.
>
> "Have we put a nigger in the white ward?" they asked, horrified.
>
> Father was snatched from the examination table lest he contaminate the "white" air, and taken hurriedly across the street in a driving downpour to the "Negro" ward.

At the time, the black ward at Grady Hospital was the only facility in Atlanta that admitted black patients. No private black hospital existed. Walter White noted that the ward was infested with rats and cockroaches and that "dinginess, misery, and poverty pressed so hard on one from every side that even a well person could not avoid feeling a little sick in those surroundings." George White had worked for the U.S. Post Office for forty-three years and had always paid his taxes on time. "But when death had come," his son bitterly remembered, "he had been ushered out of life in the meanest circumstances an implacable color line had decreed for all Negroes, whatever their character or circumstances might be."[23]

Leaders of the NMA and NHA repeated tragic stories such as the deaths of these black people to emphasize the need for their programs. It should be noted that racism, not class position, determined the outcome for these three middle-class African Americans. And if such a fate could befall them, how much more often must it have occurred among black people without the connections to make their stories heard? Black medical leaders saw the solution to the problem of black hospitalization as the development and improvement of black hospitals. These physicians stressed, as did black social scientists, educators, and other activists, that an inadequate number of hospital beds contributed to the shockingly poor health status of black Americans. In 1920, for example, the tuberculosis rate per 100,000 was 85.7 for whites and 202 for blacks; the pneumonia rate per 100,000 was 97.1 for whites and 145.9 for blacks; and the heart disease rate per 100,000 was 93.1 for whites and 126.4 for blacks. In 1925, the death rate for blacks was 48 percent higher than for whites and the black infant mortality rate exceeded that of whites by 62 percent. Yet, despite these higher morbidity and mortality rates, and a correspondingly greater need for health care, African Americans had fewer hospital beds available to them than whites. Dr. H.M. Green, then NHA president, reported in 1928 that one bed existed for every 139 white Americans, but that only one bed existed for every 1941 black Americans.

The hospital situation for African Americans in Mississippi was particularly severe. Over 900,000 black people lived in the state in 1928, but only four black hospitals with a total of forty-two beds operated to serve their needs. Green's figures on the number of hospital beds then available to black people may be low, as it is unclear whether they include beds in mixed hospitals, which usually maintained separate and inferior wards for their black patients. Nonetheless, his central point remains unassailable: the number of hospital beds was egregiously inadequate to meet the health needs of black people. These realities spurred black medical leaders, who hoped that their professional activities would improve the health status of the race. It is clear that in the minds of the black hospital reformers the interests of black patients and doctors coincided on the issue of fighting for more hospital beds.[24]

One of the first activities of the black hospital reformers was to attempt to formulate a program to standardize black hospitals, by upgrading weaker institutions to an adequate, if not ideal, level. The physicians viewed standardization of their facilities as the most urgent problem that they would face. In a 1922 address H.M. Green, then president of the NMA, challenged the 100-bed standard for accreditation used by the American College of Surgeons (ACS) and the American Medical Association (AMA). He warned that this policy stood to eliminate approximately 85 percent of the hospitals operated for and by black people. A survey conducted a year later by the NMA's Commission of Medical Education and Hospitals proved even more alarming. It found that 93 percent of the 202 black hospitals studied had fewer than fifty beds. The AMA required that hospitals approved for internship have an average daily census of at least seventy-five patients. But the organization waived this requirement for a few black hospitals in order to provide some training opportunities for black medical school graduates.[25]

Since size precluded the accreditation of all but a few black hospitals by the ACS and AMA, the NHA issued its own set of standards. Membership in the organization was not contingent on adherence to those criteria, which included the following:

> 1. Each Hospital must be in the charge of a graduate registered nurse or physician.
> 2. The institution shall make and keep a complete clinical record of all cases treated.
> 3. Hospitals operating training schools shall maintain a staff of reputable physicians who hold regular meetings at least once each month for the purpose of reviewing work being done and matters pertaining to the moral and educational status of the school.

4. The course of instruction [for nurses] shall consist of three years of a graded course covering at least the subjects required by the examining board of the state in which the school is located. A minimum of four hours a week shall be devoted to class work with standard texts as a basis.

5. The following shall be a minimum for graduating nurses: (a) 21 years of age; (b) good moral character; (c) sound body and mind; (d) completion of a 3-year graded apprenticeship, the last of which shall be taken in the institution from which she is to graduate.

In comparison with standards set six years earlier by the larger, predominantly white, national organizations, those of the NHA were rudimentary, lacking regulations for diagnostic facilities, laboratories, or physician training.[26]

The NHA did not view its guidelines as a substitute for those set by the AMA and ACS, but rather as criteria by which smaller hospitals could be judged. It urged those few black hospitals that met the size requirements of those associations to actively seek accreditation. The NHA hoped that its attempts at standardization would prevent black hospitals from meeting the same fate as most of the black medical schools. And they hoped that their development of a set of standards for the operation of black hospitals would demonstrate to their white colleagues that black physicians could keep abreast of changes in medicine.

Although the black medical organizations acknowledged that the introduction of standardization and accreditation programs into medical care threatened the existence of black hospitals, they did not criticize the policies themselves. They did, however, contend that the hospitals should be given the resources that would allow them to meet the requirements and be brought into medicine's mainstream. Black physicians accepted the establishment of standards in hospital care, praised them, and, as we have already seen, emulated them. At the 1926 annual meeting of the NHA, Dr. John A. Ward, medical director of the Tuskegee Veterans Hospital, observed that the goal of the hospital standardization movement was "not to restrict and destroy, but to extend a helping hand in hospital activities the world over." At the annual meeting the following year, Dr. Henry M. Minton, superintendent at Philadelphia's Mercy Hospital, applauded the work of the ACS. He observed that

> What the American College of Surgeons has done has been of the greatest benefit to all institutions, great and small, rich and poor. It has shown all how far from the perfect hospital their organizations were, and when they had achieved any proportion of the requirements stipulated they could view their accomplishment with much satisfaction and pride.

Ward's and Minton's acceptance of standardization may, in part, be explained by the fact that both physicians worked at two of the best and largest black hospitals. Furthermore, their institutions had more adequate assets than those of the average black hospital. The Tuskegee Veterans Hospital received federal support, and Mercy Hospital received aid from the Julius Rosenwald Fund and the Commonwealth of Pennsylvania.[27]

The record, however, is silent on the views of the operators of the smaller, poorer facilities more at risk for extinction. The leaders of the black hospital movement, on the other hand, clearly disapproved of the operation of nonstandardized hospitals. As Peter Marshall Murray observed:

> While in the past, a certain pride might have been justified in pointing to any hospital, no matter how ill equipped or inadequately fitted to meet the health needs of a community, as an example of the Negro's effort to help himself—to build his own—there is to-day no justifiable excuse for such a state of affairs.

H.M. Green held similar views. The race's hospitals, he argued, had to be "worthy or we shall be the last to welcome them. The race cannot afford to countenance the unworthy in any line of endeavor." The NHA president pledged that the association would offer help to any black hospital that wanted to meet standardization requirements.[28]

As was true in the medical profession generally, gaps existed between the ideals of medical leaders and those of the average practitioner. The NHA thus had to work hard to convince the vast majority of the black medical profession of the importance of standardization and the threat that it posed to their careers. To achieve this goal, the hospital organization provided technical assistance to hospitals, sponsored professional conferences, and produced literature about the proper operation and administration of hospitals. Topics discussed at its annual meetings included "Hospitals As Affecting the Relationship Between the Internist and Specialist," "Some Problems in the Development of Race Hospitals in the North," "Economic Hospital Buying," and "Significance of Bi-racial Staffs in Negro Hospitals." The NHA also arranged for officials of the American Medical Association, the American Hospital Association (AHA), and the American College of Surgeons to address its members about the latest developments in medical care and hospital practice.[29]

The leaders of the NMA and NHA also lobbied the major health-care organizations and urged them to take more active roles in the development of black hospitals. In August 1927, a delegation from the two black medical associations appealed to representatives of the

American Medical Association, the American College of Surgeons, and the American Hospital Association for funds to conduct a survey of black hospitals, noting accurately that there was a paucity of data on them. In order to help them plan their programs, the physicians wanted to conduct a survey that included visits to every black hospital and documentation of their activities and needs.[30]

The AMA's Council on Medical Education and Hospitals responded favorably to the request and appropriated $5000 to conduct an investigation. The funded survey, however, was to be more limited than the NHA and NMA had originally envisioned. First, it would examine only black hospitals in the South. Furthermore, the survey would be under the auspices of the AMA and not that of the NHA. A black physician with close ties to the hospital reformers, Dr. Algernon B. Jackson, was selected to conduct the study. Jackson, professor of public health at Howard University, had previously worked as the superintendent of Philadelphia's Mercy Hospital. The survey consisted of an intensive four-month study of 120 Southern facilities—sixty-three black hospitals located primarily in the North were not examined. Jackson provided detailed information on each institution that he visited and awarded each a grade—A, B, C, or D. Those receiving a D were deemed "purely mercenary and generally unworthy."[31]

Jackson painted a bleak picture of the hospitals, including both white- and black-operated facilities. Sixteen hospitals (13 percent) received A grades, while twenty-seven (22 percent) received D grades. Jackson described conditions in some of the latter hospitals as so "filthy and inadequately equipped and managed that one would hesitate to take a drink of water in them, much less submit to even the most minor surgical operation." He also found, as Ethel Johns had four years previously, deplorable educational programs at most of the nurse training schools. Jackson concluded that the quality and quantity of hospital beds for blacks in the South was inadequate and that the problem required a more comprehensive survey. He advised that the better hospitals be supported with financial and educational assistance and that the inferior ones be abolished.[32]

The survey recommended that black hospitals should generally be under black control, but did not make this an absolute requirement. It is not clear who made the final recommendations of the survey. Apparently, the AMA Council did not fully trust Jackson's perspective on the issue. After he had completed his on-site visits, the Council submitted his report for verification to a group of white physicians, "all of whom have had a lifelong contact with the negro and spent a score or more years in medical and hospital service in their midst." This committee then submitted a revised report to the

Council. The published account of the survey obscured any differences that may have existed between the two reports, but the rather unusual procedure suggests that such differences may well have been significant.[33]

The NHA also lobbied the AHA for support of the black hospital movement. However, the ties between the two organizations were relatively weak. Although the NHA held affiliate membership with the AHA, the larger organization showed little interest in its black constituency. In 1929, the AHA did make a feeble attempt to address the problems of black hospitals when it established an ad hoc Committee on Hospitalization of Colored People, chaired by a white Chicago physician, Dr. William H. Walsh, the former executive secretary of the AHA. The purpose of the Walsh committee was to examine how the AHA could assist the NHA in its reform efforts. After its investigations, the committee concluded in general terms:

> There rests at the door of the American Hospital Association a grave responsibility for colored hospitals, and we believe that more effective efforts should be made by the Association to assist in a difficult undertaking which will require many years for satisfactory accomplishment.

It also noted that the lack of a permanent office and a full-time executive secretary severely hampered the work of the NHA. The Walsh committee recommended that the AHA assist the NHA in a campaign to secure funds for an executive secretary, and also advised that its own work be continued.[34]

Despite the modesty of these recommendations, the report received a lukewarm reception from the American Hospital Association. At a meeting in September 1931, the Board of Trustees of the American Hospital Association endorsed the general aims of the National Hospital Association but failed to make any specific commitments—financial or programmatic—to the NHA. Nor did it extend the work of the Walsh committee. This noncommittal response can be explained, at least in part, by the effects of the Depression on hospitals. At a time when many white hospitals were threatened with extinction, with the AHA at the forefront of the battle to save them, the needs of black hospitals were not a priority for the organization. Of course, the AHA had not stirred itself to action on behalf of black hospitals before the economic depression, either.[35]

The NHA continued its campaign to raise funds for a full-time executive secretary who would be based in Chicago, the location of the offices of the American Medical Association, the American Hospital Association, and the American College of Surgeons. The NHA almost immediately appealed again to the AHA, and also sought money from the Julius Rosenwald Fund, the foundation for which the black hospital reformer Midian O. Bousfield worked. The fund did express some interest in financing the position, however its terms may have included a demand that the executive secretary be accountable to it, rather than to the black hospital organization. Dr. Watson Smith Rankin, director of the Duke Endowment's hospital section and an adviser to the Rosenwald Fund, recommended to Dr. Michael M. Davis, the fund's medical director, that it should maintain tight control if it decided to underwrite the position. He insisted that the executive secretary should be under the direct authority of the fund rather than that of the NHA. Rankin further advised Davis:

> After you have had someone, preferably an intelligent Negro, in your office to work on this problem of Negro hospitals for some years and have carefully determined the program and established policies, then it might be desirable to transfer such an officer to the National Hospital Association with the status of executive secretary.

The NHA and NMA, however, believed that the person selected would work under their auspices.[36]

Throughout the early months of 1932, discussions continued on whether the Rosenwald Fund would provide money for the executive secretary. A committee composed of representatives of the NHA, NMA, AMA, and ACS even met to recommend a person to be appointed to the position. NHA President Green decided not to stand for consideration because he did not want to move from his home in Knoxville to Chicago. The committee found a well-qualified candidate in Dr. J. Edward Perry (1870–1956), chairperson of the executive committee of the NHA and a former president of the NMA in 1923, who had also founded Perry Sanitarium, a private hospital, in Kansas City, Missouri in 1910. This facility operated until 1913 when it was taken over by a community organization and renamed Provident Hospital. In 1915, another organization assumed control of the hospital and it was again renamed, this time Wheatley-Provident Hospital. Perry remained active in the institution throughout all these transitions, working as superintendent until 1929, when he was named superintendent emeritus. Perry had also been instrumental in the campaign for black control of Kansas City Hospital, No. 2. Perry's credentials notwithstanding, he was never named executive secretary of the NHA. For unknown reasons, the Rosenwald Fund decided in May 1932 not to fund the position. It is not clear whether conflict over control of the appointment played any part in the fund's decision. The NHA never received the funds from any source to hire an executive secretary, and it continued to be administered on a part time and unsalaried basis by three successive presidents. H.M. Green served in this capacity until 1934, when he was replaced by another physician, Dr. E.B. Perry. In 1939, E.R. Carney, a hospital administrator who was not a physician, became president.[37]

The National Hospital Association never received any extensive financial support from outside organizations or from foundations and was forced to operate on a meager budget. Between 1923 and 1931, it never had more than $300 in its treasury and in 1931 all its funds were wiped out by a bank failure. Most of its monies came from the collection of membership dues. However, most black hospitals did not pay, or perhaps could not pay, the five dollar annual membership fee. The association had begun in 1923 with thirty-three hospitals as members, which turned out to be the peak in membership. In 1927, the number of member hospitals had declined to twenty-three, and by 1931 it dropped to fifteen. All the member hospitals were black-operated facilities. John A. Kenney lamented in 1933 that so few institutions had paid their dues that the NHA was "short of funds even for ordinary correspondence." Its fiscal situation was so precarious that at times H.M. Green had to use his own money to keep the organization running. The NHA thus lacked the financial and political muscle to implement its programs, especially the enforcement of its standardization guidelines.[38]

The NHA and NMA also suffered from the indifference of many black physicians to its goals for black hospital reform. Few, for example, attended the meetings of the NHA. Ten hospitals and seventeen individuals registered for its 1934 meeting. The next year, registrants had increased to seventeen hospitals and thirty-five individuals. But at least 186 black hospitals operated at the time. H.M. Green also complained that many hospitals did not even return questionnaires that the NHA had sent to them. After visiting Brewster Hospital, a black hospital in Jacksonville, Florida, Dr. Midian O. Bousfield complained:

> The men in Jacksonville are way behind the times and by no means equal to the demands of such a hospital . . . I tried to talk to them in the interest of better medicine—better preparation—the National Hospital Association, National Medical Association, Promotion of Specialization, etc . . . Not a single man in the place knew anything about scholarship and the opportunity for improvement.

The enormous energies that many black physicians needed in their daily struggles to maintain their practices and to survive economically probably contributed to their lack of interest in the hospital reform movement. H.M. Green attributed the physicians' actions not to indifference but to the "loose organization" and the poor finances of the NHA. Most black physicians apparently did not perceive any benefits or advantages to joining the organization.[39]

The NHA limped along until the early 1940s. Its demise was hastened by the unwillingness, for unclear reasons, of its parent organization the NMA to continue to support it. The NHA was succeeded by the National Conference of Hospital Administrators. Founded by professional hospital administrators, not physicians, the new organization reflected the trend toward the management of hospitals by people with training in hospital administration. As opposed to the NHA, membership in the National Conference of Hospital Administrators was limited to those black hospitals that had been accredited by the American College of Surgeons. Unaccredited institutions were granted associate membership.[40]

In 1938, Midian Bousfield, then director of the Negro Health Program of the Julius Rosenwald Fund, characterized the NHA as a conglomerate organization of "inspirational nature" that had made no significant contribution to the improvement of black hospitals. But, Bousfield underestimated the impact of the National Hospital Association. Although it did not achieve most of its objectives, it did play a vital role in two critical respects. The NHA provided at least some black physicians with an arena to discuss and learn about trends in hospital care. More importantly, it worked with the National Medical Association to publicize and articulate the plight of black physicians and their hospitals. The two organizations reminded foundations and health care organizations that black hospitals needed and deserved their support.[41]

The NHA's and NMA's plans for hospital reform and professional advancement were predicated on the necessity of separate facilities for African Americans. These organizations accepted the existence of segregation—at least for the time being—and shaped their policies to work within its framework. Their leaders condemned segregation in principle, but contended that racial discrimination in the medical field left the race with no immediate alternative but to establish its own hospitals and to accept those founded by whites. Although they acknowledged that the harshness of racism was more severe in the South, the black hospital reformers also called for black hospitals in the North as well. A 1929 editorial entitled "Our Hospital Problems" that appeared in *The Journal of the National Medical Association* illustrates the positions of the two medical organizations:

> Extremists say that we had better do without these benefits for fifty years more than to accept anything that smacks of segregation. In the meantime let the sick folks suffer and die for the lack of them. Let those who would render the more dignified service of nursing continue as maids or degenerate into worse. Let the young graduates in medicine fail of their certificates to practice because they cannot meet the state board's requirement for interneship. Let those who can practice in cer-

> tain states without these requirements do so and bear the stigma of inferiority.

The 1920s and 1930s represented a time of professional frustration for black physicians, and many viewed the improvement of black hospitals as a key to their professional survival. Such an approach was consistent with the tendency toward separatism and self-help often observed during periods of increased racism.[42]

At the same time that they embraced separatism, the hospital reformers made very clear their opposition to segregation and its concomitant ideology of white superiority, insisting that their activities did not constitute self-segregation. The NHA and NMA viewed first-class black hospitals as sources of community pride, social uplift, and economic opportunity—not, as critics charged, as examples of Jim Crowism. They pointed to the establishment of other ethnic hospitals as models and noted that they had opened without allegations that they fostered segregation. Spokespersons for the organizations also noted that most black hospitals did not practice racial discrimination in patient care, physician training, and staff appointments and that their activities involved white support.

Paradoxically, the hospital reformers viewed the development of separate institutions as a strategy not only for professional survival, but also as a tactic for integration in the long run. The black hospital movement sought to gain black physicians a foothold in organized medicine. Black physicians created separate institutions—hospitals, medical societies, hospital associations—as part of their arsenal in the battle to win professional acceptance. The careers of the four major black hospital reformers, described earlier, illustrate the process that they hoped to expand and accelerate. Murray, Green, and Kenney had graduated from black medical schools, and Bousfield had interned at Freedmen's Hospital. Three of the four—Murray, Green, and Bousfield—later obtained positions within white-dominated institutions.

By creating and accepting separate institutions, they appeared to be condoning that which they purported to abhor. Maintaining, however, that their activities did not conflict with the eventual goal of an integrated American society, the hospital reformers argued that quality black hospitals would provide black physicians and nurses with opportunities to demonstrate and learn the skills that would allow them to enter the mainstream of their professions. They also asserted that once black hospitals attained the standard of excellence that characterized other hospitals, all races and nationalities would seek to utilize their services. August Meier, a prominent scholar of Afro-American political ideology, has argued that this paradoxical stance of black leaders—endorsing separate facilities and yet struggling for integration—was one of the central themes of early twentieth-century African-American political thought.[43]

The stance of the NMA and NHA on racially separate facilities was not absolute. Throughout the period of the black hospital movement, most public hospitals—even those admitting black patients—excluded black physicians. Leaders of the organizations harshly criticized this practice and called for the removal of racial barriers at tax-supported institutions. Since African Americans were taxpayers, the physicians argued, they should not be barred from these hospitals either as professionals or as patients. They pointed to New York City's Harlem Hospital as a model.[44]

Harlem Hospital was one of the first municipal hospitals to admit black physicians to its staff, but not without a battle. The institution had opened in 1887 before the influx of black residents. When blacks began to move into Harlem in large numbers, the hospital's admissions reflected the changes in community composition. In 1900, 62,000 blacks lived in Harlem and by 1920, the black population had grown to 152,000. In that year African Americans represented nearly 75 percent of the patients seen at Harlem Hospital. At the same time, however, there were no black physicians on the hospital staff. One physician, Dr. Louis T. Wright, had been appointed in 1919 as clinical assistant visiting surgeon in the outpatient department. This appointment represented the lowest rung on the medical staff hierarchy and did not carry with it admitting privileges. Some white physicians strongly protested even this token integration of the medical staff. Four doctors resigned and Cosmo O'Neil, the hospital superintendent who had hired Wright, was forced to transfer to another position reportedly because he had "brought niggers into Harlem Hospital."[45]

During the early 1920s, a broad coalition of African Americans (including the North Harlem Medical Society, the Urban League, the NAACP, the black press, and some politicians) launched a drive to secure staff appointments for black physicians and employment opportunities for black nurses. The campaign was greatly assisted by the growing political power of black people in New York City. Black voters had become critical to the outcome of local elections and they were courted by politicians from both parties. They had abandoned their traditional alliance to the party of Lincoln in the 1921 mayoral election and had overwhelmingly supported the Democratic candidate, John Hylan, who received over 75 percent of the black vote in his reelection bid. The mayor, sensitive to political realities, sought a solution to the Harlem Hospital controversy that would be acceptable to both the black community and the white medical staff, recommending, initially, that the hospital become an institution exclusively for the care of black patients like Kansas City Hospital, No. 2. This suggestion was rejected by the black leaders who wanted the hospital to remain open to patients of all races *and* to be open to black physicians and nurses. They feared, with good reason, that creation of an all-black institution would result in municipal neglect and, consequently, inferior medical care.[46]

The black activists won their first victory in 1923 when black nurses were hired. The appointment of physicians proved more difficult. In 1925, black community leaders agreed to a temporary measure: five black physicians would be named as assistant visiting surgeons and physicians. They were Drs. Louis T. Wright, Douglas B. Johnson, Ralph Young, Lucien Brown, and James W. Granady. These positions were created specifically to accommodate these men and represented the lowest positions on the medical staff. The assignments were considered provisional and would remain so until the physicians had demonstrated their competence to the white staff. The black community made it clear that their goal of full staff recognition for black physicians remained intact and continued applying political pressure. The 1925 agreement also called for the establishment of a nurse training school for black nurses and the appointment of black interns. Black medical school graduates had applied for internships in the past, but they had not scored high enough on the required examinations because they were given low ratings for "personality." In 1926, three were finally admitted to the program. The integration of the medical staff proved successful. Two years after they had been named to the staff, the physicians' provisional status was dropped. By 1932, the number of black medical staff employed at Harlem Hospital had increased to fifty-five physicians, ten dentists, and fourteen interns.[47]

The Harlem Hospital precedent was a landmark for leaders of the NMA and NHA, who considered the removal of restrictions against black physicians at public hospitals to be a key component of their hospital program. By 1931, black physicians had secured positions as interns and staff physicians at six nonsegregated public hospitals. In addition to Harlem Hospital, the institutions were Bellevue Hospital in New York, Cook County Hospital in Chicago, Detroit City Hospital, Boston City Hospital, and Cleveland City Hospital. The Tuskegee Veterans Hospital; St. Louis City Hospital, No. 2; and Kansas City General Hospital, No. 2 also admitted black physicians, but these facilities had been established to care for black patients exclusively.[48]

Black medical leaders did not believe that their advocacy of the integration of tax-supported hospitals conflicted with their insistence on the need for black hospitals, arguing that the full integration of public hospitals would take many years and that the number of positions offered to black physicians would be extremely limited. Furthermore, white people tended to view the black physicians who had integrated these places as extraordinary, and not as representative of their race. When Boston City Hospital accepted its first black intern, NMA President Peter Marshall Murray even hinted that such hospitals would only allow physicians of a certain hue to pass through their doors. He observed:

> With nothing but the highest regard for this first young man and the record he has made, at the same time we have a sneaky feeling that we have made little or no headway . . . For as the old saying goes: 'Sight beats the word' and if one were looking for a Negro, sight would not have helped them much in this case.

He alleged that the intern, Dr. John B. Hall, Jr., had only been admitted because he could pass for white. Since most black medical professionals would work at black hospitals, not integrated ones, the hospital reformers concentrated their efforts on improving these facilities. The black hospital movement, they argued, would provide a "record of group achievement, which cannot be explained on the ground of 'an exceptional person.'"[49]

Not all black physicians adhered to the separatist strategy of the black hospital reformers. A small group of physicians, many of whom were associated with the NAACP, assailed the activities of the NMA and NHA and demanded the immediate integration of medical facilities. Dr. Louis T. Wright (1891–1952), the first black physician named to the staff of Harlem Hospital, was one of the most vocal and active critics of the tactics employed by the major black medical organizations.

An examination of Wright's life helps shed light on his development as a leading proponent of medical integration. Wright was born in La Grange, Georgia in 1891, the son of Ceah and Lulu Wright. Ceah Wright had graduated from Meharry Medical School and briefly practiced medicine before abandoning it to pursue a career in the ministry. He died when his son was four years old; his widow later married another physician, Dr. William Fletcher Penn, a graduate of Yale Medical School. Penn's brother, Dr. I. Garland Penn, was one of the founders of the NMA.

Louis T. Wright had a distinguished academic career. He was class valedictorian when he graduated from Clark University, a black institution in Atlanta, in 1911. Four years later, he graduated *cum laude* from Harvard Medical School. Wright's response to a racist episode while he was a student at Harvard demonstrates that his opposition to separate training for black physicians developed early in his career. At the end of his second year at Harvard, a faculty member informed him that he could not do his obstetrics clerkship at Boston Lying-In Hospital as was the usual practice for Harvard students. He would have to complete it with a black physician who practiced in Boston "because that is the way all the colored men get their obstetrics." Wright protested and won the support of his classmates in a successful fight against his separate assignment. Despite his academic record at Harvard—he graduated fourth in his class—he could not secure an internship at Massachusetts General Hospital, Boston City Hospital, or Peter Bent Brigham Hospital. He had to complete his internship at one of the black hospitals, Freedmen's Hospital in Washington, D.C. Wright had not wanted to do his training at Freedmen's Hospital because his stepfather, who had trained there, had told him "how handicapped the men there were for equipment" and for "contact with new and stimulating clinical experiences." But racial discrimination limited the options for all black medical school graduates, even one as brilliant as he. While at Freedmen's Hospital Wright once again displayed his stance on racial matters. The hospital staff had been ordered to take part in President Woodrow Wilson's 1916 peace parade, but Wright refused to participate because black people were relegated to the rear. Another time during Wright's internship, a white man approached him and asked, "Sam, where can I find the Superintendent?" "Charley, you find him yourself," Wright replied. "Why damn it, I'm a United States Senator," said the man. "Well, damn it, it's high time you learned to call a doctor a doctor." Wright's encounter with the unidentified senator almost led to his dismissal from the internship program. Instead, he received a reprimand.[50]

In 1916, after he had completed his internship, Wright returned to Atlanta to work with his stepfather in a private practice. He was quickly introduced to the realities of medical practice for black physicians in the South. When Wright arrived at the Fulton County Courthouse to register his license, the white clerk refused to call him Dr. Wright and insisted on calling him Louie or Wright. When he refused to respond to either name, the clerk kicked him and asked, "You aren't going to sell any dope are you or do any abortions?" Wright exploded, "Let me tell you something. I'll choke you right here if you open your god damn mouth again." He later recalled that he had never been so close to murder as he had been at that moment. Realizing that the South was a dangerous place for someone of his temperament and political persuasion, he left Atlanta within a year. However, during his time there he accepted an appointment that would have a profound effect on his life: he became treasurer of the recently established Atlanta branch of the NAACP. It was to be the start of Wright's thirty-six-year involvement with the civil rights organization and the beginning of a long friendship with Walter White, who was secretary of the branch.[51]

Wright went on to enjoy an illustrious medical career. After a stint in the United States Army Medical Corps, he opened a private practice in New York City in 1919. In that same year, he received his first appointment at Harlem Hospital, where, twenty-four years later, he would be director of the hospital's department of surgery. Wright also engaged in clinical research and published articles in prestigious medical journals including *Boston Medical and Surgical Journal*, *Journal of Infectious Disease*, and *Journal of the American Medical Association*. His first scientific research project, conducted while he was an intern, proved the validity of the Schick test, a diagnostic test for diphtheria, in blacks. Previously, it had been believed that dark skin pigmentation made the test useless in black patients. In 1938, Wright contributed a chapter on head injuries to an orthopedics textbook, making him the first black physician to publish in a major medical textbook. His accomplishments resulted in his election to the American College of Surgeons in 1934. He was the first black physician so honored since Daniel Hale Williams had been elected a charter member in 1913.[52]

In addition to his medical career, Wright gained prominence and drew controversy as a civil rights activist. In 1935, he became chairperson of the board of trustees of the NAACP, a post he held until his death in 1952. Wright often served as a NAACP spokesperson, presenting the organization's objections to separate medical facilities for African Americans. For example, in testimony at a 1938 national health conference convened by President Franklin D. Roosevelt, Wright articulated the stance of the civil rights organization:

> It is hoped at this time that the American people will begin to realize that the health of the American Negro is not a separate racial problem to be met by separate segregated set-ups or dealt with on a dual standard basis, but that it is an American problem that should be adequately and equitably handled by the identical agencies and met with identical methods as the health of the remainder of the population.

The NAACP considered black hospitals to be Jim Crow institutions. It argued that these facilities hindered efforts at integration because they provided white hospitals with excuses to continue their discriminatory practices. Wright's personal experience of having been turned away from the Boston hospitals of his alma mater and relegated (as he saw it) to the inferior Freedmen's Hospital may have seemed to him a vivid example of this process. Although his subsequent career had depended on the existence of Freedmen's Hospital, Wright became a vehement and persistent critic of black hospitals. In a 1935 article, "The Health Problems of the Negro," he contended that black physicians and nurses did not need "peculiar set-ups suited to their own unique needs," but rather needed equality of opportunity for training and practice in the existing institutions, especially those receiving public funds. Wright maintained that separate facilities were inherently unequal and pointed out that segregation had led to black hospitals that were understaffed, poorly financed, and inadequately equipped. In contrast to the black hospital reformers, he believed that the solution rested not in the improvement of black hospitals but in the full integration of all hospitals.[53]

The NAACP strenuously protested the establishment of black hospitals by government organizations or "extra racial" agencies, but it sanctioned private institutions maintained and directed exclusively by African Americans. Louis T. Wright himself worked at Harlem's Booker T. Washington Sanitarium, a small proprietary facility started in 1920 by black physicians. It was designed "primarily to supply the best of accommodations for colored patients," but patients of all races were welcome. Booker T. Washington Sanitarium operated until 1925, then continued as Edgecombe Sanitarium. Wright was one of the physicians who invested money for the new hospital.[54]

The NAACP noted, however, that very few black hospitals were operated exclusively by African Americans. White people often determined or greatly influenced the activities of the institutions because they supplied much-needed funds and support. The civil rights organization argued that white participation and, in some cases, supervision of institutions designed for the black community reinforced tenets of racial segregation and black subordination. Furthermore, it asserted that the comparisons between black hospitals and other ethnic hospitals were not valid. Ethnic hospitals were usually controlled exclusively by the ethnic group for which they had been established. Jews, not Gentiles, decided the policies of Jewish hospitals.[55]

In Peter Marshall Murray and Louis T. Wright, the black medical community of New York City had two effective, energetic, and forceful advocates of two conflicting approaches to the immediate problems of black physicians and patients. Tensions between the factions they represented became especially acute in the lean years of the Depression. These were compounded by the political maneuvering of the city's political leaders.

In 1929, the administration of Mayor James Walker, in an effort to gain political control of the municipal hospital system, abolished the agencies that had previously operated the city's hospitals and created a Department of Hospitals, headed by a commissioner of hospitals and a governing board, appointed by the mayor. Each municipal hospital was to be administered autonomously by its medical board, with a final review by the hospital commissioner. A year later, Dr. J.G. William Greef, the commissioner of hospitals, announced a sweeping reorganization of the medical staff at Harlem Hospital. In February 1930, twenty-five physicians, twenty-three white and two black, were abruptly forced to resign. Twelve black physicians were added to the staff. Together with the seven black physicians that remained on staff they now represented 40 percent of the medical staff. In addition, there were also an unknown number of black physicians who worked part time in the hospital's outpatient department.[56]

Ferdinand Q. Morton, the president of the United Colored Democracy, and Louis T. Wright were major figures in the staff changes at the hospital. The black political organization that Morton headed functioned as a segregated unit within the Democratic party and had played an influential role in Harlem becoming the first black community to lend significant support to the Democrats. In exchange for his loyalty, he was appointed chairperson of the Municipal Civil Service Commission and gained control of black patronage jobs. Because of his position and close ties to the city's administration, Morton emerged as the most powerful black politician in New York City. Morton and Louis T. Wright, both Harvard graduates, maintained a close friendship. The physician had benefitted in the past from this relationship: in 1929, for example, he was appointed a police surgeon for the city. The reorganization at Harlem Hospital resulted in Wright's ascending the hospital's hierarchy. He helped in the selection of the medical staff and was named secretary of the new medical board.[57]

Walter White of the NAACP hailed the reorganization of Harlem Hospital as the most decisive step that a city had taken in giving black physicians equality of opportunity. However, the changes at Harlem Hospital were not unanimously praised by African-American physicians. The Morton–Wright friendship prompted those who had not been appointed to charge that Harlem Hospital had become "Tammanyized" and that political connections, not merit, had determined the staff appointments. Political considerations were indeed at work in the restructuring. Tammany Hall supported the appointment of the black physicians as part of its efforts to control the administration of municipal hospitals. Most physicians who were selected had affiliations with the Democratic Party. Wright and his allies maintained, however, that professional qualifications had been the major criteria. W.E.B. DuBois, editor of the NAACP publication *Crisis*, hailed the reorganization and attributed the disgruntled physicians' allegations to Wright's refusal to appoint some prominent black physicians whom he considered incompetent. "To fill Harlem Hospital with such dead weight," DuBois wrote, "was to play directly into the hand of every `Nigger hater' in the land, and `prove' the inability of the Negro physician to measure up to modern, exacting standards."[58]

Appointment to the staff of Harlem Hospital had economic and professional implications. Except for Harlem Hospital and three small private black hospitals (International Hospital, Edgecombe Sanitarium, and Wiley Wilson Sanitarium), black physicians could not secure admitting privileges at any other hospital in New York City. Consequently, they viewed a position at Harlem Hospital to be financially and professionally crucial. Because of his influence in staff appointments, Louis T. Wright became the target of much criticism. For example, upon his dismissal from Harlem Hospital with the reorganization, Dr. U. Conrad Vincent called Wright, "a Negro political boss" who used the hospital for his own personal gain. Of course Vincent's assessment was influenced by his belief that Wright masterminded his removal, but it was a view shared by other black physicians in the city.[59]

Peter Marshall Murray emerged as one of Wright's chief opponents. Murray, who had worked at the hospital since 1927, resigned in March 1930, a month after the reorganization, to protest the way in which it had been carried out. The North Harlem Medical Society urged him to rescind his resignation and he consented, but he remained a critic of Wright's activities. The two physicians differed over the strategies that should be employed in the struggle for the professional advancement of black physicians. Murray, active in the hospital reform movement, supported the separatist views of the NMA and NHA, while Wright, engaged in the activities of the NAACP, pushed the integrationist agenda. Murray, a graduate of Howard University Medical School and a trustee at the institution, repudiated Wright's assumptions that graduates of black medical schools were inferior. The two physicians were also professional rivals. Before the 1930 reorganization, they each supported different men (both white) in an acrimonious fight over leadership of the surgical service. Wright sided with Dr. John Fox Connors, the eventual victor, and Marshall with Dr. Lewis Friedman, one of the physicians who was dismissed with the staff changes. With the reorganization, Connors was selected president of the medical board, rewarding Wright for his backing by helping him win election as the board's secretary. Wright, not Murray, would have access to power within the hospital's hierarchy.[60]

But Tammany Hall was not the only potential source of money and power in the medical world. As we shall see in Chapter Four, private philanthropies had come to wield substantial influence in black medical affairs. In April 1930, officials of the Julius Rosenwald Fund met with Dr. E.H.L. Corwin, President of the New York City Hospital Information Bureau, and Drs. Peter Marshall Murray and Charles Middleton, who represented the North Harlem Medical Society. The group discussed the hospital needs of Harlem and proposed to survey the community's hospital facilities to determine whether additional hospital beds were needed to care for black paying patients. The Rosenwald Fund officials committed personnel to assist the bureau with the study, but did not agree to conduct the study themselves or to build a hospital. Given the fund's broad Negro health program and its activities in other cities, black physicians in New York City assumed that its assistance with the survey was a prelude to beginning a voluntary black hospital. The North Harlem Medical Society supported the survey and hoped that it would lead to the establishment of a new hospital, but a sizeable number of its members opposed both a survey and a hospital.[61]

In May 1930, thirty of the fifty-four members of the North Harlem Medical Society, including the president and the secretary, left the organization to form a rival black medical organization, the Manhattan Medical Society. Most of the physicians who left were supporters of Louis T. Wright. Upon their departure, several of them lambasted the North Harlem Medical Society and asserted that it was engaging in conduct "undignified and unworthy of a medical society." Dr. Vernon Ayer charged that the organization had "definitely outlived its usefulness and was definitely committed to a policy of lowering the standard of medical practice and efficiency through an unwarranted and abusive attack upon Harlem Hospital." Differences over the use of separatist or integrationist strategies for the advancement of the black medical profession played a major role in the establishment of the new organization. The North Harlem Medical Society followed the position of the national medical organizations, while the Manhattan Medical Society espoused integrationism.[62]

One of the goals of the Manhattan Medical Society was to cooperate with the officials of the Department of Hospitals and at Harlem Hospital in order to build up the black medical profession. This objective clearly demonstrated the influence of Louis T. Wright, who was elected to the executive committee of the new body. The remaining members of the North Harlem Medical Society contended that Wright had attempted to turn the North Harlem Medical Society into a semi-political body that he would control and that he had left after some members objected to his maneuvers. They also charged that the other physicians had departed because Wright had exerted undue pressure on them and had made vague promises of appointments and promotions at Harlem Hospital. After the departure of Wright and his allies, Wright's rival, Dr. Peter Marshall Murray, was elected president of the North Harlem Medical Society. Dr. W. Montague Cobb, a scholar of black medical history, has observed that the dissidents established the new association in order to pursue a more vigorous program against segregation and to promote a more scientific approach to medicine than they had thought possible in the old organization. It is apparent, however, that personal jealousies and professional rivalries—as well as Wright's reportedly blunt character—cannot be discounted.[63]

The controversy over the proposed survey of hospital facilities in Harlem and the possibility of a black hospital, reflected professional and personal differences that were already present; however, ideological differences over the role of black hospitals intensified the debate. In a stormy, five-hour meeting attended by officials of the Julius Rosenwald Fund on 8 December 1930, members of the Manhattan Medical Society strongly voiced their opposition to the proposed survey, viewing it as part of a Jim Crow plan with an ultimate goal being the establishment of a hospital exclusively for African Americans. Harlem Hospital, they maintained, was not a black hospital, even though most of its patients were African Americans, because it was open to all races. The physicians also contended that the small number of black paying patients in Harlem obviated the need for such a study. During the meeting, Dr. Michael M. Davis, Medical Director of the Julius Rosenwald Fund, reiterated the fund's position: "The Julius Rosenwald Fund has no idea of promoting any colored hospital in New York City." He also informed the group that the fund had only agreed to lend personnel to the New York City Hospital Information Bureau to assist it with the survey.[64]

Davis's comments received a hostile reception. At issue was not just the fund's participation in the local study, but its entire Negro health program. Members of the Manhattan Medical Society used the occasion to vehemently criticize the need for black hospitals and the role that the fund had played in supporting them, and, in their view, in fostering a segregated medical system. A letter from Ferdinand Morton was also read at the meeting by Dr. James L. Wilson, president of the Manhattan Medical Society. Morton criticized the construction of a black hospital, calling it "vicious in principle" because it advanced Jim Crow. He also contended that such a facility was unnecessary because black patients in New York City had an adequate number of hospital beds available to them and that black physicians and nurses enjoyed equality of opportunity. Morton pledged his support and that of the Democratic Party to help the Manhattan Medical Society to defeat the "pernicious project." The meeting ended with the unanimous passage of a resolution condemning the survey and hospital as "uninvited, uncalled for, and unnecessary."

In January 1931, the Manhattan Medical Society published and widely distributed to the black press an open letter to Edwin R. Embree, President of the Rosenwald Fund, entitled, "Equal Opportunity—No More—No Less!" In this letter, the Manhattan Medical Society more fully detailed its opposition to black hospitals in the North. The organization did not discuss its position on the establishment of black hospitals in the South. The letter contended that "the Negro citizen, for his own advancement and progress along professional lines, needs no separate institutions. What the Negro physician needs is equal opportunity for training and practice—no more, no less." The Manhattan Medical Society also bitterly accused the Rosenwald Fund of "establishing and attempting to maintain a health program and a hospital program that contravenes the Constitution of the United States, bows its head before race prejudice, and offers a minimum of health protection to the American people." Fund officials believed their critics to be a "small faction which appeared to be trying to gain political ends under a screen of 'high moral principles'," but, rather condescendingly, considered the conflicts within the black medical community to be a "necessary and doubtless wholesome process."[65]

Meanwhile, the North Harlem Medical Society continued its support of the proposed survey and the work of the Julius Rosenwald Fund, contending that the study would provide valuable information about the hospitalization of black patients and the practices of black physicians. It maintained that Harlem needed a voluntary hospital in order to take care of black middle-class patients who did not want to be hospitalized at Harlem Hospital and could not afford one of the proprietary hospitals. The hospital would also benefit those physicians who found themselves locked out of the Harlem Hospital system. The North Harlem Medical Society also contended that the views of the Manhattan Medical Society represented a minority opinion and attributed its objections to a new hospital to political considerations, namely that a new hospital would be out of the hands of black Tammany. It pointed to the introduction of a letter from Ferdinand Q. Morton at the Manhattan Medical Society meeting as evidence that politics were at work in the criticisms that had been launched by the organization. On 18 December 1930, the North Harlem Medical Society unanimously passed a resolution praising the work of the Rosenwald Fund and urging the survey and the construction of a black hospital in Harlem. The National Medical Association strongly backed the stance of the North Harlem Medical

Society and the need for a voluntary black hospital in Harlem. Walter G. Alexander, general secretary of the NMA, repudiated the actions of the Manhattan Medical Society as "unprofessional and discourteous" and made clear that the new medical group had no affiliation with the national organization. The support of the NMA and North Harlem Medical Society proved futile. The survey was not conducted and a hospital was not built because of the controversy that they had provoked.[66]

The abandonment of the survey project did not eliminate tensions between the two black medical societies in Harlem. Once Wright had consolidated his position on the medical board of Harlem Hospital and was named a member of the intern committee, a new source of conflict emerged. Allegations surfaced that Wright, a Harvard graduate, was prejudiced against graduates of the black medical schools. One newspaper observed in 1933 that of the twenty-seven black physicians on the inpatient staff at the hospital, twenty-three had graduated from predominantly white medical schools. African-American graduates of such institutions were indeed uncommon at the time, representing only an estimated 14 percent of the black medical school graduates in 1932. Contending that black physicians who had graduated from the predominantly white schools had received superior training because they had access to better facilities and had had to compete with white men, Wright believed that only by competing with whites would black physicians be able to advance in the medical world. He also pledged to fight any efforts to have African Americans appointed to the staff of Harlem Hospital simply because of their race.[67]

Graduates of black medical schools chafed under the inference that they were inferior physicians, pointing out that white schools had been known to produce mediocre physicians and that some graduates of the black medical schools had achieved as much as black physicians who had graduated from the predominantly white schools. The level of the hostility that some black physicians held towards Wright manifested itself publicly in 1952 at the annual convention of the NMA. Despite his outstanding credentials, Wright received only one vote for the organization's distinguished service medal. In contrast, twelve years earlier he had received the NAACP's Spingarn medal, awarded to the black person who had "reached the highest achievement in his field of activity."[68]

During the 1920s and 1930s, divisions in the black community over the need and purpose of black hospitals were not limited to Harlem. Similar schisms were found in Detroit, Boston, Chicago, and Cleveland. Despite the intense opposition that plans for the construction of black hospitals provoked at times, the leaders of the black hospital movement were not swayed from their objectives. They continued to press for the development and improvement of black hospitals. Although they saw integration as an eventual goal, they persisted in their belief that black hospitals were crucial for their professional survival and that of the race. This position frequently placed them at odds with the NAACP. However, for a brief time in 1923, the national black medical associations and the civil rights association became unlikely allies in the campaign to place control of the national black veterans hospital at Tuskegee, Alabama, into the hands of African Americans. This battle for the Tuskegee Veterans Hospital would turn out to be one of the most explosive events of the black hospital movement.[69]

THREE

"Where Shall We Work and Whom Are We to Serve?" The Battle for the Tuskegee Veterans Hospital

❧

On 3 July 1923, several hundred members of the Ku Klux Klan marched through the streets of Tuskegee, Alabama. The demonstration culminated an especially racially tense summer in the town. Racial friction had been triggered by the federal government's pledge to allow the recently opened Veterans Bureau Hospital, No. 91, an institution exclusively for black patients, to be run eventually by a black professional staff. But the Klan and its supporters did not want a black-operated federal facility in the heart of Dixie—even though it would serve only black people.

Events at Tuskegee galvanized African Americans nationwide. Led by organizations such as the National Medical Association (NMA), the National Association for the Advancement of Colored People (NAACP), and the National Negro Press Association, they vigorously and vociferously demanded that the government uphold its promise. They condemned the Klan action and urged the government to protect the black residents of Tuskegee. Black Americans also feared for the safety of Tuskegee Institute, the school founded by Booker T. Washington. Although the school had existed peacefully in the community for forty-two years, these events during the summer of 1923 jeopardized this harmony. Several black newspapers described a reign of terror in which prominent black Tuskegeeans were forced to flee the town, and some went so far as to warn that a race war was imminent in Tuskegee.[1]

The battle over control of the Tuskegee Veterans Hospital struck a passionate chord in the black community. The depth of this response reflected the symbolism that the hospital had come to hold for African Americans: black control of the hospital stood not only as a measure of the federal government's responsibility to protect its black citizens but of the Republican party's commitment to uphold its traditional ties to African-American voters. A crucial issue for black people was whether the federal government would stand up to the Ku Klux Klan and place black physicians in charge of the hospital. Would the Klan or the federal government set the nation's race policies?

Black Americans also sought control of the hospital as recognition for their contributions to the war effort. The proposed hospital would provide both medical care for disabled black veterans and employment opportunities for black medical personnel. African Americans argued that the ex-soldiers would receive the best possible care from black physicians and nurses because they would be more caring and sympathetic to their needs. Access to the hospital was also important for black health care personnel, giving them a well-equipped and well-financed place in which to work. In addition, their appointment to the veterans' facility at Tuskegee would be a professional affirmation, demonstrating that the federal government believed in the skills and competence of black medical professionals. Exclusion of black physicians from a highly visible government hospital built for black patients would certainly have been detrimental to the profession. J.F. Lane, president of Lane College, vividly described this dilemma of black physicians and their investment in the Tuskegee Veterans Hospital when he asked, "If we can not serve our own people, where shall we work and whom are we to serve?"[2]

The decision to have a separate hospital for black veterans had been made by the Consultants on Hospitalization, a committee of medical experts, appointed in March 1921 by Secretary of theTreasury Andrew W. Mellon to advise him on the development of a national hospital system for veterans. Earlier that month, Congress had appropriated $18.6 million for the hospitals and President Woodrow Wilson on his last day in office had signed the law (P.L. 66-384). The legislative action had been prompted by the failure of a series of efforts to provide for disabled ex-soldiers in government hospitals (such as those run by the Public Health Service) and in voluntary hospitals that had contracted with the federal government. These new facilities would be organized and financed by the federal government and initially would be restricted to those veterans with service-related diseases and injuries.[3]

The care of the large numbers of veterans with tuberculosis and psychoneurotic disorders and the maintenance of proper surgical and medical standards were two major issues that the Consultants on Hospitalization would face. The committee's composition indicated the significance of these concerns. Mellon appointed Dr. William Charles White, an expert in both psychiatry and tuberculosis, chairperson. The Pittsburgh physician had previously been professor of neuropathology and clinical psychiatry at the Indiana University and during World War I had directed the Red Cross's tuberculosis hospital program in France and Italy. At the time of his appointment to the Consultants on Hospitalization, he was medical director of Pittsburgh's Tuberculosis League Hospital and a member of the executive committee of the National Tuberculosis Association.

The other physicians on the committee had equally prestigious credentials. They were Dr. Frank Billings, dean of the faculty at Chicago's Rush Medical College and a former American Medical Association president; Dr. John G. Bowman, chancellor of the University of Pittsburgh and former director of the American College of Surgeons; and Dr. Pearce Bailey, director of the National Committee for Mental Hygiene and former president of the American Neurological Association. Bailey served but three months because of ill health. He was replaced by Dr. George H. Kirby, director of the New York Psychiatric Institute at Ward's Island and former medical inspector of the New York State Hospital Commission.

The consultants, also known as the White Committee after its chairperson, worked for two years to develop a hospital system that was not only national, but rational. They were assisted by an advisory group that included representatives from the United States Public Health Service, the National Committee for Mental Hygiene, the National Home for Disabled Volunteer Soldiers, and the National Tuberculosis Association. They held hearings and heard testimony from over 100 groups—all interested in having a veterans hospital located in their area. The committee noted that such testimony "scarcely provided the data on which to build a rational hospital system," and consequently, the White Committee painstakingly collected and analyzed data on the number of veterans, their medical needs, and the number of hospitals that would be required to care for them. It sought to make its recommendations based on statistics, not political considerations. The committee had in fact been deliberately created to be an apolitical body, with decisions about the location, organization, and coordination of veterans hospitals to be made by a group of medical experts divorced from the political process and the taint of pork barrel politics.[4]

But the Consultants on Hospitalization were not immune to the racial politics of the time. In their final report, published in 1923, they recommended that a separate national hospital for black veterans be established at Tuskegee, Alabama. The original legislation that established the hospital system had not made any mention of separate facilities for black veterans, but the White Committee noted that very early in its deliberations "one of the great American problems—that of race—obtruded itself more and more." The need to provide separate facilities for black veterans had in fact been brought to the committee's attention during its first week of hearings.[5]

Approximately 385,000 black soldiers, mostly from the South, fought in World War I. After the war, hospital provisions for those who found themselves disabled only because of their participation in the "War to Make the World Safe for Democracy" were deplorable. Many Southern communities refused to hospitalize black veterans in the same facilities as white veterans. Many black veterans were unable to receive any hospital care or were housed, even those with tuberculosis, in jails and mental institutions. Some were able to gain admission to predominantly white hospitals, but were usually placed, as was the custom, in separate accommodations where they received inferior care.[6]

Black veterans poignantly and graphically described the conditions they found when they returned home. Lieutenant C.J. Adams noted that many of the ex-soldiers were "helpless not only because of color, disenfranchisement, condition of peonage, lack of representation in Congress or elsewhere nor lack of a chance for redress, but because of being wounded in France while actually engaged in battle." Issac Webb wrote in a letter to *Crisis*, the journal of the NAACP:

> I am also one of the boys who volunteered, in 1917, for services "over there"; and I have spent over six months in hospitals for the disabled . . . At Mobile, Alabama, I was handed my food out of a window, forbidden to use the front of the hospital to enter my ward, which was on the back; given no medical attention, and forced to use the same toilet facilities fellows in advanced stages of syphilis and gonorrhea used. Six beds from mine I saw a young fellow die with tuberculosis. Four hours before his death was discovered by one of his bed fellows he had not been visited by nurse or doctor. Unfortunately, there were no nurse maids in the hospital. Never in France . . . was I so humiliated and insulted, nor saw such acts of negligence and cruelty committed in the name of race superiority and blindness of race prejudice.

Segregation was not limited to Southern hospitals. It also existed in hospitals in the North that had been used to hospitalize disabled ex-soldiers. For example, in Dayton, Ohio, separate wards and toilets were maintained. These conditions led to an understandable aversion on the part of many black veterans to be hospitalized in the facilities. Their reluctance to be segregated and ill-treated and the unwillingness of some hospitals to even admit them resulted in the proportion of hospitalized black veterans being 50 to 80 percent below that of their white counterparts.[7]

The development of a policy for the hospitalization of black veterans clearly illustrated the problems and tensions inherent in the creation of a federal hospital system when racial customs and practices had to be taken into account. The White Committee acknowledged that black veterans were as entitled to government care as any other citizens of the United States, but it noted that they could not be "housed satisfactorily" with white veterans, especially in the South. The committee argued that these ex-soldiers needed hospitalization not only for their own good, but for the protection of the white community. For example, it contended that black veterans with tuberculosis could spread the disease and that "the negro insane are a danger and they are much more liable to be a danger to white than to negro."[8]

Throughout the Spring of 1921, the Consultants on Hospitalization investigated the so-called "negro problem." They sought advice from several philanthropies, including the Rockefeller Foundation, General Education Board, and the Carnegie Foundation, because of their "intensive study of the situation among the colored people." At no time did they consult any black organizations, including the National Medical Association. The consultants also sent members of their advisory committee to conduct field visits. Dr. Thomas W. Salmon, of the National Committee for Mental Hygiene, visited every institution for the black insane in the South and found that the rule was to have separate facilities. Dr. George Kirby, a member of the White committee, reinforced Salmon's findings. He thought that it was unwise to hospitalize black and white people together because "no states do, and I think it would go against the sentiments of the people very much."[9]

By June 1921, the consultants had come up with a solution. In a letter to Secretary of the Treasury Mellon, William Charles White reported that one of the committee's most important findings had been "the imperative demand for some separate provision in the South for the Negro soldier." The separate provision was not to be segregated accommodations within facilities but a national hospital for black veterans. The proposed hospital was to be built in the South because that was where most of the veterans lived and where the problems of access and segregation were most extreme. Historian Rosemary Stevens notes that this decision represented the abandonment, for African Americans only, of the national policy of caring for patients in their local communities. The Consultants on Hospitalization also thought that the construction of such a hospital would assist black uplift by providing black physicians and nurses with educational and training opportunities.[10]

Plans called for the hospital to be located so as to provide for the greatest number of ex-servicemen. Georgia and Alabama became prime contenders because in each of the states black soldiers represented more than 40 percent of the men who had fought in World War I. Factors such as proximity to a black educational institution and to a railroad station would also be taken into account.[11]

Finding a location for the black veterans hospital proved more difficult than had been anticipated. Some Southern communities vehemently opposed the construction of the hospital in their vicinities. In Montgomery, Alabama, for example, the chamber of commerce had tried to secure the hospital before it realized its purpose. At a mass meeting held in June 1921, a group of self-identified representative white citizens articulated their position. Dr. M.W. Swartz, president of the town's Woman's College, argued that the establishment of a black hospital would be against the best interests of his college because the presence of a large number of black men would jeopardize the safety of the white women students. Dr. S.W. Welch, the state health officer, observed, "There are richer things than silver and purer things than gold" and that he was altogether opposed to bringing "demoralized negroes" from France to Montgomery regardless of any commercial advantage. Furthermore he contended that the proposed hospital would bring "governmental interference in Southern affairs." However, the group unanimously passed a resolution, sponsored by Robert E. Steiner, state commander of the American Legion, supporting the construction of a white veterans hospital. Thus it appears that the group was not anxious about governmental interference in general, but afraid of the potential for government intervention in local racial policies. This pattern repeated itself two months later in Atlanta, where white residents of the city also opposed the construction of a black veterans hospital, but lobbied for a white one.[12]

Shortly after the meeting in Montgomery, Major Robert Russa Moton, Booker T. Washington's successor as principal of the Tuskegee Institute, wrote to William Charles White and vigorously campaigned for the hospital to be located in Tuskegee. Referring to the opposition in Montgomery, a mere forty miles to the northwest, Moton acknowledged that he had already discussed the project with prominent white Tuskegeeans, including the mayor, the president of the state medical association, and the owner of a local newspaper, and had found no objections. He observed that the main reason for the conciliatory attitude of the white residents of Tuskegee was "that the Tuskegee Institute with its large number of Negro teachers and students has lived during its forty years in the midst of these excellent white people of our county, and they have never experienced any disadvantage or inconvenience or embarrassment because of the presence of these black people." In addition, the school already operated a vocational rehabilitation program for black veterans. Moton urged White to send a representative to investigate the feasibility of placing the hospital at Tuskegee.[13]

The Consultants on Hospitalization had in fact considered the town—and Nashville, the home of Meharry Medical College—as potential sites because black educational institutions were already located in these communities. Locating the hospital in Nashville had certain advantages: it would allow the hospital to be attached to a medical school and would enable it to be used for training black physicians and nurses. Tuskegee Institute did not have a medical school, but did have a nurse training school. Abraham Flexner, an official at the General Education Board and an influential figure in medical education, supported constructing the hospital near Meharry. Flexner thought that the hospital would greatly improve Meharry's clinical program. There had been some early indications that the General Education Board might give money to Meharry if the hospital were placed near it. By June 1921, the White Committee appeared more interested in building the facility near Tuskegee Institute "because it is better known and would meet with less opposition." Members of the committee considered the school the "center of Negro activities for the country" and Moton an important leader of his race. As did Booker T. Washington, Moton maintained ties with influential white politicians and philanthropists and often served as an advisor to them on racial issues.[14]

In the summer of 1921, the consultants sent Major W.N. Kenzie of the Public Health Service to the South to explore possible locations for the black veterans hospital. In August, he met with Major Moton, who indicated that Tuskegee Institute might be willing to donate land for the endeavor. Kenzie also met with white Tuskegeeans and during these meetings he encountered an unexpected obstacle. White citizens demanded that before negotiations continued they needed assurances that the hospital would be controlled and operated by white Southerners who were "in touch with local conditions." As originally conceived, the staff would have been mixed. Plans had called for black physicians and nurses to be permitted on the staff of the hospital in order to give them "the fullest advantage of privileges of education and service to their own race." White personnel would also work at the hospital and would supervise its operation.[15]

After being confronted by the demands of the white Tuskegeeans, the consultants retreated from their support of the mixed staff. Kenzie received a guarantee from the consultants that the hospital would indeed be white controlled and operated. The white citizens accepted this promise and negotiations proceeded. Kenzie sought the opinions of a wide range of white residents of the town, meeting with physicians, bankers, lawyers, and city and county officials. Kenzie soon wired Surgeon General Hugh S. Cummings that 90 percent of the people he had met with supported the hospital. He attributed the success of his negotiations to the government's guarantee that the hospital would be white run and operated.[16]

All indications suggested that the proposed hospital would not disturb race relations in the town. A month after Kenzie's visit, the Board of Revenue of Macon County submitted a petition to the White Committee in which it supported the construction of the hospital, "provided the scientific personnel be white people." The backing of white Tuskegee residents for the project can be explained, in part, by economic factors. They believed that they might make money by selling land to the government for the hospital and, later, by furnishing food and other hospital supplies.[17]

Major Kenzie endorsed Tuskegee as the site for the black veterans hospital because there had been practically no racial tensions there and, as opposed to other locations, the hospital had the support of the white community. He also observed that the hospital would be a tribute to and a continuation of the work of "that marvelous man," Booker T. Washington. Although race relations had been harmonious in the town, he warned that any offers of land from Tuskegee Institute "would have to be considered in a very careful manner that does not conflict or cross wires with white citizens."[18]

On 16 September, Major Moton appeared before the Consultants on Hospitalization. He spoke in favor of the segregation of black patients and gave his support for the construction of the separate black veterans hospital. He also presented an offer from Tuskegee Institute in which the school was prepared to donate 300 acres for the project. Moton, however, urged that black physicians be allowed to practice there. In his testimony he noted, "If negroes could not go into the hospital except as patients and laborers then I would rather not have the hospital there in any way that would embarrass us." Chairman William Charles White made no mention of his pledge to the white citizens of Tuskegee, but assured the principal that the government would probably use capable black personnel. One month after Moton's testimony, Kenzie wrote a memo to Surgeon General

H.S. Cummings outlining the plans for the construction of staff quarters and stating that the hospital would be operated by white officers and scientific personnel. He made no mention of separate accommodations for black staff, which would have surely been the case in the 1920s South. Thus it appears that he did not intend to employ black physicians at the hospital. White's assurance to Moton can be explained in two ways: either the policy had not yet been finalized regarding staffing, or White had deliberately misled Moton to guarantee his cooperation and not jeopardize the Tuskegee Institute gift. Later events would make the latter interpretation more plausible. In late September, the consultants voted to accept the Tuskegee Institute offer over that of a group of private white citizens. The Institute site was less expensive to secure and provided better access to rail transportation. The hospital would be built on the 300 acres donated by Tuskegee Institute, but 140 additional acres would be bought from private individuals to protect the site.[19]

Not all African Americans supported the construction of a black veterans hospital at Tuskegee. Criticism focused primarily on the hospital's location. Although the NAACP argued that black veterans should receive care in the same hospitals as white veterans, it conceded that "if this were impossible because of race hatred, certainly the last place on God's green earth to put a segregated Negro hospital was in the lynching belt of mobridden Alabama, Georgia, Mississippi, and their ilk." The civil rights organization did support construction of the hospital in Washington, D.C.[20]

Black veterans echoed this sentiment. One disabled ex-soldier urged black newspapers and organizations to take steps to stop "colored soldiers who were gassed in France" from being sent to a hospital in "prejudice-ridden Alabama." On 1 November 1921, several members of the National Committee of Negro Veteran Relief met with William Charles White. The committee had been founded by African-American veterans of the World War in order to make sure that they received the benefits due them under the Veterans Bureau legislation. In their seven and one-half months of soliciting information and hearing testimony, the Consultants on Hospitalization had not contacted the group. In fact, White claimed that he had not even heard of the organization until its leaders had made contact. Lt. John W. Love, chairperson of the committee, noted that the group had learned of the proposed hospital through press accounts. It is unclear why the National Committee of Negro Veteran Relief waited until November to contact the consultants.[21]

What is clear is that the black veterans association opposed the construction of the hospital in the South, stressing that the region's racial situation would be detrimental to the health and safety of the men who would be hospitalized there. It also feared the hospital would further segregation. They believed that Northern black veterans would not be admitted to hospitals in their areas, but would be transported to the hospital in the South. The National Committee on Negro Veteran Relief opposed the Tuskegee location because it was not near a recognized medical center, and urged that the hospital be built in Washington, D.C., near Howard University Medical School. White vigorously defended the consultants actions, maintaining that the hospital was not intended to segregate, but to provide Southern veterans with better care. He mentioned the difficulties that had been encountered previously in hospitalizing black veterans in the South, and reassured the committee that the doors of veterans hospitals in the North would be open to African Americans. However, he did not guarantee that they would not be housed in separate accommodations. In fact, when one member of the delegation of black veterans pointed out that black veterans were separated from white ones in Northern facilities, White replied that it was "only a matter of administration." The chairperson of the Consultants on Hospitalization also made clear that he supported Tuskegee as the locale for the hospital, noting that the decision had been made after careful deliberations. Before the meeting with White ended, members of the National Committee of Negro Veteran Relief acknowledged that his statements had forced them to reconsider their stance on the project. Either they changed their opinion or they decided it was a hopeless cause. They never again contacted the consultants after this initial meeting.

Although black veterans expressed their opinions to the consultants, another group that stood to be affected by the construction of the hospital—black physicians—were surprisingly silent. It is true that the consultants never solicited their views, but at no point during 1921 was the proposed facility discussed in the *Journal of the National Medical Association*. Members of the medical association surely knew about the plans for the hospital. A colleague of Major Moton's, Dr. John A. Kenney, medical director at Tuskegee Institute's John A. Andrew Memorial Hospital, was editor of the publication. Furthermore, there was only one letter in the records of the White Committee from the National Medical Association. On 18 November 1921, Dr. J.A. Lester, secretary of the association's commission on medical education, wrote Dr. William Charles White to recommend that the hospital be built in Nashville near Meharry Medical College. Even if the White Committee would have seriously considered this input, it came much too late. Two days previously, Secretary of the Treasury Andrew W. Mellon had approved $2.5 million for the construction of a 600-bed hospital for black veterans at

Tuskegee. The hospital would consist of twenty-seven buildings spread over 300 acres.[22]

As plans for the hospital progressed throughout 1922, African Americans still believed that black medical personnel would be on staff. In June, Major Moton and Melvin J. Chisum, field secretary of the National Negro Press Association, met with Colonel Charles F. Forbes, the director of the recently created Veterans Bureau. Administration of veterans hospitals had been transferred from the Treasury Department to the new bureau the previous April. Moton and Chisum left the meeting with the understanding that Forbes supported the hiring of black personnel. A few months later, Moton and Chisum met with a representative of the Veterans Bureau who reassured them that progress was being made on the personnel issue. At this meeting Moton was asked whether he would agree to a white physician being temporarily named as superintendent of the hospital. Moton replied that this would be acceptable "if the appointee were a Northern man who would properly consider the interests of colored people." Moton left the meeting believing that he would be informed before any appointments were made. He later recommended that Major Kenzie be named head of the hospital. Kenzie, however, had no interest in the position.[23]

It soon became clear that the Veterans Bureau had been duplicitous in its discussions with Moton and Chisum. On 24 January 1923, while visiting a veterans hospital in St. Paul, Minnesota, Chisum noticed on a bulletin board a Veterans Bureau field letter about the soon-to-be-completed hospital in Tuskegee. The letter stated:

> The medical personnel will be composed of white persons. The chief nurse, chief aide, chief dietitian, and their assistants will be white. The staff nurses, aides and dietitians will be colored. The medical coordinator selected to take charge of the post will be from the Reserve Corps of the Public Health Service of Southern birth, and one who thoroughly understands the Negro.
>
> The colored people of Tuskegee and the superintendent and staff of Tuskegee Institute are giving Government officials their hearty support.

Unbeknown to the African-American community, a white man of "Southern birth," Colonel Robert H. Stanley of Greenville, Alabama, had already been appointed medical officer in charge of the institution. The new commander was a boyhood friend of Robert E. Steiner, the state commander of the American Legion, who had previously opposed construction of a black veterans hospital in Montgomery and the entrance of black people into the Alabama branch of the American Legion. Later, when Stanley arrived at his new station, he was on the hospital grounds for two days before anyone from Tuskegee Institute was even notified—an action that African Americans understandably viewed as an insult.[24]

The new hospital was dedicated on Lincoln's Birthday in a carefully staged ceremony at the Tuskegee Institute Chapel. Speakers to the capacity crowd included Vice-President Calvin Coolidge, Alabama Governor William W. Brandon, Tuskegee Principal Robert R. Moton, Assistant Treasury Secretary Edward Clifford, and Roger E. McDonald, a disabled black veteran. In his address, Coolidge underscored the tie between the Republican Party and African Americans, praising the accomplishments that black men and women had made since emancipation and applauding their patriotism at home and on the battlefield during the World War. "They have justified the faith of Abraham Lincoln," he proclaimed. Moton, in turn, thanked the government for constructing a hospital that would enable black soldiers to "have a fair and equal chance, under as perfect conditions as modern science affords, for as speedy and complete a recovery as is possible." Furthermore, he noted, the hospital had "no ear-marks of inferiority".[25]

The celebratory and congenial atmosphere of the ceremony belied tensions that were brewing over hospital staffing. The Veterans Bureau's deceit forced Moton into action. Two days after the dedication, he wrote President Warren G. Harding to push for the appointment of qualified black physicians and nurses to the hospital. Although the Veterans Bureau field letter had stated that black nurses, aides, and dietitians would be hired, L.B. Rogers, the bureau's assistant director, alleged that none were on the civil service eligibles list. Therefore all the hospital employees, with the exception of orderlies, attendants, and laborers, would be white. In his letter to the President, Moton conceded that the commanding officer of the institution could be white but urged that at least half the professional staff be black. He warned that the exclusion of black professional men and women "will bring down on my head, and on Tuskegee Institute, an avalanche of criticism which I think would be entirely justified, especially as I have been very active in bringing the hospital here." "What is more," he added, "it will bring down upon your administration throughout the country, a storm of protest on the part of the Negro press and from Negroes, North and South, which I think would be most unfortunate."[26]

Moton's threats were not idle. A few days after he wrote Harding, he contacted the NAACP to solicit its assistance. In confidential correspondence with James Weldon Johnson, secretary of the civil rights organization, Moton wrote with regard to the appointment of black professionals, "I mean to see this matter through in a way that will be satisfactory to us or else I shall have to go before the country and put the blame upon the Republican Party and the Harding administration." Johnson replied that the NAACP was prepared to give Moton any support that he would need to accomplish his goal.[27]

Moton also contacted Colonel Stanley to make sure that the hospital's commanding officer understood the stance of the African-American community. Again, he urged that black physicians and nurses be hired and even recommended the names of three black physicians, including John A. Kenney, whom he considered to be qualified for positions. Stanley was not sympathetic and made it very clear that he did not welcome black medical personnel at his hospital. He informed Moton that the hospital had been built only to provide medical care to black veterans and "that no other considerations must or shall be permitted to interfere or become paramount." He further added that the Veterans Bureau had deemed it wise to put white officers in charge and that a man of Moton's "perspicuity must fully appreciate the fact that it would be utterly impossible to function successfully with a mixed staff of white and colored officers." He noted that the bureau had not been able to find qualified black nurses; therefore "the only practical solution is to use white nurses and negro nurse maids." The black women had been hired to comply with an Alabama law that stated that white women could not be forced to care for black men. Penalties for violation of the statute were a fine of between ten and two hundred dollars. In addition, a prison sentence of up to six months could be imposed.[28]

Stanley's condescending reply confirmed black beliefs that officials at the Veterans Bureau were hostile to their objectives. Chisum of the National Negro Press Association went so far as to call them "crackers left over from the Wilson Scourge." He considered Marylander George E. Ijams, who as acting director of the Bureau had appointed Stanley, to be the ringleader of efforts to bar black professionals. Ijams advised the White House that he had filled the positions at Tuskegee with white personnel after attempts to find black personnel who met Civil Service eligibility standards had failed. Ijams's efforts were most likely feeble: he had not even asked Dr. J.R.A. Crossland, a black physician employed in the Veterans Bureau, for assistance, and he had never heard of the NMA or Freedman's Hospital, an institution with a large staff of black medical personnel that was located just a short distance from his office.[29]

Black efforts to secure positions for black physicians and nurses focused on enlisting the help of President Harding. On 23 February, Moton and other black leaders met with the President, who proved to be more sympathetic to black concerns than Stanley or Ijams. A few hours after the meeting ended, George B. Christian, the President's secretary, informed Ijams that it was the President's wish that no appointments of nurses or physicians be made to the Tuskegee Veterans Hospital until there had been a "thorough and determined effort to secure a civil service eligible list of colored citizens." The lobbying by Moton and his colleagues led to a delay in the hospital's 1 April scheduled opening. It is clear that if the hospital had opened at that time there would not have been any black medical personnel on hand.[30]

By the end of April, the President had expanded his goal. On 28 April, Christian informed the NAACP that it was "the plan of the Director of the Veterans Bureau, with the approval of the President, to man this institution completely with a colored personnel." The NAACP widely publicized the administration's pledge. It issued a press release that included Christian's letter to black newspapers and announced, "Tuskegee Hospital To Have Colored Doctors and Nurses. President Harding Allays Fears of 'Jim Crow' Institution For Colored Veterans."[31]

Harding's approval of black control can be explained by his personal attitudes toward race and by political motivations. An October 1921 speech made by the President before an interracial audience in Birmingham, Alabama, gives some insight into his stance on racial issues. In it he made clear that he did not endorse social equality or racial amalgamation, but did support political, economic, and educational equality—between separate societies. He urged the black race to "improve itself as a distinct race, with a heredity, a set of traditions, and array of aspirations all its own. Out of such racial ambitions and pride will come natural segregation." He further contended that the purpose of education for African Americans should be to develop race leaders capable of "understanding and sympathizing with such a differentiation between the races as I have suggested." His support of exclusive black control of the Tuskegee hospital fit with his views on black advancement within segregated institutions. He later wrote on his goal at the hospital, "I am sure we are in the process of doing a fine thing, not only for the hospital itself and its patients but for the colored race. It is going to afford the opportunity to prove self-dependence and capacity for outstanding service."[32]

Political expediency, however, cannot be discounted as a partial explanation for Harding's action. He was not prepared to sever the traditional ties between African Americans and the GOP. With the growing African-American migration to the North, black voters had become decisive in many local elections. Harding surely did not want to alienate them, especially in large urban areas. In addition, with the rise of a new militancy that followed World War I, African Americans demanded that their votes not be taken for granted and they increasingly criticized President Harding. They pointed out that racial segregation in the federal government had increased during his administration, that he had not appointed black people to political positions that had traditionally gone to them, and that he had not made any strong condemnation of the recently revived Ku Klux Klan. African Americans also criticized the President because he had not provided strong leadership in failed attempts to pass anti-lynching legislation. By endorsing black control of the Tuskegee Veterans Hospital, Harding hoped to appease black voters. As one black journalist put it, "The hospital at Tuskegee was to be a beacon light radiating the good wishes of the Republican party. More and more good Republican intentions have gone to pave the hell of Southern hatred."[33]

Throughout the spring of 1923, the Veterans Bureau proceeded to make plans to implement the President's policy, responsibility for which fell on Brigadier General Frank T. Hines, the new head of the Veterans Bureau. As opposed to Acting Director Ijams, Hines impressed black leaders and indicated that he supported the appointment of black staff. One of Hines's first tasks was to coordinate efforts to recruit African Americans to fill 384 positions, including physicians, nurses, dietitians, physical therapists, and clerks. Twenty-five physicians and sixty nurses would be needed to operate the facility. Harding had issued an executive order that called for a special civil service examination for black applicants. Fifteen thousand copies of the examination announcement were distributed to black institutions and to 250 black publications. The National Medical Association worked with the Civil Service Commission to publicize the examination among the approximately 2000 black physicians, dentists, and pharmacists it represented, while vigorously opposing the efforts of two prominent black Republican politicians to have the examinations waived. These politicians, Henry Lincoln Johnson of Georgia and Perry Howard of Mississippi, had wanted to seize the jobs for patronage. The NMA wanted to demonstrate unambiguously that their members were competent to serve on the hospital staff. Dr. George E. Cannon, chairperson of the association's executive committee and himself a prominent Republican, declared its support of the examinations: "We have men and women who can pass these examinations with credit." As another black physician put it, "At some period in our history we must be given an opportunity to cater to and administer the needs of our own racial group, when we are adequately prepared to do so."[34]

These efforts to name a black staff at the Tuskegee hospital provoked a heated backlash from white Southerners. The *Montgomery Advertiser* reported that rumors of black control of the facility had "filled the citizens of Macon County with indignation, and has stirred them to action." For example, Alabama Governor William W. Brandon and Robert E. Steiner of the American Legion wired Washington to protest efforts to change the staff from white to black personnel. Governor Brandon argued, "This change would be detrimental to both races and would endanger in my opinion the functioning properly in this section of the institution." Steiner warned that the change would be a "colossal mistake." He later raised the social taboo of black men coming into contact with white women and warned that white control was needed in order to maintain Southern customs and mores. Steiner claimed that "if Negroes were placed in the hospital as doctors and others as officers, they would inevitably come into contact with and control over white girls and other white people connected with the institution."[35]

Other prominent white Alabamians joined the protest. State Senator R.H. Powell criticized the federal government for attempting to break the pledge given by the Consultants on Hospitalization in 1921 that the hospital would be run by white people. He declared that "we do not want any Government institution in Alabama with niggers in charge. White supremacy in this state must be maintained at any cost, and we are not going to have any niggers in the state whom we cannot control." The town also stood to benefit financially from exclusively white operation of the hospital. The dollars spent by the workers who had come to construct the hospital had brought economic prosperity to the town. With only black personnel and patients at the hospital the boom would not continue for all local establishments because they excluded black people. Colonel Stanley, in a speech before the Montgomery Chamber of Commerce, emphasized the financial rewards of the project. "The government has staked out a gold mine at your door," he remarked. "The amount of ore you take out depends upon yourselves."[36]

In early May, Powell, accompanied by W.W. Campbell and John H. Drakeford, who were businessmen and Tuskegee Institute Trustees, met with Harding to voice the concerns of the white community. The men emphatically opposed any moves that would place black men in positions of authority, especially those from the North who might be unfamiliar with local conditions. They alleged that such actions would be fatal to the success of the project and would harm the operation of Tuskegee Institute. Harding apparently was not swayed by the men's visit. He informed them and the NAACP that he would proceed with his plans for black personnel.[37]

There were indications, not overlooked by the black community, that the Administration had already begun to retreat from its position. In May, before the visit of the white Tuskegeeans, Hines had reported that forty black nurses had passed the examinations and were to be ordered to Tuskegee at once and that as soon as qualified black physicians were found that they too would be sent. He also announced that he planned to visit the yet-unopened hospital in the near future "at which time the name of the colored surgeon-in-chief, who will have charge of the hospital, will be announced." Names of physicians who had surfaced as possible candidates for the position included those of Dr. John A. Kenney of Tuskegee and Dr. T.E. Jones, a former Army surgeon and at the time assistant to the superintendent at Freedmen's Hospital.[38]

A few days after the meeting with the white representatives, it was clear that the Harding administration had departed, at least temporarily, from its commitment to the African-American community. Hines informed Dr. George E. Cannon of the National Medical Association that because the Veterans Bureau had encountered difficulties finding black physicians who were specialists in the treatment of tuberculosis and neuropsychiatric disorders he had decided to open the hospital with an entirely white physician staff. Given the paucity of postgraduate training and employment opportunities for black physicians, the bureau may have faced some obstacles in recruiting black physicians, but Helen H. Gardner of the Civil Service Commission had informed Hines that there were qualified black physicians available in the needed fields. However, political considerations were at work. In mid-May, Harding informed a group of black representatives that the "time was not ripe" for black personnel because of local conditions. The President had discovered that he had to reconcile his policies on a black staff with conflicting demands from Southern white members of his party.[39]

African Americans saw the appointment of white physicians as an attempt by the Harding Administration to renege on its pledge to them. They stood their ground and continued to vigorously urge that the Tuskegee Veterans Hospital be black controlled and operated. As historian Raymond L. Wolters has pointed out, these demands were consistent with one of the chief tenets of the New Negro militancy that emerged after World War I: African Americans themselves should control the major institutions that shaped their lives. In the spring and summer of 1923, black people protested the exclusion of qualified black personnel from the hospital, not its inherently segregated nature. They knew that black people would be hired for low-status positions such as attendants, laborers, and cooks, but they demanded more. African Americans pushed for the hiring of black professionals because their exclusion from the hospital was seen as adding to the "public stigma of proclaiming without investigation or trial, that the Race is not qualified to care for its wounded, not intelligent enough to be given places of responsibility." Furthermore, working in a segregated facility was better than not being able to work at all.[40]

African Americans also contended that if facilities were equal to those given to whites that black veterans would receive better, more caring treatment from members of their own race. Even the NAACP, which had originally opposed the construction of the facility now supported it—if it were black controlled. James Weldon Johnson, secretary of the organization, explained its paradoxical stance: "since the hospital is built and we are confronted with the situation that it will be manned either by unsympathetic whites or by Negroes, we insist upon the demand for all-colored personnel." Walter White, the assistant secretary, pointed to another reason for the organization's stance. He claimed that if an all-black staff were not appointed, black medical personnel would be excluded. White believed that the state of race relations in Alabama in the 1920s would make it impossible to have a mixed personnel, further arguing that if black staff were barred at the hospital's inception, it would be even more difficult for them to get access to the hospital later. The NMA agreed with this stance. Dr. W.G. Alexander, the general secretary of the organization, urged members to continue to apply for positions at the hospital. "We cannot afford to let this opportunity slip by us," he contended, "for if it falls into the hands of others we may never reclaim it."[41]

By April 1923, the NAACP had emerged as the most visible advocate in the battle for black control of the hospital. In a move prompted by security and strategic concerns, Moton had retreated from any open role in the campaign. Because of developing white hostility, it had become necessary to place extra guards at the principal's home. As tensions mounted, Moton decided that in order to protect himself and Tuskegee Institute he had to remain publicly silent, but he continued to work surreptitiously for black control and turned to the NAACP for help. This was a tactic that was consistent with the way in which Booker T. Washington had handled volatile situations. Moton's strategy was outlined in a 2 April letter that his secretary, Albon L. Holsey, sent to James Weldon Johnson. Holsey noted that it had become

> necessary for Dr. Moton's friends to take up the fight through the press, and by telegrams to important Government officials with Dr. Moton left out, so that he can truthfully say that the colored people, themselves, are making the fight for the hospital, and that because of the attitude of the people here, he is leaving the matter alone.

Holsey stressed the need for utmost confidentiality "because it would be disastrous if it was known here that we at Tuskegee Institute had any part, no matter how small, in organizing the colored people away from here to protest against this despicable situation."[42]

Utilizing its traditional techniques of publicity and political pressure, the NAACP swung into action. Walter White remarked, "It seems as though we have acted nice long enough and we have to go to the mat in opposing the wishy-washy attitude of President Harding in his attempts to pacify southern sentiment." On May 14, he wrote to the editors of several publications including *The Nation*, *The New Republic*, and *The New York Times*, calling the turmoil over the staffing of the hospital "a revealing indication of the peculiar psychology of the Southern white man." "Race prejudice," he remarked, "falls with a bang before the almighty dollar—a delegation of eminent white Alabamians travel all the way to Washington to urge the President to permit whites to serve and wait upon Negro patients!" White's letter clearly demonstrates one of the strategies that the organization used: launching a publicity campaign that made Southern whites the objects of harsh ridicule. One month after White's letter appeared, W.E.B. DuBois, editor of the NAACP's journal *The Crisis*, also chastised white Southerners:

> Meantime at Tuskegee, has come the last word in segregation. A great hospital for maimed Negro soldiers has been built there against the protest of many Negroes who know Alabama and with fears of others who kept silent. Now come the Archpriests of Racial Separation in the United States, demanding, not merely asking, that the physicians, surgeons and officials in charge of this institution shall be white! This, we confess, has set our heads to whirling.

The tactic of ridiculing white Southerners had been suggested by Moton's secretary, Holsey, who wrote, "By ridicule I mean that here in the State of Alabama where the matter of segregation and Jim Crowism is the bulwark of her civilization the leading citizens in the state from the Governor down are clamoring to have white people wait upon and nurse Negro soldiers."[43]

Black newspapers nationwide also joined the campaign and unleashed articles and editorials—at times planted by the NAACP's press service—that criticized and belittled white efforts to control the hospital. Most commentary focused on the hypocrisy of "white folks [who] preach and believe in segregation and discrimination as long as neither interferes with their purse nor inconveniences them." Black newspapers emphasized that the operation of the hospital with black staff was consistent with patterns of racial division that white people themselves had established. An article in the *Atlanta Independent* typified black editorial sentiment:

> The white man has not given a single reason why he should be put in charge of the hospital at Tuskegee, and our group can see but one reason why he wants it, and that is to satisfy his lust for power and greed for money. It is not that he loves the Negro so well that he wants him to have the very best services that man is capable of rendering. He wants to boss; he wants to control; he wants to keep the Negro down and shut him out from every opportunity that will enable him to measure up as a man. It is money and power the white man wants, and not service to black men.

Many African Americans believed that white Americans wanted "the right to step on our side of the color line and order us around, tell us what to think and to do."[44]

Most black newspapers stressed that economic motivations had prompted the actions of white Southerners, taunting whites "who do not want to associate with Colored people, but rattle silver and gold and you can't shut them up." Some publications even hinted that white Southerners wanted control of the hospital as part of a racist plot to kill and sterilize African-American men and that the hospital would become an "experiment station" for mediocre white physicians. Only one major black publication, *The Messenger*, criticized the establishment of a segregated veterans hospital because "it sets a bad and dangerous precedent to advocate an all-Negro personnel in a government institution which is maintained by the taxes of the people." The left-wing journal also criticized the NAACP, "whose very foundation stone is antisegregation," for its support of the facility.[45]

The Messenger clearly expressed a minority viewpoint; most African Americans supported black command of the hospital. Ordinary black citizens, many of them ex-veterans, bombarded the White House and Veterans Bureau with letters calling for such control. Several of the letters, for example the one from Mr. James T. Bailey of Macon, Georgia, hinted that African Americans would vote their convictions in the next election. He warned, "We want our boys to have it and they must have its [sic] or else the poles [sic] of the 1924 election will stand a very poor shot for the Negro vote for a Republican president." And on 18 June 1923, 1200–1500 black men and women jammed into Washington's John Wesley A.M.E. Zion Church to protest the government's delay in appointing black people to the hospital.[46]

In spite of black agitation, when the hospital finally opened on

1 June, whites comprised the entire professional staff. Officials at the Veterans Bureau maintained, however, that the arrangement was only temporary, necessary in order to open the hospital and provide urgently needed care to black veterans. They continued their efforts to recruit black personnel. L.B. Rogers, assistant director of the bureau's medical division, advised Colonel Stanley that steps should be taken to discontinue all white personnel at the hospital and that "white physicians on duty will be replaced as soon as a colored medical unit can be secured." Rogers worked with the NMA to obtain a list of qualified black physicians; but recruitment efforts were hindered by the reluctance of black people to work in a town in which they might be the victims of racial violence. Nonetheless, by mid-June a sufficient number of black nurses had been found and by the end of the month five were sent to work at the hospital. In addition, thirty-three black physicians had qualified for the civil service eligibles list. General Hines acknowledged that it would be possible to have an entire black medical staff without lowering the standards of the Veterans Bureau. On June 18, he informed President Harding, "I hope in the very near future to be able to advise you that the hospital has been completely manned by colored personnel."[47]

These activities toward eventual black control of the hospital resulted in heightened racial tensions in Tuskegee. White Tuskegeeans saw the fight over the hospital as a "test of the supremacy of the Anglo-Saxon race" and were prepared to win the battle by any means necessary. White control, they contended, was essential in order not to "disturb local conditions" and to preserve "our friendly race relations." Several wrote letters to Hines in which they warned that placing black personnel at the hospital would result in bloodshed and endanger the operation of Tuskegee Institute. Furthermore, they noted that they would hold the federal government responsible for any racial violence that might occur, because it had broken the pledge of the Consultants on Hospitalization. The white citizens received support for their stance from such prominent politicians as Governor William W. Brandon, Senator J. Thomas Heflin, Representative W.B. Bowling, and State Representative R.H. Powell.[48]

By the time the first patients arrived at the end of June, the potential for violence and bloodshed had become increasingly apparent. Colonel Stanley, the medical officer at the hospital, observed:

> The people of Alabama are determined that no nigger officers shall be installed here. They are looking for trouble and are ready for it, and you know when a fellow goes around *looking* for trouble he usually *finds* it. For the last week I have expected every minute some hot head would do something to start it. Nearly everybody totes a gun here too.

Alabama Congressman W.B. Bowling warned Hines, "If you persist in the announced purpose of appointing a colored personnel at this Hospital, you may prepare yourself for a shock." The *Chicago Whip*, a black newspaper, reported that a mob had descended on a train when it was rumored that black physicians would be arriving on it. Fortunately, this report proved false.[49]

The racial situation in the town had become so heated that throughout the summer several prominent black Tuskegeeans, including Booker T. Washington's widow, Margaret Murray Washington; Dr. John A. Kenney; and the entire Moton family fled the town. Kenney, who had practiced medicine in the town for about twenty years, left with his family after they had received threats because of his support of black control. Moton ostensibly left Tuskegee for three months for business and health reasons. However, before his departure threats had also been made against him and Tuskegee Institute, especially after he had reportedly refused to capitulate to the demands of a committee composed of fifteen of the community's leading white citizens. The men wanted him to sign a petition that no black nurses or physicians be allowed to work at the hospital. The meeting lasted for three hours during which the principal was apprised of the potential consequences of his refusal. One man warned Moton, "Booker Washington gave 35 years of his life to build up this school and you are going to have it blown up in 24 hours." Another told him, "You understand we have the legislature, we make the laws, we have the judges, the sheriffs, the jails; we have the hardware stores, the arms." According to Moton's account of the confrontation, he stood firm and informed the men, "If I were to sign that paper, I would be deceiving my people and my country. . . . It's a Negro hospital, built for Negroes; and gentlemen, if Negroes trained for the job can't run it, you can wipe out the hospital and the school and Moton."[50]

However, it is impossible to know whether Moton's description of the meeting was self-serving or whether escalating racial tensions soon forced him to change his position, at least privately. A few weeks after the meeting, it became clear that he had backed down. On 1 July, unbeknown to the NAACP, he wrote Hines and suggested a compromise, urging that qualified black physicians be given access to the facility, but that for the time being it remain under white supervision. He feared that

> if Negroes are put in charge of the hospital, there is no doubt in my own mind but that there will be serious trouble which may mean the destruction sooner or later of much property and serious bloodshed, the effect of which would be far-reaching in its effect on the relations of the races in the South.

Moton maintained his public silence on the hospital situation, but he continued to work behind the scenes to prevent bloodshed, to keep white support of Tuskegee Institute, and to ensure black medical personnel some access to the hospital.[51]

The volatile conditions in Tuskegee prompted Hines to announce that he would not appoint any black personnel until after he had visited the town and investigated the situation. He made plans to visit in early July. Two days before his trip, however, racial tensions in Tuskegee exploded. The spark was the 3 July arrival of a young black man, John C. Calhoun, to report for duty as a bookkeeper at the hospital. The Hampton Institute graduate had passed the eligibility examinations and had been sent by the Civil Service Commission to replace Clara Hunicutt, the white woman who previously held the position but who had failed the exam. Upon his arrival, Colonel Stanley, the hospital's commanding officer, made sure that the new employee would not feel welcome, thereby supporting black beliefs that Stanley did not want black professional personnel at the hospital. He refused to give him any assignments or allow him, as was specified in his contract, to stay on the hospital grounds. Stanley later handed him a sealed letter, addressed to Calhoun but without any postmark, reading, "WE UNDERSTAND YOU ARE REPORTING TO HOSPITAL TO ACCEPT DISBURSING OFFICERS JOB. IF YOU VALUE YOUR WELFARE DO NOT TAKE THIS JOB BUT LEAVE AT ONCE FOR PARTS FROM WHENCE YOU CAME OR SUFFER THE CONSEQUENCES. KKK." Calhoun left the hospital and sought refuge a half mile away at Tuskegee Institute. Whites reveled in his departure. As the *Montgomery Advertiser* reported:

> The fact that the first negro to report for executive duty concurs that the climate would not agree with his health and the further fact that he is described as a man of exceptional courage and departed is being accepted here as meaning that others will not attempt to break down the settled determination of Tuskegee citizens that they will not tolerate negro control of the hospital.

And as a warning to any other African American who might attempt to seek a professional appointment at the hospital, less than an hour after Calhoun left the hospital, the Ku Klux Klan marched on Tuskegee.[52]

Earlier in the day, the Klan had held a mass demonstration in Montgomery to protest black personnel at the hospital. They then traveled to Tuskegee, where several hundred members, alleged to represent a membership of 50,000 in Alabama, assembled at the town's train station. Shortly after 9:00 P.M., "automobiles loaded with garbed and mysterious figures" began a parade through the streets of Tuskegee. The silent procession stretched two miles. On the outskirts of town the Klan members burned a forty-foot cross. They then headed toward Tuskegee Institute and the veterans hospital. The Klan did not enter the grounds of the school. If they had, there might have been bloodshed. Faculty members then at the school later recollected that Colonel William H. Walcott, commander of the Tuskegee Institute Cadet Corps, had placed armed students, who were prepared to defend their school, around the campus. Accounts differ as to the next action of the Klan members. Some state that they slowly proceeded past the hospital and then dispersed. Others state that they entered the hospital grounds before disassembling. Rumors also circulated, later found false, that sheets used in the march had been provided by a white Red Cross nurse at the hospital and that several of the Klan members had been served a meal by the hospital's dietitian. Although the march was not violent, the NAACP's Walter White later reported that his fair-skinned brother had infiltrated the Klan by passing as white and learned that it had made plans to kill Major Moton and blow up Tuskegee Institute.[53]

The purpose of the Klan march was to force African Americans to back down from their demand that the hospital be black controlled. It had the opposite effect. It aroused the community. The issue no longer was just control of the hospital, but whether the federal government would stand by its pledge *and* stand up to the Ku Klux Klan. Dr. George E. Cannon, chairperson of the NMA's executive committee, captured the sentiments of African Americans when he wrote to General Hines, "to recede from this promise means that the federal government will declare itself powerless to defend us against the most absurd form of race prejudice, however just and sacred be our cause." Black newspapers across the nation kept their readers abreast of the situation and continued their editorial campaign of ridiculing the actions of the white southerners. The NAACP, surreptitiously assisted by Tuskegee Institute staff, continued its activities. It called for the federal troops to protect black people in the town and the removal of Stanley as commanding officer because of his failure to protect Calhoun. The civil rights organization initiated a massive letter-writing campaign. Individual black citizens and black organizations, including churches, labor unions, women's associations, and medical groups responded, flooding the White House and Veterans Bureau with letters expressing their outrage at the Klan action and urging the government to continue with its plans for black control. The views expressed by the North Harlem Medical, Dental and Pharmaceutical Association, a constituent organization of the NMA, typified much of the correspondence. It wrote, "To attempt the treatment of shell shocked soldiers in an atmosphere replete with Ku Klux parades, mob violence, and race antipathy would be contrary to the dictates of sound medical judgment and common sense." Furthermore, to force men to receive treatment "at the hands of a prejudiced and unsympathetic personnel would be cruel in the extreme and entirely without consideration for the patients' welfare."[54]

African Americans also made plans for political action. Shelby J. Davidson, executive secretary of the Washington, D.C. branch of the NAACP, warned, "If Harding does not listen now, he will have a long time after 1924." Accordingly, at the end of July, a group of black Republicans from eighteen states met in Atlantic City, New Jersey to protest the Harding Administration's policies toward black people. The leader of the group was Dr. George E. Cannon. In addition to his activities with the NMA, the Jersey City physician served as a member of the board of directors of the NAACP and had long been active in the Republican party; he was even a member of the New Jersey State Republican Committee. The group of black Republicans insisted that the Tuskegee Hospital be black controlled and threatened to bolt the party if this and other demands were not met.[55]

On 5 July, two days after the Klan march, General Hines met for one-and-one-half hours at the Macon County Courthouse with representatives of the white community of Tuskegee. They reiterated their objections to black control of the hospital and once again urged the Veterans Bureau to uphold the pledge of the Consultants on Hospitalization. Hines informed the gathering that although competent black physicians had been found to staff the hospital none would be appointed until after President Harding returned from a trip to Alaska. He also assured them that he would "not be a party to any plan which would disturb the friendly relations which have existed between the races here or the great institute for the education of Colored men." The general asked that a committee of three be named to work with him on solving the hospital problem. Three white men, Dr. L.W. Johnston, president of the Alabama State Medical Society; R.H. Powell, a state senator; and W.W. Campbell, president of the Mechanics County Bank and a Tuskegee Institute trustee, were appointed.[56]

All white Southerners, however, did not support the efforts of the white Tuskegeeans. Major white newspapers, in agreement with black ones, pointed out the inconsistencies of white people opposing black control of a black institution. The Opelika, Alabama, *Daily News* contended, "As we see the matter, this is a Negro hospital. . . . It is no more a white man's affair than is the management of Tuskegee Institute—and we have not heard of any white educators insisting that the faculty of that Negro college should be composed of white professors." The *Savannah Journal* criticized the Klan march and argued that "generally white men concede the right of Negroes to wait on Negroes—to serve Negroes." It further noted that "the traditions of the South should settle this question. The doctrine of racial separation should prevent a controversy of such magnitude as the one now going the rounds." The *Norfolk Virginia-Pilot* maintained:

> If there is a sound objection to staffing with a competent colored personnel a hospital set aside exclusively for Negro patients in a community in which is located the best-known Negro training school, similarly staffed, nobody outside of Ku Klux circles in Alabama seems to be aware of it.

The Asheville, North Carolina, *Daily Citizen* also argued that the actions of the white citizens of Tuskegee did not represent Southern opinion on the race question. "It is an established Southern tradition that Negroes should have their own preachers, teachers, physicians," it editorialized. The newspaper further noted, "such a mode of living for the two races has come about because it represents the sanest sort of common sense with regard to the social contacts of whites and blacks."[57]

The Commission on Interracial Cooperation, an interracial organization established in 1919 to promote race relations, played a significant role in the campaign to secure black control of the hospital. Will W. Alexander, the white head of the commission, worked to obtain key endorsements and to demonstrate that the opinions of the white Tuskegeeans dissented from those of other white Southerners. For example, he persuaded the social service commission of the Methodist Episcopal Church to issue a widely publicized resolution condemning the Klan march and offering support for Tuskegee Institute. Alexander also convinced officials at Alabama Power and Light to criticize the Klan. Economic factors had prompted the utility's action: after the Klan march, several black employees, fearing for their safety, refused to return to work at a company dam project. The state's senatorial delegation was split on the Tuskegee matter. Its junior senator, J. Thomas Heflin, had already publicly endorsed the efforts of the white Tuskegeeans. However, Alexander secured the support of the state's senior senator, Oscar W. Underwood, by pointing out to his staff that events at Tuskegee might jeopardize his chances for the Democratic presidential nomination. Underwood advised the white citizens that they were "wrong in this hospital matter. You have no case. This man Moton has got you in a hole and you're bound to lose. Furthermore, the best white people in the South are with him." By the end of July, Alexander reported to Moton that the spirit of the white Tuskegeeans was much subdued and that they "are probably now or will soon be ready for most any compromise which the [Veterans] Bureau will offer which will allow them to save their faces."[58]

This division within the white community enabled the Veterans Bureau to proceed cautiously toward black control without creating a backlash from other Southern whites. Subsequent to Hines's Tuskegee visit it became increasingly clear that he was committed to a black-operated facility. A few days after his trip, the committee that had been appointed to represent the white community's interests submitted recommendations that would have allowed the hospital not to be run exclusively by whites. Its proposal would have let African Americans work in subordinate positions such as aides and nurses. Hines rejected the plan because it conflicted with the federal government's goal of black control of the hospital and would not have given black physicians and professionals access to the hospital. He informed the committee that one of the main purposes of the hospital was to give black patients the opportunity to be cared for by physicians of their own race, and also notified it that unless it came up with a more suitable plan, the Veterans Bureau would proceed with its own policy. The general was not swayed from his goal even after the Alabama State Legislature passed a resolution calling for white control of the institution. His plans were not adversely affected by the 2 August death of President Harding. The new commander-in-chief, Calvin Coolidge, also supported the bureau's plans.[59]

Throughout the rest of the summer, activities focused on implementing a compromise that would give black physicians and professionals at least some access to the hospital and temper racial hostilities. It should be noted that by mid-July, approximately 60 percent of the institution's employees were black, including all nurses and attendants. However, none of the physicians or supervisory staff were African Americans. Therefore, the issue was no longer whether black people should work at the hospital, but whether they should manage it. The compromise plan called for black professional personnel to be added gradually, but the three top supervisory positions would remain in white hands. The arrangement would be temporary, an experiment to see whether black patients actually did prefer black physicians and whether black personnel had the skills required to run the facility. On 6 August, the committee of white citizens agreed to this settlement after Hines stressed its experimental nature and assured it that the addition of black personnel would proceed slowly and gradually. Black employees would be added only as positions became available and would not be allowed to displace white ones. It was assumed, however, that many whites would want to leave as more blacks were hired. The white citizens' committee promised that it would work to alleviate local friction and trouble. Hines now contended that the implementation of the bureau's policy could proceed "with the assurance that the citizens of Tuskegee will lend their support toward the fullest possible accomplishment of the purpose for which the hospital was provided."[60]

The black community was divided over whether the compromise should be accepted. As discussed earlier, Moton had already confidentially indicated to Hines that he would support the plan as a way to ease tensions in the town. Moton, still in exile from Tuskegee, continued not to speak publicly about hospital issues, but maintained contact with the Veterans Bureau. His public silence and rumors of his endorsement of the compromise made him the target of criticism from other African Americans who persisted in their demand for a completely black-run facility. This was not the first time that Moton's actions had been condemned by other black people. During World War I, he had gone to France at the request of President Woodrow Wilson to investigate the conditions of black soldiers. His advice to the troops that upon their return to the United States they should not expect the degree of freedom that they had experienced in France and should not agitate for racial advancement drew censure from both black soldiers and civilians. His reluctance to speak out after his wife had been thrown off a Pullman car and during the 1919 race riots had also come under attack.[61]

Critics of Moton's stance on the Tuskegee hospital did not believe that white supervision would be a temporary measure, especially since no target date had been announced for the commencement of black control. In addition, they contended that such an arrangement would reinforce beliefs that black people were incompetent to operate major institutions. Benjamin Jefferson Davis, editor of the *Atlanta Independent*, advised Hines that if Moton had said that fifty-fifty personnel were acceptable then "he misrepresents the facts, because nobody had authorized him to speak for us." Melvin J. Chisum, the National Negro Press Association representative who had played such a prominent role in publicizing the hospital issue, informed the Veterans Bureau chief that the vast majority of black people still favored a 100-percent black workforce and urged him not to be "guided by what some individual who has been intimidated by the Alabama Ku Klux says do." Several black newspapers, including the *Amsterdam News*, the *Washington Tribune*, and the *New York World* portrayed Moton as an Uncle Tom, a coward, and as a double-crosser and urged him not only to return to Tuskegee, but to take a public stand on the situation at the hospital. The *Washington Tribune* even printed an editorial cartoon in which Moton was satirized as "The Modern Dr. Jekyl [sic] and Mr. Hyde." There were also calls for his resignation. Moton, however, continued to have his supporters. *The New York Age*, the *Star of Zion*, and the *Pittsburgh Courier* backed the Tuskegee principal. An editorial in the *Pittsburgh Courier* noted,

"It is easy to condemn the man whose head is in the lion's mouth for not trying conclusions with the lion." Although the *New York Age* saw the compromise as not "entirely satisfactory," it contended that the proposed settlement would yield substantial results that would not have been possible without Moton's "firm insistence and unremitting efforts."[62]

The NAACP disagreed with Moton's position and broke rank over what would be the best strategy to achieve black control of the hospital. Moton believed that the gradual addition of black personnel was the best approach and that the Veterans Bureau would eventually turn over the hospital to African Americans. The NAACP rejected this tactic. In early August, Walter White reasserted the civil rights organization's demand that a totally black workforce be placed immediately at the Tuskegee Veterans Hospital. "There should be no compromise by us on that score," he wrote. "That is our position and one which we need to reaffirm and stand by without compromise." W.E.B. DuBois, writing in the *Crisis*, called the compromise a "disgrace." The association called Moton's action a "disappointing experience" that had nullified its work and that of the black physicians and newspapers. The NAACP had not been informed of Moton's changed position and believed that he had deceived them. Representatives of the organization had discovered his new stance during a 3 September meeting with Hines in which they voiced their opposition to the compromise. The Veterans Bureau chief informed them that only a few days earlier Moton had told him that the plan "was the greatest stroke I had made and the best thing for the situation." Referring to Moton's actions, NAACP official Shelby J. Davidson charged, "It now develops that some double-crossing has been done and the work which we thought we were doing was being undone from quarters least expected." The NAACP contended that it had evidence to prove that Moton had not only agreed to the compromise, but had told the Veterans Bureau that the push for an all-black personnel was the "agitation of northern radicals who were merely trying to make propaganda out of the situation at Tuskegee." Disheartened and disgruntled, the NAACP withdrew from any further activity in the affair.[63]

The National Medical Association, however, continued its involvement and its demands for a totally black staff, and it too criticized Moton. Dr. M.O. Dumas, a representative of the organization, charged Moton with "pussyfooting" over the personnel issue and alleged that he had favored a mixed staff from the beginning. The association maintained that its support for an all black staff was the logical position because "if Negro patients are segregated, why shouldn't Negro doctors be assigned to care for them? We do not ask that we be allowed to treat white patients in the government hospitals; why should white doctors administer to men of our Race?" In mid-August, three representatives of the NMA met with Hines to present the organization's demands, including the removal of Robert Stanley as the hospital's commanding officer. Later in the month, at its annual meeting in St. Louis, the medical society passed a resolution that criticized the proposed compromise and urged its members not to accept any appointments at the hospital unless they worked under black supervision. The Tuskegee episode had put the issue of access to quality hospitals prominently on the association's agenda, and this was the meeting at which it established the NHA to coordinate its activities in the hospital field.[64]

Despite the disagreements within the black community over strategy, throughout the remaining months of 1923 Hines went forward with his efforts to implement the compromise. On 20 August, he notified Stanley that white officers would be given an opportunity to transfer to other stations as positions became available and that all vacancies at the Tuskegee Veterans Hospital, except that of commanding officer, executive officer, and clinical director, would be filled by black people. At the end of the month, he even ordered Calhoun, the target of the Klan march, to return to the facility. Hines also moved to oust Stanley as the hospital's commanding officer. During his July visit, it had become clear to him that Colonel Stanley was an obstacle to the bureau's plans for eventual black control, and he now sought to replace him with someone who was more sympathetic to the agency's goals. In early September, it was announced that Stanley would be transferred to the veterans hospital in Bayard, New Mexico. His replacement would be Major Charles M. Griffin, a Tennessean and former commanding officer of a federal hospital in Alexandria, Louisiana, whose primary responsibility was to train black physicians and officers to take control of the hospital.[65]

On 15 August, Hines announced that six black physicians would be selected for staff positions at the hospital. The announcement, only nine days after the white citizens' committee had agreed to the compromise, predictably drew criticism because of the swiftness of Hines's action. Members of the committee also attacked the continued political agitation of some black people. Senate Representative Powell lamented, "It looks as if the negroes are gradually taking things away from us by contesting every inch of the ground, refusing all compromises, and fighting to a finish." Perhaps because the federal government had made its intentions clear and other white Southerners had chided the white Tuskegeeans, the announcement did not provoke the fierce response that Calhoun's assignment had only one month earlier. The racial situation in the town had become less tense and in September both Major Moton and Dr. Kenney returned. Shortly after his return the physician reported that "it appears that the unpleasant and trying experience which we have sustained here with reference to the Veterans' Hospital will, 'ere long, be past history."[66]

Hines adhered to his plans to appoint black physicians and technical personnel, but he encountered some unexpected difficulties in recruiting them. Although the NMA continued to push for a black-operated facility and had urged its members not to work under white supervision, it worked with the Veterans Bureau to secure qualified black physicians. If it had declined to have worked with the agency, the NMA would not have had any role in determining who would work at, or eventually manage, the hospital. However, some NMA members refused to work at the Tuskegee hospital because of its recent history of racial hostilities and the continuing policy of white supervision. By November, twenty-four black physicians had been certified by the Civil Service Commission, but eleven had declined appointment. For example, Dr. Ferdinand D. Whitby, associate professor of neurology at Howard University, rejected an offer to be chief of the neuropsychiatric service at the veterans hospital. He informed Hines:

> The United States Veterans' Hospital had been thrown into a chaotic state resulting from a contention on the part of racial groups as to who should man the hospital. This being true, a sense of insecurity has arisen in my mind causing me to think it inadvisable to accept the position at the time, feeling that by so doing my present and future practice may be jeopardized.

Despite these obstacles, it became increasingly clear that throughout the fall of 1923, the hospital was "gradually assuming a darker hue." At the end of October, when the six black physicians arrived, the hospital employed 247 people, 218 of whom were African Americans, to take care of 226 patients.[67]

In January 1924, Hines took a major step toward black administration when he appointed Dr. Joseph H. Ward, a highly regarded black physician from Indianapolis, as chief surgeon. Plans called for the physician to apprentice under Major Griffith in order to gain competence in the management of the facility. Ward, a vice president of the National Hospital Association, had graduated from the Indiana University School of Medicine. Before establishing a practice and a small hospital in Indianapolis, he had worked briefly at the prestigious Mayo Clinic in Rochester, Minnesota. During World War I, he served overseas and had advanced to the rank of major in the medical corps. Reportedly, military authorities had promoted him unwittingly, not realizing that the fair-skinned Ward was black. Two months after his appointment at Tuskegee, Griffith filed a glowing assessment of Ward's performance, noting that he had made a favorable impression on both white and black people and that he had "an unusual good insight to hospital routine, internal management and diplomacy, and [was] taking hold of his work like an old, veterans hospital man." In June, Major Moton reported that since Ward had strong biracial support he could soon be made hospital head without incident. Furthermore, he reported that the racial tensions over the hospital had continued to lessen, stating that the white residents in the town were now more interested in the new railroad and the economic benefits that it might reap. Ward's competence and a stabilized racial situation convinced Hines to promote the physician in July to medical officer-in-charge of the hospital. One year after the Klan had tried to stop the appointment of a black bookkeeper to the facility, the Tuskegee Veterans Hospital was completely operated by African Americans.[68]

Several factors contributed to the black community's victory in Tuskegee. Despite some early opposition to the construction of the hospital and differences over strategies, African Americans were united in their demand that the hospital be black controlled. Even Moton, who prescribed patience and moderation, saw black control as the final goal. Black people nationwide responded to the situation in Tuskegee and tenaciously pursued the campaign, refusing to allow Klan threats or vacillation on the part of the federal government to deter them. The outpouring of letters protesting events at Tuskegee and the extensive coverage it received in black newspapers testified to the importance of the hospital not just to health care professionals who might work there or patients who might be taken care of there, but to the wider black community. The extent and depth of the response showed that the struggle for control of the hospital reflected larger social and political concerns. Black control of the hospital would demonstrate that African-American physicians had the skills and competence to run a federal facility and that the federal government could and should be held responsible for any promises that it made to the community. It would also show that a united black community could overcome hostile and racist white opposition. As one contemporary account put it, "The Negro has at last learned to marshal forces and fight, too."[69]

The black cause was also helped by the work of General Hines, who, with the backing of both the Harding and Coolidge administrations, slowly and persistently worked toward black control. As we saw earlier, one major reason that Hines was able to do so was that white Southern opinion was not firmly behind the actions of the white Tuskegeeans. Many white Southerners saw the town's position as contradictory to the tenets of segregation. Moton's endorsement of the compromise was also a key to Hines's success because it assured Hines that the plan would have some crucial black support. The compromise gave the Veterans Bureau chief an alternative that was less extreme than immediate black control of the facility. It also granted black physicians and technical personnel some access to the hospital and provided time for the racial situation to stabilize. Although Moton's action had initially provoked condemnation, former critics, including the NAACP, later acknowledged that his acceptance of the compromise had been decisive to the eventual victory.[70]

Before the desegregation of medical institutions, the Tuskegee Veterans hospital would provide black physicians with one of the best—accessible—locations in which to practice medicine. As opposed to most black hospitals that operated before 1945, it was a modern, well-equipped facility with adequate funding. In 1930, the hospital employed 344, including twenty-two physicians and fifty-two nurses, and had a capacity of over 700 beds. In addition, the hospital was one of the seventeen black hospitals approved by the American College of Surgeons. In 1932, Peter Marshall Murray, then NMA president, called the hospital, "a brilliant chapter in the annals of Negro medicine . . . [that] has also provided extraordinarily well for thousands of veterans of our race and given an opportunity to Negro professionals to demonstrate their fitness for this work."

In August 1931, the National Medical Association and the National Hospital Association voted to work for the establishment of a second black veterans hospital in order to provide more opportunities for black medical professionals. The organizations contended that the additional facility was needed because racial discrimination still limited black access to most veterans hospitals. In 1932, over 50 percent of the black veterans who had received care at a veterans hospital had received it at Tuskegee. The remainder almost always received care in segregated wards. In addition, all the black physicians employed by the Veterans Bureau worked at the Tuskegee facility. The two medical organizations proposed that the new hospital also be built in the South because of the region's more hostile racial climate, and opposed construction of the hospital in the North because they contended that racial conditions there did not warrant such a facility.[71]

The NMA, once again, acknowledged that it was "fully cognizant of the danger inherent in any segregated proposition." However, it urged the construction of the second black veterans hospital because the provision of hospital care for black patients and of professional opportunities for black physicians had "more to recommend it than loud mouthed preachment against segregation in the abstract." One target of the NMA's criticism was the NAACP. Although the civil rights organization and the medical association had been close allies in the 1923 campaign at Tuskegee, they now found themselves on opposing sides. The NAACP considered it the "height of irony to set apart veterans wounded in a war for democracy in hospitals where such separation is based on skin color." As compared to its brief opposition to the construction of the Tuskegee hospital, this time its resistance remained ironclad.[72]

The NAACP urged that all ex-soldiers be admitted to veterans hospitals without regard to skin color and that all qualified physicians be allowed to practice in them. Walter F. White maintained that the existence of the Tuskegee Hospital had hampered efforts to integrate all veterans hospitals. He claimed that black veterans were often denied admission to hospitals closer to their homes and were transferred to Tuskegee. White also criticized the NMA's support of separate, tax-supported facilities because he viewed them as a form of government-sponsored segregation. Noting that progress had been recently made in gaining access of black people to the staffs of several municipal hospitals including those in Cleveland, Boston, and Detroit, he urged the NMA to follow the "longer and more difficult" route and work for integration of the Veterans Bureau hospitals. White also reiterated the organization's position that black hospitals were acceptable only if African Americans privately owned and financed them.[73]

White also alleged that the NMA's interest in the construction of an additional black hospital was not entirely altruistic, noting that officers of the NMA had helped to select the staff at the Tuskegee hospital and stood to benefit from the construction of a new one. He accused them of exploiting segregation. "Segregation is a great enough evil when it exists over the protest of those jim-crowed," White bitterly remarked, and "it is both an actual and moral disaster when Negroes for the sake of jobs themselves ask for it."[74]

Not all black physicians supported the actions of the officers of the NMA. The Manhattan Medical Society, which had already vigorously contested the construction of a black hospital in Harlem, once again emerged as an opponent to the stance of the national medical body. It published and circulated a pamphlet, "Identical Care and Treatment by the Federal Government," in which it outlined its support of the NAACP position and its opposition to that of the NMA. The society argued that the acceptance of segregated facilities by black physicians would "lower the dignity [and] standards of the practice of medicine" by black physicians. Instead of seeking appointments in Jim-Crow government hospitals, the Manhattan Medical

Society advised black physicians who wanted to work in the Veterans Bureau "to file application and take the prescribed examination, and if they are competent, to stand up like men and fight for the right of appointment." This split over whether the hospital should be built extended to black newspapers. For example, the *Pittsburgh Courier* and the *Inter-State Tattler* supported the positions of the NAACP and the Manhattan Medical Society. On the other hand, the *New York Age* and the *New York Amsterdam News* called for construction of the hospital.[75]

Despite these criticisms, the NMA and NHA continued to push for a second black veterans hospital. In Spring 1932, Republican Senator David Reed of Pennsylvania introduced a bill, at the request of the American Legion, to build a black veterans hospital in the North. Both the two black medical organizations and the NAACP opposed this particular measure, whereas the NMA and NHA would have supported it if it had called for construction in the South. By the end of the summer, Reed withdrew the bill because he said that he had never been fully committed to the idea, but had introduced it only at the request of the American Legion. The proposal to build a second veterans hospital never gained any significant political momentum and it was never built.[76]

In June 1932, Peter Marshall Murray sent letters to several black medical leaders, including NHA president H.M. Green, in which he reported on the NMA's activities with regard to the additional hospital. He warned his colleagues that "it seems apparent that it has become necessary to fight out the issue of the so-called `Negro hospital' with the public. Otherwise a great many of our local efforts will be thwarted or cramped by the short sighted but well-intentioned efforts of our friends." It is clear that in the nine years following the struggle over the Tuskegee Veterans Hospital, the African-American community had become more divided not only over the purpose of black hospitals, but over tactics for racial advancement. Strong arguments both for and against black hospitals had surfaced. But, as we shall now see, policies towards black hospitals did not always reflect the resolution of divergent strategies within the black community. They might be shaped more by the expectations and attitudes of those agencies that financed them.[77]

FOUR

Black Hospitals and White Philanthropy

❧

One of the main objectives of the hospital reformers was to raise money to support black hospitals. But funds were not readily forthcoming. Indeed, throughout the 1920s and 1930s all hospitals grappled with the problem of financing. Government and third-party payments were uncommon and patient revenues and private donations were greatly reduced by the Depression. Financial problems were particularly severe for black hospitals, whose patients were predominantly poor and could afford neither to pay their hospital bills nor to provide the institutions with substantial charitable donations. When black hospitals were first established the small contributions made by the African-American community represented a significant portion of the institutions' budgets. However, the increased expense of operating hospitals that followed the advent of scientific medicine outstripped the capability of the community in adequately supporting the institutions. This state of affairs prompted H.M. Green to write that "as a race our group activities have not yet reached a point of cohesiveness that will long withstand the strain of backing financially such a non-productive enterprise as a hospital." As Green's comments make plain, black hospital reformers recognized that no movement for the improvement of black hospitals could succeed without the cooperation and financial assistance of whites. One source from which they sought support was the white philanthropic community. Charitable support of hospitals had traditionally been the obligation of local communities, and many foundations did not view the support of hospitals as part of their mission. However, three national philanthropies—the Julius Rosenwald Fund, the Duke Endowment, and the General Education Board—responded to the crisis and played crucial roles in both helping black hospitals and in influencing the direction of the black hospital movement.[1]

An examination of the histories of these foundations clearly illustrates the problems associated with white philanthropic support of black institutions. It also sheds light on the attitudes of white philanthropists towards the role of black physicians and their hospitals. White philanthropic support enabled some black hospitals not only to survive but to meet the standards set by national accrediting bodies, however, such support did not come without a price. White philanthropies frequently assumed that they, and not the black community, had the right to determine the policies of black hospitals. Foundation funding of black medical institutions led the white agencies to become entangled in the divisions within the black community over strategies for racial advancement. The foundations consistently backed the tactics advanced by the black hospital reformers: separate hospitals, they agreed, could best serve the interests of the African-American community. Their stance led to charges by integrationists that the philanthropies impeded racial progress by supporting the development of Jim-Crow institutions.

The motives behind the involvement of the Julius Rosenwald Fund, the Duke Endowment, and the General Education Board in the black hospital field varied. The three foundations had divergent yet complementary goals and often funded projects jointly. The Rosenwald Fund maintained a broad-based black health program that supported programs in professional education, public health, outpatient services, and hospital care. The Duke Endowment gave substantially to the operation and construction of black hospitals in North and South Carolina. The General Education Board (GEB) donated funds for educational programs at selected hospitals.

Of the three foundations, the Julius Rosenwald Fund had the most extensive black social welfare program. Julius Rosenwald, president of Sears, Roebuck, and Company, established the fund in 1917 to serve as a clearinghouse for his favorite charities. During its first ten years, the activities of the Chicago-based foundation consisted almost exclusively of constructing schools for black people in the rural South, reflecting Rosenwald's belief that education was a powerful instrument in the social advancement of African Americans. The fund also contributed to other black institutions, including black YMCAs, Tuskegee Institute, and Meharry Medical College. Rosenwald's interest in helping to improve the status of black people had developed, in part, from his friendship with Booker T. Washington, but Rosenwald's being Jewish also contributed to his commitment. He recognized that his religion made him a vulnerable member of American society and urged other Jews to work actively to improve race relations, stressing that in an environment that tolerated race prejudice, discrimination against Jews could also increase. His views were incorporated into fund policy, which stated that:

> So long as we degrade one segment of the people we set a pattern of caste and discrimination that may easily be transferred to other groups. No race or class can be firmly assured of fair play so long as we continue to treat any group unfairly.

Rosenwald's commitment to black social issues also had an economic basis. "Twelve million colored people constitute one of the great potential markets for American industry," he observed to President Herbert Hoover. Efforts to improve the quality of life of African Americans would increase their buying power, a tempting prospect for the president of a large retailing company. Regardless of his motives, the founder's dedication led the Julius Rosenwald Fund to become the philanthropy most identified with race relations and the advancement of black Americans. In fact, Rosenwald became so associated with black causes that rumors developed, which persist to the present day, that Roebuck was black.[2]

In 1928, the fund reorganized and expanded its interests to include black education and welfare, race relations, medical economics, library services, and social studies. Its administration was transferred from the Rosenwald family to a professional staff, although Julius Rosenwald and other family members remained on the board of trustees and continued to exert strong influences over the foundation's direction. Julius Rosenwald directed that the life of the restructured philanthropy be limited. In contrast to most philanthropists of his day, Rosenwald opposed the establishment of perpetual endowments, asserting that such arrangements fostered conservatism and bureaucracy because trustees and staff became more concerned with conserving funds than with financing new projects. Furthermore, changing times could render inflexible foundation mandates obsolete and allow the future to be controlled by the "dead hand." Rosenwald believed that each generation should assess its own needs and develop foundations to address its own concerns. Consequently, he stipulated that all the interest and principal of the endowment had to be expended within twenty-five years of his death. The Julius Rosenwald Fund ceased operations in 1948.[3]

Julius Rosenwald named Edwin R. Embree president of the reorganized fund. Embree was the grandson of John Gregg Fee, a militant abolitionist who in 1855 had started Berea College in Kentucky as an integrated institution. As a child, Embree lived on the Berea campus and from his relationship with his grandfather developed a strong interest in race relations. Prior to his appointment at the Rosenwald Fund, he worked at the Rockefeller Foundation, which he had joined in 1917 as secretary to its president, George Vincent. Seven years later, he became director of the Rockefeller Foundation's Division of Studies and attempted to develop a broad program in human ecology that included racial biology, human genetics, sexuality, and human development. Embree viewed the division's objective as the application of scientific models to solve social problems. His tenure was short lived; in 1926, the Rockefeller Foundation abolished the Division of Studies. Foundation officials charged that poor administration by Embree had been a major factor in the disbanding of the unit; however, changing foundation policy was probably the more significant factor. Embree's interest in social reform and social issues was inconsistent with the Rockefeller Foundation's activities, which had become increasingly focused on the advancement of society through scientific research. Embittered over the elimination of the Division of Studies, Embree resigned from the Rockefeller Foundation and joined the Julius Rosenwald Fund where his views were more compatible with the fund's social mission.[4]

Despite the reorganization of the Rosenwald Fund in 1928, black welfare issues and race relations remained major interests. The foundation gave major grants to black colleges and universities, including Atlanta University, Fisk University, Spelman College, and Meharry Medical College. It also established an extensive fellowship program that enabled African-American scholars and artists to pursue advanced study both in the United States and abroad. The fund also supported organizations that promoted interracial understanding, the most important of which was the Commission on Interracial Cooperation, the agency that had played a significant role in the campaign to secure black control of the Tuskegee Veterans Hospital.[5]

Although officials of the Julius Rosenwald Fund had a sincere interest in the improvement of the status of black Americans, they proceeded cautiously in the area of race relations and civil rights. They urged biracial cooperation and tried to place token blacks in strategic positions in predominantly white institutions. But they stopped short of advocating the full integration of African Americans into American society. The fund held that any efforts to "force progress much beyond its natural course" would increase racial animosities and further impede black progress. As part of its program, the Rosenwald Fund worked to establish and maintain racially separate institutions, viewing its support of such facilities not as encouraging Jim Crow, but, like the black hospital reformers, as a pragmatic response to the racial realities of American life.[6]

Prior to 1928, the Rosenwald Fund's programs for African Americans concentrated primarily on education. After the reorganization, the fund broadened its mission to include medical care. This focus on black health issues marked the convergence of the fund's longstanding interest in black social welfare and its new concern for medical care. As part of the expansion of the fund's mandate, Michael M. Davis was named director for medical services. Davis, the former director of the Boston Dispensary, came to the Rosenwald Fund with a reputation as an innovator in medical economics and medical organization. At the Boston Dispensary, he had pioneered a medical group practice that provided comprehensive health care to persons of moderate means. Upon arriving at the Rosenwald Fund, Davis established a Negro Health Division to oversee the black medical service programs. The division had the full support of fund president Embree. In a 1928 article in *Modern Hospital* titled, "Negro Health and Its Effect Upon the Nation's Health," Embree outlined why efforts to improve the health of African Americans needed and deserved white support, pointing out that poor health impeded black social advancement and reiterating the argument that black people with contagious diseases could infect white people. "Bacteria have a disconcerting fashion of ignoring segregation edicts," he warned. "Jim Crow laws have never successfully been set up for the germs of tuberculosis, pneumonia, typhoid or malaria." Embree also underscored that the increased black migration from the South to the cities of the North and Midwest made the black health problem a national, not just a regional, dilemma. The threat posed by African Americans to the white population was exaggerated, but it served a purpose. Fear—if nothing else—might force whites to address the health care needs of black people. At the same time, however, this approach defined the health care problems of black people solely in terms of the needs and concerns of white people. African Americans were depicted more as public health pests than as the victims of disease, racism, and inadequate medical services.[7]

In 1935, Dr. Midian O. Bousfield, the prominent black hospital reformer, was named director of the Negro Health Division of the Rosenwald Fund. Under his administration, the division had a comprehensive and ambitious agenda. It gave money to establish scholarships for black nurses and physicians, to train black public health personnel, to encourage projects to study black health care, to influence public opinion with regard to the health needs of African Americans, and to upgrade a limited number of black hospitals. Between 1917 and 1940, the Rosenwald Fund donated over $1.3 million to the black health field.[8]

One of the Rosenwald Fund's first ventures in black health care had been the creation in 1919 of a fellowship program to improve the curricula and training programs at black medical schools and hospitals. These fellowships allowed black physicians to pursue advanced studies in the basic medical sciences. Six fellowships, awarded annually, offered $1200 stipends to cover transportation, tuition, books, and living expenses. Rosenwald Fellows could study at any institution approved by the selection committee that accepted them.[9]

The career of Dr. W.S. Quinland, a 1919 graduate of Meharry Medical College, exemplified the goals of the program. Quinland, one of the first Rosenwald Fellows in Medicine, used his award to study bacteriology and pathology at Harvard University. He then returned to his alma mater to become head of the department of pathology. In 1922, Quinland became the first black physician admitted to the American Association of Pathologists and Bacteriologists. Fifteen years later, he passed his board examinations and became the first African American certified by the American Board of Pathology. Quinland's professional accomplishments certainly improved the quality of the laboratory science programs at Meharry and were clearly linked to the Rosenwald Fellowship, which had given him the opportunity to study at a prestigious university. Despite successes such as these, however, the Rosenwald Fund stopped sponsoring the program for reasons that remain unclear. A $100,000 grant from the General Education Board allowed it to continue for several more years.[10]

Under the auspices of the Negro Health Division, the Rosenwald Fund resumed its help for black physicians pursuing advanced training in clinical fields, offering stipends to physicians who sought specialty training at white as well as black hospitals. It also sponsored short-term postgraduate clinics. For example, the fund paid the expenses of Dr. Russell Minton to study radiology at Provident Hospital in Chicago. After his training, he returned home to Philadelphia and became director of radiology at Mercy Hospital.[11]

The Rosenwald Fund also supported public health activities. It funded training programs for black public health nurses and sanitarians and worked to secure them employment. It encouraged state boards of health to employ black personnel and often provided them with financial incentives to do so. The fund considered the placement of African Americans in predominantly white institutions and organizations to be an important element of its work. Midian O. Bousfield saw these efforts as part of "a propaganda effort" to overcome prejudice against black physicians and nurses and to improve the health status of black patients, but he recognized that such efforts at integration would be "slow and painful," and continued his support of black institutions. The Rosenwald Fund did have some success in integrating health departments. By 1937, health departments in North Carolina, Texas, Illinois, and Louisiana used Rosenwald monies to hire black physicians. However, it is not documented whether black physicians received the same salaries as white physicians and whether their practices were limited exclusively to black patients.[12]

The Negro Health Division also supported demonstration projects to promote health education and to control diseases such as tuberculosis and venereal diseases, which were thought to affect African Americans disproportionately. In 1930, the Rosenwald Fund, in cooperation with the United States Public Health Service, began a pilot program to control syphilis in six Southern counties. The project included a survey to determine the incidence of syphilis in blacks and development of a treatment program. The fund withdrew its support for the syphilis project two years later because it viewed long-term, comprehensive treatment programs as the responsibility of state and local agencies. In addition, the Rosenwald Fund experienced financial difficulties during the Depression and began a period of retrenchment. The loss of Rosenwald support proved to be particularly unfortunate for black citizens of Macon County, Alabama, one of the counties included in the syphilis project. Shortly after the fund's withdrawal, Public Health Service officers returned to Macon County and transformed what had initially been a treatment program into a study of the effects of untreated syphilis. The infamous Tuskegee Syphilis Study would last for forty years.[13]

Assistance to selected black hospitals was a major component of the efforts of the Negro Health Division. Fund officials recognized that no program in black health could succeed without addressing the plight of these institutions. Michael Davis acknowledged that foundation support was vital to the survival of the hospitals because they could not exist solely on payments from their patients. The fund maintained, however, that the provision of adequate hospital care to African Americans was too vast and complex a venture to be undertaken by any one foundation, and it limited its aid to hospitals that set high standards of service, training, and interracial cooperation. The specific criteria by which the Rosenwald Fund made its grants included:

> 1. Educational significance: a contribution not merely to hospital service, but to the training and experience of physicians, nurses, and others.

2. Interracial participation: in management, as by trustees; and in medical service, as to staff.

3. Objective standards of efficiency: qualifications of physicians for staff appointment or for particular functions, such as surgery, to be judged on objective and not racial standards.

4. Community support: the locality to take the major responsibility for building, equipment, and maintenance; the Fund's grants have not exceeded 25 per cent of the expenditure for buildings and equipment, and have not been for maintenance except occasionally for a few specific purposes.

By 1940, the fund had assisted fourteen black hospitals that met the above qualifications.[14]

This support was key to the survival of several of these black hospitals and to the provision of training opportunities for black physicians and nurses. In 1940, twenty-two black hospitals received accreditation from the American College of Surgeons and eight of these institutions had received fund support. The Rosenwald Fund had assisted seven of the eleven hospitals with approved internship programs and nine of the twenty hospitals with approved nurse training schools.[15]

The Rosenwald Fund made grants both to white-run black hospitals such as St. Philip in Richmond, Virginia and St. Agnes in Raleigh, North Carolina, and to black-controlled hospitals such as Mercy in Philadelphia and Provident in Chicago. These grants provided money for equipment, medical and nursing staff development, and hospital construction and renovation. In 1928, the Rosenwald Fund donated $25,000 to Mercy Hospital to help erect a new nurses' dormitory and a nurse training school building. The following year, it gave $50,000 to Charity Hospital, a forty-bed black hospital in Savannah, Georgia to help it construct a new building. A new facility was desperately needed: the hospital had been operating out of a cramped, unsafe frame structure, and it was one of two facilities that provided the only hospital care for the approximately 45,000 black people who lived in the Savannah area. The other facility, a small and inadequately equipped infirmary, did not permit black physicians to practice. The new 100-bed Charity Hospital would allow black physicians to practice and increase the number and quality of hospital beds available to black patients.[16]

The Rosenwald Fund's efforts to improve black hospitals were not without difficulties. The foundation considered a project in Knoxville, Tennessee to be particularly troublesome. In 1931, it donated $50,000 to construct and equip a sixty-bed black wing for Knoxville General Hospital. The city and county provided $200,000. In addition, the black citizens donated $1200 that had originally been raised to establish a black hospital in the city. The existing municipal hospital denied admitting privileges to black physicians and housed black patients in the basement, and therefore the intended purpose of the new black unit was to provide educational and practice opportunities for black physicians and nurses and to improve the medical care given to black patients. Accommodations would be made not only for indigent black patients at the city-run hospital, but for paying ones as well. The black unit was to be contiguous to the main building, but would have a separate entrance. To avoid expensive duplication of services, the two units of Knoxville General Hospital would share laboratory and radiology facilities. Plans for the black unit called for black physicians initially to admit their patients under the supervision of white physicians, and then after proving their competence, black doctors would be granted full staff privileges. Medical management of the unit would eventually be transferred to black hands, subject to supervision and control by the white superintendent of Knoxville General Hospital.[17]

The proposed black unit received enthusiastic support from both the National Hospital Association and the National Medical Association, the idea for the wing having originated with the NHA. Its president, H.M. Green, had vigorously worked to raise funds for the project located in his hometown. Green hailed the unit as one of the greatest achievements of the NHA, proudly observing that it would not be a small, freestanding black hospital, but a component of a grade A white hospital. Midian O. Bousfield, in his 1934 presidential address to the NMA, called the project a model for combatting the exclusion of black physicians in tax-supported institutions, especially in the South. Despite the segregation inherent in the proposal, the construction of the separate unit would at least provide black physicians access to a facility that their tax dollars helped to maintain. And it would get black patients out of the basement.[18]

Praise for the black unit at Knoxville General Hospital proved to be premature. After it opened in Spring 1933, opposition from white physicians derailed plans to appoint black physicians. Bousfield alleged that this resistance arose from white physicians' "fear of better prepared Negro physicians." Occasionally, a few black physicians, including Green, were allowed to admit patients and operate, but only under white supervision and without staff privileges. Bousfield conceded that many of the black physicians in Knoxville were inadequately prepared to be appointed to the hospital's medical staff, and as director of the Negro Health Division of the Rosenwald Fund, he worked to improve the skills of black physicians by arranging to send them elsewhere for advanced clinical instruction. For example, one physician, Dr. N.A. Henderson, was sent to New York University to receive a year's training in internal medicine. This additional training was still not enough to overcome the obstacles raised by the white medical and political establishment. Upon Henderson's return to Knoxville, the city council threatened to pass a resolution prohibiting the appointment of African-American medical personnel. The Rosenwald Fund attempted to break the impasse, and reminded the city of the original purpose of its contribution. The fund's efforts proved fruitless. It was not until 1942, after threatened legal action, that black physicians received full privileges at the hospital.[19]

When the Julius Rosenwald Fund first launched its Negro Health Division, it had only intended to finance programs at black hospitals. The policy shift to fund mixed hospitals such as the one at Knoxville General Hospital resulted from recommendations made by Dr. Watson Smith Rankin, director of the Duke Endowment's Hospital Section and an informal adviser to the fund. Rankin urged the fund not to limit its interest to black institutions. He contended that the problem of black hospitalization, especially in smaller communities, would best be handled in mixed hospitals, rather than in separate, substandard black hospitals. He believed that the establishment of separate wards or departments for black patients within white hospitals would be more practical and economical than maintaining, staffing, and building separate black facilities. Rankin also asserted that mixed hospitals would provide black patients with better treatment because the institutions had more abundant financial, administrative, and professional resources. But his assessment of the treatment black patients did and would receive in mixed hospitals missed a crucial point: these facilities almost invariably cared for African Americans in separate and inferior accommodations. The Rosenwald Fund's policy did eventually come to reflect Rankin's views, at least in part. Although it continued to support black hospitals, it began to provide financial assistance to mixed hospitals if they agreed to permit black medical personnel to practice and train in the black units. Perhaps because events in Knoxville demonstrated that it could not always enforce this stipulation, the Rosenwald Fund assistance to mixed hospitals was very limited: only two such institutions had received aid by 1940, in comparison to the fourteen black hospitals.[20]

The Rosenwald Fund and the Duke Endowment collaborated in the development of black units at two hospitals in South Carolina—Spartanburg General in Spartanburg and Tuomey in Sumter. Both institutions operated in areas with severe shortages of beds for black patients. Rankin participated in designing the black unit at Tuomey and made sure that it conformed to both medical and racial standards. He recommended that it be constructed so as to keep the races as physically separate as "economy and efficiency" permitted. Plans called for separate facilities except for the laboratory, x-ray department, and the major operating room. The Tuomey project involved the transfer of white patients to a modern facility and the renovation of the old facility for black patients. The work of the Rosenwald Fund and Duke Endowment in the establishment of mixed hospitals should therefore not be viewed as an attempt to foster *integrated* facilities. The institutions that they assisted maintained separate accommodations for black patients; the philanthropies' support for mixed hospitals was merely an effort to increase hospital efficiency and curb hospital costs. As conditions for their support of mixed hospitals, neither the Rosenwald Fund nor the Duke Endowment demanded that the separate facilities and accommodations of the black and white units be equal.[21]

The Julius Rosenwald Fund and the Duke Endowment collaborated on other projects in the black health field. In North and South Carolina, the Rosenwald Fund only assisted hospitals that had the approval of the endowment. Between 1928 and 1939, the two foundations jointly financed projects at five black hospitals in the Carolinas, and also worked together to offer technical assistance to black hospitals. At the request of the endowment, Midian O. Bousfield frequently visited black hospitals in the two states to evaluate them and offer recommendations for improvement.[22]

In contrast to the Rosenwald Fund, the Duke Endowment did not have a specific black health program. Founded in 1924 by the tobacco magnate James Buchanan Duke, the endowment supported schools, orphanages, and Methodist churches, as well as hospitals, in North and South Carolina. It maintained a hospital section that assisted qualified nonprofit general hospitals in the two states, and gave money to hospitals of all racial classifications—black only, white only, and mixed. Under the leadership of Dr. Watson Smith Rankin, former secretary of the North Carolina State Board of Health, the hospital section's primary objective was to improve local medical services, especially in rural areas, by increasing the supply of well-trained physicians and the number of adequately equipped hospitals.[23]

The hospital section donated money for operating and capital expenses and provided institutions with technical services, limiting its assistance to nonprofit general hospitals that it judged to be properly operated. Funds from the philanthropy had a substantial impact on hospitals in the Carolinas. The endowment contributed $1.00 a day toward the care of every charity patient in an eligible institution. In 1924, this dollar represented one-third of the average daily cost of patient care. If a surplus remained after these subsidies for free care, the endowment also funded capital expenditures for construction and equipment. To receive funds from the endowment, institutions had to submit a comprehensive application detailing their medical and administrative operations. The endowment used the information included in these applications to determine eligibility and level of assistance, and to compare hospitals statewide to uncover institutions that it considered to be inefficiently managed. Armed with both data and its abundant treasury, the Duke Endowment exerted considerable influence over the direction of hospital care in the Carolinas.

In 1924, twenty black general hospitals existed in the Carolinas, eleven in North and nine in South Carolina. These facilities represented fourteen percent of all general hospitals in the two states and supplied 38 percent of the general hospital beds for black patients. These hospitals fit the pattern of black hospitals nationwide: they were ill-equipped, small, and lacked clinical training programs. Black hospitals in the Carolinas averaged only twenty-eight beds and had low occupancy rates. Not one had the approval of the American Medical Association for internship training. A 1925 survey found that black hospitals had a death rate 35 percent greater than the average general hospital in the two states. These hospitals also had severe financial problems because of their small endowments and the large proportion of charity cases admitted.[24]

The inclusion of black hospitals in the Duke Endowment's mandate originated, in part, from the Duke family's longstanding association with Durham's Lincoln Hospital. The family founded the hospital in 1901 to show its appreciation "for the loyalty of the old Negroes to the white people of this vicinity during the War Between the States, and for their part in the industrial development of the City of Durham." Original plans called for the creation of a separate wing at the city hospital, however, John Merrick, a prominent black businessman, convinced the Duke family that a separate black hospital would be more beneficial to black physicians, nurses, and private patients. The funds to establish Lincoln Hospital represented the first and, for a time, the only major charitable venture of the Duke family in health care. The Duke Endowment's decision to fund black hospitals also stemmed from its recognition that its efforts to improve community health in the Carolinas would require the provision of hospital facilities for both white and black citizens, because the health statuses of the two races were inextricably linked.[25]

Rankin, director of the hospital section of the Duke Endowment, contended that black hospitals contributed to the unnecessary duplication of facilities in the Carolinas. He favored instead the development of mixed hospitals, not necessarily with any provisions for black physicians. However, he conceded that there was a limited role for black hospitals. Rankin acknowledged in a letter to H.M. Green that "strictly race hospitals" would be needed in regions of the Carolinas where a large number of black physicians practiced and where the black population was sizable. The Duke Endowment predicted that some hospitals in these areas would continue indefinitely, primarily as training centers, but that the smaller hospitals would either merge or close.[26]

The endowment hoped to develop between ten-to-twelve black district hospitals of 50-to-150 beds in North Carolina and from seven-to-eight such hospitals in South Carolina. These would be quality hospitals in which black physicians would practice, in which black nurses and interns would train, and in which black patients would be hospitalized. The endowment's plan called for white physicians to take active supervisory roles in the work of the district hospitals. Rankin observed that black-operated hospitals appealed to the racial pride of black people and, consequently, led to greater community participation in the institutions. However, he opposed placing the supervision of black hospitals under the control of black physicians, most of whom he considered to be poorly trained and incapable of running hospitals. The logic of Rankin's argument was that *all* black physicians, not simply *most,* were incompetent. Therefore, it would be impossible to find *any* black physicians capable of running a hospital. Rankin argued that the black hospital had a real place in the South only with active white supervision and assistance. White people, not black people, should determine the policies of black hospitals.[27]

The Duke Endowment's activities at Lincoln Hospital clearly demonstrated Rankin's concept of a black district hospital and the leverage he could and at times would exert to ensure that the institution complied with his vision. In 1925, Rankin called Lincoln Hospital the best black hospital in the Carolinas and a model for other black facilities in the South. Eight years later, the hospital had fallen on hard times. Patient receipts had decreased to one-fifth of its annual budget, half the collection rate of other black hospitals. Its surgical mortality rate had increased to twice that of other black hospitals. Consequently, the American College of Surgeons had rescinded its accreditation. Dr. Wilburt C. Davison, Dean of the Duke University Medical School, observed that many black patients refused to be hospitalized at Lincoln and would rather die than to go there. The Duke Endowment and the Rosenwald Fund attributed the hospital's decline to incompetent management by its superintendent, Dr. C.H. Shepherd, a black physician, and to the lethargy of its biracial board of trustees. Endowment officials charged that Shepherd was a dishonest alcoholic who had squandered funds at the hospital.[28]

Because of the connections of the Duke family to Lincoln Hospital, Rankin took an active interest in the hospital's problems. He saw white supervision of the hospital as the only remedy for the situation and proposed that the hospital be reorganized and that control be placed in the hands of white physicians from either Duke or Watts Hospitals. The charges against Shepherd gave Rankin the chance to create at Lincoln Hospital a model of a black district hospital. Durham's African-American community vigorously opposed this restructuring, with black physicians fearing that white supervision of the hospital would harm them professionally because they would lose staff privileges, income, and practice opportunities. James E. Shepherd, a Lincoln Hospital trustee and president of the North Carolina College for Negroes, reminded Rankin that the Duke family had wanted the hospital to be black controlled and operated in order to cultivate black leaders. He also argued that the proposed restructuring would "deprive the Negro of that initiative which they should have if leaders are to be developed" and would "strike a blow at our own self respect and make us question whether the education of the Negro would be worthwhile." Shepherd, it should be noted, had a personal interest in preventing the proposed changes. His brother, C.H., was the superintendent who had come under harsh criticism from the Duke Endowment and the Rosenwald Fund.[29]

Not all African Americans opposed the endowment's plans. Physicians from outside of the Carolinas who were closely linked with the black hospital movement heartily supported Rankin's recommendations. Midian O. Bousfield visited Lincoln Hospital and reported that conditions there were wretched. He, too, acknowledged that white philanthropic support and supervision were needed to improve its status. Peter Marshall Murray, then president of the National Medical Association, also strongly endorsed the proposed reorganization, urging the Rosenwald Fund and the Duke Endowment to

> abandon their role of passive observation and take an active positive stand and insist that institutions receiving their assistance should measure up and continue to measure up to certain minimum requirements of hospital organization and service. They would thus make a contribution to Negro medical progress far more valuable than the money they give.

Both Bousfield and Murray considered white philanthropic support and supervision crucial to their goal of developing high-quality black hospitals. Apparently, the loss of independence inherent in such an arrangement did not trouble them.[30]

Despite the protests from Durham's African-American community, Rankin stood firm and insisted upon the reorganization, threatening to withhold any Duke Endowment appropriations unless Lincoln went along with his proposal. Faced with the loss of much-needed

Duke funds, the trustees of the hospital accepted a compromise that created an advisory committee of white physicians. This body would have complete financial and professional responsibility for the hospital for five years. All its recommendations, however, had to be approved by the hospital's board of trustees. To allay the fears of local black physicians and to avoid possible conflicts of interest, no member of the advisory committee could have admitting privileges at Lincoln.[31]

These concessions did not diminish the considerable power that the advisory committee, bolstered by the support of the Duke Endowment, wielded at the hospital. It appointed a part-time medical and surgical supervisory staff to review difficult cases and all in-hospital deaths, to conduct a monthly medical conference, and to supervise the work of black physicians. Grants from the Duke Endowment and the Rosenwald Fund paid the salaries of the supervisory personnel. The advisory committee also observed the work of black physicians to determine who among them was qualified to retain staff privileges. As these physicians proved their competence, plans called for them to assume more responsibility in the hospital's operation.

Lincoln Hospital's high surgical mortality rates attracted special attention from the advisory committee. It assumed that the problem was incompetent black surgeons, without considering other possible complicating factors such as sicker patients or outmoded equipment. The committee's solution was to limit the access of black physicians to the operating room and to insist that all the doctors' work be supervised directly by white surgeons. Such restrictions were deemed necessary because the advisory committee considered black physicians to be inferior to white physicians. One official of the Duke Endowment patronizingly observed that black surgeons might have technical skills, but "frequently lacked surgical judgment."[32]

The reorganization called for the removal of Dr. Shepherd as superintendent and the appointment of another black man to the position. William M. Rich, a former banker from Roanoke, Virginia was named as Shepherd's replacement. To prepare him for his new responsibilities, the Duke Endowment sent Rich to Chicago's Provident Hospital and to New Orleans's Flint-Goodridge Hospital to receive training in hospital administration. At Flint-Goodridge, he worked under the tutelage of Albert W. Dent, then considered the nation's foremost black hospital administrator. Rich's appointment to the post reflected a trend in hospital management toward administrators who did not have medical or nursing backgrounds.[33]

The status of Lincoln Hospital improved dramatically after the initiation of the changes mandated by the Duke Endowment. Once again, Lincoln became a premier black hospital. The hospital's mortality rate decreased and its revenues increased. During the first year of Rich's administration, a $4000 deficit was erased. Black physicians also began to take more active roles in the hospital, as more of them qualified for staff privileges. Conditions at the hospital improved to the point that the American College of Surgeons reinstated its accreditation. In 1937, Bousfield called his involvement in the resurrection of Lincoln Hospital the most satisfactory endeavor that he had attempted since he had begun his work at the Rosenwald Fund. However, the success of the Duke Endowment's programs at the facility reinforced the notion that black people were not competent to run institutions—even black ones—except under white supervision.[34]

An examination of the Duke Endowment's activities at Waverly Fraternal and Good Samaritan Hospitals, two small black hospitals in Columbia, South Carolina, further demonstrates the endowment's willingness to use its financial muscle to dictate organizational changes. In the early 1930s, investigators from the Duke Endowment discovered evidence of fraudulent practices at both hospitals. First, the hospitals had falsified patient records in order to increase their free care subsidies from the endowment. For example, the record of one charity patient documented that she had been hospitalized at Waverly Fraternal for fifteen days after a tonsillectomy. An interview with the patient revealed that she had been admitted for only three days and had not had any surgery but had been treated with salt water gargles and aspirin. Furthermore, it was not exactly clear whether Waverly Fraternal might actually be a proprietary hospital disguised as a nonprofit one in order to dupe the Duke Endowment out of funds.[35]

The agents from the Duke Endowment also charged that the staffs and trustees of the two hospitals had pocketed funds donated for the care of fictitious or deceased patients while providing woefully inadequate care to the real living ones. One endowment official described Good Samaritan and Waverly Fraternal as "firetraps poorly adapted to be hospitals." At the request of the endowment, Midian O. Bousfield visited the two hospitals. He reported that "he had never seen a place where Negroes were so exploited by their own race as they were in these hospitals." He proposed, however, that the hospitals not be closed but upgraded, because of the need to train black physicians. Rankin thought otherwise, contending that the hospitals should be closed and their patients transferred to the black unit of Columbia Hospital, the county hospital. In 1938, the Duke Endowment withdrew its appropriations from the two mismanaged hospitals and their futures looked bleak.[36]

Local black physicians appealed to Rankin to reverse his decision because of the professional obstacles they faced at the county hospital. They pointed out that approximately 90 percent of the patients in the black unit were charity patients, but that they were allowed to treat only private patients there. During 1937, black physicians treated no more than twelve patients at Columbia Hospital. Furthermore, the physicians claimed that black patients were subjected to verbal abuse, even from white orderlies, at the county hospital. Because of these difficulties they argued that Columbia still needed a freestanding black hospital.[37]

In subsequent negotiations with black physicians and representatives of the two hospitals, the endowment stated that it would reconsider its actions only if the hospitals agreed to a list of organizational changes. These changes included the merger of the two hospitals, the formation of a biracial board of trustees, and, as previously done at Lincoln Hospital, the supervision of the hospital by white physicians. Initially, the hospitals balked because they feared the loss of their individual identities and of their autonomy as black institutions. But they could not continue to operate without money from the Duke Endowment and eventually they agreed to the endowment's demands. In January 1939, the newly merged Good Samaritan–Waverly Hospital opened.[38]

Despite its policy of limiting the role of black hospitals and encouraging mixed hospitals, the Duke Endowment emerged as the major philanthropic donor to black hospitals, including black-controlled institutions, in the Carolinas. Between 1925 and 1939, it donated approximately $1.2 million to twenty-two black nonprofit general hospitals for the care of charity patients, and between 1925 and 1937, approximately 70 percent of the black general hospitals in the Carolinas received Duke Endowment support. This financial assistance was essential for the survival of black hospitals in the two states, especially during the Depression years. For example, during the eight-year period between 1930 and 1937, Duke support represented 55 percent of the charitable contributions that the funded hospitals received toward operating costs, compared to 39 percent for white hospitals and 36 percent for mixed hospitals. However, in accepting funds from the Duke Endowment, black hospitals had to comply with the philanthropy's vision of black hospitals and allow the white community control over the direction of black institutions. This situation created a painful dilemma for African Americans; in many cases, the only other options were to close or to operate substandard facilities.[39]

The Duke Endowment also aided capital projects at seven black hospitals that it considered potential sites for district hospitals or that provided beds for black patients in severely underserved areas. The four largest black hospitals in the Carolinas—Good Samaritan, Lincoln, L. Richardson Memorial, and St. Agnes—received funds. The endowment provided funds to purchase equipment, and to remodel or build nurses' dormitories and patient accommodations. It also helped to construct Good Shepherd Hospital and Gaston County Negro Hospital in North Carolina's Craven and Gaston counties, respectively, which previously had no provisions at all for black patients.

There are indications that the quality of care improved in the black hospitals in the Carolinas because of the financial support of the Duke Endowment and the standards that it dictated. The typical black hospital in 1939 was larger, better utilized, and provided more efficient care than its 1925 predecessor. Between 1925 and 1939, the average hospital increased by ten beds, the average days of care rendered in each bed rose by 150 days, and the average stay decreased by 3.4 days. Not one black hospital in the Carolinas had received approval from any accrediting agency in 1925 but fourteen years later two hospitals, Lincoln and St. Agnes, which had received funds from the endowment, were endorsed by the American College of Surgeons and the American Medical Association for internship training. In addition to having two of the twenty approved internship programs in black hospitals, hospitals in North and South Carolina also had four of the twenty approved training schools for black nurses. The improved status of black hospitals in the two states resulted directly from the financial support and practices dictated by the Duke Endowment.[40]

While the Duke Endowment's involvement in black hospital reform had developed from its interest in the improvement of hospital care in the Carolinas and that of the Julius Rosenwald Fund from its programs in race relations and medical care, the attention of the General Education Board (GEB) grew out of its efforts in black education. John D. Rockefeller established the GEB in 1903 "to promote education within the United States of America without distinction of race, sex, or creed." Among the board's major activities were the reform of American colleges and universities, the improvement of education in the South, and the provision of adequate educational opportunities to African Americans.[41]

The GEB's interest in black education had both a pragmatic and a humanitarian basis. As was true at the Rosenwald Fund, GEB officials contended that the progress of American society was inextricably linked to the status of its black citizens. "The Negro race is numerous and widely scattered," a 1922 GEB memorandum on Negro education observed. "It is clear that the welfare of the South, not to say of the whole country—its prosperity, its sanitation, its morale—is affected by the condition of the Negro race." Economic considerations were also at work. The board acknowledged that African Americans were becoming an increasingly important productive force in the country and that the economic reconstruction of the South depended on a properly trained work force. James Anderson, who has written extensively on the relationship between Northern philanthropists and black higher education, has argued that industrial philanthropists, such as the Rockefellers and Carnegies, were more interested in black education as a means for economic efficiency and political stability than as a mechanism for the civil rights of African Americans.[42]

The GEB recognized that its educational programs for black people would have a profound social impact, but it did not regard the resolution of racial problems as part of its mandate. Jackson Davis, an assistant director of education at the foundation, aptly described its work as "education, not agitation." The GEB, like the Julius Rosenwald Fund and the Duke Endowment, designed its programs to operate within the framework of a segregated society. It was aware, however, of the onerous effect that segregation had on black Americans. The author of an unsigned 1931 confidential memo to GEB vice-president David H. Stevens observed that "no single thing irritates the colored people so much as enforced segregation. They interpret it as a badge of inferiority, and unfortunately it does frequently, if not usually mean inferior treatment or service for the same price." The GEB sought to remedy this problem, not by advocating integration, but by attempting to raise the standards of the black institutions that it funded to equal those of white institutions.[43]

Although the GEB stressed the importance of black education, it is clear that officials of the Rockefeller philanthropies did not consider blacks to be the intellectual equals of whites. In a 1903 address before Tennessee school superintendents, Dr. Wallace Buttrick, a former Baptist minister who served as the secretary and executive officer of the GEB between 1902 and 1917, informed his audience that "the Negro is an inferior race. . . . The Anglo-Saxon is superior. There cannot be any question about that." At a March 1929 meeting convened to discuss the Rockefeller philanthropies' black welfare programs, the issue was raised of whether there were sufficient data to determine whether blacks were worth educating. Beardsley Ruml, President of the Laura Spelman Rockefeller Memorial Fund, observed that although the average intelligence of blacks was lower, variability would compensate and thus make the support of black education a worthwhile endeavor for the Rockefeller philanthropies. Despite such racist attitudes on the part of Rockefeller officials, until World War I the GEB was the single largest source of funds for black education in the South.[44]

The GEB program in black education encompassed all educational levels. It provided funds to improve teaching at black public schools in the South, established endowments at black colleges such as Fisk University in Nashville and Morehouse College in Atlanta, and created teaching fellowships for black professors. In 1916, when it started an annual appropriation to Meharry Medical College, the GEB entered the field of black medical education. The board's policy in this area was greatly influenced by Abraham Flexner, who worked at the fund from 1913 to 1928. In his influential 1910 report, *Medical Education in the United States and Canada*, Flexner explained why it was important to provide adequate medical education to black physicians:

> The practice of the negro doctor will be limited to his own race, which in its turn will be cared for better by good negro doctors than by poor white ones. But the physical well-being of the negro is not only of moment to the negro himself. Ten million of them live in close contact with sixty million whites. Not only does the negro himself suffer from hookworm and tuberculosis; he communicates them to his white neighbors, precisely as the ignorant and unfortunate white contaminates him.

Flexner's interest in black medical education was motivated, in part, out of his concern to protect the health status of white Americans. Although he believed that germs have no color line, it is clear that he thought that medical education and practice should. In his report, he prescribed a restricted role for black physicians, contending that their practices would be limited to black people and that they should be taught to master the principles of hygiene rather than the techniques of surgery.[45]

Flexner asserted that of the seven black medical schools that existed in 1910, only two—Howard and Meharry—were worthy of future development, considering the other five schools to be "wasting small sums annually sending out undisciplined men, whose lack of real training is covered up by the imposing M.D. degree." The GEB eventually followed Flexner's recommendations and funded programs at Howard and Meharry. By 1924, these were the only surviving black medical colleges and until 1969 they trained the majority of black physicians. The absence of philanthropic support and the lack of affiliation with a state-run or a generously endowed private university contributed to the demise of the other schools. The GEB's decision to fund only Howard and Meharry fit closely with its overall policy to "make peaks higher": that is, to assist the strongest individuals and institutions to reach ever higher standards rather than to build up the weakest institutions.[46]

The GEB's efforts to improve the quality of medical education at the two schools represented its major work in black medical education. Between 1916 and 1944, the GEB gave approximately $8 million to Meharry Medical College, and between 1920 and 1936, it donated approximately $600,000 to Howard University School of Medicine. The funds given to Meharry provided key financial assistance at a time when the national movement to upgrade medical school curricula jeopardized its future. In 1923, the GEB appropriated $15,000 to Hubbard Hospital, Meharry's teaching hospital, for renovation of the operating rooms and the purchase of laboratory equipment and hospital supplies. The GEB also donated $88,000 to help expand the hospital's physical plant. In 1937, after Meharry was placed on probation by the AMA's Council on Medical Education and Hospitals, the GEB prompted curricular reforms at the school by threatening to withdraw its financial support. The GEB also employed its fiscal power to revamp the curriculum at Howard, where it had established a faculty fellowship program. In contrast to fellowships given at predominantly white medical schools, the purpose of the Howard grant was not to develop research-oriented medical scientists, but to provide remedial education to Howard faculty. This action illustrates the attitudes of GEB officials toward the capabilities, skills, and "place" of black physicians. Since they believed that African Americans were intellectually inferior, they did not believe that they could be trained to be research scientists, nor did the GEB use its financial muscle on behalf of expanding opportunities for black medical undergraduates at white institutions.[47]

The GEB's interest in medical education extended to graduate and postgraduate medical education as well. The board, like the black hospital reformers, considered the lack of adequate clinical opportunities for black medical school graduates to be the most serious gap in black medical education. In 1929, according to GEB figures, approximately 125 black physicians graduated from medical school, but fewer than 50 percent of them secured internships in qualified programs. Dr. Robert A. Lambert, a white medical science adviser at the GEB, wrote a memorandum in 1929 that vividly described the obstacles black physicians faced as they sought the clinical training that they needed to practice and advance in medicine:

> The negro doctor's opportunities for worth while *postgraduate* work are still more restricted so far as clinical subjects are concerned. Even in Boston, the cradle of abolition, prejudice against the negro is such that we have found it impossible to secure an opening for a well recommended Meharry teacher wanting special training in internal medicine. We would not have dared suggest a service in gynecology or obstetrics!

Officials at the GEB argued that the solution rested "not in attempting to force white hospitals to accept Negro internes and nurses, but rather in providing Negro hospitals with competent staff, at first white and eventually colored." This was the same paternalistic attitude expressed by representatives of the Duke Endowment, and which was incorporated into foundation policy mandating white supervision of activities to improve black hospitals and the training of black physicians. The GEB proposed to fund internship programs at the better black hospitals, such as Nashville's Hubbard Hospital, Washington's Freedmen's Hospital, and Chicago's Provident Hospital, selecting the latter for an ambitious pilot project designed to create the nation's foremost center for black medical education. As we shall see in the next chapter, the Provident experiment ended in failure and the GEB consequently abandoned funding internship programs.[48]

Officials at the GEB decided that a more worthwhile use of its resources would be to sponsor postgraduate refresher courses for black physicians at black hospitals. One such program was a series of two-week postgraduate courses held between 1931 and 1940 at Richmond's St. Philip Hospital, a facility operated by the Medical College of Virginia. The idea for the program had originated with the Negro Medical Association of Virginia, which had approached the exclusively white Medical Society of Virginia about sponsoring refresher courses for black practitioners, most of whom lacked hospital privileges and medical school appointments. The white medical society turned down the request, but referred it to the Medical College of Virginia because of its demonstrated interest in black medical care.[49]

The Medical College of Virginia had founded St. Philip Hospital in 1920 to care for black patients and, seven years later, it opened a nurse training school for black nurses. However, St. Philip Hospital barred black physicians. In 1929, the Medical College of Virginia proposed to open and operate a separate institution for the use of the twenty-seven black physicians who then practiced in Richmond. The Medical College of Virginia approached the GEB for assistance. The GEB considered the proposal significant because it represented the first time a white Southern medical college had agreed to cooperate with a black hospital. However, it decided against funding the project, believing that there were not enough black paying patients and black physicians to support another black hospital in Richmond. In addition, the city's African-American community made clear that if another black hospital were built in the city, they wanted it connected to a black institution, specifically Virginia Union University. They wanted a black hospital that would be controlled by black people.[50]

The GEB did express an interest in funding postgraduate courses in Richmond. With this incentive, the medical college formed a biracial committee to develop a two-week summer refresher program for black physicians, primarily those from Virginia. The course, to be held at St. Philip, would consist of lectures, clinical demonstrations, and discussions covering common problems in internal medicine, pediatrics, obstetrics, and surgery. The classes would be taught by Medical College of Virginia faculty, but guest black instructors would be invited. Enrollment in the course would be limited to around twenty and each participant would be expected to pay a ten-dollar tuition fee. In March 1931, the medical college requested $1500 from the GEB to cover faculty expenses and honoraria. The board approved the request and in June 1931, the first session was held.

The first summer program included lectures and demonstrations on physical diagnosis, infant feeding, and clinical pathology. In addition to the faculty from the Medical College of Virginia, two black physicians, Dr. Algernon B. Jackson of Howard University and Dr. H.A. Callis of the Tuskegee Veterans Hospital, gave lectures. Officials of the GEB later observed that the presence of competent and successful black physicians had a beneficial psychological effect on the physicians who attended the summer program.[51]

The program proved to be productive. By 1937, seventy-nine physicians had attended at least one of the sessions. Although the largest number of participants were from Virginia, practitioners also hailed from North Carolina, South Carolina, Georgia, Florida, Kentucky, and even Texas. The GEB estimated that by 1937 approximately 25 percent of the black physicians in Virginia had taken advantage of the courses. The success of the program at St. Philip led to the development of similar postgraduate courses at Flint-Goodridge, Negro Hospital of the Medical College of Georgia, and Provident Hospital. As a result of its involvement in the summer program, the Medical College of Virginia further extended its facilities to black physicians, all the while maintaining segregation. It opened a separate reading room for black physicians from Richmond and granted black physicians throughout the state the privilege of borrowing books by mail. Despite the medical college's interest in the careers of black physicians, however, the doors of the hospital remained closed to them. Robert A. Lambert of the GEB observed that it would have been "impracticable" to have black interns and attending physicians at St. Philip because the hospital was used for teaching white medical students who would refuse to work under black physicians.[52]

The GEB came to view postgraduate courses as a practical, inexpensive, and relatively non-controversial approach to black medical education. A 1938 board report on postgraduate training strongly praised the St. Philip project, observing that "it is doubtful whether any equal investment by the board has started so many useful ripples of education in the medical sciences." The report emphasized that with a small amount of funding the GEB had been able to offer educational opportunities to a large number of practitioners. It also concluded that the Richmond venture had done much to promote interracial understanding and cooperation. GEB support of the program ended in 1940, after the state had assumed responsibility for it.[53]

The GEB, in contrast to the Rosenwald Fund and Duke Endowment, did not provide grants for the improvement of hospital service. Its interests were exclusively focused on educational projects, and on hospitals only as necessary learning sites. The GEB did not fund hospital-based programs to the same degree as did the other two philanthropies; it allocated more resources to undergraduate medical education. Nonetheless, the GEB had a significant impact on the black hospital movement, its funds leading to improvements in clinical training at some hospitals, especially at Hubbard Hospital. Most importantly, it contributed to the professional survival of African-American physicians by providing them with improved educational opportunities, albeit in separate institutions.

White foundations supplied essential assistance to the black hospital movement, which could have accomplished little without this cooperation and support. The African-American community itself lacked the financial resources to operate first-class medical institutions at a time when the expense and technology of equipping a hospital were increasing so rapidly. Philanthropic support enabled a limited number of black hospitals and physicians to be better prepared to meet the challenges presented by the changes in hospital standardization, medical education, and clinical practice. For example, in 1939 ten black hospitals provided black physicians with approved internship training; all ten had external sources of support. Eight received funds from either the Rosenwald Fund, Duke Endowment, or the General Education Board, and three had either federal or municipal sponsorship. The three philanthropies also gave funds to ten of the nineteen black hospitals that had American College of Surgeons endorsement. Government agencies subsidized five hospitals with such accreditation. As the fate of the black medical colleges made plain, white financial support was essential for the survival of black medical institutions.[54]

Such support, however, came at a price. It enabled white philanthropies, and not the African-American community, to have a key role in controlling and determining the role and function of some black hospitals. The assisted facilities would be "for blacks" but would be supervised by whites, an arrangement that frequently denied black people a voice in determining the direction of institutions that served them. White supervision of black hospitals also reinforced a racial hierarchy within medicine that saw black physicians as inferior to their white colleagues. Black physicians maintained that it was their training and institutions, not their intellects, that were inferior. The efforts of the foundations also contributed to the advancement of a separate, and not equal, medical world for black physicians, nurses, and patients. As we have seen, the existence and necessity of separate facilities was at the center of the foundations' funding policies. Although their efforts led to the improvement of a few black hospitals and the encouragement of mixed hospitals with separate black wards, they usually did not demand that these facilities equal those provided for white people.

By funding separate black institutions, white philanthropies found themselves entangled in controversies among African Americans over the need for such institutions. Leaders of the black hospital movement supported and even praised the efforts of the white philanthropies, raising no objections to the obligations that such funding often demanded and, in some cases, even welcoming them. Walter G. Alexander, general secretary of the NMA, contended in 1931 that more professional opportunities had recently been made available to black physicians. The Julius Rosenwald Fund, he maintained, had been the "greatest force responsible for this change." John A. Kenney went so far as to proclaim that "every Negro in the United States of America should get down on his knees and thank God for Julius Rosenwald" because of the vast sums the philanthropist had spent to improve the status of black people. Such sentiments were not universal. Nationwide, during the early 1930s, segments of the African-American community committed to integrationism increasingly attacked the philanthropies' practice of establishing and maintaining separate institutions, charging that such a policy fostered segregation and perpetuated second-class citizenship for black people.[55]

Because of its extensive and visible programs in black social welfare and race relations, the Julius Rosenwald Fund became the primary target for condemnation by integrationists. We have already seen how the Manhattan Medical Society had criticized the Rosenwald Fund's involvement in the proposal to create a black hospital in Harlem and had distributed the open letter assailing the fund's position on separate institutions. The medical association was not the only critic of the fund's policies. Journalist George Schuyler, in an editorial in the *Pittsburgh Courier*, argued that if African Americans had economic power that they would not need the charity of white philanthropists. Philanthropists, such as Julius Rosenwald, whom Schuyler bitterly called a "semitic Santa Claus," gave "alms, not opportunity." Schuyler contended that although Rosenwald employed a large number of African Americans at Sears and Roebuck, they had no positions above janitors or laborers. An editorial in the *Chicago Whip* labelled Julius Rosenwald an "apostle of Jim Crow whose philanthropy . . . has stimulated the satanic bird of segregation to fly north above the Mason-Dixon line." A.C. MacNeal, the first black president of the Chicago NAACP, charged that the purpose of the Rosenwald Fund was the "segregation and separation of the races through Jim Crow schools, YMCAs, hospitals, and housing."[56]

The Julius Rosenwald Fund vigorously denied the allegations that it advanced segregation. Edwin Embree used the dedication of a nurses' residence at Philadelphia's Mercy Hospital in December 1930 to answer the fund's critics publicly. He asserted that the fund did not advocate segregation of any group, and also reaffirmed the foundation's commitment to improving the health status of African Americans and to providing training opportunities for black physicians and nurses. He maintained that black hospitals such as Mercy were necessary if the fund's efforts were to be successful. "Unless," he added, "one is ready to sacrifice the education of the Negro medical profession." Embree's repudiation of segregation did not satisfy integrationists or erase the controversy over the role of black hospitals. Tensions continued over the role of white philanthropies in funding black hospitals and reached a peak at Provident Hospital in Chicago.[57]

FIVE

"Progressive Disappointment and Defeat": The Provident Hospital Project

❧

Provident Hospital in Chicago, the institution founded by Daniel Hale Williams in 1891, was one of the nation's most highly regarded black hospitals thirty years later. Of the approximately 200 black hospitals, it was one of the few facilities accredited by national medical organizations, and was a renowned center for the training of black physicians and nurses. The hospital had become crucial to the lives of residents of Chicago's South Side, its doors remaining open to black patients when those of other Chicago hospitals were closed to them. The hospital also functioned as a center for black civic activities. Langston Hughes in his poem, "Interne at Provident," captured the importance of the hospital to both black patients and health care professionals. He wrote of physicians:

> Learning skills of surgeons
> Brown and wonderful with longing
> To cure ills of Africa,
> Democracy,
> And mankind,
> Also ills quite common
> Among all who stand on two feet.

Provident Hospital's stature received a further boost in 1929 when it affiliated with the University of Chicago. This project represented a new strategy for black hospital reform and black medical education: the partnership of a black hospital with a white university. Promoters of the affiliation wanted to create a black medical mecca in Chicago. Provident Hospital was to become the foremost center of black medical education in the United States and, at the same time, set a new standard in black hospital care. It would, supporters hoped, be equal to the best white institutions. But despite early optimism, widespread biracial support, and generous financial assistance from the General Education Board (GEB) and Julius Rosenwald Fund, the project showed signs of instability almost from its inception. The problems resulted from factors both internal and external to the affiliation, which lasted but fifteen years. One GEB official described its history as "one of progressive disappointment and defeat."[1]

An examination of the short-lived Provident Hospital project makes plain the obstacles and tensions inherent in black hospital reform during the 1920s and 1930s. This analysis further illuminates the often conflicting ideas that black physicians, white foundations, and the black public held with regard to the role of black hospitals. It also demonstrates once again that black hospitals could not be divorced from contemporary racial politics and realities. These institutions were not just medical facilities, but were also social institutions that reflected the goals, needs, and divisions within the African-American community, and the state of American race relations.

Despite its many accomplishments, Provident Hospital was not without problems. Since its establishment, it had had financial difficulties, since many of its patients were poor people who could not afford to pay. At one time, nurses lived on bread and molasses. Although the African-American community continued to make donations, these were not sufficient to cover costs and white support became increasingly critical. In 1898, white benefactors had financed the construction of the hospital's new 65-bed facility. They also had bailed out the institution after a financial judgment had been rendered against it.[2]

After Daniel Hale Williams's forced resignation in 1912, most white support vanished and the hospital fell on even harder times. Ethel Johns, the British nurse commissioned by the Rockefeller Foundation to study the status of black nurses, visited Provident Hospital in 1925. She found that the hospital was deteriorating; the physical plant was run-down and the equipment inadequate, even though the institution was "clean and orderly." Johns attributed the hospital's problems to its transfer to exclusively black control, but her assessment ignored the significant impact made by massive black migration from the South on the hospital's operations. Most of these new residents had come without adequate financial and social resources. Their arrival placed increased demands on Provident's services and worsened its already precarious financial status.[3]

Medical service at the hospital had become so deficient that one of Chicago's largest employers, Armour and Company, threatened to send its black workers elsewhere. It might have intended to hospitalize them at Cook County Hospital or at one of the segregated wards that had opened in a few of the city's voluntary hospitals. But Provident remained one of the premier black hospitals. In 1928, it was one of the seventeen black hospitals approved by the American College of Surgeons and one of the fourteen approved by the American Medical Association (AMA) for internship training. These imprimaturs again remind us that black hospitals that had received accreditation had not necessarily met the minimum standards of the organizations. It was accepted practice to educate and care for African Americans in separate and unequal facilities.[4]

In the spring of 1928, representatives of Provident Hospital, including Dr. George C. Hall, met with Dr. Franklin C. McLean, director of the University of Chicago Clinics and a trustee of the Julius Rosenwald Fund, to discuss the possible affiliation of the hospital with the university. Although an exponent of black self-help and racial solidarity, Hall was a pragmatist, recognizing that white support was necessary for the continued survival of Provident Hospital. The proposed arrangement would help the hospital upgrade its medical service and improve and expand its educational program by offering residency training. It would also enable the hospital to keep in step with the latest developments in scientific medicine and secure its position as a black hospital of national importance. Changes in medical training and the rise of academic medicine now mandated that all teaching hospitals be affiliated with medical schools. An additional benefit for the hospital would be that the participation of the university in its affairs might rekindle white interest in the institution.[5]

McLean reacted favorably to the proposal and initiated efforts to secure university support. In his appeal to university officials, he stressed that their institution would also gain from the proposed arrangement. McLean noted that the affiliation with Provident Hospital would remedy "two rather urgent problems, namely, the care of colored patients, and the clinical training of colored physicians." In 1928, university policy prohibited admission of black patients to its clinics, a policy described by McLean as "frequently embarrassing." The proposed affiliation would enable university physicians to admit their black patients at Provident and provide them with abundant clinical material. It would also obviate the necessity for construction of a separate pavilion for black patients at the university's Billings Hospital.[6]

Affiliation with Provident Hospital would also assist the University of Chicago to meet the educational needs of its black medical students. In 1928, fourteen African-American students were enrolled. This represented the highest black enrollment at any predominantly white medical school. However, these students reportedly encountered hostility from white patients during their clinical years. Dr. B.C.H. Harvey, dean of medical students, acknowledged it was not "practicable" to routinely assign black medical students to clinical clerkships. "It can be done perhaps to a small extent," he argued, "but it creates an embarrassing situation and cannot be the real solution of the problem." Black students were forced to obtain their clinical experience in the outpatient dispensary, which Harvey admitted was not sufficient. Since the school could not guarantee black students adequate clinical training, some faculty members considered it a disservice to continue to admit them and pushed for a more racially restrictive admissions policy. The proposed partnership would allow the medical school to remain open to black students because they could now do their clinical clerkships at the black hospital.[7]

The importance of the proposed affiliation went beyond Chicago. In December 1928, Dr. Richard M. Pearce, head of the Division of Medical Studies of the Rockefeller Foundation, hailed the project as a significant development in black medical education and urged foundation support. He noted that it would provide black physicians and nurses with at least one clinical training program that equalled those available to their white colleagues.[8]

Some university officials viewed the proposal with apprehension. They expressed concern that the project would substantially increase the number of black alumni, and also feared that the public would look unfavorably upon the University of Chicago's association with a black institution. McLean assured them that the number of black medical students admitted would never be large, only around ten annually. Frederic Woodward, a vice president of the university, although supportive of the project, warned that "great care should be taken to keep our hands free, so that if the greater interests of the university are seriously threatened we can withdraw." He added, prophetically, "I earnestly hope that the dangers will not prove so serious as I have sometimes feared."[9]

Perhaps aided by the Rosenwald Fund's and GEB's acknowledged interest and anticipated funds, McLean succeeded in overcoming these reservations and obtained the necessary faculty and administrative support for the project. Eventually the project received the approval of the university's Board of Trustees, where it had an ardent supporter in Trustee Julius Rosenwald. On 24 October 1929, the

University of Chicago and Provident Hospital signed a provisional contract for affiliation. This agreement was far from iron-clad, and its tentative nature paved the way for future problems. The university would have no financial obligations, its responsibilities contingent upon the successful solicitation of funds earmarked for the project. As conditions for the affiliation, Provident Hospital agreed to raise funds that would enable it to move into a lien-free facility of 100 beds. It also promised to maintain an endowment or working capital of not less than $400,000 and to seek funds for the endowment of the teaching program. Responsibility for internal operation of the hospital would continue to rest with a separate board of trustees.[10]

The university would assume control of all teaching and research activities and would create a center for the teaching of clinical medicine at all levels. The agreement called for all staff nominations to be made by the university; however, Provident retained the right to veto. The university would give preference to black physicians, but personal and professional qualifications, regardless of race, would be the determining criteria. Initially it was expected that all the resident staff and at least 60 percent of the attending staff would be black. The supervisory staff would be white as it was to be composed of university faculty. The medical school had only one black faculty member, Dr. Julian H. Lewis, the first African American on the medical school faculty, who was appointed to the department of pathology in 1922. As a pathologist, his contact with living patients was very limited. The agreement between Provident Hospital and the University of Chicago did permit patients to request consultations with physicians not on staff. This arrangement addressed Provident Hospital's concern that private practitioners who had come to depend on the hospital would not be totally shut out of it. As a consequence of the affiliation, these physicians might lose their admitting privileges, but at least they could maintain some connection, albeit very limited, with the institution.[11]

Furthermore, the segregation inherent in the project appeared to be in keeping with the interests and expectations of the institutions and communities involved, and the affiliation received widespread biracial support in Chicago. Although some black people, including Julian Lewis, regretted the loss of Provident's identity as a black institution, Thomas J. Helsom, a black civic leader and the executive secretary of Provident Hospital, articulated the prevailing view, hailing the venture as "one of the greatest forward looking projects that had been undertaken in the matter of public health and medical education in our long history of the contact of the white and colored races." Julius Rosenwald extolled the project as "one of the biggest steps in the progress of this race in America since the Emancipation Proclamation." Significantly, no voices of dissent were heard from the black community.[12]

At the beginning of what would become the Great Depression, Provident Hospital faced an overwhelming challenge: it had to raise over $2 million to bring the affiliation to fruition. Funds were needed to purchase a building, create working capital, and establish an endowment for the clinical teaching program. Instead of constructing a new facility that met the specifications of the university, the trustees of Provident Hospital opted to buy and remodel the building previously occupied by Chicago's Lying-In Hospital. The university had decided to vacate that building and erect a new facility closer to its Hyde Park campus and the new Billings Hospital after the South Side had become predominantly black. The cost of purchasing and renovating the vacated building, conveniently located a little over a mile from the University of Chicago, was estimated at between $800,000 and $900,000. Provident Hospital also had to raise $400,000 to maintain the working capital that was specified in the agreement and approximately $1 million to endow the teaching program.[13]

In the fall of 1929, the project's supporters launched a $1.5 million fund-raising campaign. Its slogan, "Germs Have No Color Line," served to remind potential white donors that the improvement of black medical education deserved their financial support, if not for humanitarian reasons, then at least for self-protection. Julius Rosenwald, a longtime supporter of the hospital, served as honorary chairman of the campaign, giving it a large boost by personally pledging $250,000, while the Rosenwald Fund pledged another $250,000. The fund's president, Edwin R. Embree, worked to solicit donations for the affiliation from other philanthropies. Even before the provisional agreement had been signed, he sent letters strongly endorsing the project to the officers of several foundations, including those of the Carnegie Foundation, the Commonwealth Fund, and the Duke Endowment. Embree also contacted his former colleagues at the Rockefeller Foundation about providing the funds for the teaching endowment.[14]

Rockefeller philanthropies had long been involved in medical education at the University of Chicago. In 1916, the GEB submitted to the Rockefeller Foundation a proposal to develop a university-based medical school at Chicago that would include a teaching hospital and a full-time clinical faculty. The Rockefeller Foundation eventually funded the proposal, its first venture into medical education. Subsequently, both the GEB and Rockefeller Foundation contributed large sums of money to the university's medical school. In 1923, on the recommendation of the Rockefeller Foundation, the university appointed Franklin C. McLean to his position as professor and chairman of the department of medicine and director of the University of Chicago Clinics. Previously, he had worked for the China Medical Board of the Rockefeller Foundation to organize the Peking Union Medical College.[15]

The development of a center of black medical education at Provident Hospital, under university auspices, fit closely with the GEB's ongoing interests in academic medicine at the University of Chicago and in the education of black physicians. Officers of the foundation acknowledged that inadequate clinical training seriously jeopardized their efforts to improve the professional status of black physicians and nurses. Therefore, they took a keen interest in the then-maturing project in Chicago. In February 1929, Dr. Robert A. Lambert, a medical science adviser to the GEB, visited three black hospitals in Chicago: Provident Hospital, Lakeside Hospital, and Dailey Hospital. He left with a favorable impression of only Provident. Lambert observed that the institution was doing good work under very difficult conditions. The following month, Richard Pearce, the Rockefeller Foundation executive who had previously backed the project, enthusiastically renewed his endorsement and urged GEB support because of its educational significance.[16]

On 16 October 1929, eight days before it signed the affiliation agreement with Provident Hospital, the University of Chicago submitted a formal request to the GEB for one million dollars to endow the clinical teaching aspects of the project. At its 21 November 1929 meeting, the trustees of the GEB approved the application. The funds were given to the University of Chicago, not to Provident Hospital. Although the allocation had been made specifically for its affiliation with Provident Hospital, terms of the agreement stated that the university could use the income for other purposes, except theological instruction. In addition, the GEB reserved the right to defer payment of the entire principal for a period of ten years, during which time interest payments only would be made.[17]

Planning for the official affiliation progressed well during 1930 and 1931, and all signs appeared propitious in spite of the still-deepening economic crisis. Provident Hospital undertook organizational changes designed to upgrade its status and acceptability within the university community. The board of trustees was strengthened by the addition of several prominent white Chicagoans, including Dr. Otto F. Ball, president of the Modern Hospital Publishing Company, and Alfred C. Meyer, president of nearby Michael Reese Hospital. In April 1930, Admiral Norman D. Blackwood, a retired white naval officer with experience in hospital management, replaced the ailing George C. Hall as medical director. Hall remained on the hospital's board until his death two months later. By February 1930, supporters of the project had even more cause for optimism: the Provident fund-raising campaign had secured over $2.2 million in pledges—$700,000 over its goal. Included in these pledges were $210,000 from black Chicagoans. In April 1930, the project received another boost when the Commonwealth Fund pledged $100,000, conditional on the campaign meeting its goals. Commonwealth Fund officials lauded the affiliation as "the first worthwhile project for the negro which has ever come to the Fund's attention."[18]

In March 1930, Franklin C. McLean, who functioned as the university liaison for the project, started preliminary work on the educational programs, and began to select black physicians who would be enrolled in an intensive training program designed to prepare them to be faculty members at the new hospital. The Julius Rosenwald Fund agreed to supply money to educate physicians for junior positions; however, in order to educate those for senior positions, funds would be needed from the GEB appropriation. Although Provident Hospital had yet to meet all the terms of its agreement with the University of Chicago, including possession of a lien-free facility and $400,000 in working capital, its progress toward meeting its contractual obligations convinced the GEB to make a $25,000 payment from its pledge.[19]

In February 1931, McLean observed that Provident Hospital continued its advancement toward meeting the terms of its contract with the university. The hospital expected to move into its new facility by September and it had secured over $1 million in contributions, over 50 percent of its total pledges. On June 15, it paid $375,000 and took on a $400,000 mortgage to buy the vacated Chicago Lying-In Hospital. It also signed a contract to renovate the facility. Subsequently, A.L. Jackson, the president of the hospital's board of trustees, informed the university that the hospital had met the conditions stipulated in the agreement. The university, in turn, requested that the GEB pay its full pledge. The GEB, however, deferred payment pending collection of the unpaid campaign pledges and completion of the renovation of the Lying-In Hospital. Instead, as permitted by its contract with the university, it authorized a $50,000 grant, which represented 5-percent interest on its full pledge.[20]

In spite of these steps toward official affiliation, by the end of 1931, rifts and doubts had begun to appear. The Provident Hospital project showed signs of trouble: administrative mismanagement, financial problems, personnel changes, and racial tensions. First, Edwin R. Embree, of the Rosenwald Fund, expressed well-founded concerns about the management of Provident Hospital, especially the activities of its president, A.L. Jackson. Jackson, a black businessman, had served in numerous capacities in the African-American community. In 1915, he began a four-year tenure as executive secretary of the Wabash Avenue YMCA, a "Y" exclusively for blacks. In 1921, the Harvard graduate became assistant to the publisher of the *Chicago Defender*, a black newspaper, and also assumed the presidency of the Provident Hospital board of trustees. Rosenwald Fund officers, however, found Jackson's leadership of the hospital to be a liability. In December 1931, Embree wrote Jackson a harsh letter in which he voiced his apprehensions about the project's future because of the organization and policies of the hospital's board. He criticized the lack of responsible board control of the hospital, the paucity of meetings, and Jackson's receipt of a salary of between $9000 and $12,000 for a traditionally voluntary position. The payment was reportedly for his fund-raising duties. Jackson had, in fact, been using his position for personal gain: he ran his real-estate business from a hospital office.[21]

The hospital's financial status also began to look bleak. A May 1932 auditors' report noted that the hospital's deficit had escalated from $10,000 in June 1929 to almost $165,000 by December 1931. The auditors blamed the increased deficit both on the Depression and on changes in hospital service mandated by the affiliation agreement. A $400,000 lien remained on the new property and the hospital had encountered difficulties in the collection of $800,000 in outstanding campaign pledges, including over $400,000 from Rosenwald sources. The auditors considered at least $200,000 to be uncollectible. The Rosenwald Fund, hard hit by the Depression because of the drop in market value of Sears and Roebuck stock, did take steps to ensure that its commitments were met. In May 1932, Lessing H. Rosenwald, president of the board of trustees of the fund, and Edwin R. Embree, its president, appealed to the GEB to underwrite some of its pledges, including those to Provident Hospital. At first, the officers of the GEB were cool to the request because they did not want to be in the position of supporting another foundation. However, they realized that the failure of the Rosenwald Fund would jeopardize some important GEB programs, and consequently, they voted to make emergency grants of up to $200,000 to selected projects in which both philanthropies cooperated. Without this support, the fund, which was virtually bankrupt, would probably not have survived the Depression.[22]

On 16 and 17 June 1932, Dr. Alan Gregg, director of the Medical Sciences Division of the Rockefeller Foundation, went to Chicago to investigate the status of the project. He examined the hospital's financial situation thoroughly and was surprised to learn that the fund-raising campaign had not been for endowment, but for capital funds that would be exhausted within four years. The campaign had been developed by Julius Rosenwald, who adamantly opposed the establishment of perpetual endowments. This difference in views represented a major split between the two foundations. Gregg informed A.L. Jackson that the GEB would not look favorably on the continuation of such a fiscal policy. He also reported that the board was not yet ready to pay its full pledge: it would continue to make annual interest payments until the hospital had paid off its mortgage.[23]

Other problems plagued the still-unofficial affiliation. In 1932, Franklin C. McLean, the director of the University of Chicago Clinics and a key supporter of the project, left, under pressure, for reasons unrelated to the project. His plan to establish a full-time faculty had been vigorously opposed by some faculty members who demanded that McLean be replaced. In order to restore harmony to a deeply divided faculty, McLean resigned. And, as if this were not enough, Michael M. Davis, medical director of the Rosenwald Fund, reported that "all is far from quiet on the Negro front." His assessment referred to the tensions that had developed over the racial composition of the medical staff. Consistent with GEB policy, the university intended that, initially, the leadership of the hospital would be white; the implicit assumption was that this was better than black control. Officials of the university and the Rosenwald Fund had expected some black opposition to the appointments. As Davis charged, "the disappointed will throw stones." Nonetheless, the university and the fund decided that such opposition would not be allowed to interfere with its plan to put the "hospital service on a high academic standard." In March 1930, Robert A. Lambert stated that although black physicians would hold most staff positions, they would be under the direction of white physicians. "The Negroes," he alleged, "prefer white responsibility in the beginning." Two months later, A.L. Jackson, in his annual report to Provident Hospital's Board of Trustees, challenged Lambert's assertion. He urged that the hospital move swiftly toward black control. Thus, seeds of discord had been sown even before the affiliation had formally begun.[24]

The contract between the hospital and university became official on 15 May 1933. It is unclear, from available records, why the contract went into effect at all, since the hospital had not yet met all its contractual obligations. Provident still held a substantial mortgage on its new facility and had not procured the required amount of working capital. Perhaps the affiliation's expected benefits and the continued financial support of the GEB and Rosenwald Fund convinced the university to sign the contract.

Despite these problems, in September 1934, Dr. Henry S. Houghton, McLean's successor as director of the University of Chicago

Clinics, expressed optimism about the project's progress. He noted that the hospital's management had become more efficient under its new medical director, Admiral Blackwood, and that four black physicians had been selected to head clinical departments at Provident. In contrast, Robert A. Lambert, the GEB liaison for the project, filed a distinctly discouraging report only three months later, voicing his doubts that the educational objectives of the affiliation were being met. He noted that the number of black medical students at Chicago had actually decreased since the inception of the project, there now being only two in the preclinical years and one in the clinical years. Lambert acknowledged that thus far, the benefits of the project had been to medical service, not to education. He reported that the hospital now provided better medical care and that its outpatient department had improved immensely. Provident's move to the new facility had increased its inpatient capacity from 65 beds to 150 beds. Whereas in 1930 over 5000 visits had been made to the hospital's three outpatient clinics, in 1933 over 7800 visits were made to its eighteen clinics. Staff salaries for several of the new clinics came from the GEB funds.[25]

In spite of these improvements in medical service, Lambert uncovered additional problems that threatened the success of the affiliation. He questioned the extent of the university's involvement and enthusiasm for the affiliation, especially after McLean's departure from his administrative post. During his site visit, he discovered that contacts between Provident Hospital housestaff and university attending physicians were minimal and that some department heads at Chicago were cold to the affiliation and considered it an extra burden. The experiences of Dr. Harsba Bouyer exemplified some of the obstacles that black physicians faced in their encounters with white physicians at the university. Bouyer, a staff physician for six years at Provident Hospital in the eye, ear, nose, and throat department, wished to undertake advanced studies in ophthalmology at Billings Hospital. When he attempted to make arrangements for the course, a hostile reception greeted him. Dr. E.V.L. Brown, chief of the ophthalmology department, verbally attacked him and refused to let him work in the department. Brown told Bouyer that the leadership at Provident was bad and that he, "together with the University of Chicago, [was] disgusted at the whole setup." He added, "I shall preserve my course for young white men only, Negroes and Jews will not be allowed to take it." Midian O. Bousfield, an official of the Rosenwald Fund and a trustee of Provident Hospital, admitted that the nationwide practice of having white physicians supervise the work of black hospitals had not lived up to expectations, pointing out that the physicians' primary responsibilities were to white hospitals and that their already overburdened schedules left them with little time to assist their black colleagues.[26]

During his December 1934 visit to Provident Hospital, Robert Lambert also found that financial problems, which he attributed to mismanagement, still plagued the hospital. He noted specifically the rapid consumption of the working capital and A.L. Jackson's continued receipt of a salary for his work as president of the hospital's board of trustees. He also charged that the GEB funds had been misappropriated, having been used not just for teaching and research expenditures, but for general operating costs as well. Lambert concluded that the project's future looked bleak, especially since it was not clear whether either Provident Hospital or the University of Chicago wanted it to continue. Representatives of both institutions now referred for the first time to the "experimental" nature of the affiliation. Foundation officials observed, in response to Lambert's report, that the time was approaching when the GEB should probably withdraw its pledge.[27]

When the GEB reviewed the project in 1935, conditions had deteriorated even further. In the forefront were escalating racial tensions. A.L. Jackson contended that the project's progress toward black medical leadership had been far too slow, and demanded that the successor to the retiring Admiral Blackwood be black. Thus a conflict developed between university officials who said they wanted the medical director to be the best person for the job, regardless of color, and Jackson and his supporters who wanted the successor to be black. Lambert characterized the situation as "excessive and unhealthy racialism."[28]

When Provident Hospital initially agreed to affiliate with the University of Chicago, the segregation inherent in the project did not arouse protest. However, in the intervening years, as demonstrated by events in Harlem, integrationists nationwide had increasingly attacked white philanthropies' practice of establishing and maintaining separate institutions for African Americans. The highly visible activities in Chicago could not escape censure. The assignment of a black medical student to a clinical clerkship at Provident in October 1934 provided the integrationists with a target. Although the placement was consistent with the agreement between the university and the hospital, vociferous accusations of Jim Crowism soon surfaced. Critics alleged that the compulsory assignment of only black medical students to Provident Hospital was an attempt to make the hospital a segregated teaching unit of the University of Chicago. In addition, they charged that the practice resulted in the students receiving an inferior education because the facilities at Provident were not equal to those at Billings Hospital. "Race students," critics claimed, "lose the value of the instruction and clinical material at Billings Hospital for which they paid and are literally forced to accept facilities offered by the Provident Hospital staff." One black leader went so far as to say that white support of Provident Hospital had been, all along, a ploy to keep African Americans out of the other Chicago hospitals.[29]

Several segments of the African-American community voiced their opposition to the events at Provident Hospital. The Cook County Physicians Association, a local black medical society, emerged as one of the primary critics. Dr. Joseph A. Berry, president of the association, charged that the Jim-Crow practices of the University of Chicago at Provident Hospital had national repercussions, contending that black medical students who were enrolled at predominantly white medical schools might be forced to complete their clinical years at Provident Hospital. This was not a farfetched accusation, but a distinct possibility if the institution had become the center of black medical education that the originators of the project had intended. Berry urged members of the medical organization to "hammer against the forces of prejudice and segregation." On 21 December 1934, over fifty members of the Cook County Physicians Association adopted a formal resolution that condemned the assignment of the medical student and any further Jim-Crow activities at the hospital. The Illinois State Conference of the National Association for the Advancement of Colored People (NAACP), the Interracial Commission, and the *Chicago Defender*, a black newspaper, supported the medical society's position. The issue was not whether Provident Hospital, under black control, should exist, but whether the hospital should be supervised and used for Jim-Crow purposes by a white university.[30]

As was true in the dispute over a black hospital in Harlem, the African-American community was split over the allegations of segregation. The affiliation continued to receive some support. On 2 January 1935, a dissident group of the Cook County Physicians Association issued a report critical of the medical organization's official stance. The report, signed by forty-four black physicians including Midian O. Bousfield and Julian H. Lewis, noted that the student assignment had been made in accordance with the agreement between the hospital and university. It contended that the Cook County Physicians Association had accepted the conditions of the affiliation, including segregation, and had raised no objections when the project had been initiated. The report argued that the affiliation had not increased the level of segregation at the institution, pointing out that, almost from its inception, Provident Hospital had been a segregated facility, and that the hospital, without any assistance from the University of Chicago, maintained a nurse training school exclusively for black women. The report also lambasted the hypocrisy of association members who had been "silent beneficiaries" of the affiliation, but who now joined the public protests against the project.[31]

The controversy over the Provident Hospital project extended beyond Chicago to the national black medical community. Physicians and organizations associated with the black hospital movement endorsed the project. When the National Medical Association (NMA) held its 1933 annual meeting in Chicago, it urged its members to visit the "finest Negro hospital in the world." A 1933 editorial in the *Journal of the National Medical Association* lavishly praised the new Provident Hospital as a "new adventure in Negro medical training, and hospitalization" and as a "modern, up-to-date, down-to-the minute-hospital, not just another Negro hospital." Dr. John A. Kenney, editor-in-chief of the journal and secretary of the National Hospital Association, lamented that, in spite of the vast benefits of the project, the affiliation had been labelled "Jim Crowism." On the other hand, the Manhattan Medical Society and its most prominent member, Dr. Louis T. Wright, harshly criticized the project and those black physicians who supported it. Wright saw the project as "a menace to the training of the Negro in medicine" because it "set him apart from all other citizens as being a different kind of citizen, and a different kind of medical student and physician." Jim-Crow institutions, he maintained, "establish in the minds of the white doctor and citizen a superiority complex and they also establish in the minds of the colored doctor and citizen an inferiority complex." Wright called the affiliation a "morally wrong and intellectually dishonest arrangement" and urged black physicians to withdraw quickly from this "unworthy and unholy type of professional enslavement."[32]

The indefatigable A.L. Jackson immediately attempted to defuse the controversy by appointing a committee composed of hospital trustees to investigate the educational program and attempt to renegotiate Provident's contract with the university. He named the eminent black journalist Claude A. Barnett to head the committee. In addition to his responsibilities at the hospital, Barnett was founder and president of the Associated Negro Press, a news service for black newspapers. The Barnett committee recognized that the policy of assigning black students exclusively to the hospital had led to "unfortunate repercussions" in the community that had "possibilities of seriously impairing the usefulness of the hospital." It acknowledged that the practice resulted in a stigma being attached to black medical students. The committee hoped to convince the university to change its policy by assigning white students as well as black students to clerkships at Provident, arguing that this arrangement would "not place upon the University the stigma of actually seeking to bar or segregate their Negro students . . . and not place Provident Hospital in the position of being party to a limitation of the opportunities for Negro students." The committee, however, was not able to sway the university.[33]

After the negotiations of the Barnett committee failed, the wily A.L. Jackson came out in support of the project's critics and backed the Jim Crow charges. The university, the GEB, and the Rosenwald Fund all considered his mismanagement of the hospital a liability and wanted him out. By gathering support in the black community over the Jim Crow issue, Jackson hoped to make it more difficult to force his departure. In the end, despite his strong ties to the African-American community, Jackson's power-play failed and he was forced from his sinecure. Provident Hospital's board of trustees came to consider Jackson's continued presence a liability to the affiliation as well as a financial drain. They forced his resignation in the spring of 1936 and replaced him with Claude A. Barnett, but irreparable damage had already been done.[34]

Tense relations between the other participants further strained the project. The GEB criticized the university and the Rosenwald Fund for not assuming adequate responsibility in connection with the hospital's finances. The GEB also accused the University of Chicago of giving in to the local racial situation. In a May 1935 report, Dr. Arthur C. Bachmeyer, then director of the University of Chicago Clinics, had recommended that a black physician be named medical director of Provident. The GEB viewed the suggestion as a violation of its principle that merit, regardless of race, should govern personnel selections. It is clear that the foundation did not conceive that a black person could possibly be the most qualified person. Nonetheless, when Blackwood retired in 1936 the black radiologist John W. Lawlah succeeded him. Lawlah, a 1931 honors graduate of Rush Medical School, had become Blackwood's assistant in 1935.[35]

The GEB reserved its harshest criticism for the alleged misappropriation of funds by the University of Chicago. Gregg and Lambert noted that GEB monies had not been used exclusively for teaching and research expenditures, but instead had gone for operational costs, administrators' and technicians' salaries, and the payment of fellowships to black physicians not associated with the teaching program. The university did not take kindly to such criticism. Its president, Robert Hutchins, annoyed by the accusations, reminded the GEB officials that, according to its contract with Chicago, the funds could be used for any purpose except theology. When the university requested a $50,000 appropriation from its GEB grant in May 1935, the philanthropy demonstrated its dissatisfaction with the events in Chicago. It appropriated only $40,000 and notified the university that, until further notice, it should not make any further financial commitments based on expectations of monies from the GEB. The GEB made clear its "willingness to take the initiative, and the blame associated with it, in a move to terminate the project."[36]

Although the GEB had become pessimistic about the project, the Rosenwald Fund had not. Midian O. Bousfield, noting that the hospital had more approved residencies than any other black hospital, hailed Provident as "the proudest spot in Negro medicine." Edwin R. Embree continued to advocate the project and took an active role in trying to keep it alive. For example, he assisted in reorganizing the hospital's board of trustees. Franklin C. McLean, a long-term supporter of the project and now a consultant in Negro health at the Rosenwald Fund, was one of the people Embree selected for the board.[37]

Embree also assisted in efforts to stabilize the hospital's still precarious fiscal situation. He reported that the financially revitalized Rosenwald Fund would be willing to donate $33,333 annually for two to three years because he anticipated that the new board of trustees would bring more efficient management to the hospital. Embree (again as he did at the inception of the project) sought funds from other foundations, including the Josiah Macy, Jr. Foundation, the Albert P. Sloan Foundation, and the John and Mary Markle Foundation. He asked the foundations to give a donation to an endeavor "which might be thought of as discharging your obligations nationally in the Negro field." Embree admitted that relations between the hospital and university were not yet perfect, but emphasized that this did not negate the uniqueness and importance of the project. He described the project as "the only movement in America toward that continuous graduate experience and instruction for Negroes which is the privilege of practically all white physicians." Embree's efforts to raise funds from the philanthropies were unsuccessful. He also tried to secure the Commonwealth Fund's unpaid $100,000 pledge, and, again, he failed. Barry Smith, director of the Commonwealth Fund, informed Embree that not only had he become disillusioned by the tactless demands of A.L. Jackson, but that funding black hospitals was outside of the Fund's current interests.[38]

In a last attempt to save the project, Embree called a meeting of Rosenwald Fund and GEB officers. At this 30 November 1938 meeting, Embree agreed that the project had not yet lived up to its expectations but asserted that the problems could be resolved. He stressed the project's importance to black medical education, not—as originally proposed—in the areas of undergraduate medical education and internship training, but in the provision of postgraduate training to a small number of physicians. Embree also conceded that since the inception of the project it had become easier for black physicians to get clinical training in white institutions. However, he feared that a resurgence of "race feelings" could negate hard-won gains in this area.[39]

The GEB officers remained firm. They considered the affiliation an educational failure. Most important, the number of black medical students had declined at the University of Chicago: between 1931 and 1938, only seven black medical students had graduated. Provident Hospital also had difficulty finding black interns and had begun to recruit foreign white doctors. Apparently the deans at Howard and Meharry, the predominantly black medical schools, thought the clinical programs at Provident to be inadequate. In 1938, not one graduate of Meharry chose to go to Provident Hospital for an internship. Robert A. Lambert, the GEB liaison for the project, did acknowledge that because of the Depression the number of black students nationwide had decreased, while the number of internships available to them had increased. Consistent with foundation policy, he concluded that the conversion of Provident Hospital to a first-rate teaching hospital would have required the major services to be headed by white men because there were no black physicians with the necessary qualifications.[40]

Lambert questioned whether heavily subsidized black hospitals were necessary for the training of black physicians, noting that not one black physician who had been awarded a postgraduate fellowship by the GEB had chosen to study at Provident Hospital. In spite of occasional racial difficulties, all had selected predominantly white institutions, although they had to return to black hospitals in order to practice. Lambert thought that GEB money would be better spent by improving the medical school curricula at Meharry and Howard and by subsidizing additional postgraduate refresher courses for black physicians such as the one at Richmond's St. Philip Hospital. The GEB officer did discern one important educational benefit of the Provident Hospital project. He noted that it had provided the foundation with "several useful lessons in race relations" and demonstrated "that while backward or under-privileged people may want material help, they do not always welcome guidance and direction." Lambert's candid remarks gives us insight into the racist and patronizing attitudes that certainly influenced foundation policies throughout this period.[41]

Despite Embree's efforts, by the end of 1938 the university and the GEB had begun negotiations to abrogate their contract. Initially, the university balked at withdrawing from the contract because it did not want to be the focus of local racial antipathies. It also did not want to antagonize the GEB, a very generous contributor to the university, and use the money for other purposes. However, the GEB pushed for withdrawal and in early 1939, the university requested the termination of the contract.

Correspondence between the university and the GEB reveals the tensions that had developed because of the project. On 25 February 1939, Robert Hutchins, president of the University of Chicago, acerbically informed Raymond B. Fosdick, president of the GEB, of the university's decision to cancel the pledge. He wrote:

> I arise from a bed of pain to tell you . . . that the Board of Trustees of the University of Chicago at its meeting on February 9 agreed to the ungenerous suggestion of the Rockefeller Foundation in regard to the Provident Hospital.

On 6 March, Fosdick responded in an equally sardonic tone:

> I am sorry to hear about that bed of pain, but I am glad to know that the Trustees of the University have agreed to our suggestion about Provident Hospital–generous or ungenerous. After all the largesses which the University of Chicago has received from Rockefeller sources, I am surprised that the distinguished President of that institution confuses the General Education Board with the Rockefeller Foundation. But we will charge that up to the bed of pain. I hope you are well past your agony.

At its 6 April 1939 meeting, the GEB trustees canceled the grant but authorized a five-year terminal appropriation of $75,000.[42]

The decision to terminate the contract can be attributed to several factors, including policy differences, financial problems, the university's indifference, and racial politics. First, the two philanthropies held differing views as to the project's scope. The General Education Board saw the project as an educational undertaking, while the Rosenwald Fund saw it as an educational *and* hospital service endeavor. The GEB decided to withdraw its funds after the project did not live up to its educational expectations. On the other hand, the fund's interest continued because, as even the GEB agreed, the medical service at the hospital had improved with the affiliation. The Rosenwald Fund also had longstanding ties to Provident Hospital. In sum, the GEB did not think that it got a fair return on its investment; the Rosenwald Fund did.

Provident Hospital's precarious financial situation also contributed to the project's demise. Jackson's mismanagement certainly played a role in the hospital's financial woes, although the Depression clearly was a more significant factor. Because of the Depression, the hospital could not collect pledges, and, at the same time, saw the number of relief and free patients increase. In 1938, Provident Hospital estimated that it lost approximately $63,000 on relief patients and an additional $6000 on free patients.[43]

The University of Chicago's indifference to the affiliation can also be counted as a factor in the project's termination. After McLean's departure, no one at the university assumed a key advocacy role. Claude A. Barnett observed that the teaching program at Provident Hospital never became an integral component of the university's work. "Provident Hospital," he maintained, "appeared to be an appendage which they [university officials] had as soon be without." Dr. Emmet Bey, a university faculty member who supervised the medical service at Provident Hospital, even questioned the merit of black medical education, contending that without a long period of preparation, black physicians would not immediately demonstrate themselves to be the equal of their white counterparts. President Robert Hutchins stated that he had not liked the idea of affiliation because it represented an "extra-mural, charitable enterprise" and that he had only accepted the idea because of the GEB's and Rosenwald Fund's enthusiasm. The University of Chicago never provided the strong support necessary to guarantee the success of the project.[44]

The project's entanglement in racial politics and in the ideological divisions within the black community also contributed to its ultimate failure. The project at Provident had been based on the premise—supported by the black hospital reformers—that black medical professionals and patients would be provided for in separate facilities. The affiliation eventually became a primary target for integrationists who considered it an insidious way of perpetuating Jim Crowism in medical care. Once the project had become racially controversial, the University of Chicago and the GEB had little interest in continuing it.

Despite its many problems and unfulfilled expectations, the Provident Hospital–University of Chicago affiliation played an important role in the professional survival of black physicians. Funds raised for the project enabled Provident to begin residency training and expand its clinical facilities. In 1940, it was one of the seven black hospitals nationally that offered specialty training, and it also had more approved residency programs than any other black hospital. In the same year, most of the black physicians in the United States who had become board certified in specialties had trained at Provident Hospital. Two of the three black physicians certified by the American Board of Surgery, four of the six certified by the American Board of Radiology, four of the five certified by the American Board of Pediatrics, and three of the four certified by the American Board of Ophthalmology had all trained at the hospital. The Provident Hospital project had offered these black physicians the opportunity to train, practice, and become specialists, at a time when their options were extremely limited.[45]

The affiliation between the University of Chicago and Provident Hospital officially ended on 30 June 1944. Racial ideology within the black community had changed significantly since the project's inception fifteen years earlier. Although the university had offered to continue the affiliation on an advisory basis, Provident Hospital now rejected this offer because of the racist practices of the university in its medical school and clinics. The hospital's action reflected the increasing influence of integrationism as a strategy for racial advancement. An association of a black institution with a discriminatory white one would no longer be acceptable to many African Americans. This increasing integrationism, however, did not completely stop the movement to establish and maintain black hospitals.[46]

SIX

Cleveland—A Black Hospital at Last

❧

In January 1948, an article entitled "The Color Line in Medicine" appeared in the *Saturday Evening Post*. The authors, Henry F. Pringle and Katharine Pringle, harshly attacked segregation in medicine and detailed its consequences, including inadequate facilities for the training of black physicians and nurses and the delivery of inferior health care to black patients. They painted a bleak picture of the substandard situations in which most black physicians were forced to practice. They did note a few bright spots, however. Conditions in Cleveland were especially praised. Cleveland City Hospital had named its first black physician to the outpatient department in 1928, and three years later it appointed its first black intern. By 1948, thirty African-American interns had trained at the hospital and six African-American physicians taught at Western Reserve Medical School.[1]

These achievements, however, did not stop black physicians from seeking to establish a black hospital in the city. These practitioners, many of whom had been beneficiaries of the integration of Cleveland City Hospital, argued that the integration of City Hospital only benefitted a few black doctors and that they still needed a place in which to hospitalize their private patients. On 4 August 1957, fifty-six years after Provident Hospital led the way, Forest City Hospital, Cleveland's first black hospital, opened its doors. Black physicians had initially started the campaign for the hospital in 1939, but financial difficulties and charges of Jim Crowism had hampered that movement.

The 1939 drive for a black hospital was not the first time that such an effort had been made in Cleveland, but earlier attempts had all been unsuccessful. The first campaign occurred in 1915, when Dr. Ellis A. Dale, a 1900 graduate of Cleveland Homeopathic Medical College, proposed construction of a hospital, under the control and management of black people. His proposal did not receive widespread support even among the city's eight black physicians who disagreed over whether the hospital was necessary. Black ministers opposed the plan because they feared that the institution would "become the entering wedge of Jim-crowism, so detestable to all self-respecting Negroes the world over." In addition, the Cleveland Association of Colored Men, an organization of black businessmen that had been established to promote racial advancement, also criticized the venture. The association argued that the black community lacked the financial resources to support such a facility. Opposition to the hospital also came from another significant quarter—the black press. Both the moderate *Cleveland Advocate* and the militant *Cleveland Gazette* harshly criticized Dale's plan because they viewed it as encouraging segregation.[2]

Opponents of a separate black hospital received additional ammunition when in 1920 the Cleveland Hospital Council published the results of a survey of hospitals and health facilities conducted the previous year. The survey did find that opportunities for the nineteen black physicians who then practiced in the city were severely restricted. Only one, Dr. Charles H. Garvin, had been able to obtain a hospital appointment. In 1919, Lakeside Hospital, a major teaching affiliate of Western Reserve University School of Medicine, appointed him assistant surgeon for genito-urinary diseases in its dispensary. Garvin thus became the first African American to serve on the staff of a Cleveland hospital. The council did acknowledge black citizens' concerns that the paucity of black appointments to the staffs of hospitals and dispensaries effectively deprived them of adequate medical care, but the final report of the survey contained some contradictions. It also claimed that "it is a fine testimony to the spirit and policy of the hospitals of Cleveland that so far as Negro patients are concerned, there has been absolutely no complaint by the Negroes about discrimination." The council, therefore, concluded that the construction of a separate black hospital would be "unnecessary and undesirable." As the council saw it, however, there was only one solution to this problem, namely that hospital appointments should be based solely on merit.[3]

Despite the rosy assertions of the survey, racial discrimination did exist in Cleveland's hospitals and health facilities. Only one black physician had access to a hospital in the city. It is true that the medical school at Western Reserve University had a long tradition of admitting black students. Dr. Charles B. Purvis, for example, graduated in 1865 and was one of the eight black physicians appointed to the medical corps of the Union Army during the Civil War. In 1881, he became surgeon-in-chief at Freedmen's Hospital. Black medical students, however, complained that at times they were barred from some clinical courses because the school feared that white patients would not accept care from them. In addition, after graduation they could not secure internships in Cleveland. Black women also had limited opportunities for admission to nurse training programs in the city. And, if fortunate enough to receive training in Cleveland or elsewhere, they had difficulty finding employment. For example, Jane Edna Hunter, a graduate of Dixie Hospital and Training School at Hampton Institute, Virginia, arrived in the city in 1905. When she first sought employment, one physician told her "to go back South—that white doctors did not employ 'nigger' nurses." Hunter eventually did find employment and also went on to receive a law degree. Through her experiences as a nurse, she became aware of the problems that poor black women faced and the paucity of institutions that existed in Cleveland to address their needs. In 1911, Hunter established the Phillis Wheatley Association, a residential and job-training center for black women.[4]

Blacks also encountered obstacles in seeking care. In his study of African Americans in Cleveland, historian Kenneth L. Kusmer argues that prior to 1915 hospitals admitted patients on a nondiscriminatory basis. However, as was true in other Northern cities, the city's black population expanded rapidly during the first three decades of the twentieth century, growing from 8448 in 1910 to 34,451 in 1920 and to 71,899 in 1930. This influx led to increased white hostility and a racism mirrored in Cleveland's institutions. Kusmer notes that after the "Great Migration" began several hospitals adopted more discriminatory policies, starting to separate black and white patients and limit the number of beds available to black patients. For example, in 1915, Women's Hospital, under the pretense of establishing a specialty clinic, instituted a policy of admitting black people only on Saturdays. "What does this mean?" one black woman asked. "Are we to arrange to get sick on Saturday or is it possible that we are to be exempted from privileges enjoyed by every other nation or nationality?"[5]

Because of the problems faced by black health-care professionals and patients, in February 1921 Dr. Joe T. Thomas revived the effort to establish a black hospital. He contended that Cleveland was "far behind other northern cities in taking advanced steps to promote its Negroes in medical and surgical work and in the field of nursing." For this reason, Thomas organized the Cleveland Hospital Association and sought to raise $250,000 to build the Abraham Lincoln Memorial Hospital. The association solicited individual contributions and appealed to the Cleveland Hospital Council of the Welfare Federation for funds. Thomas's endeavor received enthusiastic support from the National Medical Association. In September, Dr. H.M. Green, then president of the medical society, addressed the Cleveland Medical, Dental, and Pharmaceutical Association, the local constituent of the NMA. He strongly urged its members to establish a hospital of their own.[6]

However, as was true with Dale's attempt six years previously, Thomas's efforts to build Lincoln Memorial Hospital provoked harsh criticism from segments of the black community. Again, black physicians were divided over whether the hospital was necessary. Dale offered his support, but Dr. George C. Sutton argued that the hospital would escalate segregation in the city. In a letter published in the *Cleveland Gazette* he wrote, "A hospital for Negroes in the city of Cleveland is a further step to other institutions of a separate nature and a warning further of 'crackerdom' in Cleveland from which thousands sought the northern clime as a haven." Another physician, O.A. Taylor, had initially endorsed Thomas's plan, but withdrew his support because he alleged that Thomas had misrepresented the plan to him.[7]

The black press, both the *Cleveland Advocate* and the *Cleveland Gazette*, again attacked the proposed hospital, alleging that the construction of Lincoln Hospital would make it possible for other Cleveland hospitals to close their doors to African Americans. A particular issue of contention was that the Cleveland Hospital Association had approached the Cleveland Hospital Council for funds. Both newspapers acknowledged that they would support a private black hospital: that is, "one supported without the aid of endorsements from any white men." They would not support a separate black hospital that had been built with dollars from the government or cash from the white community. The Hospital Council, however, denied Thomas's request for funds. And since he was unable to raise the money from other sources, his attempt to build Lincoln Hospital failed.[8]

In 1926, the Cleveland Hospital Association, now under new leadership, renewed its efforts to establish a black hospital. Its board of trustees consisted of several prominent African-American leaders, including William R. Green, a lawyer; Herbert Chauncey, a successful businessman; and Jane Edna Hunter, the founder of the Phillis Wheatley Association. Although no physicians served on the association's board, three—Dr. M.H. Lambright, Dr. L.O. Baumgardner, and Dr. Charles H. Garvin—worked on subcommittees. Garvin's connection with the association was especially significant; he was the most distinguished black physician in Cleveland.

Charles H. Garvin (1891–1968), a native of Jacksonville, Florida, graduated in 1915 from Howard University Medical School. A year later, after he had completed an internship at Freedmen's Hospital, he moved to Cleveland. Quickly gaining both local and national prominence in the medical profession, he was the first black physician to attend the Army Medical School and first of the 356 African-American physicians to be commissioned into the United States Army during World War I. During the war he rose to the rank of captain and served as a commanding officer of an ambulance company in the 92nd division, a black unit. In 1919, he received the appointment at Lakeside Hospital that made him the first black physician to serve on the medical staff of a Cleveland hospital. He was later named to the faculty of the genito-urinary department at Western Reserve University Medical School. However, it appears that Garvin's responsibilities were limited to the outpatient department and that these appointments did not offer him privileges to admit patients to the hospital.[9]

After the war, Garvin involved himself in various activities to improve the status of black physicians and patients. He served on the editorial board of the *Journal of the National Medical Association* and wrote several articles on black medical issues. In 1925, he helped to establish the Cleveland Medical Reading Club, an organization to help black physicians keep abreast of recent developments in medicine. He also studied and wrote on African medical history and the contributions of Africans to the development of modern medicine.[10]

Garvin urged his colleagues to conduct research on those diseases, such as tuberculosis and pellagra, that were thought to affect African Americans disproportionately or idiosyncratically. He contended that such research was needed to dispute theories that attributed the race's high tuberculosis rates to inherent biological inferiority. "We seriously question," Garvin wrote, "if under similar environment—long hours of hard labor; limited, often faulty diet, restriction in proper hospital and medical care, and faulty sanitation—any race would have shown such a marked improvement in its tuberculosis rate." He also insisted that black physicians investigate racial diseases because "heretofore in literature, as in medicine, the Negro has been written about, exploited, and experimented upon sometimes not to his physical betterment or to the advancement of science, but the advancement of the Nordic investigator." Moreover, he charged that "in the past, men of other races have for the large part interpreted our diseases, often tinctured with inborn prejudices." Although Garvin stressed the importance of African-American physicians becoming experts on "black-related" diseases, he did not believe that they should restrict their knowledge to such conditions.[11]

Garvin did not limit his activities to the medical sphere. He participated in various community and political organizations, and served on the boards of trustees of the Cleveland branches of the NAACP and the Urban League. He also helped found two black businesses, Dunbar Life Insurance Company and Quincy Savings and Loan.

Garvin also established himself, at great personal risk, as a staunch advocate of the legal rights of African Americans. His move to a white neighborhood in the fall of 1925 sparked white hostility and violence. When white people in the area learned that their new neighbor would be black, they harassed the men building the house and distributed a flyer that urged white people to oppose the move—violently, if necessary. A neighborhood organization also tried to prevent Garvin's residency by offering to buy the house even before he had settled in. The physician refused to sell. White harassment continued and escalated. Shortly after the Garvin family moved into their new home racist graffiti were scrawled on the house. Three weeks later, on 26 January 1926, a firebomb exploded at 10:00 P.M. while Mrs. Garvin was entertaining friends. Fortunately, no one was hurt and the damage to the house was minor. Six months later, another firebombing was attempted, but the device was discovered before it exploded. Despite these incidents and the advice of friends to move, Garvin remained steadfast. As Mabel Clark, the physician's sister, observed, "he has made a home for himself and will stay there, all he wants is to be let alone."[12]

The threats against the Garvin family drew both local and national attention. Shortly after the discovery of the second bomb, Cleveland police officers chosen by the Garvin family began to guard the home. The national office of the NAACP offered its assistance to the organization's Cleveland branch and issued press releases about the family's predicament. Walter White also sent a letter to Edwin D. Barry, the Cleveland director of public safety, urging continued police protection, and pointing out parallels between the situation in Cleveland and a more widely publicized incident that had occurred in Detroit the previous year involving another black physician, Ossian H. Sweet. Sweet and his family had been harassed after they too had moved into a white neighborhood. The family's request for police protection was denied. On 8 September 1925, an angry white mob gathered in front of the house and shots were fired into the Sweet home. Shots were returned and a member of the mob was killed. Subsequently, Dr. Sweet and other members of his family were tried for murder. The NAACP retained Clarence Darrow, the renowned criminal defense attorney, to defend the family. The first trial ended in a hung jury and the second in an acquittal. White stressed to Barry that the killing could have been prevented had the Detroit police offered the family the protection that they had requested. The harassment of the Garvins did not result in bloodshed. After the police withdrew, black and white friends of the family took their places. By March 1927, acts of intimidation had ceased.[13]

An examination of Garvin's political and medical activities underscores the problems that can occur categorizing a person either as an "integrationist" or as a "separatist." On the one hand, Garvin participated in organizations that worked for integration, fought for his right to live in a white neighborhood, and worked as the only black physician on a white hospital staff. On the other hand, he advocated the development of black institutions, celebrated African achievements, and vigorously supported the establishment of a black hospital in Cleveland. Garvin's strategy for racial advancement was not fixed, but fluid. As was true of George Cleveland Hall in Chicago, he was a pragmatist. Although he had benefitted from his hospital appointment, he recognized that his affiliation was hardly typical. Thus, he vigorously supported the work of the Cleveland Hospital Association to establish a black hospital to meet the needs of the city's other black physicians.

The Cleveland Hospital Association launched a $200,000 fund-raising campaign in Spring 1926. Association officials solicited contributions primarily from the African-American community, intending, however, to ask the Community Chest for help. But dollars from all sources only trickled in: by August, just $2000 had been donated. Nonetheless, hospital proponents remained undaunted. In early 1927, they reorganized as the Mercy Hospital Association and continued their efforts. This time they ambitiously attempted to raise even more money—$220,000.[14]

The Mercy Hospital Association sought to convince the African-American community that it needed the facility. At public meetings black physicians testified about the racial discrimination that they and their patients encountered. At a meeting held on 12 March at Mt. Zion Temple Congregational Church, Dr. Garvin spoke of the "unpleasant experiences" to which he had been subjected when he tried to attend to his patients at a predominantly white hospital. Dr. Middleton H. Lambright, Sr. echoed his colleague's sentiments. He observed that at "Lakeside it is asked whether or not a patient is white or colored and there is never no [sic] room for colored." He also told the gathering the story of a patient of his who, although critically ill, had been denied admission at several hospitals because of his race. "If they don't make a place for us," Lambright argued, "we should make a place for ourselves."[15]

The Mercy Hospital Association also distributed a pamphlet, "Does Cleveland Need A Negro Manned Hospital?: Facts Are the

Answer," to publicize the importance of the hospital and to convince African Americans to support the endeavor financially. The leaflet, mirroring the efforts to start hospitals in other cities, detailed the exclusion of black physicians and nurses from most hospitals in Cleveland. Only three of the forty-three black physicians in practice had hospital affiliations, and not a single institution would accept black interns and nursing students. It noted that the need for hospital beds for black patients had been "alarmingly accentuated" because of the recent increase in the city's black population. The new facility, the pamphlet pointed out, would be a place for black physicians and nurses to train and practice and a center for the investigation of health problems that most affected African Americans. The pamphlet went on to say that the "sponsors of Mercy Hospital, like every self-respecting group, oppose segregation that proscribes, limits or restricts the social, economic or political life of any group." Although the hospital would be controlled by African Americans, the hospital, like its predecessors in Chicago and Philadelphia, would be open to all.[16]

By publicly stating its position on segregation, the Mercy Hospital Association hoped to stem opposition from other segments of the black community who saw the hospital itself as a Jim-Crow institution. Such critics included Harry C. Smith, owner and managing editor of the *Cleveland Gazette* and George A. Myers, a wealthy and politically well-connected barbershop proprietor. In addition, several clergymen and physicians opposed the hospital.

Harry C. Smith, a militant and uncompromising integrationist, had served three terms as a Republican member of the lower house of the Ohio General Assembly where he sponsored civil rights and anti-lynching legislation. He also had participated in the Niagara Movement, the political effort initiated by W.E.B. Dubois in 1905 to organize black radicals to fight for the full equality of black people into American society. Smith had used his newspaper, founded in 1883, as a platform for his political and ideological positions. He vehemently opposed the establishment of separate schools and recreational facilities for African Americans, harshly attacking black people who sought to create separate institutions, especially if they accepted white dollars to achieve their goal. Jane Edna Hunter observed that the "most cruel and outspoken obstruction" to her starting the Phillis Wheatley Home had been Harry C. Smith. The *Gazette* editor contended that the establishment of facilities such as the Wheatley Home and Mercy Hospital would be the entering wedges for increased segregation in Cleveland. As he saw it, existing institutions would not be under any pressure or obligation to meet the needs of African Americans.[17]

Dr. Daniel Hale Williams. *Courtesy of Provident Hospital of Cook County, Chicago, Illinois.*

Provident Hospital, Chicago, 1891. *Courtesy of Provident Hospital of Cook County, Chicago, Illinois.*

Frederick Douglass Memorial Hospital and Training School, Philadelphia, Pennsylvania, circa 1897. *Courtesy of the Historical Collection, Library of the College of Physicians of Philadelphia.*

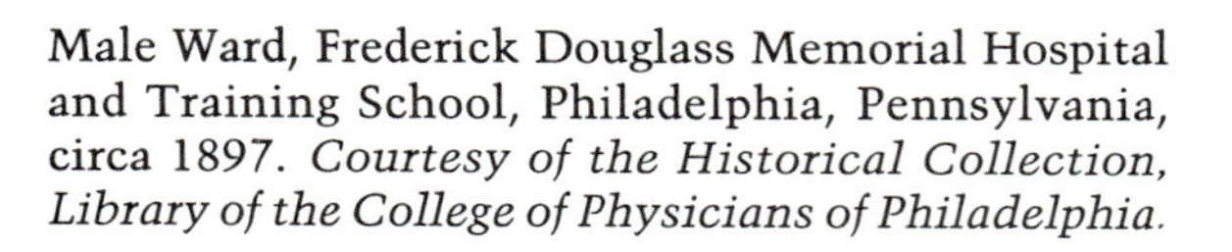

Male Ward, Frederick Douglass Memorial Hospital and Training School, Philadelphia, Pennsylvania, circa 1897. *Courtesy of the Historical Collection, Library of the College of Physicians of Philadelphia.*

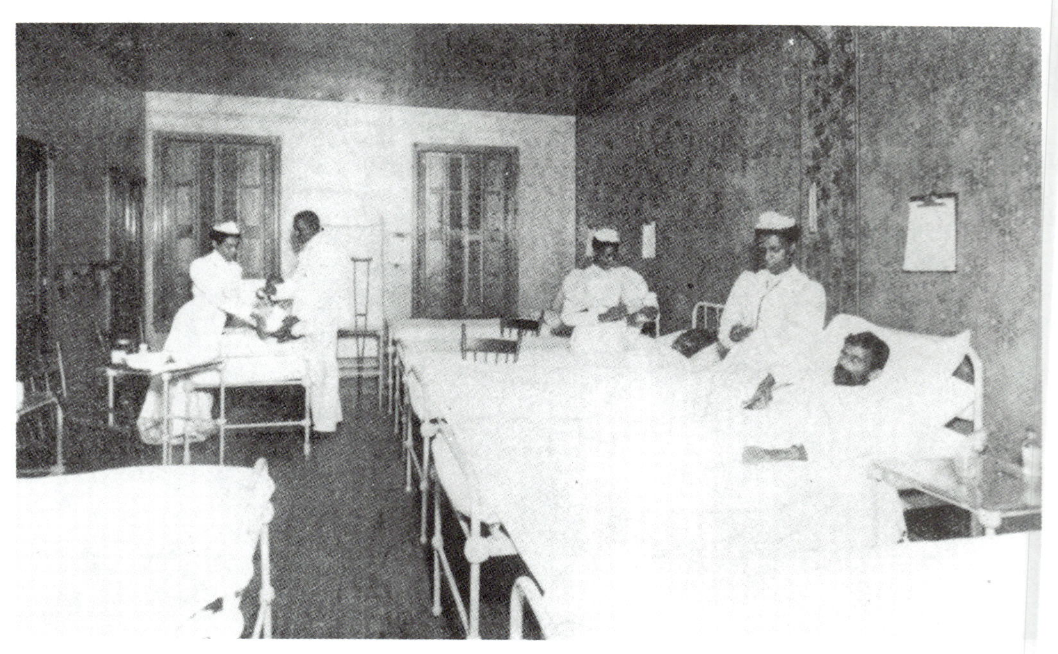

Dr. Peter Marshall Murray. *Courtesy of the Photographs & Prints Division, Schomburg Center for Research in Black Culture, The New York Pubic Library, Astor, Lenox and Tilden Foundations, and Scurlock Studio, Washington, D.C.*

Dr. Nathan Francis Mossell. *Courtesy of University of Pennsylvania Archives, Philadelphia, Pennsylvania.*

Residents and Nurses of Mercy Hospital and School for Nurses, Philadelphia, 1930. *Courtesy of the Center for the Study of the History of Nursing, School of Nursing, University of Pennsylvania, Philadelphia, Pennsylvania.*

Dr. Midian O. Bousfield. *Courtesy of the* Crisis.

Dr. H. M. Green and his wife, Henri Henderson Green. *Courtesy of Beck Cultural Exchange Center, Knoxville, Tennessee.*

Dr. John A. Kenney. *Courtesy of Dr. John A. Kenney, Jr.*

Dr. Louis T. Wright. *Courtesy of Francis A. Countway Library of Medicine, Harvard University School of Medicine, Boston, Massachusetts.*

Editorial Cartoon, Criticizing Government Position on Tuskegee Veterans Hospital, *Chicago Defender*, 21 July 1923. *Courtesy of* Chicago Daily Defender.

Major Robert Russa Moton. *Courtesy of the Photographs and Prints Division, Schomburg Center for Research in Black Culture, The New York Public Library, Astor, Lenox and Tilden Foundations.*

Dr. Charles H. Garvin. *Courtesy of the Western Reserve Historical Society, Cleveland, Ohio.*

Dr. Ulysses G. Mason. *Courtesy of Historical Division, Cleveland Medical Library Association, Cleveland, Ohio.*

r. W. Montague Cobb. *Courtesy of the hotographs and Prints Division, Schomurg Center for Research in Black Culture, he New York Public Library, Astor, Lenox nd Tilden Foundations.*

Provident Hospital of Cook County, 1993. *Courtesy of Provident Hospital of Cook County, Chicago, Illinois.*

In several editorials that appeared throughout early 1927, Smith vehemently assailed the supporters of Mercy Hospital, calling them "jim-crow Negroes, the bane of the race" who sought to retard racial advancement. He even made a connection between "The Lord Have Mercy Movement" and that of the Ku Klux Klan. The 26 March edition of the *Cleveland Gazette* carried the headline: "How the Kluxers Won Them To Their Vicious Segregation Idea." The accompanying article read in part:

> This week the *Gazette* was informed, by those in a position to know, that the segregation of our people of this city in a separate or "jim-crow" hospital was primarily promoted by the local Ku Klux Klan and that their "Negro" allies were gained by the promise to secure ten thousand dollars and the use of an old, unused building in Woodland Avenue, owned by the city, for the proposed "jim-crow" hospital.

Smith alleged that the KKK charges had "foundation in fact," but he never presented any evidence to prove them. The allegations were probably false. Nonetheless they served a purpose. They struck an emotional chord in the African-American community and stirred up negative sentiment toward the hospital project. Smith also rejected the argument of the Mercy Hospital Association that the hospital was needed to provide black nurses and physicians with a place to train and work, arguing that such opportunities would be provided if African Americans took "the only stand they can take in a situation like this and FIGHT for the opening of opportunities to which we are justly entitled in present institutions."[18]

Smith worked with George A. Myers to discourage white support of the hospital project. The wealthy proprietor of a barbershop that catered almost exclusively to a white clientele, Myers was an influential black politician and had strong ties to Cleveland's Republican machine. He had been a delegate to the Republican National Conventions in 1892, 1896, and 1900 and had served three terms on the Republican State Executive Committee around the turn of the century. Both Smith and Myers wrote letters to influential white leaders such as William R. Hopkins, Cleveland City Manager; Ben P. Bole, editor of *The Cleveland Plain Dealer*; and Charles F. Thwing, former president of Western Reserve University, detailing their opposition to Mercy Hospital. They also made sure that these leaders received copies of the *Gazette* that contained articles critical of the project. Their lobbying undoubtedly helped prevent the campaign from receiving funds from the Community Chest.[19]

Myers went so far as to state that racial discrimination was not a problem in Cleveland hospitals either for patients or for professionals, and contended that he had not heard of any incidents where black people who were able to pay had been refused a private room. In addition, he noted that many white physicians also did not have hospital appointments, but that "outstanding ability will always be recognized, regardless of color or creed."[20]

Both Myers and Smith shared an antipathy for separate black institutions and black people who tried to establish them. Both had opposed the construction of the Phillis Wheatley Home. Myers and Smith represented, as had Dr. Daniel Hale Williams in Chicago, the old elite of the black community who espoused integration and had economic and professional connections with the white community. The Cleveland men contended that those who supported Mercy Hospital were "overnight migrants" from the South who did not understand the ways of the North and were retarding racial progress in the city because of their activities.[21]

Critics of Mercy Hospital further contended that the African-American community did not have the financial resources to construct and maintain a hospital. They argued that black physicians had a right to establish a small private clinic or hospital that would be financed with patient fees and without appealing to the general public for support. Echoing the views of the national office of the NAACP, they pointed out that when Jewish and German hospitals had been organized, the founders had not sought funds from outside their respective communities. The opponents of Mercy Hospital feared, however, that if a black hospital were established, it would be a Jim-Crow institution because it would eventually need funds from either the municipal government or white philanthropy. It would be a separate black institution supported by white dollars. For the opponents of the hospital, the risk of establishing a segregated institution in Cleveland outweighed the "selfish ambitions" of a few black doctors.[22]

To demonstrate that the black community could not afford the costs associated with operating a hospital, Smith published in the *Gazette* lists of the indebtedness of several black organizations, including twenty-six churches and the Phillis Wheatley Home. According to the newspaper, the churches owed over $450,000 and the Wheatley Home over $150,000. Smith argued that in the face of the financial struggles of the black institutions that already existed it was "ridiculous and out of the question" for a few "backward" physicians to ask the community to finance and support a hospital for them. The editor published the lists for an additional reason: it was part of a strategy to remind other black institutions, particularly churches, that if Mercy Hospital were built, it would compete with them for a limited pool of funds.[23]

Smith's tactic appeared to have had some effect on the ministers, a powerful force within the black community. Reverend Horace C.

Bailey, the former minister of the Antioch Baptist Church, one of the city's largest black churches, came out strongly against the hospital because of its cost and the effect it would have on the financial stability of existing black institutions, including churches. Bailey, emphasizing the poverty of many of the recent migrants from the South, wrote, "These people have not (many of them) got their 'bearings' as yet and why thrust upon or decoy them into *unnecessary* burdens? They are groaning and writhing now with great church debts. . . . Doctors give, I pray you, a breathing spell to our 'overworked' people." Reverend Charles Ailer, pastor of Zion Hill Baptist Church and secretary of the Ministers Association, an interdenominational organization that represented fifty-six black churches, urged his congregation to boycott those physicians who supported the Mercy Hospital movement. The other black ministers group, the Baptist Ministers' Conference, rejected the Mercy Hospital Association's request for the churches' membership rolls to be used for fund-raising. There were ministers who supported the hospital, but none served as officers of the Mercy Hospital Association. Furthermore, their backing was not enough to win the hospital endorsements from either the Ministers' Association or the Baptist Ministers' Conference. Another important black organization, the Negro Welfare Association, also chose not to endorse the hospital. With individual board members aligned on both sides of the issue, the association voted to remain neutral.[24]

Throughout Spring 1927, the debate over Mercy Hospital continued to divide the black community. Charles W. White, the president of the local branch of the NAACP, described the situation as "red hot." As in previous attempts to build a hospital, Cleveland's black medical community was not unified, and only six of the city's forty-three black physicians actively worked with the Mercy Hospital Association. Dr. Garvin complained that most of the others were apathetic on the issue. For some reason, veterans of previous campaigns to organize hospitals, Dr. Ellis A. Dale and Dr. Joe T. Thomas, did not support the current effort. Dr. Dale's position may be explained by the fact that in January 1927 he had received staff privileges at Huron Road Hospital. Dr. E.J. Gregg questioned whether the hospital was even necessary, maintaining that he had been asked only once about the race of a patient that he wanted to have hospitalized. He urged that the black community use the ballot to force the city to open up City Hospital to black physicians and nurses.[25]

Tensions over Mercy Hospital also "rather hopelessly separated" the local branch of the NAACP and placed it in a "messy situation." "On the one hand," lamented branch president Charles W. White, "it is being bitterly opposed as a self-inflicted bit of jim-crowism. On the other hand, it is being espoused as a very much-needed institution for the training of Negro physicians and nurses who at present have no such facilities for training anywhere in Cleveland." Members of the executive committee of the civil rights organization lined up on both sides of the hospital controversy. William R. Green, not only an executive committee member but the branch's former president, supported the Mercy Hospital Association and served as its executive director. Dr. James Owen was another of the most ardent supporters of Mercy Hospital. Other members of the NAACP's executive committee, including Russell Jelliffe, a white settlement house director, and Rev. Russell S. Brown, a black minister, opposed the construction of the hospital.[26]

White sought to ease tensions within the branch and have it develop a definite policy on the hospital question. He recognized that it was a complicated issue that could not be rejected with the simple assertion that it represented self-segregation, because "the roots of the problem run deeper than that." To assist him in sorting out his dilemma and in gauging public opinion, White organized a mass meeting on 12 March 1927 to hear testimony on the proposed hospital. He also sought guidance privately from Robert Bagnall, director of branches of the NAACP and former rector of Cleveland's St. Andrews Episcopal Church. Bagnall advised White:

> colored hospitals which refuse all but colored patients should be opposed as advocating a policy which brings much misery to the race when practiced by others, and against which all self-respecting Negroes are protesting. If the proposed Mercy Hospital is to be a private hospital, serving all groups and appealing to the general public for funds, and not supported by city, county or state, its existence does not run counter to the principles of the National Association.

Significantly, Bagnall's directive did not include sanctions against those black hospitals that received private funds from the white community, as did later NAACP policy. The Cleveland branch remained deadlocked and never issued any policy statements on Mercy Hospital. Kenneth Kusmer has observed that the NAACP's stance constituted an attempt to avoid divisiveness without adopting an accommodationist position; however, in later controversies surrounding the establishment of a black hospital in Cleveland, the organization would not be as acquiescent.[27]

Despite the mounting opposition to the proposed hospital, the Mercy Hospital Association pushed forward throughout the spring of 1927 with its fund-raising activities. The drive, however, was not successful, collecting only $1500—less than one percent of its goal. By May, the campaign for the hospital showed signs of impending failure. The treasury of the hospital association had dwindled to $100, a circumstance that prompted charges of financial mismanagement. Administrative problems had also developed. Several officials of the association had resigned and its executive secretary had left after his salary had been cut. "The movement seems to be about dead," the *Gazette* enthusiastically proclaimed, "funeral in the near future." In June, a few diehard supporters, including Dr. Garvin, attempted to rally support for the hospital, but their efforts were unsuccessful. Once again, an attempt to organize a black hospital in Cleveland had ended in failure.[28]

Several factors contributed to the collapse of the Mercy Hospital project. Its supporters failed to win endorsements from key black associations such as the Negro Welfare Association and the two coalitions of black clergy. While individual members supported both sides, the organizations, wishing to avoid the controversy, professed neutrality. Furthermore, the proposal failed to elicit widespread support from physicians, a group who purportedly would have greatly benefitted from the construction of the hospital. The majority, in fact, did not take active roles in the hospital movement. The Mercy Hospital Association's inability to develop into an administratively stable organization also contributed to the failure of the hospital project. The association reorganized twice between January and June 1927. These organizational problems made it difficult for the Mercy Hospital Association to conduct a successful fund-raising effort or to counter the charges that its opponents had lodged against it. Even Garvin, one of the most active supporters of the hospital association, described its management as "improper and misguided." Finally the opposition waged a vigorous campaign in which they successfully portrayed the project as Jim Crowism and as financially unfeasible.[29]

Although the movement for a black hospital had failed, it had focused the black community's attention on racial discrimination in Cleveland's hospitals, especially Cleveland City Hospital. Although the hospital admitted black patients, it had no black physicians or nurses on staff or in its training programs. Organizations and individuals who had found themselves on opposite sides on Mercy Hospital subsequently joined forces and began a push to integrate Cleveland City Hospital. In the fall of 1927, black leaders met with Dudley S. Blossom, the city's director of public health and welfare, to present their demands. They did not find a sympathetic audience. Reportedly Blossom was "aggravatingly insulting" and replied, "No, I am not going to allow Negro boys and girls to train at City Hospital." In the November election, voters rejected a city bond proposal that would have raised money for Cleveland City Hospital. The opposition of the black community to the measure greatly contributed to its defeat. African Americans voted against it to voice their displeasure with Blossom and the policy of excluding black physicians and nurses. They threatened to use the ballot again if it was necessary to integrate the hospital.[30]

The protest ballot had an effect. In December 1927, at the urging of the Interracial Committee of the Federated Churches, City Manager William R. Hopkins appointed a committee to make recommendations about the feasibility of admitting black nursing students and interns to the programs at Cleveland City Hospital. The committee was to investigate hospital integration in other cities and survey opinions about the training of black physicians and nurses. City officials maintained that the decision to add black interns and nurses to the hospital's staff would not be based solely on local conditions and politics, and that any change in policy would be largely governed by the experiences of other institutions with integration. However, George A. Myers spoke for many members of the African-American community when he contended, "We care nothing about what is being done in other cities or how they handle the situation there. We are only concerned about the situation here and the opening of the City hospital."[31]

Members of the committee included P.J. McMillan, the hospital's superintendent; Estelle C. Koch, principal of its nurse training school; Carl A. Hamann, the former dean of Western Reserve Medical School; J.C. Placak, Chief of the Division of Tuberculosis at Cleveland City Hospital; John H. McMorries, a black physician who had practiced medicine in the city since 1916; and Blossom. Throughout December, the group toured twenty hospitals and medical schools in seven Midwestern and Northeastern cities. It is not clear how the committee selected its itinerary, but each of the cities on it had large public hospitals. The committee may have been attempting to visit locations that had institutions comparable to Cleveland City Hospital. Its trip included facilities that admitted black health-care trainees and those that did not, and it also conducted interviews with both black and white health-care personnel. In January 1928, the committee filed its final report. An examination of this report provides insight as to why the decision to integrate was deferred for two years, and also documents graphically the pervasiveness of racism in medical and nursing education in the late 1920s and the justifications used to exclude African-American health professionals from majority institutions.[32]

The report vividly depicted the enormous pressures and obstacles that black men and women faced as they sought to enter medicine and nursing. It underscored the assessment of an assistant dean at Harvard Medical School who informed members of the committee that the black medical students at his institution had "very tough sledding." He told them that the black students were housed in separate accommodations and that the white medical students usually did not socialize with them. Furthermore, he noted that the presence of black students on clinical rotations "creates much ill feeling." The medical school administrator added that African-American medical students "invariably" graduated in the lower third of the class and that this indicated "the lower mentality" of the black race.[33]

The committee found that similar conditions existed for medical students at the University of Pennsylvania School of Medicine. Since the 1882 matriculation of Nathan Francis Mossell, the school had admitted two or three black male students each year. The school's dean, Dr. William Pepper, III, informed the committee that the "mortality is heavy" among these students and that usually only one graduated annually. He also concurred with his colleague from Harvard that the presence of black students led to difficulties. For example, he noted that in the autopsy room they had difficulties "unless care [was] taken that the other three men working at the same time [had] no special prejudices." Black medical students were usually prohibited from working with white patients "except in exceptional instances" where the patients had been "hand-picked or otherwise prepared." Furthermore, the students were not allowed in the dormitories, but had to find accommodations off campus. It should be emphasized that at both Harvard and Pennsylvania the officials viewed the source of the problem as the presence of African-American medical students, not the existence of racial discrimination.[34]

The committee discovered that only five municipal hospitals admitted black medical school graduates to their training programs. These facilities were Harlem Hospital and Bellevue Hospital in New York; Kansas City General Hospital, No. 2; St. Louis City Hospital, No. 2; and Cook County Hospital in Chicago. Three institutions served predominantly black patient populations; Bellevue and Cook County's patients were predominantly white. The two Missouri hospitals, established as segregated facilities, supplied twenty-two positions for black interns. Although Harlem Hospital had not been established to serve African-American patients exclusively, by 1927, because of demographic changes in the hospital's community, 60 percent of its patients were black. At the time, seven of the twenty-one interns and all eighty of the student nurses were black. The opportunities for black interns at Bellevue and Cook County were extremely limited. At the time of the committee's investigation, Bellevue had only one black intern, a woman, and Cook County had two.[35]

The Cleveland delegation also learned that the nurse training schools affiliated with municipal hospitals provided few opportunities for black women. As was true for black interns, most of the positions were found in institutions such as Harlem Hospital that served large numbers of black patients. And, where black women did secure admission to programs at predominantly white hospitals, they were not treated as the equals of their white classmates. Black student nurses were frequently excluded from social activities and housed in separate accommodations. Many of the nursing educators who met with the committee also reinforced stereotypes about the emotional and intellectual inferiority of black students. The principal of the nurse training school at Harlem Hospital claimed that the work of black students equalled that of white students in the classroom, "but fell down miserably in their work on the wards where initiative and judgment were demanded."[36]

All the white physicians and nurses interviewed by the committee urged it not to "mix" white and black interns and nurses at Cleveland City Hospital, arguing that such an experiment would surely end in failure and would jeopardize the quality of the hospital's training programs. Furthermore, they contended that white patients would object to such a change in policy. Dr. J.G. Doane, Superintendent of Philadelphia General Hospital and the president of the American Hospital Association, emphatically stated that he believed that his institution would suffer for years if black people were added to its staff. As evidence, he observed that the quality and quantity of internship applications at Jersey City Hospital had declined after it had accepted two Jewish interns. The dean of the Georgetown University Medical School reiterated Doane's position, stating that it would be a "serious mistake" to attempt to admit black interns and nurses on an equal basis with white personnel. An assistant medical school dean from Harvard told the committee that many of the school's graduates would not apply to Cleveland City Hospital if it admitted black interns. An official of the New York State Board of Education, who headed the division responsible for nurse training schools, argued that allowing black women into the hospital's nurse training school would "absolutely wreck" it. She warned that if they were admitted that she would recommend that the school be dropped from her state's list of hospitals approved for student programs. Dr. Edward A. Balloch, the white physician who served as the dean of the Howard University Medical School, even claimed that it would be detrimental to black women to place them in a predominantly white nursing school. He argued that they would be "so lonesome and so 'out of it,' even so heart-broken, that they could not show to the best advantage, and would very likely fail of their purpose."[37]

The white physicians and nurses consulted by the committee recommended that if it was necessary to admit black people that great efforts had to be made to ensure that "exceptional" or "the right type" of black people be recruited: people, as one nurse put it, who would be able to take their "humiliation without complaint." According to several of the white health professionals, a better alternative would be to establish a separate hospital for the training of African Americans.[38]

Most of the black physicians and nurses who met with the committee also urged that a separate black hospital be built. They, too, did not support placing black physicians and nurses at Cleveland City Hospital. Dr. John E. Perry, chairperson of the executive committee of the NHA and the superintendent of Wheatley-Provident Hospital in Kansas City, Missouri, informed the Cleveland delegation that black hospitals provided the most successful mechanism to educate African Americans for careers in medicine and nursing. "Wherever [the] mixture of white and colored is tried, it results in humiliation, ignoring, and embarrassment," the physician asserted. "Instead of trying to batter your way into hospitals where you are unwelcome, why not spend your time, money, and effort in establishing your own colored hospitals." Dr. William A. Warfield, the superintendent at Freedmen's Hospital, concurred with Dr. Perry, noting, however, that having black interns attend to black patients exclusively was not an ideal situation, but it was the only way to solve their training problem. Even Dr. Peter Marshall Murray, then on staff at Harlem Hospital, doubted that the integration of black interns and nurses at Cleveland City Hospital would work. He noted that the admission of black interns to Harlem Hospital had been successful only because the policy of its nurse training school had been changed to accept only black women. He did not believe that white women would be willing to work under the supervision of black interns.[39]

Only one black physician, Dr. Henry Minton, superintendent of Mercy Hospital in Philadelphia, opposed the construction of a separate hospital. Minton, a graduate of the city's Jefferson Medical College, argued that one black intern could be placed at the hospital without any difficulty, observing that during his medical education he had been confronted with embarrassing situations, but that he "never was thrown into a state of mind where he wanted 'to give up.'"[40]

Minton's opinion did not hold much sway with the committee. Almost all of the physicians and nurses whom it had interviewed had argued against opening up the hospital to black interns and nurses. They saw such a move as a radical step that would place the institution outside the limits of acceptable hospital practice and would jeopardize its training programs. Their contentions proved much more persuasive. In its final report, the committee recommended that the policy of excluding African Americans be continued, concluding that "for the good of the whole, the time is not ripe for trying an experiment which seems so void of promise of success and so full of danger of a serious and a disastrous failure." Dr. McMorries, the only African American on the committee, also signed the report, although later accounts have contended that he dissented. The committee's report went beyond keeping the doors of the hospital closed to black physicians and nurses. As Dr. Charles Garvin observed, it sustained "the prejudice and narrow arguments previously made against the admission of colored professional men and women into the hospital." In other words, the report reinforced stereotypes about the competence of black health-care professionals.[41]

The committee did, however, make a concession to the black community's demand that it have some representation at the hospital. It recommended that discussions be initiated with Western Reserve University School of Medicine about the possibility of placing a reputable black physician on the hospital's outpatient department staff and another on its visiting staff. At the time, all staff appointments had to be approved by the medical school. The committee perceived this move as carrying with it "the least danger of serious failure." Six months after the recommendation was made, Dr. McMorries became the first African American named to the staff of Cleveland City Hospital. The Howard University graduate was named to a position in its surgical outpatient department. Surprisingly, no charges emerged that McMorries had signed the committee's report on the promise of a position at the hospital. Charles W. White, branch president of the NAACP, lauded McMorries appointment, but he observed, "We are not content that the matter rest here." The appointment would not stop the campaign for more black representation on the hospital staff and the admission of black interns and nursing students.[42]

In June 1928, Dr. E.J. Gregg, a physician and one of three black city councilmen, introduced a proposal designed as a compromise to the full integration of Cleveland City Hospital. His plan called for the establishment of a new municipal hospital on Cleveland's East Side, a predominantly black area of the city. A new hospital would not be constructed; rather, an abandoned building would be renovated. This facility would be open to black physicians and nurses; therefore, it would no longer be necessary to push for the integration of the existing hospital on the town's West Side. Yet the new hospital would give black physicians and nurses more representation in publicly supported institutions. Gregg's plan received the backing of City Manager Hopkins and most of the city's black physicians. Hopkins maintained that it would be easier to place black staff at the East Side facility because there would be "no long established precedents to break."[43]

As was true in the case of Mercy Hospital, Gregg's proposal split black public opinion. African Americans remained adamant that they have more access to publicly financed institutions, although they differed over the strategies to increase it. Gregg's plan prompted charges of publicly financed Jim Crowism from segments of the black community, including the NAACP, and, predictably, from *Gazette* editor Harry C. Smith.

The Cleveland Branch of the NAACP, which had remained neutral in the controversy over Mercy Hospital and had never been actively involved in hospital issues, emerged as one of the leading and most vociferous opponents of the proposed East Side hospital and of hospital discrimination in Cleveland. In his 1929 annual report, Charles W. White noted that he had been a member of a delegation of black leaders that had toured Cleveland City Hospital earlier in the year, and had found that, despite the denials of the hospital superintendent, "segregation [was] openly and brazenly practiced." The group discovered that black patients were kept in separate wards and that not a single black person was employed at the hospital in any capacity. The NAACP demanded that all racial barriers at the hospital be removed.[44]

Charles W. White, in keeping with the policy of the national office, made clear the branch's opposition to the use of public funds to establish what it perceived to be a separate hospital for black people. "Our opposition is not to a Negro Hospital, privately supported, nor to an East side branch of City Hospital with a mixed staff, designed to and adequate to serve the whole East side and to which all patients on the East side shall be required to go," the branch president wrote. "We stand against a branch of the City Hospital which whether originally intended or not, will eventuate in a short while into what to all intents and purposes is a Negro branch of City Hospital." White refuted claims that the hospital would be similar to Harlem Hospital, noting that the latter had not been originally established in an all-black area and that 40 percent of the patients treated there were white. White acknowledged the plight of black physicians and nurses but stated that the branch was "not willing to compromise such a fundamental [principle] by acquiescing to the introduction of a pernicious double system of municipality owned and operated hospitals."[45]

White was not alone in his criticism of the East Side hospital. Harry C. Smith, in his usual style, bitterly attacked not only the proposal, but the proposer, exhorting the physician-councilman, a native of Alabama, to "go back south . . . ! And for God's sake and that of your people of this city stay there until you can 'take that red bandanna off your head.'" The editor once again argued, as he had in the previous efforts to build private black hospitals, that the establishment of the new municipal hospital would close the existing one to African Americans.[46]

Gregg's fellow black councilmen, Rev. Russell S. Brown, pastor of Mt. Zion Congregational Church, and Clayborne George, a lawyer and former president of the local NAACP, also vigorously opposed the plan. Brown and George argued that the measure was "plain 'jim-crow'" because black people would be able to work in the city institution on the East Side, but not on the West Side. In April 1929, Brown introduced a resolution that would have opened up the existing city hospital to all citizens of Cleveland regardless of race, creed, or color. Gregg did not support the measure, believing that the time was not yet right to push such legislation through the council. After Gregg's position to the Brown bill was made public, allegations surfaced that he had opposed it because Hopkins had promised that he would head the proposed hospital. Both men later denied the charges.[47]

Most black physicians in the city supported the construction of the East Side branch. The Cleveland Medical, Dental, and Pharmaceutical Association—the local black medical society—adopted a resolution supporting the creation of the new facility. Signers of the resolution included Drs. Garvin, McMorries, and, not surprisingly, Gregg. The physicians argued that the East Side facility would be more convenient and accessible to patients than the city hospital on the West Side, and that it would also provide black health-care professionals with a place to train and work. They further contended that the hospital would not be a Jim-Crow institution because white patients, physicians, and nurses would not be barred from using it. The organization noted, however, that its endorsement of the East Side hospital would not affect "its determination to participate in existing facilities."[48]

Representatives of the NMA visited Cleveland to investigate the situation. After meeting with Hopkins and members of the black community, the medical society came out in favor of the actions of its local branch. A July 1929 editorial in the *Journal of the National Medical Association* called for the construction of the hospital and decried the appearance of the "segregation bogy" once again in the establishment of a hospital that was meant to serve the needs of African Americans.[49]

Yet, an East Side branch of City Hospital was not established. In the November 1929 election, Gregg was turned out of office. His stand on the hospital and his support of a Polish candidate, instead of a black one, for a seat on the city's civil service commission were the primary factors behind his defeat. Before he left office, Gregg attempted to have the finance committee of the city council allocate $350,000 to construct the new medical facility. Strenuous opposition from Brown and George killed the measure.[50]

The November council elections proved pivotal in the campaign to integrate Cleveland City Hospital. Again, three black men were selected to serve on the body. George was reelected, attorney Lawrence O. Payne replaced Brown, and dentist LeRoy Bundy defeated Gregg. All three men had run on a platform vowing to change the policies at Cleveland City Hospital. Historian Christopher Wye has argued that the election of this triumvirate dramatically altered the temper of black politics in Cleveland during the early 1920s. Under the direction of Bundy, the men worked to increase the political power of the African-American community and the amount of political patronage allotted to it. Shortly after their election they got an opportunity to do both when a power struggle developed in the council over who would be named city manager. A movement had arisen to remove Hopkins as city manager and replace him with Daniel E. Morgan. However, excluding the votes of the black members, the council was evenly split between the two men. The triumvirate clearly held the balance of power in the selection of the new city manager. In exchange for their votes, they extracted a promise from Morgan that he would support the admission of black interns and nurses to Cleveland City Hospital and the appointment of African Americans to municipal offices. The political power that the African-American community had gained in the city was undoubtedly the key to the eventual integration of Cleveland City Hospital. Despite Hopkins's earlier protestations, it was local conditions, not external factors, that determined the outcome. Political considerations helped to override the recommendations of the committee that had previously advised that black interns and nurses not be admitted to the facility.[51]

On 13 January 1930, the Cleveland City Council unanimously passed a resolution introduced by Dr. F.M. Walz that instructed the city manager "to provide an equal opportunity for all citizens of Cleveland to receive training as nurses and interns at the Cleveland City Hospital." The local branch of the NAACP attributed its passage to the support of Dr. Walz, an eighty-year-old physician, and the work of the three black councilmen "who would not let the matter sleep." In one of his last actions as city manager, William R. Hopkins signed the measure.[52]

By September, the first black women entered the hospital's nurse training school; however, the first black intern did not start until July 1931—over a year after the council resolution. The need to conduct a "very searching investigation" had delayed the appointment. Indeed, the quest for the intern was thorough and methodical. Black community leaders, aware of the obstacles that the person would face and the burden that he would carry, proceeded very cautiously. In line with the opinions expressed earlier by the physicians and nurses who had been interviewed by the committee investigating the integration of the hospital, they were convinced that they had to find the "right type of person." Consequently, they surveyed some of the leading medical schools looking for their top black students. Council member Lawrence O. Payne visited Harvard and urged a brilliant student, Frederick Douglass Stubbs, to apply for the position. Black leaders compiled a list of five names to present to the executive board of Cleveland City Hospital. Stubbs's name soon emerged as the leading candidate.[53]

Stubbs (1906–1947), a native of Wilmington, Delaware, had an impeccable social background and unimpeachable academic credentials. His father was a physician and his mother was related to Dr. Daniel Hale Williams, the founder of Chicago's Provident Hospital. The family reportedly passed as white until Stubbs, with his slightly darker complexion, was born. Although darker than the other members of his family, Douglass Stubbs was still fair and this would later be one of the factors in his appointment. But his impressive academic record played a more significant role. In 1927, Stubbs graduated magna cum laude from Dartmouth College, where he had been elected to Phi Beta Kappa. Four years later he graduated first in his class from Harvard Medical School. At Harvard he became the first African American admitted to the school's chapter of Alpha Omega Alpha, the medical school honor society. Stubbs's academic career clearly challenged the stereotypes that many medical educators, including those at his alma mater, held regarding the capabilities of black medical students. But such stereotypes were unyielding. Stubbs maintained that Harvard Medical School decided not to admit any more black medical students after his matriculation in 1927 and that thirteen years later it had not altered its policy. Despite Stubbs's distinguished academic record, "light complexion and pleasing personality," attempts were made by white citizens to block his nomination. Dudley S. Blossom only approved his application after City Manager Daniel E. Morgan threatened to fire him. White physicians also tried to stop the appointment, taking their protest to Morgan. But he stood firm. "Gentlemen," he reportedly told them, "We once fought a war over that in this country."[54]

Not all members of the black community welcomed Stubbs as the first black intern at Cleveland City Hospital. Dr. Joe T. Thomas, who ten years earlier had attempted to establish a black hospital in the city, protested that the candidate was someone "whose parents have never paid a dime in taxes to maintain our City Hospital." Thomas maintained that there were black medical school graduates from Cleveland who had the qualifications to fill the position. Thomas, however, represented a minority viewpoint. Most African Americans believed that they had found the right person to break the color line at the hospital.[55]

While Douglass Stubbs was at Harvard, he had been the only black student in his class and encountered several incidents of racial discrimination. For example, no one in his dormitory would speak to him. The coping mechanisms that Stubbs had developed to survive racist experiences at Harvard would again be useful during his internship, which began on 1 July 1931. At the time approximately fifty housestaff worked at the hospital and several were from the deep South. The interns worked in pairs and Dr. James E. Morgan was assigned to be Stubbs's partner. Fifty years later, Morgan described some of the obstacles that Stubbs faced during the year. Some of the housestaff would leave if Stubbs sat down at a table and some patients would refuse to let him treat them. Stubbs himself observed that some black patients found it difficult to believe that a black person could be a physician. He recalled that during his internship two black patients once argued over his nationality. One believed that he was Chinese; the other that he was Japanese. According to Morgan, Stubbs handled these situations with "intelligence, tact, and style" and successfully completed his internship. The next year, two black interns were admitted. None of the dire warnings of the medical and nursing educators about the impact of integration on the integrity of the program came to pass.[56]

Two years after Stubbs's pioneering acceptance into the program at Cleveland City Hospital, two black interns were again admitted. They too encountered racist incidents. When they walked into the dining hall on their first day, several of the other housestaff walked out. After this episode, they usually waited until the end of the meal hour when almost everyone had left. One southern intern, after drinking a great deal, decided that he was going to put one of the men "in his place." He put ether under his door and lit it. Fortunately, the target of this violence was not harmed. The black interns also had to deal with the racism of white patients. An alleged prostitute from the South "raised an uproar with screams and racial vituperation" when one of the interns tried to treat her in the syphilis clinic. One of the interns' white colleagues later noted that a "few emergency room patients were less concerned with their injuries than that they should be treated by a black man, and raised nasty refusals."[57]

Despite the problems that they faced, at least one to three black interns entered the program at Cleveland City Hospital each year throughout the 1930s. But opportunities for advanced specialty training still remained beyond reach. Even Douglass Stubbs was not able to obtain a residency at the hospital because "the time hadn't arrived that the powers that be could award a residency to a black." However, Dr. Sam Freedlander, the head of the department of surgery, created a one-year fellowship in thoracic surgery especially for Stubbs. By 1939, five black residents had been appointed: two in pathology, one in neuropsychiatry, one in surgery, and one in internal medicine.[58]

The first African-American resident in internal medicine at Cleveland City Hospital was Dr. Ulysses G. Mason, a 1936 graduate of the University of Chicago School of Medicine. Mason finished his internship at Cleveland City Hospital in 1937 and completed his two-year residency in 1939. During the last year of his postgraduate training, he served as chief resident and supervised the work of twenty-three interns. Mason's work was so highly regarded that after he had finished his residency he was appointed to the visiting staff of the hospital where he joined two other black physicians, John McMorries and L.O. Baumgardner.[59]

The successful integration of Cleveland City Hospital did not deter the leaders of the NMA from their position on black hospitals. They argued that the institutions were still needed because "token" integration of municipal hospitals would only benefit a few black physicians. The vast majority would still be dependent on black hospitals. A 1931 editorial in the *Journal of the National Medical Association* noted that in Cleveland, despite widespread suffrage and three black councilmen, positions at City Hospital had been obtained only for one intern, seven nurses, and one staff physician. It disdainfully observed that the staff physician, John McMorries, was a "real whitewash . . . almost 98% white. No patient will ever take him for a Negro." The improvement and establishment of black hospitals would remain a cornerstone of NMA activities.[60]

Dr. Douglass Stubbs and Dr. Ulysses G. Mason had both profited from the integration of Cleveland City Hospital; however, both physicians became strong advocates of the NMA position. Stubbs, after his fellowship year, moved to Philadelphia in 1933 to complete a surgery residency at Douglass Hospital because he could not obtain one in Cleveland. This was the physician's first affiliation with a black institution, and the hospital was to become an integral part of his later career. When he finished his residency, Stubbs entered private practice, but he wanted to seek additional postgraduate education. In 1937, he began a residency in thoracic surgery at New York

City's Sea View Hospital, one of the nation's premier institutions for the treatment of tuberculosis.

On completion of his residency at Sea View, Stubbs became the first black physician formally trained in thoracic surgery. At the time the specialty consisted mostly of performing thoracoplasties and phrenicectomies for the treatment of tuberculosis. When Stubbs returned to Philadelphia these skills proved critical because of the high incidence of tuberculosis among African Americans. In 1938, he was named chief of thoracic surgery at Douglass, and as part of his duties, he supervised the hospital's tuberculosis ward. He later noted with pride its success. "We . . . feel that the work being done there," he stated, "compares in actual work done as well as in final results with similar institutions throughout the country regardless of their racial identity." Stubbs admitted that the 100-bed Douglass Hospital could easily be absorbed by other hospitals, however he fought to keep it open because it was the only hospital in the country where black physicians could perform thoracoplasties.[61]

Douglass Stubbs's surgical skills and work in tuberculosis helped him rise rapidly in the mainstream medical world until his untimely death in 1947 at the age of 40. In 1943, he became the first black board-certified surgeon in Philadelphia. Three years later he was admitted to the American College of Surgeons. He was the first African American appointed to the medical staff at Philadelphia General Hospital, and at the time of his death was acting chief of the tuberculosis division at the hospital.

Stubbs conceded, however, that his professional success in predominantly white institutions was out of the ordinary, acknowledging that black hospitals continued to be essential for the professional lives of the vast majority of black physicians and nurses. A 1944 speech at the annual meeting of the Booker T. Washington Community Hospital Association of Newark, New Jersey, clearly illustrated Stubbs's position. He maintained that without the efforts of Daniel Hale Williams and Nathan Francis Mossell to build hospitals, the black nursing and medical professions would be virtually nonexistent. He observed that 95 percent of all black nurses and physicians were "products of wholly Negro institutions," further stating that although it was important for black physicians and nurses to work in predominantly white institutions, "the privileged few cannot significantly affect the fate of the group." Black hospitals, he argued, were necessary because

> every Negro doctor who aspires to hospital practice must have a place to work in peace, to develop his own potential destiny, and every Negro patient who needs hospitalization and desires to retain the service of his own Negro physician must be granted this important privilege.

Throughout, his short career, Douglass Stubbs remained a staunch advocate of black hospitals.[62]

Ulysses G. Mason also emerged as a strong supporter of black hospitals. His appointment to a staff position at Cleveland City Hospital did not stop him from becoming the leading force in the fourth, and only successful, movement to establish a black hospital in the city. In this capacity he was following in the footsteps of his father, also a physician, who had in 1917 established Northside Infirmary, a small hospital, in Birmingham, Alabama. Mason praised the strides that had been made in hospital integration in Cleveland, but noted that the arrangement did not fully solve the professional problems that black physicians faced. He concurred with Stubbs that integration of municipal hospitals only benefitted a few doctors. Mason pointed out that cities with black hospitals—for example, Philadelphia, Chicago, and Washington, D.C.—had the highest number of black specialists, arguing that most of the city's black physicians still did not have access to private facilities in which to hospitalize their paying patients. Mason himself had been turned down for staff positions at several of the city's private hospitals.[63]

In 1939, only eleven of Cleveland's thirty-five black physicians had staff positions at hospitals. Black physicians claimed that it was "embarrassing . . . professionally and economically" to be forced to refer patients to other physicians solely because they could not obtain hospital appointments. Mason also maintained that the exclusion of black physicians from hospitals resulted in "intellectual stagnation and decay." Even those physicians who had staff appointments encountered professional restrictions. Most held outpatient positions; therefore, even they could not admit patients to the facilities. Furthermore, those few who were able to admit patients often had to be supervised by white physicians. A black physician might find himself reduced to being either an assistant or an observer in an operation involving his own patient.[64]

Obstacles also continued to exist for black patients who sought hospital care in Cleveland. Racial discrimination ranged from the maintenance of separate wards to the total exclusion of African Americans. For example, in one incident well-publicized by the NAACP, a young boy was denied admission to Charity Hospital after his physician had sent him to the hospital's emergency ward. Upon the boy's arrival, a physician at the hospital called the referring physician. "Why didn't you say this boy was a 'Negro' boy; we have no bed for a 'Negro' boy?" he asked. The boy's physician retorted, "I have no right to discuss the race of my patient and you had better take care of this boy." The boy was admitted after threats were made. In another incident, St. Luke's hospital transferred a black woman and her newborn baby to a segregated ward that did not have the facilities needed for their care. African Americans also charged that even if they did gain access to hospitals they were frequently treated with disdain and disrespect.[65]

The racially discriminatory practices at Cleveland hospitals had prompted the earlier movements to start a black hospital. They also proved to be the catalyst for the final campaign. In October 1939, Mason called together a meeting of the city's African-American physicians to discuss the possibility of establishing their own hospital. In the letter announcing the meeting, he wrote:

> the time has come for us to unite and formulate a program which will eventuate in the procurement and development of an institution where we can take our patients and not be hampered by the restrictions which so severely limit us at present.

Twenty-six of the city's thirty-five black physicians attended the gathering, voting to establish a temporary organization that would "study the hospital question with the ultimate view of obtaining a hospital" and electing Ulysses G. Mason president of the new organization.[66]

Nine months later, the organization incorporated as the Forest City Hospital Association, a voluntary, nonprofit corporation. Its board of trustees included the following physicians: Ulysses G. Mason; Charles Garvin; M.H. Lambright, Sr.; E.B. Spencer; and L.O. Baumgardner. All these men, it should be noted, had appointments at other hospitals in the city. For unknown reasons, however, Garvin and Spencer would not be active members of the association. Neither man attended meetings regularly, raised funds for the endeavor, or promoted the hospital at public meetings. From the outset, supporters of Forest City Hospital, undoubtedly cognizant of the allegations that had been launched against previous hospital campaigns, claimed that the proposed facility would not be a "separate setup." Although the hospital would be geared toward serving the African-American community, and all twenty-one members of its board were black, it would welcome all races and nationalities.[67]

The immediate challenge faced by the Forest City Hospital Association was raising funds. The physicians on the board of trustees pledged to pay five dollars a month into the hospital fund. Memberships to the hospital association were sold to the public at large for a one-dollar fee. Members of the board, including board president Mason, visited black churches and community organizations to solicit donations and support, reminding their audiences that the new hospital would not only provide medical care, but would bring jobs to the community. In 1940, a women's auxiliary was created to assist the hospital association. Its members also spoke to several groups to gather financial support for the hospital. The women's auxiliary also held an annual "Spring Style Show and Dance" to raise funds. Despite these various efforts, by the end of 1940 the Forest City Hospital Association had less than $1200 in its treasury—nowhere near enough to build the proposed 100-bed facility.[68]

Throughout the early 1940s, the Forest City Hospital Association struggled financially. By April 1942, it had raised only $2800. The hospital association realized that in order to be successful it had to widen its financial base beyond the African-American community. At a January 1943 meeting, "after frank discussion," it voted to expand and integrate its board. This resolution may also have been intended to stem growing criticism from some African Americans who viewed the hospital project as Jim Crowism. After the integration of its board, the hospital association modified its mission somewhat. It now stressed that Forest City Hospital would be an "interracial" hospital, rather than a "Negro" one. The hospital, however, would still be located in a black neighborhood.[69]

The decision to integrate the board proved pivotal. Prominent white Clevelanders who were named trustees included Dr. R.W. Scott, chief of staff at Cleveland City Hospital and professor of medicine at Western Reserve School of Medicine; Dr. J.B. Stocklen, controller of tuberculosis for Cuyahoga County; and Walter Weil, president of the National Smelting Company. These men worked to gather support for the hospital from the city's chief medical institutions. Their efforts proved successful. In 1943, the Forest City Hospital Association received endorsements from Mayor Harold Burton's Joint Hospital Committee, the Hospital Council, Welfare Federation, and the Academy of Medicine. The hospital association also began to receive financial support from the white residents of Cleveland. In November 1943, the treasury of the hospital association had risen to a scant $5000. By December that amount had tripled because of a $10,000 donation from Trustee Walter Weil.[70]

Throughout the 1940s and 1950s tentative steps were made toward the establishment of the hospital. A paucity of funds, however, continued to plague the project. A turning point came in 1945 when the hospital association became a participant in the Greater Cleveland Hospital Fund. The fund had been launched in 1945 to raise $9.5 million to expand hospital services in the metropolitan Cleveland area. In 1947, the board of the hospital association accepted the fund's proposal that it establish Forest City Hospital at the site that had recently been vacated by Glenville Euclid Hospital. The hospital would receive the property, which was located in a predominantly black neighborhood, and $450,000 to help with renovations. In 1953, the hospital association received the unencumbered deed to the property. The opening of Forest City Hospital was delayed until 1957 because the original allocation proved inadequate in large part because of skyrocketing labor and construction costs. The hospital association still had to raise an additional $850,000 for renovations and operating expenses. The fund-raising efforts were only partially successful, and the hospital was forced to obtain a $400,000 bank loan before it was able to open.[71]

As with the previous movements to start a black hospital, the campaign to found Forest City Hospital provoked charges of Jim Crowism from other segments of the black community. The NAACP, which had been neutral in the campaign to establish Mercy Hospital, but vociferous in its opposition to the East Side branch of Cleveland City Hospital, emerged as the primary opponent of Forest City Hospital. The hospital association's pronouncements that the hospital would be interracial, rather than black, did not move the civil rights organization from its opposition. The NAACP charged that the "'interracial' cry [was] a mere smoke screen for the actual creation of more segregation in health and hospital facilities." It pointed out that other hospitals, such as Chicago's Provident Hospital, had been established as interracial facilities, but had evolved into institutions that served a predominantly, if not exclusively, African-American clientele. When two members of the executive committee of the Cleveland branch of the NAACP visited Provident Hospital in February 1944, they reported that the facility had "a mere semblance of the proposed inter-racial atmosphere, and [was] badly in need of qualified physicians to man it." The report accurately noted that some progress had been made in integrating the staffs of Cleveland Hospitals and that not all black physicians supported the activities of the hospital association. The NAACP feared that the establishment of Forest City Hospital would be used "to frustrate or postpone the meeting of the legitimate demands of qualified Negro doctors and nurses for admission to tax-supported and tax-exempted institutions." The NAACP contended that the efforts of the black community should be directed toward integrating the already established hospitals in the city, not in creating a separate facility. In other words, *all* hospitals in Cleveland should be made interracial.[72]

The national office of the NAACP actively supported the efforts of the Cleveland branch to halt the opening of Forest City Hospital. In February 1948, Dr. W. Montague Cobb, a member of the NAACP's National Medical Committee and one of the leaders of the growing medical civil rights movement, met with representatives of the local branch. Cobb, an anatomist and a physician, was familiar with Cleveland. In 1932, three years after he had obtained his M.D. from Howard, he had earned a Ph.D. from Case Western Reserve. He urged a vigorous and well-publicized campaign to oppose the hospital, harshly criticizing Forest City Hospital as an example of the "old-clothes to Sam" pattern of black hospital development. Forest City Hospital would not be a new facility, but one created out of a vacated and outmoded facility. Cobb noted that similar patterns had been employed in the establishment of the new Provident Hospital.[73]

The major black newspaper, however, did not support the NAACP stance. In contrast to the *Gazette's* previous campaigns to oppose a black hospital, the black press did not come out against Forest City Hospital. The *Gazette* had ceased publication in 1941 with the death of Harry C. Smith. In the early 1940s, the most prominent black newspaper was the *Cleveland Call and Post*. Its editor, William O. Walker, who did not have Smith's zealous integrationism, served on the boards of both the Forest City Hospital Association and the NAACP. Walker charged that the NAACP position on Forest City Hospital was "all wet." He maintained that the hospital was needed, and urged the civil rights organization to spend less time and energy fighting Forest City Hospital and more on fighting to integrate the existing Cleveland hospitals.[74]

Walker was not the only NAACP board member to criticize the civil rights organization's position on Forest City Hospital. Charles W. White, the former branch president, also opposed it. As branch president, White had led the campaign to fight the construction of the East Side branch of City Hospital, however, he vigorously supported the establishment of Forest City. He, too, served on the boards of both the NAACP and the hospital association. At a April 1954 meeting attended by representatives of the hospital committee of the NAACP and of Forest City Hospital, White argued that the NAACP's stance was an error that was based upon "fanciful fear." He contended that the hospital would be an interracial institution, not a segregated one, noting that the hospital's board had recently adopted a resolution that reaffirmed its commitment to integration and its opposition to segregation. For example, the resolution ordered the hospital's credentials committee to divide staff positions on an equitable basis between black and white physicians.[75]

Although the African-American community did not unanimously support the establishment of Forest City Hospital, the campaign was ultimately successful. Two major factors distinguished this final effort from previous movements to found a black hospital in the city. First, the black newspaper did not attack the hospital and arouse public sentiment against it. Second, the Forest City Hospital Association was able to procure the funds necessary to open the hospital. As opposed to earlier attempts to establish hospitals, the Forest City Hospital Association's fund-raising activities went beyond the black community. It was able to solicit funds from the white community. Without the hospital's participation in the Greater Cleveland Hospital Fund, it is doubtful that it would have been established. However, when Forest City Hospital finally opened its doors in 1957, the nascent medical civil rights movement and its uncompromising integrationism had gained momentum. These medical civil rights activists rejected the notion of separate black and pseudo-interracial institutions. Their movement would pose new challenges for all black hospitals and call into question their very existence. As W. Montague Cobb described it, "The Forest City Hospital clearly belongs to the old order and not to the new."[76]

CONCLUSION

The Black Hospital—A Vanishing Medical Institution

❧

By 1945, the energies of black medical organizations, even the previously separatist National Medical Association (NMA), shifted from the creation of black hospitals to the dismantlement of the "Negro medical ghetto" of which black hospitals were a major component. This change reflected the predominance of integrationism as the major strategy for racial advancement in the years following World War II. Civil rights activists renounced the establishment of separate black institutions by either black or white people, and instead pushed for the full integration of African Americans into all segments of American society. Their efforts would pose new challenges for black hospitals and would call into question the need for such facilities.

The NMA and National Association for the Advancement of Colored People (NAACP) led the campaign for medical civil rights. The medical association had embraced integrationism by the end of World War II; in 1945 the NMA's Board of Trustees outlined a program to promote the desegregation of hospitals. Two years later, NMA President Dr. Walter Younge recommended that the organization join forces with the NAACP to push its activist agenda. The appointment in 1949 of Dr. W. Montague Cobb, an active member of the NAACP's National Medical Committee, as the new editor of the *Journal of the National Medical Association* also signaled a change in the medical society's political stance and its growing connection with the longstanding goals of the civil rights organization.

The NMA's emerging civil rights activism was clearly demonstrated in a 1951 *JNMA* editorial, "Integration Only Practicable Goal," which contended that equal justice for African Americans was impossible under segregation. It urged NMA members "to discard the timid and forced misgivings which many have had in the past about 'moving too fast,' 'being too radical,' or 'attempting the impossible.'" The NMA now contended that black physicians should not be content to function on the periphery of American medicine in segregated institutions, but should demand to be part of its mainstream.[1]

Black medical leaders had come to recognize the limitations of their hospital reform movement and of the establishment of separate black hospitals. In 1940, Dr. John A. Kenney, who ten years earlier had enthusiastically vowed a "Negro Hospital Renaissance," conceded that his promise had been overly optimistic: most black hospitals were struggling simply to keep their doors open. He pointed out that even those that had been accredited were inadequate in their "physical, financial, and professional equipment." "They are simply making the most of an embarrassing situation, and doing the best they can," he observed.[2]

The black hospital movement, however, had been crucial for the survival of the black medical profession in a period of extreme racism and segregation. It had forestalled the feared extinction of the black hospital in the face of mounting accreditation and standardization pressure, and it had enabled black physicians to train and practice at a time when their options were severely restricted. The efforts of the black hospital reformers and the dollars of white philanthropists had produced some improvements in historically black hospitals by World War II. But these changes were limited to only a few institutions. In 1923, approximately 202 black hospitals operated. Only six had internship programs and not one had a residency program. Of the approximately 169 black hospitals that existed in 1929, the American Medical Association (AMA) approved fourteen for internship training and two for residencies; the American College of Surgeons (ACS) accredited only seventeen. By 1944, the number of black hospitals had decreased to 124. The AMA now approved nine of the facilities for internships and seven for residencies; the ACS fully approved twenty-three and provisionally approved three, an undistinguished record at best. In addition, two institutions had won certification for graduate training in surgery or a surgical specialty. The overall number of black hospitals that were recognized by accrediting agencies had increased by 1944, but most facilities still remained unaccredited.[3]

Although the number of approved internship programs at black hospitals declined over two decades, the number of positions offered in the accredited programs had actually increased: between 1929 and

1939 the number of slots grew from 68 to 168. At the same time, however, the number of black medical school graduates declined. Between 1929 and 1938, the annual number of graduates decreased by 50 percent—from 120 to 60—primarily as a result of the Depression. The inadequate number of internships for black physicians had been one of the major factors that prompted the black hospital movement, but the combination of greater opportunities in black hospitals and in some municipal hospitals and fewer graduates largely solved this problem by the 1940s. The surplus of internships created a new dilemma for black hospitals; they now had difficulty filling available positions.[4]

The nearly 40-percent decrease in the number of black hospitals between 1923 and 1944 primarily reflected the closing of small, poorly equipped, unaccredited facilities. These hospitals, for the most part, lacked financial resources, and the Depression hastened their demise. All the black hospitals that had received certification by the national medical organizations had been able to secure external sources of support from either white philanthropies or governmental agencies. This assistance enabled select hospitals to build new facilities, purchase needed equipment, and provide advanced training for their medical staff. Despite the significant improvements at a few hospitals, by World War II most black hospitals remained unchanged by the hospital movement.

The narrow scope of the black hospital movement can be explained by a number of factors. The effectiveness of the National Medical Association and the National Hospital Association was limited. The organizations functioned impressively as advocates for the concerns of black physicians and offered their members the only forum in which they could keep abreast of trends in medical and hospital care. However, the National Hospital Association and the National Medical Association lacked the resources to implement most of their objectives. The muted response of the major white health-care organizations toward the plight of black hospitals also limited the reach of the efforts to improve them. The American Medical Association and the American Hospital Association only gave minimal support to the hospitals. Although both organizations sponsored studies of black hospitals, their activities did not go much beyond surveying the institutions, and they never allocated funds or personnel to help the black institutions.

The rise of integrationism as the predominant strategy for racial advancement and its adoption by organizations that had previously espoused separatism also limited the scope of the black hospital movement. After World War II the NMA joined the NAACP in arguing that a segregated health-care system resulted in the delivery of inferior medical care to black Americans. The organizations charged that a poorly financed black medical ghetto existed, centered around two medical schools, fourteen hospitals with approved teaching programs, and about ninety-eight additional hospitals. They argued that these facilities could not adequately meet the health and professional needs of black people and rejected the establishment of additional separate institutions to address those needs. The NMA and NAACP instead called for the integration of existing hospitals and the building of truly interracial hospitals. The medical civil rights activists vociferously pointed out the detrimental effects of hospital segregation, charging that a segregated health care system contributed to the high cost of medical care because of the expense required to duplicate services. The activists also graphically documented—and widely publicized—the tragic consequences of segregation: the maiming of black patients and the loss of black lives. In the past, such tragedies had been used to advance the development of black hospitals. Those occurrences were now cited to push for the desegregation of medical facilities.[5]

The activists selected the Veterans Administration hospital system as their first target. It was a shrewd choice. Segregation in this federal system especially underscored America's hypocrisy with regard to the rights of African Americans. Approximately 1.2 million black men and women had served valiantly in a war allegedly to defend democracy against Fascism and Nazism, but upon the war's conclusion, they found themselves either segregated in, or barred from many veterans hospitals. Dr. W. Montague Cobb spoke for many African Americans when he remarked, "The Federal Government could give no clearer indication to the Negro that the democracy he fought for in the two World Wars included him, too, than by the elimination of segregated practices in the Veterans Administration system." A year later, Cobb reported that of the 127 Veterans Administration hospitals in operation as of 3 November 1947, twenty-four had separate wards for black patients and nineteen Southern facilities had no accommodations at all for black veterans. The extent of segregation at the remaining eighty-four institutions is unclear because Cobb did not comment on them.[6]

Efforts to desegregate veterans hospitals began shortly after World War II. In October 1945, representatives of civil rights groups and black medical and nursing organizations, including the NAACP, National Association of Colored Graduate Nurses, the NMA, and the Medico-Chirurgical Society of the District of Columbia, met with General Paul R. Hawley, the medical director of the Veterans Administration. The black leaders demanded the complete integration of the agency's hospitals. Progress toward their goal was slow. It took six years for the civil rights activists to score their first victory, and that a limited one. On 6 June 1951, the U.S. House of Representatives rejected, 222–117, a proposal to establish a black veterans hospital at Booker T. Washington's birthplace in Franklin County, Virginia. Some members of Congress probably voted against the bill, not out of civil rights convictions, but simply because it did not have the support of the Veterans Administration. The bureau opposed the measure because it already had a surplus of hospital beds and had encountered difficulties recruiting qualified personnel to staff already existing facilities. In addition, it believed that black veterans were adequately cared for in hospitals in the vicinity of the proposed new one.[7]

The proposal to build the segregated hospital had been sponsored by Representative John E. Rankin (D., Mississippi), chairman of the House Veterans Committee. The congressman argued, as had the black supporters of the Tuskegee Veterans Hospital thirty years earlier, that black ex-servicemen would receive better treatment in a racially exclusive hospital. But sentiments in the black community had changed drastically since the establishment of the facility at Tuskegee. African Americans, buoyed by the successful integration of black nurses into the armed forces during World War II and by President Harry S. Truman's 1948 order desegregating the armed forces, now banded together not to support the construction of a black veterans hospital, but to oppose it. Two black members of the House, Adam Clayton Powell, Jr. (D., New York) and William L. Dawson (D., Illinois) led the floor fight against Rankin's bill. Powell and Dawson argued that the proposal was racially discriminatory and that building a separate hospital would be a large and unnecessary expense. The black community won a more significant battle in 1953 when the Veterans Administration ordered an end to segregation in all its hospitals, including the one at Tuskegee, Alabama. Shortly after this order was issued, white patients were admitted to the hospital. The Tuskegee facility exists to the present day, serving veterans of all races.[8]

At the same time that civil rights activists launched the campaign to integrate, Congress passed the Hill-Burton Act, which in effect, fostered the establishment of additional segregated hospitals. This 1946 legislation, also known as the Hospital Survey and Construction Act, provided federal monies to public and voluntary hospitals for construction. The legislation also made a weak attempt to address the problem of hospital segregation, containing an antidiscrimination clause stipulating that hospitals receiving Hill-Burton funds could not discriminate on the basis of race, creed, or color. However, communities could obtain waivers to this policy if they maintained "separate-but-equal" facilities. Dr. Vane M. Hoge, the white chief of the Division of Hospital Services of the United States Public Health Service, hailed the antidiscrimination and separate-but-equal clauses of the Hill-Burton Act as concrete steps toward improving hospital service for African Americans.[9]

Hoge's optimistic predictions did not convince black medical organizations, who maintained that the act's separate-but-equal clause would encourage the continuation of segregation and inequality in hospital care. Dr. John A. Kenney, editor-in-chief of the *Journal of the National Medical Association*, pointed out that interpretation of the clause was under state, not federal control, and that the act had been championed as a states' rights bill in the Senate by one of its sponsors, Lister Hill (D., Alabama). Kenney further noted that the legislation specifically barred federal regulation of hospital policy. The predictions of black physicians proved correct. Hill-Burton monies were widely used to build racially exclusive hospitals. By March 1964, the program had assisted in the construction of 104 segregated hospitals, 20 black and 84 white. But by increasing federal involvement in hospital care, the Hill-Burton Act, as we shall see, ultimately provided a tool for the chipping away of hospital segregation.[10]

The use of Hill-Burton monies to build segregated hospitals was not without incident. The building of a black hospital in Evanston, Illinois was particularly controversial. It sparked tensions among African Americans centering on the continued necessity of black hospitals. Community Hospital had been founded in 1914 by two black physicians, Drs. Isabelle G. Butler and Elizabeth Hill, to provide hospital service to black residents of Chicago's North Shore. By the early 1950s, conditions at the hospital had so deteriorated that one observer commented, "Albert Schweitzer's hospital in the middle of French Equatorial Africa must be better."[11]

A plan to construct a new facility immediately divided the community. Proponents argued, as they did in Cleveland, that the new hospital would be an interracial institution, rather than a black one, noting that the board of trustees and the medical staff would be biracial. Supporters conceded that most patients would be black, but this, they maintained, reflected residential patterns, not enforced segregation. Opponents countered that residential segregation produced institutional segregation and that Community Hospital *was* a black hospital. They viewed the construction of the new hospital building as a perpetuation of racial segregation and as a ploy to forestall the integration of Evanston Hospital. In spite of this opposition, a new fifty-four bed Community Hospital opened on 5 October 1952.[12]

The controversy provoked by the construction of the hospital in Evanston makes it plain that divisions and ambiguities still persisted in postwar America over the establishment of separate racial institutions. At issue was, once again, whether separate institutions should be tolerated because they met immediate community needs or whether they should be resisted because they prevented the integration of American society. This complex dilemma even affected the NAACP when, in 1951, its Memphis branch endorsed the construction of a black unit at John Gaston Hospital, a municipal facility. The Memphis branch of the civil rights organization argued that the city's black population desperately needed the unit. The national office, however, maintained that "civil rights should prevail over practicalities." It threatened to rescind the local association's charter unless it withdrew its endorsement. The Memphis branch eventually complied with the directive from the national office.[13]

Medical civil rights activists were not to be swayed from their demand that medical facilities and organizations be desegregated. Their actions included grassroots efforts such as the one in Charlotte, North Carolina led by Dr. Reginald Hawkins, a black dentist and an ordained minister. In March 1962, he organized demonstrations at the city's major hospitals to protest their racially discriminatory policies. The pickets' signs included slogans that read "This hospital built on a rock of segregation" and "Is this Christian tradition? Segregated hospitals."[14]

Armed with the precedent set by the 1954 *Brown v. Topeka Board of Education* Supreme Court decision, the medical civil rights activists also began a legal assault on hospital segregation. *Simkins v. Moses H. Cone Memorial Hospital* proved to be the pivotal case. On 12 February 1962—Lincoln's birthday—black physicians, dentists, and patients from Greensboro, North Carolina filed the first suit designed to challenge the separate-but-equal clause of the Hill-Burton Act. They sought to prohibit racially discriminatory practices at Moses H. Cone Memorial Hospital and Wesley Long Community Hospital, voluntary hospitals that had together received $2.8 million in Hill-Burton funds.[15]

The hospitals did openly discriminate in both patient admissions and in staff appointments. Cone Hospital refused to admit any black patients except those who required services not available at L. Richardson Memorial Hospital, a voluntary black institution. Cone and Long excluded black physicians and dentists from their staff, and Long completely barred black patients. The white hospitals maintained that their racial policies "protected" the black institution, and that full integration would force Richardson Hospital to close because patients would not want to use the antiquated facility. The two white hospitals further contended that since Richardson Hospital had also received Hill-Burton funds, the federal mandate for equal provision of hospital service had been met.

In 1961, a group of black physicians and dentists led by Dr. George C. Simkins, a dentist and president of the Greensboro branch of the NAACP, petitioned the hospitals to end their exclusionary policies. The group's request was turned down. The next year, the physicians and dentists brought suit, asking that the separate-but-equal clause of the Hill-Burton Act be declared unconstitutional on the grounds that it violated the due process clause of the Fifth Amendment and the equal protection clause of the Fourteenth Amendment. The Justice Department and the American Public Health Association filed *amicus curiae* briefs on behalf of the plaintiffs. The District Court dismissed the case, ruling that although there was clear evidence of racial discrimination, no state or federal action was involved.[16]

The plaintiffs appealed. On 1 November 1963, the Fourth Circuit Court of Appeals ruled that there *was* evidence of state action and reversed the lower court's decision. It found that voluntary hospitals receiving Hill-Burton funds were instruments of the state because such facilities were integral parts of a state and federal plan to allocate resources effectively for the promotion and maintenance of the public's health. The Court issued an injunction prohibiting the hospitals from discriminatory practices in staff appointments and patient admissions. It also declared the separate-but-equal clause of Hill-Burton Act unconstitutional. Since the Supreme Court refused to hear the case on appeal, the decision of the lower court stood.

The Simkins decision represented a significant victory in the battle for medical civil rights. It extended the principles of the Brown decision to hospitals, including those not publicly owned and operated, although its authority was limited to hospitals receiving Hill-Burton funds. However, a 1964 federal court decision, *Eaton v. Grubbs*, broadened the prohibitions against racial discrimination to include hospitals that did not receive such funds.[17]

The early history of the Eaton case predated that of Simkins. In 1955, three black physicians, Hubert Eaton, Daniel Roane, and Samuel Gray, because of their race were denied courtesy privileges at James Walker Memorial Hospital, a voluntary hospital in Wilmington, North Carolina. At the time, Walker Hospital did not allow African-American physicians to admit their patients. Black physicians admitted their patients to Community Hospital, a black hospital that had a biracial, but predominantly black medical staff. Walker Hospital maintained twenty-five beds for black patients, who had to be admitted by white physicians. The black patients were housed in a wing separate from the main building and had to be taken outdoors, regardless of the weather, in order to receive treatment in some units of the hospital, including the operating room, the delivery room, and the radiology department. In March 1956, the three physicians, joined by two of their patients, filed suit against the hospital, charging, as in Simkins, that the hospital's policies violated the Fifth and Fourteenth Amendments. Walker Hospital, in contrast to the facilities in Greensboro, did not receive Hill-Burton funds. *Eaton v. Grubbs* focused on whether a private, voluntary hospital that did not receive substantial government funding could be defined as an instrument of the state. The hospital argued that it received only a small amount of its revenues from city and county sources, and therefore it should not be considered to be an agent of the state. It held that as a private institution, it could set its own racial policies. The District Court agreed and dismissed the suit in June 1958. Five months later and five years before it decided Simkins, the Fourth Court of Appeals concurred with the lower court. The Supreme Court refused to hear the case.

After the Simkins victory, the plaintiffs resubmitted their suit. In April 1964, the Fourth Court of Appeals reversed its earlier decision. It now found evidence that Walker Hospital was indeed an arm of the state and, therefore, bound to the constitutional restrictions against racial discrimination. As indications of state action, the Court pointed to the hospital's receipt of federal funds prior to the passage of the Hill-Burton Act, its exemption from property taxes, and its allocation of funds from local tax appropriations. In addition, it noted a reverter clause in the hospital's deed stipulating that if the hospital ceased operations, the property must be returned to the city and county. The city and county, in essence, controlled the use of the land on which the hospital sat. The Eaton decision was significant: it broadly defined the links between voluntary hospitals and the state and greatly expanded the prohibitions against hospital discrimination.

The 1964 Civil Rights Act extended these judicial decisions. Title VI of the Act stated:

> No person in the United States shall, on the ground of race, color, or national origin, be excluded from participation in, be denied the benefits of, or be subjected to discrimination under any program or activity receiving federal financial assistance.

In 1965, the Department of Health, Education, and Welfare issued regulations mandating that hospitals had to be in compliance with Title VI in order to be eligible for federal assistance or to participate in any federally assisted program. The 1965 passage of Medicare and Medicaid legislation made virtually all hospitals potential recipients of federal funds and therefore obligated to comply with federal civil rights legislation. However, federal enforcement of these policies often proved lax.[18]

In addition to challenging segregation at hospitals, the medical civil rights activists also targeted the racial policies of medical societies, especially of those in the South. The inability of black physicians to obtain membership in local medical organizations had been used to exclude them from hospital staffs, since membership in the American Medical Association and its local constituent society was often a requirement for a hospital appointment. In 1950, as a result of pressure from black physicians and their white allies, the AMA urged local medical societies to take steps to eliminate racially restrictive membership policies. Most associations in the North had already allowed black physicians to join. By 1956, every Southern state, except Louisiana and North Carolina, had agreed to admit African Americans.[19]

The historically black hospitals had been established to provide medical care and professional training for African Americans within a segregated society. The advances of the civil rights movement raised questions about what role these institutions would play in a desegregated society. In 1965, Dr. Charles D. Watts and Dr. Frank W. Scott, black physicians associated with Durham's Lincoln Hospital, observed, "As we pass from a period of segregation in medical care and medical education, Lincoln and hospitals like it are having to look for new roles to play or run the risk of becoming obsolete."[20]

The historically black hospitals have indeed struggled to find new missions, and most have lost the battle. In the years since the end of legally sanctioned racial segregation, the number of black hospitals has declined sharply. In 1944, 124 black hospitals operated. In 1993, the number was eight and the future for several of them looks grim. The widespread closing of black hospitals prompted Dr. Calvin C. Sampson, assistant editor of *The Journal of the National Medical Association*, to warn in 1974:

> It will be a sad commentary and a blight on all black pioneers in medicine if we allow our black community hospitals to succumb to inaction and expediency. If the trend continues, the black community hospital, as we know it, will become extinct.

As did his medical predecessors in the 1920s and 1930s, Sampson urged black physicians to take active roles to support and save the institutions. For the most part, his advice has gone unheeded and black hospitals have continued to shut their doors, including Durham's Lincoln Hospital in 1976 and Cleveland's Forest City Hospital in 1978.[21]

In their attempts to survive, black hospitals have undergone significant organizational changes through conversions, mergers, and consolidations. Nathaniel Wesley, director of planning at Howard University Hospital, has reported that between 1961 and 1985, fifty-two hospitals closed and thirteen facilities changed their organizational structures. These transitions have often resulted in the loss of the hospitals as independent black institutions. For example, Baltimore's Provident Hospital ceased operations in July 1986. One month later, it reopened, but not as an autonomous black institution. It had merged with Lutheran Hospital to become Liberty Heights Medical Center, which does not consider itself a black hospital. Another is the forthcoming merger of George W. Hubbard Hospital of Meharry Medical College with Metropolitan Nashville General Hospital, a public hospital. As is true with most of the surviving black hospitals, Hubbard Hospital has encountered financial difficulties because of the large amount of free care that it gives to poor people. In a move intended to strengthen the institution, Dr. David Satcher, then president of Meharry Medical College, proposed in 1988 that Meharry/Hubbard consolidate with Metropolitan General Hospital. This action would benefit both the city and the medical college. Plans call for patients to be transferred from the antiquated municipal hospital to Hubbard, a facility built in 1974 but that has never operated at full capacity. Physicians from Meharry would control clinical services at the consolidated hospital; previously, the medical staff at Metropolitan General was dominated by white physicians from Vanderbilt University School of Medicine. Satcher's proposal met with resistance from members of the white community who did not believe that physicians from Meharry could operate the hospital adequately. Supporters of the affiliation contended that racism had prompted the opposition. Whites, they argued, did not want to see a white-dominated institution become a black-dominated one. However, opposition to the merger has been overcome because of financial considerations: the city cannot afford to build a new municipal hospital. The merger of Hubbard Hospital with Nashville Metropolitan General Hospital, expected to be completed in 1995, will surely challenge its status as a black hospital, but will bolster the position of one of the few remaining black medical schools.[22]

The desegregation of medical facilities has been the primary factor accelerating the demise of the historically black hospitals and contributing to the vulnerability of the few that remain. As early as 1967, Hiram Sibley, the Executive Director of the Hospital Planning Council of Metropolitan Chicago, went so far as to proclaim, "The Negro Hospital is dead. The Civil Rights Act killed it." Fifteen years later, Haynes Rice, the former executive director of Howard University Hospital, offered a similar assessment. "Integration provided for the elimination of black institutions," he argued, "the community could not support black institutions *and* integration." Civil rights legislation increased the access of black people to previously white health-care facilities. Consequently, black hospitals faced an ironic dilemma: they now competed for patients with hospitals that had once excluded black patients and professionals.[23]

Many civil rights activists had believed that the integration of medical facilities would be a two-way process: black patients and staffs would integrate white hospitals and white patients and staff would integrate black hospitals. But the physicians soon discovered that their assumptions had been overly optimistic. Integration proved to be a one-way street—out of black hospitals. Where white physicians had once used these facilities to admit and treat their black patients, they abruptly cut their ties. For example, immediately prior to the passage of the 1964 Civil Rights Act, 407 white and 43 black physicians had staff privileges at Atlanta's Hughes Spaulding Pavilion for black patients. After the bill's ratification, 75 percent of the white physicians stopped admitting there.[24]

Black physicians have also abandoned black hospitals over time. Most now train and practice in predominantly white hospitals and are not forced to depend exclusively on black medical institutions. As recently as 1967, approximately 83 percent of the country's 6000 practicing black physicians had obtained their medical education at either Howard or Meharry. Twenty years later, the four predominantly black medical schools awarded only 20 percent of the medical degrees granted to African Americans. Only two of the eight remaining black hospitals, Hubbard and Howard, offer residency training programs. As black physicians have successfully struggled for and gained entry into the mainstream medical profession, black hospitals have become marginal to their careers. Compared to their predecessors, most contemporary black physicians do not have strong allegiances to black medical institutions.[25]

Loss of physician support contributed to declines in both patient admissions and revenues at black hospitals. Civil rights legislation also played a role, making it legally feasible for black patients to receive medical care at previously segregated hospitals. Medicare, Medicaid, and third-party payment have made it economically possible for African Americans to look beyond black institutions for treatment. With the gradual erosion of residential segregation, middle-class patients have moved from the neighborhoods in which black hospitals exist. Black hospitals have become facilities that treat, for the most part, poor people who are uninsured or on Medicaid. The situation has become especially critical as Medicaid reimbursement has fallen farther and farther behind the actual costs of health care. This pattern of decreased physician support, reduced patient occupancy, and diminished patient revenues have forced many black hospitals to close.

One casualty was Chicago's Provident Hospital, the first black-controlled hospital and once the premier black medical institution, which closed in September 1987. Provident's last years belied its rich history. In 1976, the hospital's building—the renovated facility that it had occupied in 1931 when the prospects for affiliation with the University of Chicago seemed bright—had so deteriorated that it was cited by city inspectors for health and safety code violations. Its accommodations and laboratory facilities were also obsolete. These problems prompted the hospital to embark on a fund-raising campaign to build a new 300-bed Provident Hospital, which opened in 1983. The hospital's administration hoped that the modern patient accommodations and up-to-date medical facilities would attract middle-class patients and their physicians. Their expectations were not met: most of the patients whom they had wanted to attract no longer lived in the hospital's historic South Side neighborhood, and Provident had acquired an unenviable reputation as an institution that did not provide quality medical care. The hospital continued to suffer from low occupancy rates and high deficits. In April 1987, Robert T. Smith, Provident's chief operating officer, estimated that 75 percent of the hospital's patients received public medical assistance and another 8 percent did not have any medical insurance at all. Provident Hospital was also plagued by allegations of financial mismanagement and infighting between members of the medical staff and the board of trustees. When the hospital closed five months later it had a census of only eighty-six patients and a $40-million debt. Provident reopened in August 1993, not as an independent black institution, but under the control of a government agency, the Cook County Bureau of Health Services. It is now known as Provident Hospital of Cook County.[26]

The current plight of the historically black hospitals suggests that the gains of the civil rights movement have rendered them obsolete. However, in recent years, African Americans have begun to reassess the value of black-controlled institutions and organizations. Escalating racial tensions, frustration over the unfulfilled dreams of the civil rights movement, and anger over the continued estrangement of African Americans from the country's political and economic systems have prompted the reevaluation. As in the past, a period of black discouragement and growing white hostility has resulted in an increased emphasis on black self-reliance and the importance of black organizations. Advocates of black self-help cover the political spectrum: from black conservatives to the Nation of Islam. Supporters of black hospitals note that the health status of blacks continues to lag behind that of whites, and claim that well-run and fiscally sound black community hospitals could help bridge the gap. These hospitals could develop into research and treatment centers dedicated to diseases that disproportionately affect African Americans, and that function as advocates of black health-care needs.[27]

Many African Americans point out that there is merit in having black-controlled institutions, arguing that these institutions give black people the opportunity to determine the direction of establishments that serve them and provide black professionals with the autonomy and power that they might not have in majority enterprises. For example, in 1951, the National Association of Colored Graduate Nurses (NACGN), voted to disband. From its founding in 1908, the NACGN had viewed itself as a vehicle for professional survival and integration. After black nurses began to gain entry into mainstream nursing organizations, the NACGN disbanded, believing that its activities were no longer needed. The optimism of the black nurses proved to be temporary; black nurses found that institutional racism persisted within the American Nurses' Association (ANA). Very few black women reached leadership positions within the ANA, and the organization failed to acknowledge significantly the contributions of black nurses. Black nurses decided that, in addition to the ANA, they needed another organization to address their professional needs and the health care problems of the African-American community. In 1971, they established the National Black Nurses Association.[28]

Despite these arguments supporting the importance of black-controlled institutions, the future for the historically black hospital remains bleak. The larger institutions, such as the 500-bed Howard University Hospital, are in a better position to survive, but not without a struggle. In 1990, the hospital ran a $13.8-million deficit on its $150-million budget. The following year, financial problems forced the hospital lay off of 218 employees. In an era of cost containment, the financial constraints on all hospitals make small black hospitals even more vulnerable and less competitive. They will be forced to close or merge.[29]

The historically black hospitals have had a significant impact on the lives of African Americans. Originally created to provide health care and education within a segregated society, they evolved to become symbols of black pride and achievement. They supplied medical care, provided training opportunities, and contributed to the development of a black professional class. The hospitals were once crucial for the survival of African Americans, professionally and personally. They have now become peripheral to the lives of most black people and are on the brink of extinction. As was true throughout their history, no consensus exists among black or white Americans as to whether this is a good or bad thing. In this, the debate over the black hospital continues to reflect tensions that remain very much alive in modern America.

Manuscript Collections

Chicago Historical Society, Chicago, Illinois
    Claude Barnett Papers (Microfilm edition)

Cleveland Health Sciences Library, Cleveland, Ohio
    Forest City Hospital Archives

Duke University, Durham, North Carolina
    Duke Endowment Archives
    Watson Smith Rankin Papers

Fisk University Library, Nashville, Tennessee
    Julius Rosenwald Fund Papers

Howard University, Moorland-Spingarn Research Center, Washington, D.C.
    Peter Marshall Murray Papers
    Louis T. Wright Papers

Library of Congress, Washington, D.C.
    National Association for the Advancement of Colored People (NAACP) Papers

National Archives, Suitland, Maryland
    Records of the Bureau of War Risk Insurance, Director's Correspondence File (Director's File)

National Archives, Washington, D.C.
    Records of the Public Building Service, Records of the Consultants on Hospitalization (Consultants' Records)

Ohio Historical Society, Columbus, Ohio
    George A. Myers Papers (Microfilm edition)

Rockefeller Archive Center, Pocantico Hills, North Tarrytown, New York
- General Education Board (GEB) Papers
- Rockefeller Family Papers
- Rockefeller Foundation Archives

Tuskegee University, Hollis Burke Frissell Library, Tuskegee, Alabama
- Robert Russa Moton Papers
- Tuskegee Institute News Clipping File (TCF)

University of Chicago, Regenstein Library, Chicago, Illinois
- Julius Rosenwald Papers
- Harold H. Swift Papers

University of Pennsylvania, University Archives, Philadelphia, Pennsylvania
- Nathan Francis Mossell Papers

Western Reserve Historical Society Library, Cleveland, Ohio
- Charles H. Garvin Papers
- Daniel E. Morgan Papers
- National Association for the Advancement of Colored People (NAACP) Papers
- Urban League Papers

ABBREVIATIONS USED ON NOTES

JAMA — *Journal of the American Medical Association*
JNMA — *Journal of the National Medical Association*

Notes

Introduction

1. "Hospitals and Nurse Training Schools," in *The Negro Year Book and Annual Encyclopedia of the Negro*, ed. Monroe N. Work (Tuskegee Institute, Ala.: Negro Yearbook Co., 1918/19), pp. 424–26; Eugene H. Bradley, "Health, Hospitals, and the Negro," *Modern Hospital* 65 (August 1945): 45. The eight historically black hospitals that were in operation in 1993 are Provident Hospital of Cook County, Chicago, Illinois; Howard University Hospital, Washington, D.C.; Norfolk Community Hospital, Norfolk, Virginia; Newport News General Hospital, Newport News, Virginia; Memorial Hospital of Greensboro (formerly L. Richardson Memorial Hospital), Greensboro, North Carolina; George W. Hubbard Hospital of Meharry Medical College, Nashville, Tennessee; Riverside General Hospital, Houston, Texas; and Richmond Community Hospital, Richmond, Virginia. Provident Hospital is now under the control of the Cook County Bureau of Health Services. A merger of Hubbard Hospital with Metropolitan General Hospital, a public hospital, is expected to be completed in 1995.

2. Steven Shea and Mindy Thompson Fullilove, "Entry of Black and Other Minority Students into U.S. Medical Schools," *New England Journal of Medicine* 313 (1985): 936; and Robert E. Tomasson, "Goals for Racial Inclusion Elude the Latest Crop of Young Doctors," *New York Times*, 1 April 1992, National Edition, p. B7.

3. W.E.B. DuBois, "The Woman's Medical College," *Crisis* 26 (1923): 154.

4. Examples of work that examine the issue of race and American medicine include Darlene Clark Hine, *Black Women in White: Racial Conflict and Cooperation in the Nursing Profession, 1890–1950* (Bloomington: Indiana University Press, 1989); Todd L. Savitt, *Medicine and Slavery: The Diseases and Health Care of Blacks in Antebellum Virginia* (Urbana: Uni-

versity of Illinois Press, 1978); David McBride, *Integrating the City of Medicine: Blacks in Philadelphia Health Care, 1910–1965* (Philadelphia: Temple University Press, 1989); David McBride, *From TB to AIDS: Epidemics Among Urban Blacks Since 1900* (Albany: State University of New York Press, 1991); and Edward H. Beardsley, *A History of Neglect: Health Care for Blacks and Mill Workers in the Twentieth Century South* (Knoxville: University of Tennessee Press, 1987).

5. Charles E. Rosenberg, *The Care of Strangers* (New York: Basic Books, 1987); David Rosner, *A Once Charitable Enterprise: Hospitals and Health Care in Brooklyn and New York, 1885–1915* (Cambridge: Cambridge University Press, 1982); Rosemary Stevens, *In Sickness and In Wealth* (New York: Basic Books, 1989); Morris Vogel, *The Invention of the Modern Hospital: Boston, 1870–1930* (Chicago: University of Chicago Press, 1980); and Virginia G. Drachman, *Hospital with a Heart: Women Doctors and the Paradox of Separatism at the New England Hospital, 1862–1969* (Ithaca, N.Y.: Cornell University Press, 1984).

6. For an analysis of the role of African-American women in health activities see Susan Smith, "'Sick and Tired of Being Sick and Tired': Black Women and the National Negro Health Movement, 1915–1950" (Ph.D. diss., University of Wisconsin—Madison, 1991); Cynthia Neverdon-Morton, *Afro-American Women of the South and the Advancement of the Race, 1895–1925* (Knoxville: University of Tennessee Press, 1989); and Earline Rae Ferguson, "The Woman's Improvement Club of Indianapolis: Black Women Pioneers in Tuberculosis Work, 1903–1938," *Indiana Magazine of History* 84 (1988): 237–61.

7. "Pros and Cons for the Mercy Hospital Association," Clipping, n.d. (circa 1926), Box 3, Garvin Papers.

8. Drachman, *Hospital with a Heart*.

9. Alan M. Kraut, review of *Integrating the City of Medicine: Blacks in Philadelphia Health Care, 1910–1965*, by David McBride, *Bulletin of the History of Medicine* 65 (1991): 146.

1. Roots of the Black Hospital Reform Movement

1. Daniel Hale Williams, "The Need of Hospitals and Training Schools for Colored People in the South," *National Hospital and Sanitarium Record* 3 (April 1900): 4; John A. Kenney, *The Negro in Medicine* (Tuskegee, Ala., 1912), pp. 42–44; "Hospitals and Nurse Training Schools," in *The Negro Year Book and Annual Encyclopedia of the Negro*, ed. Monroe N. Work (Tuskegee Institute, Ala.: Negro Yearbook Co., 1918/19), pp. 424–26.

2. Charles E. Rosenberg, *The Care of Strangers: The Rise of America's Health Care System* (New York: Basic Books, 1987); David Rosner, *A Once Charitable Enterprise: Hospitals and Health Care in Brooklyn and New York, 1885–1915* (Cambridge, U.K.: Cambridge University Press, 1982); Morris Vogel, *The Invention of the Modern Hospital: Boston, 1870–1930* (Chicago: University of Chicago Press, 1980); Harry Dowling, *City Hospitals: The Undercare of the Underprivileged* (Cambridge, Mass.: Harvard

University Press, 1982); and Joan E. Lynaugh, *The Community Hospitals of Kansas City, Missouri, 1870–1915* (New York: Garland Publishing, 1989).

3. James O. Breeden, ed., *Advice Among Masters: The Ideal in Slave Management in the Old South* (Westport, Conn.: Greenwood Press, 1980), p. 183. Studies of plantation medicine include Weymouth T. Jordan, "Plantation Medicine in the Old South," *Alabama Review* 3 (1950): 83–107; Elizabeth Barnaby Keeney, "Unless Powerful Sick: Domestic Medicine in the Old South," in *Science and Medicine in the Old South*, eds. Ronald L. Numbers and Todd L. Savitt (Baton Rouge, La.: Louisiana State University Press), pp. 276–94; William Dosite Postell, *The Health of Slaves on Southern Plantations* (1951; reprint, Gloucester, Mass.: Peter Smith, 1970); Todd L. Savitt, *Medicine and Slavery: The Diseases and Health Care of Blacks in Antebellum Virginia* (Urbana: University of Illinois Press, 1978); Richard Harrison Shryock, "Medical Practice in the Old South," *The South Atlantic Quarterly* 29 (April 1930): 160–78 [reprinted in Shryock, *Medicine in America: Historical Essays* (Baltimore: Johns Hopkins University Press, 1966), pp. 49–70]; and Felice Swados, "Negro Health on the Antebellum Plantation," *Bulletin of the History of Medicine* 10 (1941): 460–72.

4. "Georgia Infirmary," pamphlet celebrating its 100th anniversary, pp. 8–11, copy available at Tuskegee University Archives; "Infirmary for Negroes at Savannah, Geo.," *Charleston Medical Journal and Review* 7 (1852): 724; and Postell, *The Health of Slaves*, p. 140.

5. Charles E. Rosenberg, "And Heal the Sick: Hospital and Patient in Nineteenth Century America," *Journal of Social History* 10 (1977): 432.

6. Paul Skeels Peirce, *The Freedmen's Bureau: A Chapter in the History of Reconstruction* (Iowa City: The University of Iowa, 1904), pp. 87–94; Todd L. Savitt, "Politics in Medicine: The Georgia Freedmen's Bureau and the Organization of Health Care, 1865–66," *Civil War History* 28 (1982): 45–64; Gail S. Hasson, "Health and Welfare of Freedmen in Reconstruction Alabama," *Alabama Review* 35 (1982): 94–110; J. Thomas May "The Louisiana Negro in Transition: An Appraisal of the Medical Activities of the Freedmen's Bureau," *Bulletin of the Tulane University Medical Faculty* 26 (1967): 29–36; Marshall Scott Legan, "Disease and the Freedmen in Mississippi during Reconstruction," *Journal of the History of Medicine* 28 (1973): 257- 67; Gaines M. Foster, "The Limitations of Federal Health Care for Freedmen, 1862–1868," *Journal of Social History* 48 (1982): 350–72; and Alan Raphael, "Health and Social Welfare of Kentucky Black People," *Societas* 2 (1972): 143–57. For information on Freedmen's Hospital see W. Montague Cobb, "A Short History of Freedmen's Hospital," *JNMA* 54 (1962): 271–87; Thomas Holt, Cassandra Smith-Parker, and Rosalyn Terborg-Penn, *A Special Mission: The Story of Freedmen's Hospital, 1862–1962* (Washington, D.C.: Academic Affairs Division, Howard University, 1975); and William A. Warfield, "A Brief History of Freedmen's Hospital," *Freedmen's Hospital Bulletin* 1 (1934): 1–2.

7. Howard N. Rabinowitz, *Race Relations in the Urban South 1865–1890* (Urbana: University of Illinois, 1980), pp. 128–51. "Germs Have No Color Line" served as the slogan for a fund-raising campaign in the 1920s

to create a center for black medical education at Chicago's Provident Hospital. Stuart Galishoff, "Germs Know No Color Line: Black Health and Public Policy in Atlanta, 1900–1918," *Journal of the History of Medicine and Allied Sciences* 40 (1985): 29. For an extensive discussion of the "Negro health problem" see Vanessa Northington Gamble, ed., *Germs Have No Color Line: Blacks and American Medicine, 1900–1940* (New York: Garland Publishing, 1989). Julius Rosenwald Fund, compiled by Harrison L. Harris and Margaret L. Plumley, *Negro Hospitals: A Compilation of Available Statistics* (Chicago: Julius Rosenwald Fund, 1931), p. 15.

8. Ethel Johns, "A Study of the Present Status of the Negro Woman in Nursing, 1925," Exhibit K (Atlanta), pp. K-7–8; Box 122, Record Group 1.1, Series 200C, Rockefeller Foundation Archives; Alice Mabel Bacon, "The Dixie and Its Work," *Southern Workman* 20 (November 1891): 244; Cora M. Folsom, "The Dixie in the Beginning," *Southern Workman* 55 (March 1926): 121–26; Patricia A. Sloan, "Commitment to Equality: A View of Early Black Nursing Schools," in *Historical Studies in Nursing*, ed. Louise Fitzpatrick (New York: Teachers College Press, 1978), p. 76; and Johns, "Negro Woman in Nursing," Exhibit H (Hampton, Virginia), pp. H-1–3.

9. Johns, "Negro Woman in Nursing," Exhibit J (Raleigh, North Carolina), pp. H-1–3; W. Montague Cobb, "St. Agnes Hospital, Raleigh, North Carolina, 1896–1961," *JNMA* 53 (1961): 441–42.

10. Accounts of the founding of the hospital and biographical information on Unthank can be found in Clyde Reed Bradford, "History of Kansas City General Hospital, Colored Division," *Jackson County Medical Journal* 26 (October 8, 1932): 6–15; and in Samuel U. Rodgers, "Kansas City General Hospital, No. 2: A Historical Summary," *JNMA* 54 (1962): 523–44.

11. *Annual Report of the Board of Hospital and Health for the Year Ending April 14, 1909* (Kansas City, Mo.), p. 83.

12. Bradford, "History of Kansas City General Hospital," p. 9.

13. Johns, "Negro Woman in Nursing," Exhibit C (Kansas City, Mo.), p. C-2.

14. W. Montague Cobb, *Medical Care and the Plight of the Negro* (New York: The National Association for the Advancement of Colored People, 1947), pp. 20–29. For histories on the development of the hospital see Homer G. Phillips Hospital, *The History and Development of Homer G. Phillips Hospital* (St. Louis: 1945); H. Phillip Venable, "The History of Homer G. Phillips Hospital," *JNMA* 53 (1961): 541–51; and Frank O. Richards, "The St. Louis Story: The Training of Black Surgeons in St. Louis, Missouri," in *A Century of Black Surgeons: The U.S.A. Experience*, eds. Claude H. Organ, Jr. and Margaret Kosiba (Norman, Okla.: Transcript Press, 1987), pp. 197–247.

15. August Meier, *Negro Thought in America 1880–1915: Racial Ideologies in the Age of Booker T. Washington* (Ann Arbor: University of Michigan Press, 1966); Herbert Shapiro, *White Violence and Black Response: From Reconstruction to Montgomery* (Amherst: University of Massachusetts Press, 1988); Allan H. Spear, *Black Chicago: The Making of a Negro Ghetto, 1890–1920* (Chicago: University of Chicago Press, 1967); and St. Clair Drake and Horace R. Cayton, *Black Metropolis*, rev. ed. (New York: Harper and

Row, 1962). For discussions of the self-help tradition in the African-American community see Richard W. Thomas, "The Historical Roots of Contemporary Urban Black Self-Help in the United States," in *Contemporary Urban America: Problems, Issues, and Alternatives*, ed. Marvel Lang (Lanham, Maryland: University Press of America, 1991), pp. 253–91; and Lenwood G. Davis, "The Politics of Black Self-Help in the United States: An Historical Overview," in *Black Organizations: Issues on Survival Techniques* (Washington, D.C.: University Press of America, 1980), pp. 37–50.

16. Rosenberg, *The Care of Strangers*, p. 346. For analyses of the transformation of the American hospital and the rise of scientific medicine see George Rosen, "The Impact of the Hospital on the Physician, the Patient, and the Community," *Hospital Administration* 9 (Fall 1964): 15–33; Rosemary Stevens, *In Sickness and in Wealth* (New York: Basic Books, 1989); Paul Starr, *The Social Transformation of American Medicine* (New York: Basic Books, 1982); Rosenberg, *The Care of Strangers*; Rosner, *A Once Charitable Enterprise*; and Vogel, *The Invention of the Modern Hospital.*

17. For tables providing statistics on the number of black physicians see Todd L. Savitt, "Entering a White Profession: Black Physicians in the New South, 1880–1920," *Bulletin of the History of Medicine* 61 (1987): 510–11.

18. W.E.B. DuBois, *The Philadelphia Negro: A Social Study* (1899; reprint, New York: Schocken, 1967), p. 113.

19. Darlene Clark Hine, *Black Women in White: Racial Conflict and Cooperation in the Nursing Profession, 1890–1950* (Bloomington: Indiana University Press, 1989). For extensive discussions of the professionalization of nursing see Barbara Melosh, *The Physician's Hand: Work Culture and Conflict in American Nursing* (Philadelphia: Temple University Press, 1982); and Susan M. Reverby, *Ordered to Care: The Dilemma of American Nursing, 1850–1945* (Cambridge: Cambridge University Press, 1987).

20. "Proceedings of the Imhotep National Conference on Hospital Integration," *JNMA* 49 (1957): 197; Eugene B. Elder, "The Management of the Race Question in Hospitals," *Transactions of the American Hospital Association* 9 (1907): 128; and "Carson's Private Hospital, Washington, D.C.," *JNMA* 22 (1930): 148.

21. H.M. Green, *A More or Less Critical Review of the Hospital Situation Among Negroes in the United States*, n.d. (circa 1930), pp. 4–5; and *Third Annual Report of the Frederick Douglass Memorial Hospital and Training School* (Philadelphia: The Hospital, 1898), p. 9. The annual reports of Douglass Hospital are available at The Library of the College of Physicians of Philadelphia. Thomas Wallace Swan, "Pennsylvania's Memorial to Frederick Douglass," *Howard's Magazine* 4 (October 1899): 6. For more information on medical experimentation on slaves see Savitt, *Medicine and Slavery*, pp. 281–307; Savitt, "The Use of Blacks for Medical Experimentation and Demonstration in the Old South," *Journal of Southern History* 48 (1982): 819–27; Diana E. Axelsen, "Women as Victims of Medical Experimentation: J. Marion Sims' Surgery on Slave Women, 1845–1850," *Sage* 2 (Fall 1985): 10–13; David C. Humphrey, "Dissection and Discrimination: The Social Origins of Cadavers in America, 1760–1915," *Bulletin of the New*

York Academy of Medicine 49 (1973): 819–27; and F. N. Boney, "Slaves as Guinea Pigs: Georgia and Alabama Episodes," *Alabama Review* 37 (1984): 45–51.

22. Rosenberg, *The Care of Strangers*, p. 112.

23. Meier, *Negro Thought*; and Louis R. Harlan, *Booker T. Washington: The Wizard of Tuskegee, 1901–1915* (New York: Oxford University Press, 1983).

24. John A. Kenney, "Home Infirmary, Clarksville, Tennessee" and "Fair Haven Infirmary," in *The Negro in Medicine* (Tuskegee, Alabama: 1912), pp. 47–48.

25. Accounts of the founding of Provident Hospital and biographical information on its founder can be found in Cassius Ellis, "Daniel Hale Williams, M.D., F.A.C.S.," in *A Century of Black Surgeons*, pp. 311–332; Helen Buckler, *Daniel Hale Williams: Negro Surgeon*, 2nd ed. (New York: Pitman, 1968); W. Montague Cobb, "Daniel Hale Williams, M.D., 1858–1931," *JNMA* 45 (1953): 379–85; Ulysses Grant Dailey, "Daniel Hale Williams: Pioneer Surgeon and Father of Negro Hospitals" (Paper presented at the meeting of the National Hospital Association, Chicago, Illinois, 18 August 1941), Provident Medical Center, Chicago, Illinois; Henry B. Matthews, "Provident Hospital Then and Now," *JNMA* 53 (1961): 209–24; Theresita Norris, "An Historical Account of Provident Hospital," Chicago Medical Society, unpublished, n.d. (circa 1940), State Historical Society of Wisconsin, Madison, Wisconsin; and Rayford W. Logan and Michael R. Winston, eds., *Dictionary of American Negro Biography* (New York: W.W. Norton, 1982), pp. 654–56. For a general history of Chicago medicine see Thomas Neville Bonner, *Medicine in Chicago, 1850–1950*, 2nd ed. (Urbana: University of Illinois Press, 1991).

26. Susan Lynn Smith, "The Black Women's Club Movement: Self-Improvement and Sisterhood, 1890–1915" (M.A. thesis, University of Wisconsin, 1986), pp. 79–100; and Buckler, *Daniel Hale Williams*, pp. 70–73.

27. Williams, "Need of Hospitals," p. 7.

28. Ibid., p. 4.

29. Norris, "Provident Hospital," p. 3; Robert McMurdy to William C. Graves, 30 December 1912, Rosenwald Papers, cited in Spear, *Black Chicago*, p. 98.

30. Williams did not perform the first successful open-heart surgery, as has often been stated. His 1893 operation on the pericardium followed, by two years, that of the St. Louis physician H.C. Dalton. See C. Walton Lillehei, "Invited Commentary," in *A Century of Black Surgeons*, pp. 332–34. McMurdy to Graves, 30 December 1912, cited in Spear, *Black Chicago*, p. 98.

31. Norris, "An Historical Account," p. 5; and Spear, *Black Chicago*, pp. 99, 141. The classic study of black social development in Chicago is Drake and Cayton, *Black Metropolis*. See also Spear, *Black Chicago*.

32. Buckler, *Daniel Hale Williams*, pp. 175–76; and Spear, *Black Chicago*, pp. 72–73, 99–100. For biographical information on Hall see Spear, *Black Chicago*, pp. 72–73; Buckler, *Daniel Hale Williams*, p. 77; "Some Chicagoans of Note," *Crisis*, 10 (September 1915): 241; "Doctor George C.

Hall," *JNMA* 14 (1922): 216; and John W. Lawlah, "George Cleveland Hall, 1864–1930: A Profile," *JNMA* 46 (1954): 207–10.

33. Spear, *Black Chicago*, pp. 51–89; and Charles Bentley to Julius Rosenwald, 16 October 1917, Rosenwald Papers, cited in Spear, *Black Chicago*, p. 174.

34. Dailey, "Daniel Hale Williams," p. 2; and Lawlah, "George Cleveland Hall," p. 208.

35. Nathan Francis Mossell, "Biographical Sketch," unpublished manuscript, n.d. (circa 1946), p. 7, Mossell Papers. When the author used these papers, the manuscripts were in the possession of Dr. Mossell's granddaughter, Mrs. Gertrude Cunningham. However, the papers have now been deposited in the University of Pennsylvania Archives. For additional information about Mossell and the founding of Douglass Hospital see W. Montague Cobb, "Nathan Francis Mossell, M.D., 1856–1946," *JNMA* 46 (1954): 118–30; Edward S. Cooper, "Mercy-Douglass Hospital: Historical Perspective," *JNMA* 53 (1961): 1–7; Elliot M. Rudwick, "A Brief History of Mercy-Douglass Hospital in Philadelphia," *Journal of Negro Education* 20 (Winter 1951): 50–66; and Rayford W. Logan and Michael R. Winston, eds., *Dictionary of American Negro Biography* (New York: W.W. Norton, 1972), pp. 457–58.

36. Mossell, "Biographical Sketch," p. 15.

37. Ibid., p. 16; and Cobb, "Mossell," p. 122.

38. Cobb, "Mossell," p. 118.

39. *Seventh Annual Report of the Frederick Douglass Memorial Hospital and Training School* (Philadelphia: The Hospital, 1902), p. 12. The hospital's annual reports are available at the Library of the College of Physicians of Philadelphia. Swan, "Pennsylvania's Memorial," p. 4; and Alfred Gordon, "Frederick Douglass Memorial Hospital and Training School," in *Philadelphia—World's Greatest Medical Centre* (Philadelphia, n.d.), p. 59. The group that met to organize the hospital included Rev. R. Heywood Stitt, pastor, Zion Wesley AME Church; Jacob C. White, Jr., retired principal, Robert Vaux Grammar School; Rev. Matthew Anderson, pastor, Berean Presbyterian Church and founder of Berean Building and Loan Association; Rev. L.G. Jordan, pastor, Union Baptist Church; S.J.M. Brock, a leading black businessman; Dr. William A. Jackson, a dental surgeon; P.A. Dutreuille, caterer; Aaron A. Mossell, attorney and youngest brother of the physician; Mrs. Bishop B.T. Tanner, the widow of Bishop Tanner of the AME Church; Henry M. Minton, a pharmacist, and Alma G. Sommerville, a volunteer in many charitable causes.

40. Roger Lane, *William Dorsey's Philadelphia & Ours: On the Past and Future of the Black City in America* (New York: Oxford University Press, 1991), p. 181.

41. Nathan Francis Mossell, "Frederick Douglass Memorial Hospital," unpublished manuscript, n.d. (circa 1946), p. 3, Mossell Papers.

42. DuBois, *The Philadelphia Negro*, p. 230; "A Fair Question," *The Weekly Tribune*, 7 September 1895, n.p.; "That Hospital," *The Weekly Tribune*, 21 September 1895; and clipping from *Weekly Tribune*, n.d. All the newspaper articles are contained in scrapbooks owned by Dr. Mossell, and are among the Mossell Papers.

43. *Second Annual Report of the Frederick Douglass Memorial Hospital and Training School* (Philadelphia: The Hospital, 1897). The information on the early history of the hospital, except where noted, was obtained from the hospital's annual reports from 1896 to 1904, not including 1899, which were not in the collection at the College of Physicians of Philadelphia.

44. "A Hospital for Colored People," *Colored American* (Washington, D.C.), 7 September 1895, n.p., Mossell Scrapbooks; and *Fifth Annual Report of the Frederick Douglass Memorial Hospital and Training School* (Philadelphia: The Hospital, 1900), p. 13.

45. *Fifth Annual Report*, p. 13.

46. *Eighth and Ninth Annual Report of the Frederick Douglass Memorial Hospital and Training School* (Philadelphia: The Hospital, 1903–1904), p. 16; and *Seventh Annual Report of the Frederick Douglass Memorial Hospital and Training School* (Philadelphia: The Hospital, 1902), p. 12.

47. *Eighth and Ninth Annual Report*, p. 16; *Seventh Annual Report*, p. 12; and *First Annual Report*, pp. 10–12.

48. Mossell, "Douglass Hospital," p. 15.

49. "Dr. N.F. Mossell, Chief of Staff Asked to Resign His Place," *The Weekly Tribune*, 21 January 1905, n.p., Mossell Scrapbooks, Mossell Papers.

50. *First Annual Report*, p. 14; Stevens, *In Sickness and in Wealth*, p. 53; and Cobb, "Mossell," p. 21.

51. "Friends of Douglass Hospital Rallying To Aid It," *Weekly Tribune*, January 1903, n.p.; "Dr. N.F. Mossell, Chief of Staff Asked to Resign Place," *Weekly Tribune*, 21 January 1905, n.p.; and "Dr. Mossell Not Responsible," *Courant*, 4 February 1905, n.p., Mossell Scrapbooks, Mossell Papers.

52. Nathan Francis Mossell, "The Modern Hospital: Its Construction, Organization, and Management," *JNMA* 1 (1909): 98.

53. Cobb, "Mossell," pp. 124–25; and "Colored Physicians Start A New Hospital," *Weekly Tribune*, 31 March 1906, n.p., Mossell Scrapbooks, Mossell Papers.

54. Harold E. Farmer, "An Account of the Earliest Colored Gentlemen in Medical Science in the United States," *Bulletin of the History of Medicine* 8 (1940): 615. After years of struggling independently, Mercy Hospital and Douglass Hospital merged in 1949 to form Mercy-Douglass Hospital.

55. Nathan Francis Mossell, "An Institution That's Doing A Great Job," *Christian Banner*, 13 April 1906, n.p., Mossell Scrapbooks, Mossell Papers.

56. John A. Kenney, "Hospitals and Nurse Training Schools, Etc.," in his *The Negro in Medicine* (Tuskegee, 1912), pp. 42–44; Monroe N. Work, ed., "Hospitals and Nurse Training Schools," in *The Negro Year Book and Annual Encyclopedia of the Negro* (Tuskegee Institute, Ala.: Negro Year Book Co., 1912), pp. 155–57, and 1921–1922 pp. 370–72. The exact number of black hospitals is unclear. Kenney listed 144 for 1922. Both authors listed hospitals and training schools without distinguishing between the institutions. Therefore, the estimate for the number of hospitals may be high.

57. "Editorial," *JNMA* 1 (April–June 1909): 105.

58. Peter Marshall Murray, "Memoirs—Clinic" (March 1954), p. 1, Box 6, Murray Papers.

59. Todd L. Savitt, "Entering a White Profession," p. 532.

60. For extensive discussion of hospital standardization see Edward T. Morman, ed., *Efficiency, Scientific Management, and Hospital Standardization* (New York: Garland Publishing, 1989); Stevens, *In Sickness and in Wealth*, pp. 52–79.

61. Rosemary Stevens, *American Medicine and the Public Interest* (New Haven: Yale University Press, 1971), p. 118. For additional information on the Flexner Report and its impact on medical education see Kenneth M. Ludmerer, *Learning to Heal: The Development of American Medical Education* (New York: Basic Books, 1985); Barbara Barzansky and Norman Gevitz, eds., *Beyond Flexner: Medical Education in the Twentieth Century* (New York: Greenwood Press, 1992); Robert P. Hudson, "Abraham Flexner in Perspective: American Medical Education, 1865–1910," *Bulletin of the History of Medicine* 56 (1972): 545–61; and Howard Berliner, "A Larger Perspective on the Flexner Report," *International Journal of Health Services* (1975): 573–92.

62. Isabella Vanderwall, "Some Problems of the Colored Woman Physician," *The Woman's Medical Journal* 27 (1917): 156–58.

63. Roscoe C. Giles to Peter Marshall Murray, 1 March 1931, Box 5, Murray Papers; W. Montague Cobb, "Roscoe Conkling Giles, M.D., F.A.C.S., F.I.C.S., 1890–1970," *JNMA* 62 (1930): 254–56; Fitzhugh Mullan, *White Coat, Clenched Fist: The Political Education of an American Physician* (New York: Macmillan, 1976), pp. 117–21; and Johns, "The Negro Woman in Nursing," Exhibit K (Atlanta), pp. K-2–3.

64. Cobb, "Mossell," pp. 125–27; Gordon, "Frederick Douglass Memorial Hospital," p. 60; Mossell, "Douglass Hospital," pp. 17–26; and "Racial 'Jim Crow' Inspired Douglass," *Philadelphia Tribune*, 8 August 1936, p. 1.

65. Johns, "Negro Woman in Nursing," Exhibit E (Philadelphia), pp. E-8–9; and Mossell, "Douglass Hospitals," p. 26. Mossell's comment on selling one's birthright for a mess of pottage is a Biblical allusion. It refers to Esau's selling his birthright to his brother Jacob (Genesis, XXV, 29–34).

2. At the Vanguard: The National Medical Association and the National Hospital Association

1. H.M. Green, "Annual Address of the President of the National Medical Association," *JNMA* 14 (1922): 216; and "The National Hospital Association," ed., *JNMA* 17 (1925): 207. The ten schools that existed in 1900 were Howard University, Washington, D.C.; Meharry Medical College, Nashville, Tennessee; Leonard Medical College of Shaw University, Raleigh, North Carolina; Louisville National Medical College, Louisville, Kentucky; Flint Medical College of New Orleans University, New Orleans, Louisiana; Chattanooga National Medical College, Chattanooga, Tennessee; State University Medical Department, Louisville, Kentucky; Knoxville Medical College, Knoxville, Tennessee; University of West Tennessee College of Medicine and Surgery, Jackson, Tennessee; Medico-Chirurgical and Theological

College of Christ's Institution, Baltimore, Maryland. By 1923, only Howard and Meharry remained. See Todd L. Savitt, "Abraham Flexner and the Black Medical Schools," in *Beyond Flexner: Medical Education in the Twentieth Century*, eds. Barbara Barzansky and Norman Gevitz (New York: Greenwood Press, 1992), p. 67. For further information on the history of black medical education see James L. Curtis, "Historical Perspectives," in his *Blacks, Medical Schools, and Society* (Ann Arbor: University of Michigan Press, 1971), pp. 1–27; Darlene Clark Hine, "The Pursuit of Professional Equality: Meharry Medical College, 1921–38, A Case Study," in *New Perspectives on Black Educational History*, eds. Vincent P. Franklin and James D. Anderson (Boston: G. K. Hall, 1978), pp. 173–92; Hine, "The Anatomy of Failure: Medical Education Reform and the Leonard Medical School of Shaw University, 1882–1920," *Journal of Negro Education* 54 (1985): 512–25; Leonard W. Johnson, "History of the Education of Negro Physicians," *Journal of Medical Education* 42 (1967): 439–46; Herbert M. Morais, *The History of the Negro in Medicine* (New York: Publishers' Company, 1967), pp. 39–48; Savitt, "The Education of Black Physicians at Shaw University, 1882–1918," in *Black Americans in North Carolina and the South*, eds. Jeffrey J. Crow and Flora J. Hatley (Chapel Hill: University of North Carolina Press, 1984), pp. 160–88; Savitt, "Lincoln University Medical Department—A Forgotten 19th Century Black Medical School," *Journal of the History of Medicine and Allied Sciences* 40 (1985): 42–65; and James Summerville, *Educating Black Doctors: A History of Meharry Medical College* (University, Alabama: University of Alabama Press, 1983).

2. Miles V. Lynk, *Sixty Years of Medicine: Or the Life and Times of Dr. Miles V. Lynk* (Memphis: Twentieth Century Press, 1951); Herbert Morais, *The History of the Negro in Medicine* (New York: Publishers Company for the Association for the Study of Negro Life and History, 1967), pp. 64–65; and Abraham Flexner, *Medical Education in the United States and Canada: A Report to the Carnegie Foundation for the Advancement of Teaching*, Bulletin no. 4 (New York: Carnegie Foundation for the Advancement of Teaching, 1910), p. 305.

3. "National Medical Association," *JNMA* 14 (1922): 255; John A. Kenney, "Some Notes on the History of the National Medical Association," *JNMA* 25 (1933): 97–105; Monroe N. Work, ed., "Medical Organizations," in *The Negro Year Book and Annual Encyclopedia of the Negro* (Tuskegee Institute, Alabama: Negro Yearbook Co., 1914/15): 335–38; W. Montague Cobb, "The Black American in Medicine," *JNMA* supplement 73 (1981): 1225. For information on the history of the Medico-Chirurgical Society of the District of Columbia see W. Montague Cobb, *The First Negro Medical Society* (Washington, D.C.: Associated Publishers, 1939); and Herbert W. Nickens, "A Case of Professional Exclusion in 1870," *Journal of the American Medical Association* 253 (1985): 2549–52.

4. "Report of Committee on Medical Education on Colored Hospitals," *JNMA* 2 (1910): 283–91.

5. "National Hospital Association," *JNMA* 15 (1923): 286–87.

6. John A. Kenney, "The National Hospital Association," *Southern Workman* 56 (February 1927): 62.

7. W.T. Sanger to Robert A. Lambert, 7 March 1935, Box 696, GEB Papers; Lambert to Sanger, 12 March 1935, Box 696, General Education Board (GEB) Papers; W. Montague Cobb, "Peter Marshall Murray, M.D., 1888–," *JNMA* 59 (1967): 71–74; "The President–Elect," *JNMA* 23 (1931): 36; and Rayford W. Logan and Michael R. Winston, eds., *Dictionary of American Negro Biography* (New York: W. W. Norton, 1982) 465–67.

8. Peter Marshall Murray, "Hospital Provision for the Negro Race," *Bulletin of the American Hospital Association* 4 (1930): 44.

9. "The President–Elect," *JNMA* 24 (1932): 40–41; Logan and Winston, *Dictionary of American Negro Biography*, pp. 51–52; and Peter Marshall Murray, "Midian O. Bousfield, M.D., 1885–1948," *JNMA* 40 (1948): 120.

10. M.O. Bousfield, "Reaching the Negro Community," *American Journal of Public Health* 24 (1934): 211.

11. John A. Kenney, "In Memoriam: Dr. H.M. Green," *JNMA* 31 (1939): 225; and Flexner, *Medical Education in the United States and Canada*, pp. 303–4.

12. H.M. Green, "A More or Less Critical Review of the Hospital Situation Among Negroes in the United States," n.d. (circa 1930), p. 14.

13. W. Montague Cobb, "John A. Kenney, M.D., 1874–1950," *JNMA* 42 (1950): 175–77; John A. Kenney, "Kenney Memorial Hospital," *JNMA* 22 (1930): 156–57; John A. Kenney," "The Negro Hospital Renaissance," *JNMA* 22 (1930): 109–112; and Community Hospital, Newark, New Jersey, "Historical Sketch of the Community Hospital," June 1939, p.5.

14. L.A. West, "Presidential Address to the National Medical Association," *JNMA* 22 (1930): 176; and U. G. Dailey, "The Future of the Negro in Medicine," *JNMA* 21 (1929): 116.

15. "National Hospital Association," *JNMA* 15 (1923): 286; Julius Rosenwald Fund, compiled by Harrison L. Harris and Margaret L. Plumley, *Negro Hospitals: A Compilation of Available Statistics* (Chicago: Julius Rosenwald Fund, 1931), p. 16; "Investigation of Negro Hospitals," *Journal of the American Medical Association* 92 (1929): 1375–76; Julius Rosenwald Fund Minutes, 16 November 1929, Box 2 (Addenda), Rosenwald Papers; and Numa P.G. Adams, "An Interpretation of the Significance of the Homer G. Phillips Hospital," *JNMA* 26 (1934): 15. The exact number of black hospitals in 1929 is not known. The Rosenwald report listed 122 and, in the latter study, Dr. Algernon B. Jackson surveyed 120 institutions. Only seventy-three hospitals appeared on both lists.

16. Julius Rosenwald Fund, *Negro Hospitals*, p. 15; Numa P.G. Adams, "The Fifth Year Training of the Negro Medical Student," *JNMA* 24 (1932): 28.

17. For comprehensive studies of black nurses see Darlene Clark Hine, *Black Women in White: Racial Conflict and Cooperation in the Nursing Profession, 1890–1950* (Bloomington: Indiana University Press, 1989); and Mary Elizabeth Carnegie, *The Path We Tread: Blacks in Nursing, 1854–1984* (Philadelphia: J.B. Lippincott Co., 1986).

18. Ethel Johns, "A Study of the Present Status of the Negro Woman in Nursing, 1925," (p. 23 for the quotation), Box 122, Record Group 1.1, Series 200C, Rockefeller Foundation Archives; H. M. Green, "Annual Address to the National Hospital Association," *JNMA* 21 (1929): 173; and

Johns, "Negro Woman in Nursing," Exhibit O (Nashville, Tennessee), pp. O–10. For an analysis of the Johns report see Darlene Clark Hine, "The Ethel Johns Report: Black Women in the Nursing Profession, 1925," *Journal of Negro History* 67 (Fall 1982): 212–28.

19. Carter Godwin Woodson, *The Negro Professional Man and the Community* (1934; reprint ed., New York: Negro Universities Press, 1969), p. 121; and Algernon B. Jackson, "Public Health and the Negro," *JNMA* 15 (1923): 258.

20. G.S. Moore to L.H. Wood, 23 January 1930, Box 7, Murray Papers.

21. L.H. Allyn to L.H. Wood, 28 January 1930, Box 7, Murray Papers.

22. "Juliette Derricotte: Her Character and Her Martyrdom," *Crisis* (March 1932): 84–87.

23. Walter F. White, *A Man Called White* (New York: Viking Press, 1948), pp. 134–38.

24. Charles S. Johnson, "Negro Health in the Light of Vital Statistics," *Proceedings of the National Conference of Social Work* 55 (1928): 173–75; Eugene Kinckle Jones, "Some Fundamental Factors in Regard to the Health of the Negro," *Proceedings of the National Conference of Social Work* 55 (1928): 176–78; H.M. Green, "Hospitals and Public Health Facilities for Negroes," *Proceedings of the National Conference of Social Work* 55 (1928): 179; and H.M. Green, "The Annual Address to the National Hospital Association," *JNMA* 21 (1929): 169–74.

25. Green, "Annual Address of the President of the National Medical Association," p. 216; "National Hospital Association," *JNMA* 15 (1923): 286; and Rosenwald Fund, *Negro Hospitals*, p. 15.

26. "National Hospital Association, Minutes of the Third Annual Session," *JNMA* 17 (1925): 231.

27. John A. Ward, "Hospitals," *JNMA* 19 (1927): 61; and Henry M. Minton, "Some of the Problems of Hospital Administration," *JNMA* 20 (1928): 71.

28. H.M. Green, "The Hospital Survey," *JNMA* 21 (1929): 14; and Murray, "Hospital Provision for the Negro Race," p. 44.

29. "National Hospital Association, Third Annual Meeting," *JNMA* 18 (1926): 152; "National Hospital Association," *JNMA* 19 (1927): 134–5; E.B. Perry, "Are We Conscious for Better Hospitals," editorial, *JNMA* 27 (1935): 166; and "National Hospital Association, Minutes of the Seventh Annual Session," *JNMA* 22 (1930): 227–28.

30. H.M. Green, "The Hospital Survey," *JNMA* 21 (1929): 13–14; H.M. Green, "President's Address: The National Hospital Association," *JNMA* 19 (1927): 16–21; and "Investigation of Negro Hospitals," pp. 1375–76.

31. H.M. Green, "President's Address: The National Hospital Association," *JNMA* 19 (1927): 16–21.

32. "Investigation of Negro Hospitals," p. 1375.

33. Ibid., p. 1375.

34. William H. Walsh, "Report of the Committee on Hospitalization of Colored People," *Transactions of the American Hospital Association* 32 (1930): 53–61 (Quote, p. 57).

35. American Hospital Association, "Report of the Board of Trustees, 28 September 1931," *Transactions of the American Hospital Association* 33 (1931): 33–38.

36. W.S. Rankin to M.M. Davis, 30 November 1931, Box 2, Rankin Papers.

37. H.M. Green to P.M. Murray, 18 March 1932, Box 10, Murray Papers; "Three Hospitals—Frederick Douglass Memorial Hospital and Training School; Wheatley-Provident Hospital; General Hospital, No. 2." *JNMA* 22 (1930): 155; W. Montague Cobb, "John Edward Perry, M.D.," *JNMA* 48 (1956): 292–96; Martin Kaufman, Stuart Galishoff, and Todd L. Savitt, eds., *Dictionary of American Medical Biography*, 2 vols. (Westport, Conn.: Greenwood Press, 1985), 2: 592; "National Hospital Association, Program of the Ninth Annual Session," *JNMA* 25 (1933): 28; and "National Hospital Association, Minutes of the Twelfth Annual Session," *JNMA* 27 (1935): 89. For more information on the life of Dr. J. Edward Perry see John Edward Perry, *Forty Cords of Wood: Memoirs of a Medical Doctor* (Jefferson City, Mo.: Lincoln University Press, 1947).

38. "National Hospital Association, Minutes of the Third Annual Session," p. 230; "National Hospital Association, Minutes of the Fourth Annual Meeting of the National Hospital Association," *JNMA* 20 (1928): 206; "National Hospital Association, Minutes of the Sixth Annual Session," *JNMA* 21 (1929): 207; "National Hospital Association, Minutes of the Seventh Annual Session," *JNMA* 22 (1930): 231; "Atlanta: What Next?" *JNMA* 73 (1931): 171; "National Hospital Association, Minutes of the Eighth Annual Meeting," *JNMA* 23 (1931): 189; and John A. Kenney, "Meeting of the National Hospital Association, Chicago, Illinois, August 13–14, 1933," *JNMA* 25 (1933): 84.

39. E.B. Perry, "Are We Conscious For Better Hospitals?", editorial, *JNMA* 27 (1935): 166; H.M. Green, "Annual Address to the National Hospital Association," *JNMA* 21 (1929): 171; and M.O. Bousfield to P.M. Murray, n.d. (circa 1932), Box 4, Murray Papers.

40. "Minutes of the Trustee Board Meeting," *JNMA* 34 (1942): 128; "National Conference of Hospital Administrators," *JNMA* 36 (1944): 31; and "National Conference of Hospital Administrators," *JNMA* 36 (1944): 68–69.

41. M.O. Bousfield, "Program for Negro Health," 9 October 1936, Box 76, Rosenwald Fund Papers.

42. The racial ideology of the National Hospital Association and the National Medical Association is detailed in H.M. Green, "President's Address: The National Hospital Association," *JNMA* 19 (1927): 16–21; H.M. Green, "Annual Address of H.M. Green, M.D., President National Hospital Association," *JNMA* 22 (1930): 191–93; John A. Kenney, "Why the Community Hospital?" in *Historical Sketch of the Community Hospital* (Newark: The Hospital, 1939), p. 5; W.H. Miller, "What is Ours, We Should Conserve," *JNMA* 24 (August 1932): 30–34; Peter Marshall Murray, "National Medical Association," *JNMA* 18 (1926): 138–39; and "Our Hospital Problems," *JNMA* 21 (1929): 114–16 (Quote, p. 116). An extensive discussion of black political ideology can be found in August Meier, *Negro Thought*

in America 1880–1915: Racial Ideologies in the Age of Booker T. Washington (Ann Arbor: University of Michigan, 1966); Herbert Shapiro, *White Violence and Black Response: From Reconstruction to Montgomery* (Amherst: University of Massachusetts Press, 1988); Allan H. Spear, *Black Chicago: The Making of a Negro Ghetto, 1890–1920* (Chicago: University of Chicago Press, 1967); and St. Clair Drake and Horace R. Cayton, *Black Metropolis,* rev. ed. (New York: Harper and Row, 1962). For discussions of the self-help tradition in the African-American community see Richard W. Thomas, "The Historical Roots of Contemporary Urban Black Self-Help in the United States," in *Contemporary Urban America: Problems, Issues, and Alternatives,* ed. Marvel Lang (Lanham, Maryland: University Press of America, 1991), pp. 253–91; and Lenwood G. Davis, "The Politics of Black Self-Help in the United States: An Historical Overview," in *Black Organizations: Issues on Survival Techniques* ed. Lennox S. Yearwood (Washington, D.C.: University Press of America, 1980), pp. 37– 50.

43. Peter Marshall Murray to Walter White, 10 June 1932, Box 7, Murray Papers; and Meier, *Negro Thought,* p. 8.

44. Midian O. Bousfield, "Presidential Address," *JNMA* 26 (1934): 155; and Peter Marshall Murray, "Hospital Provision for the Negro Race," *Bulletin of the American Hospital Association* 4 (1930): 44.

45. Midian O. Bousfield, "Presidential Address," *JNMA* 26 (1934): 155; Murray, "Hospital Provision for the Negro Race," p. 44; H.M. Green, "A More or Less Critical Review of the Hospital Situation Among Negroes in the United States," n.d. (circa 1930), p. 8; Aubre de L. Maynard, *Surgeons to the Poor: The Harlem Hospital Story* (New York: Appleton-Century Crofts, 1978), p. 2; and "The Negro in Harlem Hospital," n.d. (circa 1935), p. 1., Box 7, Wright Papers.

46. Maynard, *Surgeons to the Poor,* pp. 18–22; Michael L. Goldstein, "Black Power and the Rise of Bureaucratic Autonomy in New York City Politics: The Case of Harlem Hospital," *Phylon* 41 (1980): 189–95; and Cheryl Lynn Greenberg, *Or Does It Explode?: Black Harlem in the Great Depression* (New York: Oxford University Press, 1991), p. 95.

47. "New Harlem Hospital Policy is Not Unanimously Approved," *New York Age,* 4 July 1925, Tuskegee Institute News Clipping File, Tuskegee University, Hollis Burke Frissell Library, Tuskegee, Alabama [hereafter TCF] (Hospitals—1925, New York); "Recognition for the Doctors," *New York Age,* 4 July 1925, TCF; "Citizens Welfare Council Successful in its Fight for Representation on Staff of Harlem Hospital," *New York Amsterdam News,* 1 July 1925, TCF; "Negroes at Last Win Recognition on Hospital Staff," *New York City World,* 28 June 1925, TCF; E.H.L. Corwin and Gertrude E. Sturges, *Opportunities for the Medical Education of Negroes* (New York: Charles Scribner's Sons, 1936), pp. 24–26; Harlem Hospital, "The Fight for Negroes in New York City Hospitals," 8 May 1935, pp. 1–2, Box 14, Wright Papers, Howard; and "The Negro in Harlem Hospital," pp. 1–2.

48. Bousfield, "Presidential Address," p. 155; Murray, "Hospital Provision for the Negro Race," p. 44; Louis T. Wright, "Health Problems of the Negro," *Interracial Review* 8 (January 1935): 6–8; Louis T. Wright, "The

Negro Physician," *Crisis* 36 (1929): 305; NAACP Press Release, "Negro Physician Appointed To Staff of Cleveland City Hospital," 27 July 1928, Box G158, NAACP Papers, Library of Congress; Memorandum, Dudley S. Blossom to Daniel E. Morgan, 30 March 1931, Container 1, Morgan Papers; Memorandum by Dr. Louis T. Wright, 19 June 1931, Box G158, NAACP Papers, Library of Congress; and Memorandum to Daniel E. Morgan from Dudley S. Blossom, 30 March 1931, Container 1, Morgan Papers. During World War I, New York City's Bellevue Hospital began to admit a few black interns. The Tuskegee Veterans Hospital employed its first African-American physicians in 1924. In 1928, Cleveland City Hospital appointed a black physician to its outpatient department. Three years later the hospital and Boston City Hospital appointed their first black interns. Also, in 1931, the mayor of Detroit named three African-American physicians to the staffs of municipal hospitals in the city.

49. Murray, "National Medical Association President's Address," p. 6; and "Nat. Medical Ass'n President Sees Need Of It," *Norfolk (Virginia) Journal and Guide*, 24 January 1931, TCF (Hospitals—1931, New York).

50. Louis T. Wright, "I Remember," n.d., pp. 22–23, 62, 64, Series A, Box 1, Wright Papers, Howard; and "Dr. Louis T. Wright Fought For Rights," *New York Amsterdam News*, 25 April 1953, p. 53.

51. Wright, "I Remember," p. 71.

52. Louis T. Wright, "Head Injuries," in *The Treatment of Fractures*, 11th ed., ed. Charles Scudder (Philadelphia: W.B. Saunders, 1938), pp. 416– 59.

53. Interdepartmental Committee to Coordinate Health and Welfare Activities, *Proceedings of the National Health Conference*, 18, 19, 20 July 1938, p. 87; and Wright, "Health Problems of the Negro," p. 6.

54. "Charitable Segregation," *The Fraternal Review* 10 (January 1931): n.p.; and "Sanitarium in Harlem Open to Physicians of the Race," *New York Age*, 8 May 1920, p. 1.

55. "Charitable Segregation."

56. Goldstein, "Black Power and the Rise of Bureaucratic Autonomy," pp. 196–98; Memorandum, City of New York, Department of Hospitals, copy in Peter Marshall Murray Scrapbook, vol. 1, Murray Papers; Cobb, "Louis T. Wright," pp. 140–41; Corwin and Sturges, *Opportunities for the Medical Education of Negroes*, pp. 23–28; Maynard, *Surgeons to the Poor*, pp. 61–66; and "Harlem Hospital Staff is Reorganized, Giving Place To Nineteen Negro Doctors," *New York Age*, 22 February 1930, p. 1.

57. Gilbert Osofsky, *Harlem: The Making of a Ghetto* (New York: Harper and Row, 1963), pp. 169–70.

58. "Medico 'Debutantes' Replace Veterans at Harlem Hospital," *New York Amsterdam News*, 19 February 1930, pp. 1, 3; William M. Kelley, "'Doc' Ferdinand Q. Morton Takes Over the Practice of Medicine," *New York Amsterdam News*, 17 December 1930, p. 20; Goldstein, "Black Power and the Rise of Bureaucratic Autonomy," pp. 191–98; "Dr. DuBois Defends N.A.A.C.P. Policy," *New York Amsterdam News*, 26 February 1930, p. 2; and W.E.B. DuBois, "Postscript: Harlem Hospital," *Crisis* 40 (1933): 45.

59. James L. Wilson, "History of Private Sanitariums in Harlem," n.d., Box 1, Wright Papers, Harvard; and "Dr. U.C. Vincent Resigns From Harlem

Hospital," clipping found in Wright Scrapbook, No. 4, Wright Papers, Harvard.

60. Report of Hospital Committee to North Harlem Medical Society, 10 March 1930, Peter Marshall Murray Scrapbook, vol. 1, Murray Papers; and Maynard, *Surgeons To The Poor*, pp. 56–66.

61. Kelley, "'Doc' Ferdinand Q. Morton," p. 20; Memorandum, Edwin R. Embree to Julius Rosenwald Fund Trustees, 6 April 1931, Box 3 (Addenda), Rosenwald Papers; and Michael M. Davis to P.M. Murray, 21 February 1958, Box 4, Murray Papers.

62. "Doctors Quit North Harlem Society To Form New Medical Body; Old Body Repudiated," *New York Age*, 24 May 1930, pp. 1, 3; "Doctors Who Resigned From North Harlem Medical Society Have Now Formed The Manhattan Med. Society," *New York Age*, 31 May 1930, p. 1.; Kelley, "'Doc' Ferdinand Q. Morton," p. 20; and "North Harlem Medical Society," *New York Amsterdam News*, 28 May 1930, p. 2.

63. Cobb, "Louis T. Wright," pp. 141–42.

64. "Negroes Reject Rosenwald Gift," *New York World*, 10 December 1930, p. 6; "Harlem Doctors Reject Survey Plan Proposed by Rosenwald Fund, Chicago," *New York Amsterdam News*, 10 December 1930, p. 2; "Negroes Vote Down Race Hospital Plan," *New York Times*, 10 December 1930, p. 34; Kelley, "'Doc' Ferdinand Q. Morton," p. 20; "Harlem Doctors Disagree on Plan Proposed By Rosenwald Fund That Provides For Negro Hospital Here," *New York Age*, 20 December 1930, p. 1; "When Doctors Disagree," editorial, *New York Age*, 20 December 1930, p. 4; and Maynard, *Surgeons to the Poor*, pp. 75–80.

65. Manhattan Medical Society, "Equal Opportunity,"; Memorandum, E.R. Embree to Julius Rosenwald Fund Trustees, 6 April 1931, Box 3 (Addenda) Rosenwald Papers; and Memorandum to Julius Rosenwald Fund Trustees, 2 May 1931, Box 2 (Addenda) Rosenwald Papers.

66. "North Harlem Medical Society Endorses and Invites Hospital Survey in Harlem For Rosenwald," *New York Age*, 27 December 1930, p. 3; "Harlem Doctors Disagree on Plan," pp. 1, 3; "When Doctors Disagree," p. 4; Kelly, "'Doc' Ferdinand Q. Morton," p. 20; "New York's Rejection of Rosenwald Offer Made in Unprofessional Way," *Pittsburgh Courier*, 17 January 1931, p. 1; "Nat. Medical Ass'n President Sees Need of It," *Norfolk (Virginia) Journal and Guide*, 24 January 1931, TCF (Hospitals—1931, New York); Lester A. Walton, "Disagreement Dulls Interest in its Survey," *Norfolk (Virginia) Journal and Guide*, 10 January 1931, TCF (Hospitals—1931, New York); and "Medical Clash Causes Rift in Hospital Plan," *New York News and Harlem Home Journal*, 28 March 1931, p. 2.

67. "Secret Harlem Report Exposes Louis Wright," clipping from *The Amsterdam News*, n.d., Louis T. Wright Scrapbook, vol. 4, Wright Papers, Harvard; Corwin and Sturges, *Opportunities for the Medical Education of Negroes*, pp. 28–30; and DuBois, "Postscript: Harlem Hospital," p. 45.

68. "That Harlem Hospital Report," *Daily Age*, 12 December 1933, copy in Peter Marshall Murray Scrapbook, Murray Papers; Julian H. Lewis, "Number and Geographic Location of Negro Physicians in the United

States," *Journal of the American Medical Association* 104 (1935): 1273; Maynard, *Surgeons To The Poor*, p. 53; and Cobb, "Louis T. Wright," p. 132.

69. Richard W. Thomas, *Life For Us Is What We Make It: Building Black Community in Detroit, 1915–1945* (Bloomington: Indiana University Press, 1992), pp. 180–184; and articles in Tuskegee Clipping File (Hospitals—1928, Massachusetts): "Why Colored People Object To Proposed Plymouth Hospital," *The Guardian* (Boston), 21 January 1928; "Means Exclusion, Says Dr. J.J. Smith," *The Guardian* (Boston), 21 January 1928; "Boston Post Says To Abandon Hospital Scheme," *The Guardian* (Boston), 28 January 1928; "No Hospital For Colored," *Boston Post*, 18 March 1928. Events in Chicago are discussed in Chapter 5 and those in Cleveland in Chapter 6.

3. "Where Shall We Work and Whom Are We to Serve?" The Battle for the Tuskegee Veterans Hospital

1. For example see Robert T. Brady, "South Lose to Race War," *Boston Post*, 5 July 1923, Tuskegee Institute News Clipping File, (hereafter TCF) (Hospitals—Alabama, 1923); and "Fear Race Clash At Tuskegee," *Chicago Defender*, 14 July 1923, pp. 1, 2.

2. J.F. Lane to Robert R. Moton, 2 June 1923, Box 90, Moton Papers.

3. For accounts of the development of a national hospital system for veterans and the establishment of the Consultants on Hospitalization see Rosemary Stevens, "Can the Government Govern? Lessons from the Formation of the Veterans Administration," *Journal of Health Politics, Policy and Law* 16 (Summer 1991): 281–305; United States Department of the Treasury, *Report of the Consultants on Hospitalization Appointed by the Secretary of the Treasury to Provide Additional Hospital Facilities under Public Act 384* (Washington, D.C.: U.S. Government Printing Office, 1923), pp. 1–10; Robert D. Leigh, *Federal Health Administration in the United States* (New York: Harper & Brothers, 1927), pp. 161–215; and Robinson E. Adkins, *Medical Care of Veterans* (Washington, DC: U.S. Government Printing Office, 1967), printed for the use of the Committee on Veterans' Affairs, 90th Cong., 1st session., House Committee Print no. 4, pp. 87–120.

4. *Report of the Consultants on Hospitalization*, p. 7.

5. *Report of the Consultants on Hospitalization*, p. 18. The Consultants on Hospitalization held its first meeting on 16 March 1921. The need to provide segregated facilities was first mentioned at its 23 March meeting in testimony presented by Captain John A. Murphy, assistant to Rear Admiral E.R. Stitt, United States Navy. Minutes of the Consultants on Hospitalization, 23 March 1921, Records of the Public Building Service, Records of Consultants on Hospitalization, Record Group (RG) 121, Box 220, National Archives, Washington, D.C., (hereafter Consultants Records).

6. *Report of the Consultants on Hospitalization*, p. 18; and Consultants on Hospitalization to Andrew W. Mellon, 20 September 1921, RG 121, Box 194, Consultants Records.

7. "Hospital For Negro Soldiers Under Discussion; Some White Citizens of Montgomery Are Opposed To Idea," *Birmingham Reporter*, 25 June 1921, TCF (Hospitals—1921); Issac Webb, Letter to the Editor, *Crisis* 26

(August 1923): 166; *The Gazette (Cleveland)*, 21 February 1921, p. 2; and Consultants to Mellon, 20 September 1921.

8. Minutes of the Consultants on Hospitalization, 9 May 1921, RG 121, Box 219, Consultants' Records.

9. William Charles White to George Vincent, 16 May 1921; William Charles White to Henry F. Pritchett, 25 May 1921; and William Charles White to Abraham Flexner, 28 May 1921, RG 121, Box 194, Consultants' Records; and Minutes of the Consultants on Hospitalization, 9 May 1921, RG 121, Box 219, Consultants' Records.

10. William Charles White to Andrew Mellon, 11 June 1921, RG 121, Box 207, Consultants' Records; Rosemary Stevens, *In Sickness and in Wealth: American Hospitals in the Twentieth Century* (New York: Basic Books, 1989), pp. 126–28.

11. Minutes of the Consultants on Hospitalization, 15 May 1921, RG 121, Box 219, Consultants' Records.

12. "Hospital For Negroes Is Opposed Here," *Montgomery Advertiser*, 18 June 1921; "Mayor Opposes Hospital For Wounded Vets," *Chicago Defender*, 6 August 1921; and "Oppose Using Gordon For Wounded Soldiers," *Atlanta Constitution*, 31 July 1921, TCF (Hospitals—1921).

13. Robert R. Moton to Charles William White, 27 June 1921, RG 121, Box 211, Consultants' Records. Although Moton used the title Major, he had not seen military service. The title had been bestowed on him in 1891 when he was appointed commandant of the male student cadet corp at Hampton Institute. He held the position for twenty-five years, but maintained the title for the rest of his life.

14. T.W. Salmon to Charles William White, 25 May 1921 and Charles William White to Abraham Flexner, 28 May 1921, RG 121, Box 194, Consultants' Records; and Minutes of Consultants on Hospitalization, 10 June 1921 and 9 September 1921, RG 121, Box 219, Consultants' Records. For biographical information on Moton see Mary White Ovington, *Portraits in Color* (1927; reprint, Freeport, NY: Books for Libraries Press, 1971), pp. 64–77; and William Hardin Hughes and Frederick D. Patterson, eds., *Robert Russa Moton of Hampton and Tuskegee* (Chapel Hill: University of North Carolina Press, 1956).

15. Minutes of the Consultants on Hospitalization, 16 September 1921, RG 121, Box 219, Consultants' Records; William Charles White to Andrew W. Mellon, 11 June 1921, RG 121, Box 207, Consultants' Records; Minutes of the Consultants on Hospitalization, 10 June 1921, RG 121, Box 219, Consultants' Records; William Charles White to George Vincent, 16 May 1921, RG 121, Box 207, Consultants' Records; and Minutes of the Consultants on Hospitalization, 10 June 1921, RG 121, Box 219, Consultants' Records.

16. W.N. Kenzie to Hugh S. Cummings, 22 August 1921, RG 121, Box 211, Consultants' Records; and W.N. Kenzie to Charles William White, 24 August 1921, RG 121, Box 211, Consultants' Records.

17. Memorandum, Board of Revenue of Macon County to Consultants on Hospitalization, n.d. (circa September 1921), RG 121, Box 211, Consult-

ants' Records; W.N. Kenzie to William Charles White, 31 August 1921, RG 121, Box 211, Consultants' Records.

18. W.N. Kenzie to the Consultants on Hospitalization, 27 August 1921, RG 121, Box 211, Consultants' Records.

19. Minutes of the Consultants on Hospitalization, 16 September 1921, RG 121, Box 219, Consultants' Records; Memorandum, W.N. Kenzie to H.S. Cummings, 8 October 1921, RG 121, Box 211, Consultants' Records; and Robert R. Moton to Andrew W. Mellon, 17 November 1921, Box 95, Moton Papers.

20. W.E.B. DuBois, "The Tuskegee Hospital," editorial, *The Crisis*, 26 (1923): 106–7; and James Weldon Johnson to John W. Love, 3 November 1923, Box C410, NAACP Papers, Library of Congress.

21. "Does Not Want To Go South For Hospital Treatment Says Wounded Soldier," Letter to the Editor, *Afro-American*, 15 August 1921, TCF (Hospitals—1921); and Minutes of Meeting of the Consultants on Hospitalization with the National Committee of Negro Veteran Relief, 1 November 1921, RG 121, Box 226, Consultants' Records.

22. J.A. Lester to William Charles White, 18 November 1921, RG 121, Box 194, Consultants' Records; and Consultants on Hospitalization to Andrew W. Mellon, 16 September 1921, RG 121, Box 219, Consultants' Records.

23. Melvin C. Chisum, "The Whole Truth About the Tuskegee Hospital," *Pittsburgh Courier*, 30 June 1923, pp. 1, 11; "Notes on the Tuskegee Hospital Situation," 11 April 1923, Box C410, NAACP Papers, Library of Congress; *Report of the Consultants on Hospitalization*, p. 29; Memorandum, "Negro Veteran's Hospital at Tuskegee," 31 December 1923, Box C410, NAACP Papers, Library of Congress; Robert R. Moton to William Charles White, 16 September 1922, Box 95, Moton Papers; and Kenzie to Moton, 19 January 1923, Box 95, Moton Papers.

24. "Veterans Bureau Field Letter, No. 78," 3 February 1923, Box C410, NAACP Papers, Library of Congress; and Carlyle Alfred Ward, "Calvin Coolidge Is Principal Speaker at Tuskegee," *Montgomery Advertiser*, 13 February 1923, TCF (Hospitals—Alabama, 1923). Unless specified, all remaining references in this chapter to holdings in the TCF will be found in this file.

25. Ward, "Calvin Coolidge"; "Coolidge Dedicates Negro U.S. Hospital," *Chicago Daily News*, 12 February 1923, TCF; "Coolidge Dedicates Tuskegee Hospital," 13 February 1923, TCF; "Coolidge Lauds Negroes," *New York Times*, 13 February 1923, p.4; and "Dedicate $2,500,000 Hospital at Tuskegee," *Chicago Defender*, 24 February 1923, p. 1. The most complete account of the ceremony is "Vice-President Praises Valor of Negro Soldiers in Dedicating New Government Hospital Near Institute," *The Tuskegee Student*, 33 (March 1–15, 1933), pp. 1–2. "Speech of Hon. Calvin Coolidge, Vice President of the United States at Dedication of Government Hospital for Colored Veterans of World War, Tuskegee, Alabama." Lincoln's Birthday, 12 February 1923, RG 121, Box 211, Consultants' Records; and Robert R. Moton, "Address in Connection With Dedication of the Government Hospital at Tuskegee, February 12," Box 95, Moton Papers.

26. L.B. Rogers to Edith Howland, 6 February 1923, Box 95, Moton Papers; and Robert R. Moton to Warren G. Harding, 14 February 1923, Box C410, NAACP Papers, Library of Congress.

27. Robert R. Moton to James Weldon Johnson, 19 February 1923 and Johnson to Moton, 24 February 1923, Box C410, NAACP Papers, Library of Congress.

28. Robert R. Moton to Robert H. Stanley, 20 February 1923, Box 95, Moton Papers; Robert H. Stanley to Robert R. Moton, 24 February 1923, Box 95, Moton Papers; Pauli Murray, comp., *States' Laws on Race and Color*, (Cincinnati, Oh.: Women's Division of Christian Service, Board of Missions and Church Extension, Methodist Church, 1950), p. 31; Melvin J. Chisum to Herbert J. Seligman, 15 May 1923, Box C410, NAACP Papers, Library of Congress; and "The Muddle at Tuskegee Hospital," editorial, *Houston Informer*, 28 April 1923, TCF.

29. Chisum, "The Whole Truth About the Tuskegee Hospital," p. 11; Melvin J. Chisum to Robert R. Moton, 21 March 1923, Box C410, NAACP Papers, Library of Congress; George E. Ijams to George B. Christian, 20 February 1923, Record Group (RG) 15, Box 71, Bureau of War Risk Insurance, Director's Correspondence File (hereafter Director's File); Robert R. Moton to J.R.A. Crossland, 16 March 1923, Box 90, Moton Papers; and Albon L. Holsey, "A Man of Courage," in *Robert Russa Moton: Of Tuskegee and Hampton*, eds. Hughes and Patterson p. 139.

30. George B. Christian to George E. Ijams, 23 February 1923, Box C410, NAACP Papers, Library of Congress.

31. George B. Christian to Herbert J. Seligmann 28 April 1923, Box C410, NAACP Papers, Library of Congress; and NAACP Press Release, 1 May 1923, Box C410, NAACP Papers, Library of Congress.

32. "Address of the President of the United States, 26 October 1921, At the Celebration of the Semicentennial of the Founding of the City of Birmingham, Alabama," RG 121, Box 164, Consultants' Records; and Warren G. Harding to Henry Lincoln Johnson, 8 May 1923, RG 15, Box 71, Director's File. For an examination of Harding's policies toward African Americans see Richard B. Sherman, *The Republican Party and Black America: From McKinley to Hoover, 1896–1933* (Charlottesville, Va.: University of Virginia Press, 1973), pp. 145–73; and Robert K. Murray, *The Harding Era: Warren G. Harding and His Administration* (Minneapolis: University of Minnesota Press, 1969), pp. 397–403.

33. For accounts of the anti-lynching campaigns see Sherman, *The Republican Party*, pp. 174–99; and Robert L. Zangrando, *The NAACP Crusade Against Lynching, 1909–1950* (Philadelphia: Temple University Press, 1980), pp. 51–97. "To Oust Whites At Tuskegee Hospital," *Chicago Defender*, 21 April 1923, p. 2.

34. The previous director, Charles R. Forbes, was forced to resign amidst allegations of improprieties in his administration of the Veterans Bureau on 28 February. He was later convicted on charges of fraud and bribery and sent to Leavenworth prison. Hines took over the bureau on the day that Forbes resigned. "Hines Chosen Head of Veteran Bureau," *New York Times*, 28 February 1923 p. 7; and Stevens, "Can the Government Govern?",

pp. 294–95. Albon L. Holsey to Robert R. Moton, 26 March 1923, Box 90, Moton Papers; Chisum, "The Whole Truth About the Tuskegee Hospital," p. 11; Memorandum, "Publicity: Veterans Bureau Hospital, Tuskegee, Alabama," RG 15, Box 71, Director's File; Walter G. Alexander to Warren Harding, 1 May 1923, RG 15, Box 71, Director's File; Memorandum, "Conference Between John E. Nail, Albon L. Holsey, and Walter F. White," 7 May 1923, Box C410, NAACP Papers, Library of Congress; and Frank T. Hines to George E. Ijams, 4 May 1923, RG 15, Box 71, Director's File. For more on the activities of Johnson and Howard see Pete Daniel, "Black Power in the 1920s: The Case of Tuskegee Veterans Hospital," *Journal of Southern History* 36 (1970): 373–75; and Raymond L. Wolters, "Major Moton Defeats the Klan: The Case of the Tuskegee Veterans Hospital," in his *The New Negro on Campus: Black College Rebellions of the 1920s* (Princeton: Princeton University Press, 1975), pp. 170–71. Memorandum, "Negro Veteran's Hospital At Tuskegee," 31 December 1923, Box C410, NAACP Papers, Library of Congress; and J.R.A. Crossland to Robert R. Moton, 28 March 1923, Box 90, Moton Papers.

35. "Tuskegee Opposes Negro Supervision," *Montgomery Advertiser*, 29 March 1923, TCF; William W. Brandon to Warren G. Harding, 24 March 1923; and Robert E. Steiner to Frank T. Hines, 24 March 1923, RG 15, Box 71, Director's File; and "Plan to Exclude Colored Medicos From Hospital," *Norfolk Journal and Guide*, 7 April 1923, TCF.

36. R.H. Powell, quoted in Holsey, "A Man of Courage," pp. 131–32; Wilma Dykeman and James Stokeley, *Seeds of Southern Change: The Life of Will Alexander* (Chicago: University of Chicago Press, 1962), p. 160; and "Montgomery to Get Hospital Benefits," *Montgomery Advertiser*, 2 March 1923, TCF.

37. "Ask Brandon To Visit Capital on Tuskegee," *Montgomery Advertiser*, 7 May 1923, TCF; "Governor Is Unable To Go To Washington, *Montgomery Advertiser*, 8 May 1923, TCF; "Alabama Delegates Pleased With Trip," *Montgomery Advertiser*, 10 May 1923, TCF; "Ask Harding Put Whites at Hospital," *Chicago Defender*, 12 May 1923, p. 2; George B. Christian to the Associated Negro Press, 11 May 1923, Box 90, Moton Papers; and George B. Christian to Herbert J. Seligmann, 14 May 1923, Box C410, NAACP Papers, Library of Congress.

38. Announcement, 5 May 1923, Director's File, RG 15, Box 71; Albon L. Holsey to Melvin J. Chisum, 4 May 1923, Box 139, Moton Papers; Frank T. Hines to George E. Cannon, 10 May 1923, RG 15, Box 71, Director's File; and Memorandum, "Information Received From Dr. William A. Warfield, Head of Freedman's Hospital." n.d., RG 15, Box 71, Director's File.

39. Helen H. Gardner to Frank T. Hines, 20 June 1923, RG 15, Box 71, Director's File; and Shelby J. Davidson to Walter F. White, 12 May 1923, Box C410, NAACP Papers, Library of Congress.

40. Wolters, *The New Negro On Campus*, p. 150; and Charles T. Isom to Warren G. Harding, 25 June 1923, RG 15, Box 71, Director's File.

41. Isom to Harding, 25 June 1923 and James Weldon Johnson to R.B. Lemus, 11 August 1923, Box C410, NAACP Papers, Library of Congress; Walter F. White to William R. Valentine, 14 May 1923, Box C410, NAACP

Papers, Library of Congress; and "The Veterans Hospital," *JNMA* 15 (1923): 204.

42. Albon L. Holsey to James Weldon Johnson, 2 April 1923, Box C410, NAACP Papers, Library of Congress.

43. For an analysis of the strategies employed by the NAACP during this time see Zangrando, *The NAACP Crusade Against Lynching, 1909–1950*; and Charles Flint Kellogg, *NAACP: A History of The National Association for the Advancement of Colored People, Volume I* (Baltimore: Johns Hopkins Press, 1967), esp. pp. 117–54 and 183–246. Walter F. White to William R. Valentine, 14 May 1923, Box C410, NAACP Papers, Library of Congress; Walter F. White to Editors, 14 May 1923, Box C410, NAACP Papers, Library of Congress; W.E.B. DuBois, "The Fear of Efficiency," *The Crisis*, 26 (June 1923): 56; and Holsey to Johnson, 2 May 1923, Box C410, NAACP Papers, Library of Congress.

44. "The Muddle at Tuskegee Hospital," editorial, *Houston Informer*, 28 April 1923, TCF; "Dr. Moton and the Veterans Hospital," *Atlanta Independent*, 24 May 1923, TCF; "Negro Opportunity in Alabama," editorial, *Norfolk Journal and Guide*, 30 June 1923, TCF; "Negro Veterans' Hospital at Tuskegee Institute Is To Have Colored Personnel, *New York Age*, 9 June 1923, TCF; and "The Remedy Worse Than Migration," *The Atlanta Independent*, 7 June 1923, TCF, and W.E.B. DuBois, "Tuskegee and Moton," *Crisis*, 28 (1924): 200.

45. Roscoe Simmons, "The Tuskegee Muddle," *Chicago Defender*, 14 April 1923, Section 2, p. 1; "The Veterans Hospital at Tuskegee", *Washington Tribune*, 19 May 1923, TCF; "Klan Halts March on Tuskegee," *Chicago Defender*, 4 August 1923, TCF; "Tuskegee Hospital Episode," editorial, *The Messenger*, 5 (June 1923): 734; and "Tuskegee", editorial, *The Messenger*, 5 (September 1923): 807. Years later the hospital did become an experiment station for black men. It was one of the facilities used in the infamous Tuskegee syphilis study. This United States Public Health Service study examined from 1932–1972 the effects of untreated syphilis in a group of black men from the area. The men had not been informed that they were part of a study and had been led to believe that they were receiving therapy.

46. James T. Bailey to Frank T. Hines, 27 June 1923, RG 15, Box 71, Director's File; and J.R.A. Crossland to Frank T. Hines, 19 June 1923, RG 15, Box 71, Director's File.

47. Frank T. Hines to George E. Cannon, 1 June 1923, RG 15, Box 71, Director's File; L.B. Rogers to Robert H. Stanley, 9 June 1923, RG 15, Box 71, Director's File; "The Veterans Hospital," *JNMA* 15 (1923): 203–4; L.A. Moyer to Helen H. Gardner, 27 June 1923, RG 15, Box 71, Director's File; "Five Nurses Sent From Greenville to Tuskegee Veterans' Hospital, 91," *New York Age*, 30 June 1923, TCF; L.B. Rogers to Frank T. Hines, 14 June 1923, RG 15, Box 71, Director's File; Frank T. Hines to Honorable Lamar Jeffers, 27 June 1923, RG 15, Box 71, Director's File; and Frank T. Hines to Warren G. Harding, 18 June 1923, RG 15, Box 71, Director's File.

48. Atticus Mullin, "Negro Dentists Reach Tuskegee Is Report Sunday," *Montgomery Advertiser*, 25 June 1923, TCF; and R.H. Powell, "How U.S. Government Broke Faith With Whites and Blacks of Tuskegee, AL,"

Montgomery Advertiser, 23 June 1923, TCF. For examples of the correspondence sent to the Veterans Bureau from White Tuskegeeans see R.H. Powell et. al, to Hines, 25 June 1923, J. Thomas Heflin to Frank T. Hines, 26 June 1923, and Lawrence C. Lewis to Frank T. Hines, 27 June 1923, RG 15, Box 71, Director's File.

49. Robert H. Stanley to Helen H. Gardner, 26 June 1923, RG 15, Box 71, Director's File; W.B. Bowling to Frank T. Hines, 25 June 1923, RG 15, Box 71, Director's File; and "Boycott, Race Riot, Menace New Hospital," *Chicago Whip*, 30 June 1923, TCF.

50. "Ask Federal Troops to Guard Hospital Against Klansmen," *Chicago Whip*, 14 July 1923, TCF; Holsey, "A Man of Courage," p. 132; and "Minutes of the 'Silver Jubilee' and Twenty-fifth Annual Meeting of the National Negro Business League and Affiliated Organizations," Chicago, Illinois, 20–22 August 1924, pp. 57–59, Tuskegee University.

51. Robert R. Moton to Frank T. Hines, 1 July 1923, Box 95, Moton Papers.

52. Holsey, "A Man of Courage," p. 134; KKK to John H. Calhoun, n.d., RG 15, Box 71, Director's File; L.A. Moyers to Frank T. Hines, 4 July 1923, RG 15, Box 71, Director's File; "U.S. Officer A Messenger For Ku Klux," *Afro-American* (Baltimore), 13 July 1923, TCF; Frank T. Hines to George Ijams, 13 July 1923, TCF; "Colonel Stanley, Commander of Veterans' Hospital, Failed To Protect U.S. Employee," *New York Age*, 14 July 1923; and Walter Harper, "Negro Vanishes When White Robed Band Assembles," *Montgomery Advertiser*, 4 July 1923, TCF.

53. Daniel, "Black Power in the 1920s," p. 378. There was extensive newspaper coverage of the Klan march. Holdings in the Tuskegee Institute News Clipping File include Walter Harper, "Negro Vanishes When White Robed Band Assembles," *Montgomery Advertiser*, 4 July 1923; Robert T. Brady, "South Close To Race War," *Boston Post*, 5 July 1923; "Hospital Issue is Now Between Government and Ku Klux Klan," *Washington Tribune*, 7 July 1923; "700 Klansmen Parade," *New York World*, 5 July 1923; "1000 Robed Klansmen Parade in Tuskegee In Protest on Negro Hospital Personnel," *New York Times*, 4 July 1923; "Klan Appears in Silent Protest," *Southern Christian Recorder*, 5 July 1923; "A Thousand Masked Ku Klux Klansmen Threaten Tuskegee," *Norfolk Journal and Guide*, 7 July 1923; "Ku Klux Klan Demonstration at Tuskegee Causes Much Agitation Throughout Country," *Savannah Tribune*, 12 July 1923; and "Telegrams Demand That U.S. Troops Be Sent To Keep Order," *Pittsburgh Courier*, 14 July 1923. See also NAACP Press Release, n.d. (circa July 1923), "Charge Ku Klux Used Tuskegee Government Hospital Sheets In Parade," Box C410, NAACP Papers, Library of Congress; Hines to W. J. Burns, 20 August 1923, Box C410, NAACP Papers, Library of Congress; J.C. Logan to Walter White, 31 August 1923, Box C410, NAACP Papers, Library of Congress; and Walter White, *A Man Called White* (New York: Viking Press, 1948), p. 70.

54. George E. Cannon to Frank T. Hines, 15 July 1923, RG 15, Box 71, Director's File. The Tuskegee Institute News Clipping File includes numerous examples of editorials and articles in black newspapers including "Ku Klux Klan Demonstration at Tuskegee Causes Much Agitation throughout

Country," *Savannah Tribune*, 12 July 1923; "Fear Race Clash at Tuskegee," *Chicago Defender*, 14 July 1923; Alfred Anderson, "Will U.S. Stand For Klan Rule?", editorial, *Chicago Defender*, 14 July 1923; "Southern Inconsistency," *New York Age*, 7 July 1923; Lester A. Walton, "Negroes Aroused Over Battle for Veteran Hospital," *New York City World*, 15 July 1923; and "100 Percent Greed," *The Afro-American* (Baltimore), 13 July 1923. The Director's Correspondence Files at the National Archives (RG 15, Box 71) contain several letters from African Americans expressing their outrage. For descriptions of the activities of the NAACP see Walter White to Albon L. Holsey, 7 July 1923, Box C410, NAACP Papers, Library of Congress; NAACP Press Release, 10 July 1923, Box C410, NAACP Papers, Library of Congress; James Weldon Johnson to Hines, 24 July 1923, Box C410, NAACP Papers, Library of Congress; James Weldon Johnson to Warren G. Harding, 24 July 1924, Box C410, NAACP Papers, Library of Congress; Memorandum Walter F. White to James Weldon Johnson, 7 July 1923, Box C410, NAACP Papers, Library of Congress. North Harlem Medical, Dental and Pharmaceutical Association to Hines, 24 July 1923, RG 15, Box 71, Director's File.

55. Davidson quoted in "Tuskegee to Cost G.O.P. Black Vote," *New York World*, 27 July 1923, TCF; Robert Talley, "Negroes Threaten Harding in Hospital Row," *Birmingham Post*, 27 July 1923, TCF; "Negroes Threaten A Republican Bolt," *New York Times*, 22 July 1923, p. 7; Edgar G. Brown, "Race Threatens Republican Bolt," *Pittsburgh Courier*, 28 July 1923, pp.1 and 8; "Colored Leaders At Atlantic City Form National Convention," *New York Age*, 28 July 1923, TCF; and Dennis Clark Dickerson, "George E. Cannon: Black Churchman, Physician, and Republican Politician," *Journal of Presbyterian History* 51 (1973): 421–24.

56. Robert T. Brady, "Big Klux Parade At Tuskegee Town, Ala., Halts Appointment of Colored Doctors," *Guardian (Boston)*, 7 July 1923, TCF; Hartwell Hatton, "Tuskegee Crisis Probably Passed With Hines Visit," *Montgomery Advertiser*, 6 July 1923; and Hines to C.E. Sawyer, 12 July 1923, RG 15, Box 71, Director's File.

57. *Daily News (Opelika, Alabama)*, 17 May 1923, quoted in "The Veterans Hospital Situation," *JNMA* 15 (1923): 287; "K.K.K. Objects to Negroes Serving Negroes at Tuskegee," *Savannah Journal*, 7 July 1923, TCF; *Norfolk Virginia-Pilot*, quoted in "Press of South Strikes High Note on Tuskegee Tangle," *Norfolk Journal and Guide*, 21 July 1923, TCF; and *Daily Citizen*, quoted in Lester A. Walton, "Southern Opinion on the Tuskegee Hospital," *Outlook (New York City)*, 135 (5 September 1923): 14.

58. Dykeman and Stokeley, *Seeds of Southern Change*, pp. 160–61; "Negro Institute Gets Approval of Methodist Episcopal Church, *Houston Post*, 10 July 1923, TCF; "Church Leaders Rise to Tuskegee's Defense," *Broad Ax*, 21 July 1923, p. 2; "Race Guards Patrol Grounds at Veterans' Hospital," *Pittsburgh Courier*, 15 September 1923, p. 3; and Will W. Alexander to Moton, 25 July 1923, Box 89, Moton Papers.

59. Conference Committee to Hines, 6 July 1923, RG 15, Box 71, Director's File; Hines to L.W. Johnston, 16 July 1923, RG 15, Box 71, Director's File; "Klan Demonstration At Tuskegee Hospital Had Reaction

Not Expected," *New York Age*, 28 July 1923, TCF; and Alabama Senate Joint Resolution, No. 85, 13 July 1923, RG 15, Box 71, Director's File.

60. "Hines Anxious To Finish Personnel," *Montgomery Advertiser*, 19 July 1923, TCF; R.H. Powell to Hines, 6 August 1923, RG 15, Box 71, Director's File; "Report of Com. in Hospital Matter," *Tuskegee News*, 16 August 1923; Hines to Thomas S. Harten, 30 August 1923, RG 15, Box 71, Director's File; Powell to Hines, 25 August 1923, RG 15, Box 71, Director's File; and Hines to James Weldon Johnson, 13 August 1923, RG 15, Box 71, Director's File.

61. Wolters, "Major Moton Defeats the Klan," pp. 147–50.

62. Benjamin Jefferson Davis to Hines, 7 July 1923 and Melvin J. Chisum to Hines, 7 July 1923, RG 15, Box 71, Director's File. The Tuskegee Institute News Clipping File contains numerous examples of newspaper articles both condemning and supporting Moton. Articles critical of him include "Moton Should Resign," editorial, *Amsterdam News*, 11 July 1923; "Where is Our Wandering Major Tonight?", editorial, *Amsterdam News*, 25 July 1923; "Moton May Be Given Hot Reception by Irate Negroes," *Amsterdam News*, 15 August 1923; "Why So Much Secrecy About the Tuskegee Situation?" editorial, *Washington Tribune*, 28 July 1923; "Major Seems to be For White and Colored at the Same Time," *Washington Tribune*, 11 August 1923; "The Modern Dr. Jekyl [sic] and Mr. Hyde," *Washington Tribune*, 11 August 1923; and "Negroes Demand Moton Take Stand in Hospital Fight," *New York World*, 29 July 1923. Supportive articles include "Star of Zion Defends Dr. Moton," *Atlanta Independent*, 13 September 1923; "The Tuskegee Tangle," editorial, *Pittsburgh Courier*, 14 July 1923; and "Compromise At Tuskegee," *New York Age*, 15 September 1923.

63. White to Shelby J. Davidson, 9 August 1923, Box C410, NAACP Papers, Library of Congress; W.E.B. DuBois, "No Compromise," editorial, *Crisis*, 27 (November 1923): 7–8; Davidson to White, 14 August 1923, Box C410, NAACP Papers, Library of Congress; and Memorandum, "The Negro Veterans Hospital at Tuskegee Institute," 31 December 1923, NAACP Papers, Library of Congress.

64. "Airs Tuskegee Situation," *Atlantic City New Jersey Gazette*, 7 September 1923, TCF; "Medical Association Favors Complete Staff at Veterans Hospital," *St. Louis Argus*, 31 August 1923, TCF; "Resolutions Call For Tuskegee Negro Personnel," *New York World*, 9 September 1923; and "National Hospital Association," *JNMA* 15 (1923): 286–87.

65. Hines to Stanley, 20 August 1923, Hines to C.E. Sawyer, 12 July 1923, and Hines to Charles M. Griffith, 22 August 1923, RG 15, Box 71, Director's File; "Colonel Stanley Moved to Bayard," *Montgomery Advertiser*, 2 September 1923, TCF; and "Tuskegee Head Transferred," *Montgomery Advertiser*, 2 September 1923, TCF.

66. "Order Negro Doctors To Tuskegee Hospital," *New York Times*, 16 August 1923, p. 15; "Negro Physicians Assigned To Tuskegee Veterans Hospital," *Atlanta Constitution*, 16 August 1923, TCF; Powell to Hines, 25 August 1923, W.W. Campbell to Hines, 25 August 1923, RG 15, Box 71,

Director's File, and Kenney to M.O. Dumas, 24 September 1923, RG 15, Box, 71, Director's File.

67. "Protest at Continued Efforts to Employ Mixed Staff Explain Letters of Refusal of Physicians Chosen for Staff at Tuskegee Hospital," *Dallas Express*, 20 October 1923, TCF; "Doctors Refuse Positions at Vets Hospital," *Washington Tribune*, 6 October 1923, TCF; "Dr. Whitby Sends His Refusal To Director Hines," *Washington Tribune*, 13 October 1923, TCF; "Col. Leaves; Six Colored Doctors Placed by Gen. Hines," *Pittsburgh Courier*, 15 September 1923, p. 3; Hines to C. Bascom Slemp, 7 November 1923, and Hines to Carl Murphy, 6 November 1923, RG 15, Box 71, Director's File.

68. "The Tuskegee Hospital," *Kansas City (Missouri) Sun*, 5 January 1924, TCF; "Dr. Ward Sent To Tuskegee As Chief Surgeon," *Chicago Defender*, 5 January 1924, TCF; Charles M. Griffith to Hines, 11 March 1924, Box 90, Moton Papers; Moton to M.O. Dumas, 21 June 1924, Box 90, Moton Papers; "Dr. Joseph H. Ward Heads The Veterans Hospital At Tuskegee," editorial, *JNMA*, 16 (1924): 203–4; Ethel Johns, "A Study of the Present Status of the Negro Woman in Nursing, 1925," Exhibit M (Tuskegee, Alabama), p. M-9, Box 122, Record Group 1.1, Series 200C, Rockefeller Foundation Archives; "Veterans Hospital Under Colored Control," *Dallas Express*, 26 July 1924, TCF; and "Tuskegee Medical Officer To Be Negro," *Biloxi (Mississippi) Herald*, 10 July 1924, TCF.

69. "Col. Leaves; Six Colored Doctors Placed By Gen. Hines," *Pittsburgh Courier*, 15 September 1923, p. 3.

70. W.E.B. DuBois, "Tuskegee and Moton," editorial, *Crisis* 28 (1924): 200–202; and "Vindication of Dr. R.R. Moton One of Notable Developments of Year," *Pittsburgh American*, 9 September 1924, TCF.

71. J.H. Ward, "U.S. Veterans' Hospital," *JNMA* 22 (1930): 133–34; Peter Marshall Murray to White, 10 June 1932, Box 7, Murray Papers; National Medical Association, "Minutes of the 36th Annual Session of the National Medical Association and Auxiliaries," *JNMA* 23 (1931): 183; and Peter Marshall Murray, "National Medical Association President's Address," *JNMA* 24 (November 1932): 6–7.

72. Murray to Oscar DePriest, 12 March 1932, Box 4, Murray Papers; and White to American Legion, 28 April 1932, Box 7, Murray Papers.

73. White to Murray, 16 June 1932, Box 7, Murray Papers.

74. Ibid.

75. Manhattan Medical Society, "Identical Care and Treatment by the Federal Government: An Open Letter To The American Legion," New York City, New York, 15 August 1932, pp. 9–10, Wright Papers, Harvard; The Peter Marshall Murray Scrapbook, Vol. 2, Murray Papers. Murray Papers contain the following newspaper editorials: "The N.A.A.C.P. is Right," *Pittsburgh Courier*, n.d.; "What Price Segregation?", *Inter-State Tattler*, June 1931; "Separate Hospitals," *New York Age*, 10 September 1932; and "There Are None So Blind," *Amsterdam News*, 6 July 1932.

76. Manhattan Medical Society, "Identical Care and Treatment," pp. 3–

7; "Senator To Drop Jim-Crow Bill," *Amsterdam News*, 30 August 1932, TCF; Peter Marshall Murray Scrapbook, Vol. 2, Murray Papers.

77. Murray to various physicians, 11 June 1932, Box 10, Murray Papers.

4. Black Hospitals and White Philanthropy

1. H.M. Green, "Some Observations on and Lessons from the Experiences of the Past Ten Years," *JNMA* 26 (1934): 23.

2. Edwin R. Embree, *Julius Rosenwald Fund: Review of the Two-Year Period 1938–1940* (Chicago: The Fund, 1940), p. 3; and Julius Rosenwald to Herbert Hoover, 12 November 1929, Box 185, Swift Papers. For general histories of the philanthropy and its founder see Edwin R. Embree and Julia Waxman, *Investment in People: The Story of the Julius Rosenwald Fund* (New York: Harper, 1949); M.R. Werner, *Julius Rosenwald: The Life of a Practical Humanitarian* (New York: Harper, 1939); and Kathleen D. McCarthy, *Noblesse Oblige: Charity and Cultural Philanthropy in Chicago, 1849–1929* (Chicago: University of Chicago Press, 1982), pp. 110–11.

3. Julius Rosenwald, "Principles of Public Giving," *Atlantic Monthly* 143 (1929): 599–609; and Julius Rosenwald, "Trends Away From Perpetuities," *Atlantic Monthly* 145 (1930): 741–49.

4. For biographical information on Embree see Charles S. Johnson, "Edwin Rogers Embree," *Phylon* 7 (1946): 317–34; and John H. Stanfield, "Edwin Rogers Embree and the Julius Rosenwald Fund," in his *Philanthropy and Jim Crow in American Social Science* (Westport, Conn.: Greenwood Press, 1985), pp. 97–118. A fuller account of Embree's work in the Division of Studies is given in Robert E. Kohler, "A New Policy for the Advancement of Science: The Rockefeller Foundation, 1924–29," *Minerva* 16 (Winter 1978): 480–515.

5. For an extensive, if overly descriptive, study of the fund's programs in race relations see A. Gilbert Belles, "The Julius Rosenwald Fund: Efforts in Race Relations, 1928–1948" (Ph.D. diss., Vanderbilt University, 1972).

6. Memorandum, Julius Rosenwald Fund Trustees Meeting, 16 November 1929, Box 2, Addenda, Rosenwald Papers.

7. Edwin R. Embree, "Negro Health and Its Effect Upon the Nation's Health," *Modern Hospital* 30 (April 1928): 49–54 (Quote, p. 52).

8. For an extensive summary of the activities of the Negro Health Division see M.O. Bousfield, "Program for Negro Health," 9 October 1936, Box 76, Rosenwald Fund Papers; Edwin R. Embree, *Julius Rosenwald Fund: Review of Two Decades, 1917–1936* (Chicago: The Fund, 1936), p. 36; Edwin R. Embree, *Julius Rosenwald Fund: Review for the Two Year Period, 1936–1938* (Chicago: The Fund, 1938), p. 39; and Embree, *Rosenwald Fund, 1938–1940*, p. 44.

9. Kenneth R. Manning, *Black Apollo of Science: The Life of Ernest Everett Just* (New York: Oxford University Press, 1983), p. 123; and *Crisis* 20 (1920): 193.

10. "Meharry Professor Qualifies," *JNMA* 29 (1937): 114; and Abraham

Flexner to Ernest Everett Just, 29 December 1922, Box 695, General Education Board (GEB) Papers, cited in Manning, *Black Apollo*, p. 144.

11. M.O. Bousfield, "Negro Health," 1 August 1937, Box 76, Rosenwald Papers, p. 4.

12. "A Program for Negro Health," 29 April 1928, Box 2, Addenda, Rosenwald Papers, pp. 24–25; Bousfield, "Negro Health," 9 October 1936, pp. 1–2; and Bousfield, "Negro Health," 1 August 1937, p. 1.

13. For detailed analyses of the Rosenwald Fund's involvement in the demonstration project and the project's evolution to a study of untreated syphilis see Allan M. Brandt, "Racism and Research: The Case of the Tuskegee Syphilis Study," *The Hastings Center Report* 8 (December 1978): 21–29; and James H. Jones, *Bad Blood*, 2nd edition, (New York: Free Press, 1993).

14. Michael M. Davis, "Problems of Health Service for Negroes," *Journal of Negro Education* 6 (1937): 444; Julius Rosenwald Fund, compiled by Harrison L. Harris and Margaret L. Plumley, *Negro Hospitals: A Compilation of Available Statistics* (Chicago: The Fund, 1931), pp. 2–4; Embree, *Rosenwald Fund, 1917–1936*, p. 36; and Bousfield, "Negro Health," 9 October 1936, pp. 15–16.

15. E.R. Carney, "Hospital Care for Negroes," *National Negro Health News* 10 (January–March 1942): 42.

16. Minutes of the Executive Committee of the Julius Rosenwald Fund, 13 June 1928, Box 1, Addenda, Rosenwald Papers; and Minutes of the Executive Committee of the Julius Rosenwald Fund, 11 May 1929, Box 2, Addenda, Rosenwald Papers.

17. Memorandum to Julius Rosenwald Fund Trustees, 14 November 1930, Box 2, Addenda, Rosenwald Papers; and Docket of the Executive Committee of the Julius Rosenwald Fund, 25 June 1931, Box 1, Addenda, Rosenwald Papers, p. 12.

18. Green, "Some Observations ," p. 24; H.M. Green, "Our Hospital Problems," *JNMA* 26 (1935): 74; and Midian O. Bousfield, "Presidential Address," *JNMA* 26 (1934): 155.

19. Midian O. Bousfield, "Negro Health," 13 December 1937, Box 76, Rosenwald Fund Papers, p. 5; Bousfield, "Negro Health," 9 October 1936, pp. 13–14; and J.J. Cary, "The Hospital Unit, Knoxville, Tenn.," *JNMA* 34 (1942): 131.

20. W.S. Rankin to Michael M. Davis, 27 March 1929, Box 2, Rankin Papers; Docket, Executive Committee of the Trustees of the Julius Rosenwald Fund, 18 December 1929, Box 1, Addenda, Rosenwald Papers, pp. 9–12; and Julius Rosenwald Fund, *Negro Hospitals*, pp. 2–4.

21. W.S. Rankin to H.L. Shaw, 25 January 1930, Box 184, Duke Endowment Papers.

22. Minutes of the Trustees of the Julius Rosenwald Fund, 16 November 1929, Box 2, Addenda, Rosenwald Papers. The jointly funded projects included the construction of Good Shepherd Hospital in New Bern, North Carolina; the hospital staff reorganization at Lincoln Hospital, Durham, North Carolina; and the remodeling and building of facilities at St. Agnes Hospital, Raleigh, North Carolina, at L. Richardson Memorial Hospital,

Greensboro, North Carolina, and at Good Samaritan Hospital, Charlotte, North Carolina.

23. A copy of James Buchanan Duke's indenture creating the Duke Endowment can be found in Robert F. Durden, *The Dukes of Durham, 1865–1929* (Durham: Duke University Press, 1975), pp. 268–80. For information on the activities of the hospital section see George P. Harris, "The Work of the Duke Endowment with South Carolina Hospitals," *Journal of the South Carolina Medical Association* 38 (1942): 282–84; W.S. Rankin, "The Interest of the Duke Endowment in Medical Education," *JAMA* 92 (1929): 1274; and W.S. Rankin, "The Hospital Program of the Duke Endowment," Box 6, Duke Endowment Archives.

24. The Duke Endowment, *Annual Report of the Hospital Section, 1925* (Charlotte: The Endowment, 1926), pp. 96–97, 208–9.

25. "One First in Which We May Take Justifiable Pride," *The Health Bulletin* (North Carolina State Board of Health) 45 (March 1930): 6; "Aaron McDuffie Moore," *JNMA* 16 (1924): 73; Durden, *Dukes of Durham*, pp. 104–5; P. Preston Reynolds, "Watts Hospital, 1895–1976: Paternalism and Race: The Evolution of A Southern Institution in Durham, North Carolina" (Ph.D. diss., Duke University, 1986), pp. 17–22, 51–60; and "Inadequate Negro Hospitals," *Charlotte Observer* 20 (November 1945): p. 12, Box 171, Duke Endowment Archives.

26. The Duke Endowment, *The Annual Report of the Hospital Section, 1937* (Charlotte: The Endowment, 1938), pp. 24–25; and W.S. Rankin to H.M. Green, 5 November 1931, Box 2, Rankin Papers.

27. W.S. Rankin to Edwin R. Embree, 8 June 1928, Box 180, Duke Endowment Archives; W.S. Rankin to C.V. Reynolds, 17 January 1941, Box 178, Duke Endowment Archives; and W.S. Rankin to Wilburt C. Davison, 23 February 1934, Box 181, Duke Endowment Archives; and W.S. Rankin to Michael M. Davis, 12 April 1929, Box 2, Rankin Papers.

28. W.S. Rankin to A.H. Sands, 16 September 1925, Box 181, Duke Endowment Archives; M.O. Bousfield, "Negro Health," 9 October 1936, pp. 16–7; W.S. Rankin to Wilburt C. Davison, 25 May 1936, Box 181, Duke Endowment Archives; George P. Harris, "Lincoln Hospital," memorandum, 10 May 1933, Box 181, Duke Endowment Archives; Davison to Rankin, 4 April 1934, Box 181, Duke Endowment Archives; and George P. Harris, memoranda, 17 June 1934 and 20 November 1934, Box 181, Duke Endowment Archives.

29. W.S. Rankin to Wilburt C. Davison, 23 February 1934, Box 181, Duke Endowment Archives; and James E. Shepherd to W.S. Rankin, 31 March 1934, Box 181, Duke Endowment Archives.

30. Bousfield, "Negro Health," 9 October 1936, p. 16; and Peter Marshall Murray to M.O. Bousfield, 17 November 1932, Box 4, Murray Papers.

31. George P. Harris, "Lincoln Hospital," memorandum, 20 November 1934, Box 181, Duke Endowment Archives; M. Eugene Newson to Wilburt C. Davison, 30 April 1934, Box 181, Duke Endowment Archives; James F. Gifford, *The Evolution of a Medical Center: A History of Medicine at Duke University to 1941* (Durham: Duke University Press, 1972), pp. 163–67; and Reynolds, "Watts Hospital," pp. 155–59.

32. George P. Harris, 17 June 1934, Box 181, Duke Endowment Archives.

33. For information on the history of hospital administration see David Rosner, "Doing Well or Doing Good: The Ambivalent Focus of Hospital Administration," in Diana Elizabeth Hall and Janet Golden, eds., *The American General Hospital* (Ithaca: Cornell University Press, 1989), pp. 157–169; and Morris J. Vogel, "Managing Medicine: Creating A Profession of Hospital Administration in the United States, 1895–1915," in *The Hospital in History*, Lindsay Granshaw and Roy Porter, eds. (London: Routledge, 1989), pp. 243–60.

34. Bousfield, "Negro Health," 9 October 1936, p. 16.

35. George P. Harris, "Negro Hospital Situation in Columbia, South Carolina," 20 September 1933, Box 180, Duke Endowment Archives; "Waverly Fraternal Hospital," memorandum, 20 September 1938, Box 180, Duke Endowment Archives; Graham L. Davis, "Waverly Fraternal Hospital," n.d. (circa 1938), Box 180, Duke Endowment Archives; and Edward H. Beardsley, *A History of Neglect* (Knoxville: University of Tennessee Press, 1987), pp. 122–26.

36. Davis, "Waverly Fraternal Hospital"; and Memorandum, 26 April 1935, Box 180, Duke Endowment Archives.

37. Ibid; and George P. Harris, "Some Observations Concerning the Negro Hospital Situation in Columbia, South Carolina," memorandum, 20 September 1938, Box 180, Duke Endowment Archives.

38. M.O. Bousfield to B. Herbert, 18 April 1938, Box 180, Duke Endowment Archives; and W.S. Rankin to B. Herbert, 23 July 1938, Box 180, Duke Endowment Archives.

39. George P. Harris, "Record-Keeping Procedures in the Small General Hospital," paper presented at the Tri-State Conference of Hospital Administrators, Lincoln Hospital, Durham, NC, 24–25 October 1940, Box 181, Duke Endowment Archives. The percentage of hospitals that received endowment funding was calculated from information in the *Annual Reports of the Hospital Section, 1925–1937*. The percentage of assisted hospitals ranged from 50 percent in 1927 to 88 percent in 1934. The annual reports for 1938 and 1939 did not include adequate information to calculate the percentage of assisted hospitals.

40. Harris, "Record-Keeping Procedures"; and "Hospitals Registered by the American Medical Association," *Journal of the American Medical Association* 114 (1930): 1195–1258.

41. *General Education Board: Review and Final Report, 1902–1964* (New York: The Board, 1964), p. 3. For a general history of the GEB see Raymond B. Fosdick, *Adventure in Giving: The Story of the General Education Board* (New York: Harper & Row, 1962).

42. Raymond B. Fosdick, Wickliffe Rose, and James H. Dillard, "Negro Education," 6 October 1922, Box 331, GEB Papers, p. 24; and James D. Anderson, "Philanthropic Control Over Private Black Higher Education," in *Philanthropy and Cultural Imperialism*, ed. Robert F. Arnove (Boston: G. K. Hall, 1980), pp. 153–58.

43. J. Davis to P.B. Young, 16 May 1944 cited in Fosdick, *Adventure in Giving*, p. 183; and Memorandum, 17 February 1931, Box 260, GEB Papers.

44. *Proceedings of the Conference of Tennessee School Superintendents at Nashville, April 8–9, 1903* (Chapel Hill: University of North Carolina), cited in Waldemar A. Nielsen, *The Big Foundations* (New York: Columbia University Press, 1972), p. 335; and Minutes of the Interboard Committee on Negro Problems, 3 March 1929, Box 260, GEB Papers.

45. Abraham Flexner, *Medical Education in the United States and Canada* (New York: Carnegie Foundation for the Advancement of Teaching, Bulletin No. 4, 1910), p. 10. For a more comprehensive discussion of the impact of Flexner on black medical education see Todd L. Savitt, "Abraham Flexner and the Black Medical Schools," in *Beyond Flexner: Medical Education in the Twentieth Century*, eds. Barbara Barzansky and Norman Gevitz (New York: Greenwood Press, 1992), pp. 67–81.

46. Flexner, *Medical Education in the United States and Canada*, p. 10; Steven Shea and Mindy Thompson Fullilove, "Entry of Black and Other Minority Students Into U.S. Medical Schools," *New England Journal of Medicine* 313 (1985): 936. The aphorism, "making peaks higher," has been attributed to Wickliffe Rose, president of the GEB from 1923 to 1928. See Fosdick, *Adventure in Giving*, p. 230.

47. Fosdick, *Adventure in Giving*, pp. 176–77; James Summerville, *Educating Black Doctors: A History of Meharry Medical College* (Birmingham: University of Alabama Press, 1983), p. 97; and Darlene Clark Hine, "The Pursuit of Professional Equality: Meharry Medical College, 1921–1938, A Case Study," in *New Perspectives in Black Educational History*, eds. Vincent P. Franklin and James D. Anderson (Boston: G.K. Hall, 1978), pp. 173–92. The effects of the racist attitudes of philanthropies on the career of one African American scientist are explored in Manning, *Black Apollo of Science*.

48. Memorandum, Richard M. Pearce to Trevor Arnett, "Problems in Negro Education," 19 March 1929, Box 260, GEB Papers; Robert A. Lambert, "University of Chicago—Provident Hospital Project," 24 October 1929, Box 699, GEB Papers; and Thomas B. Appleget, "Report of Provident Hospital and Free Dispensary of Baltimore," memorandum, November 1927, Record Group 2, Office of Messrs. Rockefeller, Medical Interests Series, Box 21, Rockefeller Family Papers.

49. Robert A. Lambert, "Negro Hospital in Richmond, Virginia," memorandum, 23 November 1929, Box 696, GEB Papers; "Medical College of Virginia—St. Philip Hospital of Nursing," memorandum, April 1944, Box 696, GEB Papers; and Lee E. Sutton, "The St. Philip Hospital Postgraduate Clinic for Negro Physicians: A Five Year Report," *The Southern Medical Journal* 29 (1936): 690–94.

50. Lambert, "Negro Hospital in Richmond," pp. 2–3.

51. "Postgraduate Training for Negro Physicians," *GEB Trustee Bulletin*, April 1938, n.p.

52. Robert A. Lambert, diary, 19 April 1929, Box 212, GEB Papers.

53. "Postgraduate Training for Negro Physicians."

54. "Hospitals Registered by the American Medical Association," *JAMA* 114 (1940): 1195–1258.

55. "Medico Says Race Should Offer Concrete Results of Own Ability,"; *East Tennessee News* (Knoxville, Tennessee), 22 January 1931; and "'Every Negro in America Should Thank God to Julius Rosenwald'—Dr. Kenney," *Pittsburgh Courier*, 14 March 1931 [both articles in Tuskegee Institute News Clipping File (TCF), (Hospitals—1931, New York)].

56. Manhattan Medical Society, "Equal Opportunity—No More—No Less! An Open Letter to Mr. Edwin R. Embree, President of the Julius Rosenwald Fund," New York City, 28 January 1931, Box 76, Rosenwald Fund Papers; George S. Schuyler, "News and Reviews," *Pittsburgh Courier*, 13 December 1930, clipping in Louis T. Wright Scrapbook, Box 3A, Wright Papers, Harvard; George S. Schuyler, "Notes From the Inner Sanctum," *National News*, 3 March 1932, p. 5; and *Chicago Whip*, 20 June 1931, clipping in Louis T. Wright Scrapbook, Box 3A, Wright Papers, Harvard.

57. "Edwin R. Embree of Rosenwald Fund Clarifies Stand on Negro Hospitals," *New York Amsterdam News*, 31 December 1930, p. 20.

5. "Progressive Disappointment and Defeat": The Provident Hospital Project.

1. Langston Hughes, "Interne at Provident," in his *Selected Poems* (New York: Vintage Books, 1974), p. 184; and Alan Gregg, "University of Chicago and Provident Hospital," memorandum, 5 July 1938, Box 699, General Education Board (GEB) Papers. This was not the first affiliation of a black hospital with a white medical college. Richmond's St. Philip Hospital was affiliated with the Medical College of Virginia. However, the hospital barred black physicians. The project in Chicago did represent the first affiliation of a black hospital with a white medical school for the purpose of training black medical professionals.

2. Robert McMurdy to William C. Graves, 24 May 1913, Box 31, Rosenwald Papers.

3. Ethel Johns, "A Study of the Present Status of the Negro Woman in Nursing, 1925," pp. B. 2–3, Box 122, Record Group 1.1, Series 200C, Rockefeller Foundation Archives; Allan H. Spear, *Black Chicago: The Making of a Negro Ghetto, 1890–1920* (Chicago: University of Chicago, 1967), p. 141. For a comprehensive study of black migration to Chicago see James R. Grossman, *Land of Hope: Chicago, Black Southerners and the Great Migration* (Chicago: University of Chicago Press, 1989).

4. H.G. Ellerd to M. George Arthur, 21 February 1929, Box 242, Rosenwald Fund Papers.

5. Memorandum on Provident Hospital, n.d., Box 130, Swift Papers; and Kenneth M. Ludmerer, *Learning To Heal: The Development of American Medical Education* (New York: Basic Books), pp. 219–233.

6. Franklin C. McLean to Robert M. Hutchins, 13 September 1929, Box 242, Rosenwald Fund Papers.

7. "Medical Education in the United States: Annual Presentation of Educational Data for 1928 by the Council on Medical Education and Hospitals," *JAMA* 91 (1928): 480; and B.C.H. Harvey, "Provision For Training Colored Medical Students," *JNMA* 22 (1930): 480.

8. Richard M. Pearce, "Negro Medical Education," memorandum, 4 December 1928, Box 260, GEB Papers.

9. Memorandum to Committee on Instruction and Equipment of the University of Chicago by Franklin C. McLean, 28 June 1929; and Frederic Woodward to David H. Stevens, 2 July 1929, Box 130, Swift Papers.

10. "Agreement for Cooperation Between the University of Chicago and Provident Hospital and Training School Association," 24 October 1929, Box 699, GEB Papers.

11. *Crisis* 24 (1922): 108, 110; "Dr. Julian H. Lewis to Teach in University of Chicago," *JNMA* 14 (1922): 200–201; and A.L. Jackson to Franklin C. McLean, 14 May 2929, Box 130, Swift Papers.

12. Robert A. Lambert, "Negro Hospitals in Chicago," memorandum, 1 March 1929, p. 3, Box 699, GEB Papers; Thomas J. Helsom, "The New Provident Hospital and Training School," *JNMA* 22 (1930): 129; and M.R. Werner, *Julius Rosenwald: The Life of a Practical Humanitarian* (New York: Harper, 1939), p. 274. A systematic review of the *Chicago Defender* from July 1929 to December 1929 did not reveal any opposition to the proposed affiliation.

13. Thomas Lee Philpot, *The Slum and the Ghetto* (New York: Oxford University Press, 1978), p. 274.

14. Subscription list, 26 February 1930, Box 699, GEB Papers; and Edwin R. Embree to Foundation Presidents, 9 July 1929, Box 244, Rosenwald Fund Papers.

15. "Rockefeller Foundation Source Material, vol. 10," pp. 2651–52, Rockefeller Archive Center; and Marshall R. Urist, "Phoenix of Physiology and Medicine: Franklin Chambers McLean," *Perspectives in Biology and Medicine* 19 (Autumn 1975): 31–34.

16. Lambert, "Negro Hospitals in Chicago," p. 2; and Richard Pearce, "Negro Medical Education," 19 March 1929, Box 260, GEB Papers.

17. Robert M. Hutchins to Trevor Arnett, 16 October 1929, Box 699, GEB Papers; GEB Pledge M-58, GEB Papers.

18. L.R. Steere to W.W. Brierly, 12 March 1930, Box 699, GEB Papers; and "Report of the General Director to the Directors of the Commonwealth Fund," 9 April 1930, Box 242, Rosenwald Fund Papers.

19. Franklin C. McLean to L.R. Steere, 4 March 1930; and Robert A. Lambert, diary, 28 March 1930, Box 699, GEB Papers.

20. Franklin C. McLean to Alan Gregg, 26 February 1931; A.L. Jackson to McLean, 12 September 1931; and GEB Appropriation No. 117, 30 September 1931, Box 699, GEB Papers.

21. For biographical information on Jackson see Thomas Yenser, ed., *Who's Who in Colored America*, 5th ed. (New York: Yenser, 1940), p. 275; and Edwin R. Embree to A.L. Jackson, 16 December 1931, Box 242, Rosenwald Fund Papers.

22. Memorandum on Provident Hospital Agreement, 26 May 1932, Box 699, GEB Papers; Lessing H. Rosenwald and Edwin R. Embree to Raymond B. Fosdick, 25 May 1932; and Max Mason to Trevor Arnett, 10 June 1932, Box 212, GEB Papers.

23. Alan Gregg to Franklin C. McLean, 21 June 1932; and Alan Gregg, "Provident Hospital," memorandum, 20 June 1932, Box 699, GEB Papers.

24. Urist, "Phoenix of Physiology and Medicine," pp. 44–46; M.M. Davis to E.R. Embree, 4 February 1931, Box 103, Rosenwald Fund Papers; Robert A. Lambert, diary, 28 March 1930, Box 699, GEB Papers; and "Annual Report, President of the Board of Trustees, A.L. Jackson to Members of the Provident Hospital and Training School Association," 31 May 1930, Box 245, Rosenwald Fund Papers.

25. Robert A. Lambert, interview with Henry S. Houghton, 14 September 1934; Robert A. Lambert, "GEB Grant to University of Chicago for Negro Medical Education," memorandum, December 1934, Box 699, GEB Papers; and *Provident Hospital and Training School Annual Report for 1933*, p.15.

26. Harsba F. Bouyer to Claude A. Barnett, 3 July 1936, Reel 5, Barnett Papers; and Midian O. Bousfield, "Program for Negro Health," 9 October 1939, p. 29, Box 76, Rosenwald Fund Papers.

27. Lambert, "GEB Grant to University of Chicago for Negro Medical Education,"; and Alan Gregg, interoffice memorandum, n.d., (circa December 1934), Box 699, GEB Papers.

28. A.L. Jackson, "Report of the Chairman of the Executive Committee," 17 April 1934, Box 244, Rosenwald Fund Papers; and Lambert, interview with Houghton, 14 September 1934.

29. "Charitable Segregation," *The Fraternal Review* 10 (January 1931): n.p.; Manhattan Medical Society, "Equal Opportunity—No More—No Less!: An Open Letter to Mr. Edwin R. Embree, President of the Julius Rosenwald Fund," New York, 28 January 1931, Box 76, Rosenwald Papers; George S. Schuyler, "Notes From the Inner Sanctum," *National News*, 3 March 1932, p. 5; A.N. Field, "Use Provident Hospital as 'Jim-Crow' School," *Chicago Defender*, 26 January 1935, p. 1,; and Philpot, *The Slum and the Ghetto*, p. 310.

30. A.N. Field, "Use of Chicago Color Line Hits Provident Hospital," *Chicago Defender*, 13 November 1934, p. 13; J.A. Berry and E.M. Johnson to G.R. Arthur and other Provident Hospital Trustees, 29 December 1934, Box 243, Rosenwald Fund Papers; A.C. MacNeal to Board of Trustees of the University of Chicago, 8 May 1935, Box 130, Swift Papers; and A.N. Field, "Use Provident Hospital," pp. 1, 4.

31. Open Letter to the Board of Trustees of Provident Hospital, 2 January 1935, Box 254, Rosenwald Fund Papers.

32. "Greater Provident Hospital," *JNMA* 25 (1933): 25; "The Chicago Meeting," *JNMA* 25 (1933): 171; John A. Kenney, "A Reasonable Program for Our Hospitalization Movement," *JNMA* 23 (1931): 158; and Louis T. Wright, "Health Problems of the Negro," *Interracial Review* 8 (January 1935): 7.

33. A.L. Jackson to Educational Committee, 17 October 1934; A.L. Jackson to Claude A. Barnett, 17 October 1934; A.L. Jackson to Educational

Committee, 18 October 1934; Handwritten notes, no author, n.d. (circa January 1935); and Barnett to Jackson, 25 January 1935, Reel 2, Barnett Papers.

34. Robert A. Lambert, interview with Frederic Woodward, 2 April 1935; and Robert A. Lambert, "Negro Education, Provident Hospital," memorandum, 29 November 1938, Box 699, GEB Papers.

35. Robert A. Lambert, interview with Edwin R. Embree, 22 March 1935 and Arthur C. Bachmeyer, memorandum to Board of Trustees of Provident Hospital, 29 May 1935, Box 699, GEB Papers.

36. Robert A. Lambert, interview with Frederic Woodward, 2 April 1935; Alan Gregg, interview with Arthur Bachmeyer, 30 July 1935; and Robert A. Lambert, interview with William H. Taliaferro, 26 February 1935, Box 699, GEB Papers.

37. Midian O. Bousfield, "Negro Health," 13 December 1937, Box 76.

38. Edwin R. Embree to Various Foundation Presidents, 22 April 1938; and E.R. Embree to M. McKeown, 25 August 1938, Box 243, Rosenwald Fund Papers.

39. Robert A. Lambert, interoffice memorandum, 9 January 1939, Box 699, Folder 7202, GEB Papers.

40. Robert A. Lambert, "Negro Education, Provident Hospital," memorandum, 29 November 1938, pp. 1–5; and Edwin R. Embree and Robert A. Lambert, telephone interview, 12 April 1938, Box 699, GEB Papers.

41. Robert A. Lambert, "Negro Education, Provident Hospital," p. 4.

42. Robert Hutchins to Raymond B. Fosdick, 25 February 1939; Fosdick to Hutchins, 6 March 1939; and W.W. Brierly to Hutchins, 18 April 1939, Box 700, GEB Papers.

43. *Annual Report of Provident Hospital for 1938* (Chicago: The Hospital, 1939), pp. 10–12. There was a capitation scheme for relief patients that did not fully reimburse hospitals for the care of these patients.

44. Claude Barnett, "Memorandum to Trustees," n.d. (circa 1938), Reel 3, Barnett Papers; Emmet Bey, Interview with Robert A. Lambert, 18 November 1935, Box 699, GEB Papers; and Alan Gregg, Interview with R. Hutchins, 10 March 1936, Box 699, GEB Papers.

45. John W. Lawlah, "Review of the Educational Training Program for Negroes in Clinical Medicine at Provident Hospital, Chicago, Illinois, for the Years 1930 to 1941," n.d. (circa 1951), Provident Medical Center.

46. Dietrich C. Reitzes, *Negroes and Medicine* (Cambridge: Harvard University Press, 1958), pp. 124–25.

6. Cleveland—A Black Hospital at Last

1. Henry F. Pringle and Katharine Pringle, "The Color Line in Medicine," *Saturday Evening Post*, 24 January 1948, pp. 69–70.

2. Russell H. Davis, *Black Americans in Cleveland* (Washington, D.C.: Associated Publishers, 1972), pp. 177, 180; "To Be—Or Not to Be?", editorial, *Cleveland Advocate*, 26 February 1921, n.p., Tuskegee Institute News Clipping File (TCF), (Hospitals—1921); Robert I. Drake, "The Negro in Cleveland," *Cleveland Advocate*, 18 September 1915, p. 4; *The Gazette (Cleve-*

land), 12 June 1915, p. 3; and "New Segregation Efforts," *The Gazette (Cleveland)*, 28 June 1915, p. 2.

3. Cleveland Hospital Council, *Cleveland Hospital and Health Survey* (Cleveland: The Council, 1920), p. 863.

4. For biographical information on Purvis see W. Montague Cobb, "Charles Burleigh Purvis, M.D., 1842–1929," *JNMA* 45 (1953): 79–82; Kenneth L. Kusmer, *A Ghetto Takes Shape: Black Cleveland, 1870–1930* (Urbana: University of Illinois Press, 1976), pp. 63–64; and Jane Edna Hunter, *A Nickel and a Prayer* (Cleveland: Elli Kani Publishing, 1940), pp. 70–71.

5. Kusmer, *A Ghetto Takes Shape*, pp. 10, 60.

6. "'Jim Crow' Segregation," *The Gazette (Cleveland)*, 12 February 1921, p. 3; *The Gazette (Cleveland)*, 19 February 1921, p. 3; "Colored Hospital Not Needed, Or Wanted," 26 February 1921, p. 3; "To Be—Or Not to Be?", editorial, *Cleveland Advocate*, 26 February 1921, n.p., TCF (Hospitals—1921); and "A Jim Crow Hospital," *The Gazette (Cleveland)* 10 September 1921, p. 1.

7. "Opposed To A Colored Hospital," *The Gazette (Cleveland)*, 26 February 1921, p. 1.

8. "To Be—Or Not to Be?", *Cleveland Advocate*.

9. For additional biographical information on Garvin see W. Montague Cobb, "Charles Herbert Garvin, 1889–1968," *JNMA* 61 (1969): 85–89; Russell H. Davis, *Black Americans in Cleveland* (Washington: Associated Publishers, 1972), p. 178; Rayford W. Logan and Michael R. Winston, eds., *Dictionary of American Negro Biography* (New York: W.W. Norton, 1982), pp. 256–57; David D. Van Tassel and John J. Grabowski, eds., *The Encyclopedia of Cleveland History*, (Bloomington: Indiana University Press), p. 436; Kusmer, *A Ghetto Takes Shape*, pp. 250–51; and Herbert M. Morais, *The History of the Negro in Medicine* (New York: Publishers Company, 1967), pp. 111– 12.

10. Articles written by Garvin include "Negro Health," *Opportunity* 2 (November 1924): 341–42; "Immunity to Disease Among Dark-Skinned People," *Opportunity* 4 (August 1926): 242–45; and "White Plague and Black Folk," *Opportunity* 8 (August 1930): 232–35. Garvin wrote an unpublished manuscript on African contributions to medical history. A copy of the manuscript, "Africa's Contribution to Medicine: The Negroid Peoples' Role in its Evolution," can be found in Box 2 of the Garvin Papers.

11. Garvin, "White Plague and Black Folk," p. 233; and "The 'New Negro' Physician," unpublished manuscript, n.d., Box 1, Garvin Papers.

12. Davis, *Black Americans in Cleveland*, pp. 225–26; "Bomb Explodes in Dr. Garvin's House" and "Doctor's Home Rocked by Bomb," clippings found in Cleveland, Ohio, Branch Files, Box G157, NAACP Papers, Library of Congress; and Mabel Clark to James Weldon Johnson, 12 July 1926, Cleveland, Ohio, Branch Files, Box G157, NAACP Papers, Library of Congress.

13. NAACP Press Release, 11 February 1926; James Weldon Johnson to Mabel Clark, 13 July 1926; Harry E. Davis to Johnson, 15 July 1926; Johnson to Davis, 19 July 1926; Clayborne George to Walter White, 20 July 1926; White to Edwin D. Barry, 24 July 1926; NAACP Press Release 30 July 1926; Clark to Johnson, 24 March 1927, Cleveland, Ohio, Branch Files, Box

G157, NAACP Papers, Library of Congress; and Kusmer, *A Ghetto Takes Shape*, pp. 168–69. For more information on the Sweet trial see Walter White, *A Man Called White* (New York: Viking Press), pp. 72–79; and Richard W. Thomas, *Life for Us Is What We Make It: Building Black Community in Detroit, 1915–1945* (Bloomington: Indiana University Press), pp. 137–40.

14. For a more extensive discussion of the Mercy Hospital movement see William Giffin, "The Mercy Hospital Controversy Among Cleveland's Afro-American Civic Leaders," *Journal of Negro History* 61 (1976): 327–50.

15. "Pros and Cons for the Mercy Hospital Association in Conference," clipping, n.d. (circa 1926), Box 3, Garvin Papers.

16. "Does Cleveland Need A Negro Manned Hospital?: Facts Are The Answer," n.d., Western Reserve Historical Society Library.

17. Harry C. Smith to George A. Myers, 28 March 1927, Box 18, Myers Papers. For biographical information on Smith see Van Tassel and Grabowski, *The Encyclopedia of Cleveland History*, p. 902; Kusmer, *A Ghetto Takes Shape*, pp. 130–32; and Russell H. Davis, *Memorable Negroes in Cleveland's Past* (Cleveland: Western Reserve Historical Society, 1969), pp. 32–33. For an analysis of Smith's political activities see William Giffin, "Black Insurgency in the Republican Party of Ohio, 1920–1932," *Ohio History* 82 (1973): 25–45; and Hunter, *A Nickel and a Prayer*, p. 94.

18. *The Gazette (Cleveland)* contains several examples of Smith's vitriolic editorials against the proposed hospital: "Kluxers and 'Jim-Crow' Negroes," 5 March 1927, p. 2; "No Mercy Hospital," 19 March 1927, p. 2; "Ku Klux Klan! Church Debts!", 22 April, p. 2; "Mercy Hospital Advocates," 26 March 1927, p. 1. Harry C. Smith to George A. Myers, 2 April 1927, Box 18, Myers Papers; and "Owe Over Half A Million," *The Gazette (Cleveland)*, 19 March 1927, p. 1.

19. For biographical information on Myers see Davis, *Memorable Negroes*, pp. 30–31; Van Tassell and Grabowski, *The Encyclopedia of Cleveland History*, pp. 708–9; and Kusmer, *A Ghetto Takes Shape*, pp. 122–23. Smith to Myers, 19 February 1927 and 24 February 1927, Box 18, Myers Papers; Myers to William R. Myers, 7 March 1927, Box 18, Myers Papers; and "Opposed To Mercy Hospital," *The Gazette (Cleveland)*, 5 March 1927, p. 1.

20. "A 'Jim Crow' Hospital Wanted," *The Gazette (Cleveland)* 2 April, 1927, p. 1; and "Opposed to Mercy Hospital Move," *The Gazette (Cleveland)*, 5 March 1927, p. 1.

21. George A. Myers to William R. Hopkins, 29 December 1927, Box 18, Myers Papers; and "Some 'Negroes' Who Are Wanting More Segregation!", *The Gazette (Cleveland)*, 12 February 1927.

22. "Lord Have Mercy," *The Gazette (Cleveland)*, 5 March 1927, p. 2; and "Some 'Negroes' Who Want More Segregation," *The Gazette (Cleveland)*, 5 February 1927, p. 2.

23. "Mercy Hospital Advocates," *The Gazette (Cleveland)*, 2 April 1927, p. 2; and Harry C. Smith to George A. Myers, 2 February 1927, Box 18, Myers Papers.

24. Horace C. Bailey to Harry C. Smith, *The Gazette (Cleveland)*, 5 March 1927, p. 1; "Mercy Hospital Advocates," *The Gazette (Cleveland)*,

26 March 1927, p. 1; "Mercy Hospital Scheme Busted," *The Gazette (Cleveland)*, 12 March 1927, p. 1; and "Minutes of the Negro Welfare Association," 7 April 1921 and 5 May 1927, Box 3, Cleveland Branch, Urban League Papers.

25. Charles W. White to Robert Bagnall, 28 March 1927, Cleveland, Ohio, Branch Files, Box G157, NAACP Papers, Library of Congress; and Charles H. Garvin, "The Negro Physicians and Hospitals of Cleveland," *JNMA* 22 (1930): 125. The six physicians were Garvin, James Owen, Linnell Rodgers, Middleton H. Lambright, Sr., Armin Evans and L.O. Baumgartner. "Want More 'Jim Crow'," *The Gazette (Cleveland)*, 1 May 1926, p. 2; "Dr. Ellis A. Dale Honored," *The Gazette (Cleveland)*, 29 January 1927, p. 2; and "No Mercy Hospital," *The Gazette (Cleveland)*, 19 March 1927, p. 2.

26. Charles W. White to Robert Bagnall, 28 March 1927; Russell W. Jelliffe to Bagnall, 7 May 1926, Cleveland, Ohio, Branch Files, Box G157, NAACP Papers, Library of Congress; Jelliffe to Bagnall, 7 May 1926, Cleveland, Ohio, Branch Files, Box G157, NAACP Papers, Library of Congress; and Newspaper clipping, "Pros and Cons for the Mercy Hospital Association in Conference," Box 3, Garvin Papers.

27. Charles W. White to Robert Bagnall, 21 February 1927, Cleveland, Ohio, Branch Files, Box G157, NAACP Papers, Library of Congress; Newspaper clipping, "Pros and Cons for the Mercy Hospital Association in Conference," Box 3, Garvin Papers; Bagnall to White, 31 March 1927, Cleveland, Ohio Branch Files, Box G157, NAACP Papers, Library of Congress; Louis T. Wright, "Health Problems of the Negro," *Interracial Review*, 8 (January 1935): 6–8; and Kusmer, *A Ghetto Takes Shape*, p. 268.

28. *The Gazette (Cleveland)*, 21 May 1921, p. 2 ; 11 June 1927, p. 2.; and 7 May 1927, p. 3; and "Another Frost," *The Gazette (Cleveland)*, 11 June 1927, p. 2.

29. Garvin, "The Negro Physicians," p. 125.

30. George A. Myers to William R. Hopkins, 6 February 1928, Box 18, Myers Papers; Resolution from Quinn A.M.E. Church, 2 March 1930, Box 1, Morgan Papers; "They Struck Back," *The Gazette (Cleveland)*, 19 November 1927, p. 1; and Myers to Hopkins, 13 December 1927, Box 18, Myers Papers.

31. Harry E. Davis to James Weldon Johnson, 1 November 1927, Cleveland, Ohio, Branch Files, Box G157, NAACP Papers, Library of Congress; and Myers to Hopkins, 13 December 1927, Box 18, Myers Papers.

32. The committee's tour included visits in Chicago, Illinois, to Cook County Hospital, Municipal Sanatorium for Tuberculosis, and Provident Hospital; in Kansas City, Missouri, to Kansas City General Hospital, No. 2, Wheatley Hospital, and St. Luke's Hospital; in St. Louis, Missouri, to City Hospital, No. 1 and City Hospital, No. 2; in Washington, D.C., to Freedmen's Hospital, Howard University Medical School, City Tuberculosis Sanatorium, and City General Hospital; in Philadelphia, Pennsylvania, to Philadelphia General Hospital, Mercy Hospital, and the University of Pennsylvania School of Medicine; in New York City, New York, to Harlem Hospital, Lincoln Hospital, and Bellevue Hospital, and in Boston, Massachusetts, to Harvard University Medical School and one anonymous hospital. Report,

"Committee Investigating the Admittance of Colored Interns and Nurses to the Staff of Cleveland City Hospital," 12 December 1927, Western Reserve Historical Society Library.

33. Ibid., p. 25 and Exhibit #2, p. 5.

34. Ibid., pp. 18, 19. The medical school, however, did not admit a black woman until 1960. On the other hand, the doors of the school had been opened to white women since 1914. George W. Corner, *Two Centuries of Medicine: A History of the School of Medicine, University of Pennsylvania* (Philadelphia: J.B. Lippincott, 1965), p. 249; and Personal Correspondence, Office of Minority Affairs, University of Pennsylvania School of Medicine.

35. "Committee Investigating," pp. 2, 19, 24.

36. Ibid., p. 20.

37. Ibid., pp. 4, 13, 17, and 23.

38. Ibid., pp. 10–12.

39. Ibid., p. 6; pp. 11–12; and p. 22.

40. Ibid., pp. 17–18.

41. Ibid., n.p.; Charles H. Garvin, "Pioneering in Cleveland," *The Women's Voice*, September 1939, p. 15.

42. "Committee Investigating," n.p.; NAACP Press Release, "Negro Physician Appointed To Staff of Cleveland City Hospital," Cleveland, Ohio, Branch Files, Box G158, NAACP Papers, Library of Congress; and Charles W. White to James Weldon Johnson, 23 July 1928, Cleveland, Ohio, Branch Files, Box G158, NAACP Papers, Library of Congress.

43. Garvin, "The Negro Physicians," p. 125.

44. Cleveland Branch, NAACP, "Annual Report of the President," 21 November 1929, pp. 4–5, Cleveland, Ohio, Branch Files, Box G158, NAACP Papers, Library of Congress.

45. Ibid., pp. 5–6.

46. "Go Back 'Home' Gregg!", *The Gazette (Cleveland)*, 13 April 1929; and "Gregg's Latest Hospital Idea!", *The Gazette (Cleveland)*, 20 April 1929.

47. Garvin, "The Negro Physicians," p. 125; "Brown To Act," *The Gazette (Cleveland)*, 16 March 1929, p. 1; "Not Time," *The Gazette (Cleveland)*, 6 April 1929, p. 2; "Opposed to 'Jim Crow' Hospital!," *The Gazette (Cleveland)*, 13 April 1929, p. 1; and "Gregg's Latest Hospital Idea!", *The Gazette (Cleveland)*, 20 April 1929, p. 2.

48. Newspaper clipping, "City Hospital on East Side Urged," n.d. (circa September 1929), Box 3, Garvin Papers.

49. "Our Hospital Problems," *JNMA* 21 (1929): 115–16.

50. "Exit Gregg," *The Gazette (Cleveland)*, 16 November 1929, p. 2; "'Jim Crow' Hospital," *The Gazette (Cleveland)*, 16 November 1929, p. 2; and "Brown Makes A 'Murphy' Finish!", *The Gazette (Cleveland)*, 23 November 1929, p. 1.

51. "Hopkins Out! Blossom Must Go Now!", *The Gazette (Cleveland)*, 18 January 1930, p. 1; Davis, *Black Americans in Cleveland*, pp. 232–36; Christopher G. Wye, "Midwest Ghetto: Patterns of Negro Life and Thought in Cleveland, Ohio, 1929–45" (Ph.D. dissertation, Kent State University,

1973), pp. 339–44; and Thomas F. Campbell, *Daniel E. Morgan, 1877–1949: The Good Citizen in Politics* (Cleveland: Western Reserve University Press, 1966), pp. 115–17.

52. "Hopkins Out! Blossom Must Go Now!," *Gazette (Cleveland),* 18 January 1930, p. 1; and Charles W. White to Walter White, 14 January 1930, Cleveland, Ohio, Branch Files, Box G158, NAACP Papers, Library of Congress.

53. Walter White to Harry Davis, 20 June 1931, Cleveland, Ohio, Branch Files, Box G158 NAACP Papers, Library of Congress; and Middleton H. Lambright, Jr., "Invited Commentary," in *A Century of Black Surgeons: The USA Experience,* vol. 2, eds., Claude Organ and Margaret Kosiba (Norman, Okla.: Transcript Press, 1987), p. 555.

54. J. E. Morgan, "Frederick Douglass Stubbs: A Pioneer, Including Some Experiences in Integration," *Cleveland Physician* 69 (September 1984): 3–5; Frederick Douglass Stubbs, "Remarks Delivered at the Health Session," Annual Conference of the National Association for the Advancement of Colored People, 20 June 1940, Philadelphia, p. 7, NAACP Papers, Library of Congress, Part I, Microfilm edition, Reel 10; and Campbell, *Daniel E. Morgan, 1877–1949: The Good Citizen in Politics,* p. 117. For biographical information on Stubbs see W. Montague Cobb, "Frederick Douglass Stubbs, 1906–1947, An Appreciation," *JNMA* 40 (1948): 24–26; Charles A. Tollett, Sr., "Frederick Douglass Stubbs, M.D., F.A.C.S.," in Organ and Kosiba, eds., *A Century of Black Surgeons,* vol. 2, pp. 529–54; and Morgan, "Frederick Douglass Stubbs."

55. Joe T. Thomas to Maurice Maschke, 24 January 1931, Box 1, Morgan Papers.

56. Morgan, "Frederick Douglass Stubbs," pp. 3, 5; and Stubbs, "Remarks Delivered at the Health Session," p. 9.

57. Laurance M. Weinberger, "Racism and Other Prejudices: Notes on an Internship Fifty-Six Years Ago," *Pharos* (Fall 1989): 17–18.

58. Morgan, "Frederick Douglass Stubbs," p. 5; and Garvin, "Pioneering," p. 20.

59. Garvin, "Pioneering," p. 20; and "Biographical Sketch of Dr. Ulysses G. Mason," Box 1, Forest City Hospital Archives.

60. "A Recommended Hospital Program," editorial, *JNMA* 23 (1931): 143.

61. Frederick D. Stubbs, "Closed Intrapleural Pneumolysis in the Treatment of Pulmonary Tuberculosis," *JNMA* 31 (1939): 98; and "Negro Health," *Time,* 8 April 1940, p. 41. At the time thoracoplasty and phrenicectomy were operations performed to treat tuberculosis. Thoracoplasty consisted of resecting ribs in order to collapse the underlying lung. Phrenicectomy involved the cutting of the phrenic nerve, which supplies the diaphragm.

62. Frederick D. Stubbs, "The Purpose of the Community Hospital," *JNMA* 36 (1944): 152–54.

63. Interview, Ulysses G. Mason, 6 June 1989, Cleveland, Ohio.

64. Ulysses G. Mason to Roscoe C. Giles, 31 December 1940, Box 1, Forest City Hospital Archives; Ulysses G. Mason, "Problems Incidental to

Negro Staff Training in Hospitals," *Hospitals* 18 (March 1944): 71–72; Garvin, "Pioneering," pp. 14–15, 20–21; and Interview, Ulysses G. Mason, 6 June 1989, Cleveland, Ohio.

65. "Some Cases Under Investigation By The Local N.A.A.C.P. Branch," February–March 1933; and "NAACP Activities, Cleveland Branch, 1932–1933," Cleveland, Ohio, Branch Files, Box G159, NAACP Papers, Library of Congress.

66. Mason to various physicians, 10 October 1939, Box 1, Forest City Hospital Archives; and Minutes of the First Meeting, 26 October 1939, Box 2, Forest City Hospital Archives.

67. Articles of Incorporation, Forest City Hospital Association, 15 July 1940, Box 1, Forest City Hospital Archives; and "Hospital Association Gets Charter," *Cleveland Call and Post*, 31 August 1940, pp. 1, 2.

68. Minutes, Forest City Hospital Association, 12 December 1940, Box 2, Forest City Hospital Archives; and Ulysses G. Mason, "Needed—One Hospital: A Prospectus," (circa 1941), Box 1, Forest City Hospital Archives.

69. Minutes, Forest City Hospital Association, 4 April 1942 and 17 January 1943, Box 2, Forest City Hospital Archives.

70. Ulysses G. Mason, "The Story of Forest City Hospital," 23 September 1964, Box 1, Forest City Hospital Archives; Minutes, Forest City Hospital Association, 7 November 1943, Box 2, Forest City Hospital Archives; and Ulysses G. Mason to Walter Weil, 19 December 1943, Box 1, Forest City Hospital Archives.

71. Mason, "The Story of Forest City Hospital"; H.P. Ladds and Harry Affelder to J. E. Rauschkolb, 23 July 1948, Box 1, Forest City Hospital Archives; and Minutes, Forest City Hospital Association, Box 1, 17 March 1957.

72. "Report of Cleveland Branch NAACP Hospital Committee on Forest City Hospital," n.d,. Cleveland, Ohio, Branch Files, Box 4, NAACP Papers, Western Reserve Historical Society (WRHS); N.K. Christopher and James E. Levy, "Report on Provident Hospital," n.d. (circa February 1944), Cleveland, Ohio, Branch Files, Box 4, NAACP Papers, WRHS; "Study of the Proposed Forest City Hospital by Cleveland Branch National Association for the Advancement of Colored People, August 1945, Box 1, Forest City Hospital Archives; and NAACP, Press Release, 11 September 1945, Cleveland, Ohio, Branch Files, Box 4, NAACP Papers, WRHS.

73. Minutes, Cleveland Branch of the NAACP, 8 February 1948, Cleveland, Ohio, Branch Files, Box 4, NAACP Papers, WRHS; and W. Montague Cobb, *Medical Care and the Plight of the Negro* (New York: The National Association for the Advancement of Colored People, 1947), pp. 20–29, 73.

74. Charles Price, "Doctors Here Promise to Integrate Hospitals," *Cleveland Call and Post*, 26 June 1954, p. 2A.

75. Minutes, Hospital Committee of the NAACP and Representatives of Forest City Hospital Association, 21 April 1954, Cleveland, Ohio, Branch Files, Box 35, NAACP Papers, WRHS.

76. W. Montague Cobb, "Cleveland's Forest City Hospital Celebrates First Birthday," *JNMA* 51 (1959): 153.

Conclusion: The Black Hospital—A Vanishing Medical Institution

1. Walter A. Younge, "The President's Annual Address," *JNMA* 39 (1947): 236; and "Integration Only Practicable Goal," editorial, *JNMA* 43 (1951): 340. The strategies and activities of the two organizations are discussed in W. Montague Cobb, "National Health Program of the National Association for the Advancement of Colored People," *JNMA* 45 (1951): 333–39; "The Old Order Changeth," editorial, *JNMA* 46 (1954): 65–67; "Proceedings of the Imhotep National Conference on Hospital Integration," *JNMA* 49 (1957): 189–201, 272–73, 352–56; and 50 (1958): 66–76, 142–44, 224–33.

2. John A. Kenney, "The Negro Hospital Renaissance," *JNMA* 22 (1930): 109–12; and John A. Kenney, "A Shortage of Negro Doctors: With Special Reference To Residents and Internes," *JNMA* 32 (1940): 113.

3. "National Hospital Association," *JNMA* 15 (1923): 286; Julius Rosenwald Fund, compiled by Harrison L. Harris and Margaret L. Plumley, *Negro Hospitals: A Compilation of Available Statistics* (Chicago: Julius Rosenwald Fund, 1931), pp. 16, 19; "Investigation of Negro Hospitals," *Journal of the American Medical Association* 92 (1929): 1375–76; and Eugene H. Bradley, "Health, Hospitals, and the Negro," *Modern Hospital* 65 (August 1945): 43.

4. M.O. Bousfield, "Internships, Residencies, and Post Graduate Training," *JNMA* 32 (1940): 25–26; John A. Lawlah, "How the Facilities of Our Medical Schools Could Be Enlarged to Meet the Prospective Shortage of Negro Doctors," *JNMA* 35 (1943): 28.

5. W. Montague Cobb, *Medical Care and the Plight of the Negro* (New York: The National Association for the Advancement of Colored People, 1947), pp. 6–7; and "Proceedings of the Imhotep National Conference on Hospital Integration," *JNMA* 49 (1950): 200. One particularly powerful publication was the Southern Conference Educational Fund's *The Untouchables: The Meaning of Segregation in Hospitals*. This brochure graphically detailed nationwide hospital segregation over a twenty-year period. See Alfred Maund, *The Untouchables: The Meaning of Segregation in Hospitals* (New Orleans: Southern Conference Educational Fund, 1956).

6. Herbert Morais, *The History of the Negro in Medicine* (New York: Publishers Company for the Association for the Study of Negro Life and History, 1967), p. 131; and W. Montague Cobb, "Progress and Portents for the Negro in Medicine," *Crisis* 55 (April 1948): 119–20.

7. Cobb, *Medical Care and the Plight of the Negro*, p. 32; "Negro Veterans Administration Hospital Proposal Defeated," *JNMA* 43 (1951): 343; and U.S. Congress, House, *Providing for the Establishment of a Veterans Hospital for Negro Veterans at the Birthplace of Booker T. Washington in Franklin County, VA*, 82nd Cong., 1st sess., 1951, Report No. 230, pp. 1–3.

8. Herbert M. Morais, *The History of the Negro in Medicine,* p.36; Robinson E. Adkins, *Medical Care of Veterans* (Washington, D.C.: U.S. Government Printing Office, 1967), printed for the use of the Committee

on Veterans Affairs, 90th Cong., 1st sess., House Committee Print No. 4, pp. 248–50; and "Veterans Hospital at Tuskegee," *JNMA* 46 (1954): 140. For a full account of the integration of nurses into the armed services during World War II see Darlene Clark Hine, *Black Women in White: Racial Conflict and Cooperation in the Nursing Profession, 1890–1950* (Bloomington: Indiana University Press, 1989), pp. 162–86.

9. Rosemary Stevens, *In Sickness and in Wealth: American Hospitals in the Twentieth Century* (New York: Basic Books, 1989), pp. 216–19; Institute of Medicine, Division of Health Care Services, *Health Care in a Context of Civil Rights* (Washington, D.C.: National Academy Press, 1981), p. 168; Vane M. Hoge, "The National Construction Program," *JNMA* 40 (1948): 102–6; and Vane M. Hoge, "What the Hospital Act Means to Negroes," *National Negro Health News* 15 (April—June 1947): 1–3.

10. John A. Kenney, "Federal Versus State Control," editorial, *JNMA* 38 (1946): 74; "Medical Legislation," editorial, *JNMA* 39 (1947): 175; Morais, *The History of the Negro in Medicine*, p. 181.

11. Homer A. Jack, "Is Segregation Really Necessary?" *Modern Hospital* 76 (June 1951): 52.

12. Arguments for both sides can be found in Amos H. Carnegie, "But Integration is Empty Talk," *Modern Hospital* 76 (June 1951): 55–56, 142; Jack, "Is Segregation Really Necessary?", pp. 52–55, 138–40; and "The New Community Hospital of Evanston, Illinois," *JNMA* 45 (1953): 74–75.

13. "Memphis NAACP Branch Rescinds Endorsement of Negro Hospital," *JNMA* 44 (1952): 314–15.

14. Edward C. Halperin, "Desegregation of Hospitals and Medical Societies in North Carolina," *New England Journal of Medicine* 318 (1988): 61.

15. Edward H. Beardsley, *A History of Neglect: Health Care For Blacks and Mill Workers in the Twentieth Century South* (Knoxville: University of Tennessee Press, 1987), pp. 245–72; Halperin, "Desegregation of Hospitals and Medical Societies in North Carolina," pp. 59–63; "Federal Court Rules Bias in Federally Aided Hospitals Unconstitutional," *JNMA* 55 (1963): 558; "Greensboro, North Carolina Group Files Historic Suit Against Hospital Exclusion," *JNMA* 54 (1962): 259; J.F. Horty, "Simkins Case Creates Civil Rights Pattern: Simkins vs Moses H. Cone Memorial Hospital," *Modern Hospital* 102 (June 1964): 40–44, and 158; and "Of Hospitals, Doctors, and the Constitution," *Hospitals* 38 (1 June 1964): 116–17.

16. The Fifth Amendment prohibits the federal government from denying a person due process of law. The Fourteenth Amendment prohibits a state from denying a person due process and equal protection of the law.

17. Halperin, "Desegregation of Hospitals," pp. 60–61; "Court Finds Voluntary Hospital Subject to Fourteenth Amendment," *Modern Hospital* 102 (May 1964): 183; "Of Hospitals, Doctors, and the Constitution," *Hospitals* 38 (1 June 1964): 116–17; "Proceedings of the Imhotep National Conference on Hospital Integration," *JNMA* 49 (1957): 199–200; and "Second Suit Filed Against Wilmington, North Carolina Hospital," *JNMA* 53 (1961): 531.

18. M.L. Parker, "Civil Rights Act of 1964," *Health, Education, and Welfare Indicators* 8 (August 1964): xii; "Implementation of the Civil Rights Act in Medical Areas: Federal Rules and Regulations," *JNMA* 57 (1965): 157–63; and Institute of Medicine, *Health Care in a Context of Civil Rights*, pp. 159–78.

19. "The AMA Resolutions," *JNMA* 42 (1950): 324; Paul Cornely, "Segregation and Discrimination in Medical Care in the U.S.," *American Journal of Public Health* 46 (1956): 1077–78; Halperin, "Desegregation of Hospitals," pp. 61–62; and Beardsley, *History of Neglect*, pp. 251–53.

20. Charles D. Watts and Frank W. Scott, "Lincoln Hospital of Durham, North Carolina: A Short History," *JNMA* 57 (1965): 183.

21. Bradley, "Health, Hospitals, and the Negro," p. 43; and Calvin C. Sampson, "Death of the Black Community Hospital: Fact or Fiction?" editorial, *JNMA* 66 (1974): 165.

22. Nathaniel Wesley, Jr., "Black Hospitals Listing and Selected Commentary: Tradition, Competition, and the Management of Change," Washington, D.C., 1986 (Unpublished), pp. 31–36; Peter Applebome, "Two Nashville Hospitals Debate a Plan to Merge," *New York Times* (National Edition), 30 April 1989, p. 24; "Black Hospital to be Included in Merger Plan," *New York Times* (National Edition), 28 October 1991, p. A14; Wayne Hearn, "Meharry Meets the Future," *American Medical News*, 2 November 1992, pp. 29, 31; and Maria Odom, "Black Hospitals Work to Find a Modern Role," *New York Times* (National Edition), 12 August 1992, p. B6.

23. Sampson, "Death of the Black Community Hospital", p. 165; Emily Friedman, "Private Black Hospitals: A Long Tradition Faces Change," *Hospitals* 55 (1 July 1981): 65–68; Deborah Pinkney, "Future Looks Bleak For Black Hospitals," *American Medical News*, 10 April 1987, p. 50; John T. Foster, "What's Ahead for Negro Hospitals?," *Modern Hospital* 109 (November 1967): 114; and Interview, Haynes Rice, Howard University Hospital, Washington, D.C., 8 October 1982.

24. "Integration Only Practicable Goal," p. 340; and Frances Ridgway, "Atlanta Opinions Clash Over Role of the Negro Hospital," *Modern Hospital* 109 (November 1967): 118.

25. Robert Wood Johnson Foundation, *Special Report: The Foundation's Minority Medical Training Programs* (Princeton, N.J.: The Foundation, 1987), p. 8. The four schools are Howard University School of Medicine, Washington, D.C.; Meharry Medical College, Nashville, Tennessee; Morehouse School of Medicine, Atlanta, Georgia; and Charles R. Drew Postgraduate Medical School. Howard, Meharry, and Morehouse are four-year schools. Drew provides two years of clinical training for minority students who have completed their basic science courses at UCLA.

26. Interview, Julius Alexander and Aretha M. Mills, Provident Hospital, Chicago, Illinois, 15 October 1981; "The New Provident Hospital Medical Center," *JNMA* 75 (1983): 727; Pinkney, "Future Looks Bleak for Black Hospitals," p. 50; John Kass and Devonda Byers, "Provident Hospital Shutting Down," *Chicago Tribune*, 15 September 1987, p. 2; Deborah S. Pinkney, "Nation's Oldest Black Hospital Closes," *American Medical News*, 2 October 1987, p. 14; and Chinta Strausberg, "Provident Hosp. of

Cook County to Open June '93," *Chicago Defender*, 3 September 1992, pp. 1, 9.

27. Steve Taravella, "Black Hospitals Struggle to Survive," *Modern Healthcare*, 20 (2 July 1990): 20–26; and Odum, "Black Hospitals," p. B6.

28. Hine, *Black Women in White*, pp. 184–93.

29. Karen Grassmuck, "University Hospital Struggles to Solve Its Big-City Woes," *Chronicle of Higher Education*, 27 March 1991, p. A28; and Odum, "Black Hospitals," p. B6.

Index

Abraham Lincoln Memorial hospital (Cleveland), efforts to build, 154
Accreditation
  by American College of Surgeons. *See* American College of Surgeons
  by American Medical Association. *See* American Medical Association
  H. M. Green's challenge of, 48
  as threat to black medical profession, 36
ACS. *See* American College of Surgeons
Adams, C. J., 73
African-American community
  division over black hospitals, xi, 15–16, 22–23, 28–29, 61–62, 65–69, 129–30, 142–44, 152, 154, 158–63, 168–70, 179–80
  establishment of hospitals by, late nineteenth century, 12
  health status of, 195
  middle-class, function of black hospitals for, 13
  political power of, in Cleveland, efforts to improve, 171
  support of black hospitals, 105, 195
    for establishment of Forest City Hospital, 180
    of Frederick Douglass Memorial Hospital and Training school, 24–25
  views
    on black-controlled hospitals, early twentieth century, 14–15
    on black hospital movement, xvi
Agnew, D. Hayes, 20
Ailer, Charles (Rev.), 161
Alabama, 75
Alabama Power and Light, 95
Alabama State Legislature, resolution calling for white control of Tuskegee Veterans Hospital, 96
Alabama State Medical Society, 94
Albert P. Sloan Foundation, 146
Alexander, Walter G., 68
  on white philanthropic funding for black hospitals, 129
Alexander, Will W., 95
Allyn, Louise, 45–46
Almshouses, 4
AMA. *See* American Medical Association
American Board of Ophthalmology, 149
American Board of Pathology, 110
American Board of Radiology, 149
American College of Surgeons (ACS), 50, 61, 117, 120, 122, 174, 175
  accreditation of black hospitals by, 102, 133
    early twentieth century, 42
    of education programs, 183
    H. M. Green's challenge of, 48
  evaluation of hospitals by, 30
  list of approved hospitals, 30
  NMA and NHA lobbying of, 51
  standardization of hospitals, 49–50
    NHA and, 35

American hospital(s), function of
early-nineteenth century, 4
transformation, xiii–xiv
American Hospital Association (AHA), 50
ad hoc Committee on Hospitalization of Colored People, 52
endorsement of National Hospital Association aims, 52
NHA lobbying of, 52
American Legion, 75, 80, 85, 104
American Medical Association (AMA), 50
accreditation of black hospitals by, 133, 183
early twentieth century, 42, 43
H. M. Green's challenge of, 48
of internship training, 116, 122
Council on Medical Education and Hospitals, 30, 43
Meharry Medical College and, 125
funding of surveys on black hospitals by, early twentieth century, 51–52
integration of, efforts for, 37
journal of, 61
membership in, racial policies related to, 29, 191
NMA and NHA lobbying of, 50–51
standardization programs of, NHA and, 35
American Nurses' Association (ANA), institutional racism in, 195
American Public Health Association, 189
Amsterdam News (newspaper), 97
ANA. *See* American Nurses' Association
Anderson, James, 123
Anesthesia, 11
Approval of black hospitals, early twentieth century, 42–43
Armed forces, black nurses in, during World War II, 186
Armour, Philip D., 15, 17
Armour and Company, 133
Asepsis, 11
Associated Negro Press, 144
Atlanta Constitution (newspaper), 7
Atlanta Independent (newspaper), 97
Atlanta University, 108

Bagnall, Robert, 162
Bailey, Horace C. (Rev.), 160–61
Bailey, James T., 89
Bailey, Pearce, 72
Bailey, R. W., 24
Ball, Otto F., 137
Balloch, Edward A., 166
Baptist Ministers' Conference (Cleveland), 161
Barnes Medical College (St. Louis), 10
Barnett, Claude A., 144, 149
Barry, Edwin D., 156
Baumgardner, L. O., 154, 177
Bayard, New Mexico, veterans hospital in, 99
Beardsley, Edward H., xiii
Bellevue Hospital (New York), 4, 58
black interns admitted to, 165
Bennett Eclectic Medical College, 18
Berea College, 108
Berry, Joseph A., 143
Bey, Emmett, 149
Billings, Frank, 17, 72
Billings Hospital (Chicago), 133, 136, 142
Birth of a Nation, The (film), 21
Black community. *See* African-American community
Black hospital(s)
arguments for, 195
conflicts over, xi, 15–16, 22–23, 28–29, 61–62, 65–69, 129–30, 142–44, 152, 154, 158–63, 168–70, 179–80
control of, by white philanthropies, 128–29
demise of, 184, 192–93
early twentieth century, 34, 42
effect on lives of African Americans, 195–96
establishment of, xv, 11
by white community, 7
first, 11
fund-raising for. *See* Fund-raising
growth of, 3–4
early twentieth century, 28–29
NHA members, 38
nonstandardized, 50
opposition to, 68
organizational changes in, 191–92
policies, determination of, 106
records of, xvii
role of, 191
ideological differences related to, 66
segregated, xiv–xv
supporters of, 1990's, 195
types of, xiv–xv
unfamiliarity with, xii–xiii
white participation in, 62
Black hospital movement
African-Americans view on, xvi
AHA and, 52
funding for, by white philanthropies, support of, 129
history of, xiii
impetus for, 35, 36

indifference of black physicians to, 54
launching of, 35
leading advocates of, 38–39
H. (Henry) M. Green, 41. *See also* Green, H. (Henry)
John A. Kenney, 41. *See also* Kenney, John A.
Midian O. Bousfield, 40. *See also* Bousfield, Midian O.
Peter Marshall Murray, 39. *See also* Murray, Peter Marshall
limitations of, 183, 184
necessity of, 183, 184
obstacles and tensions inherent in, 132
physicians view of, xv–xvi
roots of, 3–34
Black hospital reformers, xiv, xv
attempts to standardize black hospitals, 48
objectives of, 105
separatism and, xv–xvi, 36–37, 55–57, 67–68, 170
Black medical schools, 41
graduates of
decline in, 184
views on, 68
number of, early twentieth century, 36
medical degrees granted, 1980's, 193
Black medical students
options available to, xii
population of, early twentieth century, 42
racism and, 20, 32–33, 125–26, 134, 142–43, 144–45, 153, 164–67, 173
Black nurses. *See* Nurses, black
Black patients. *See* Patients, black
"Black Patti." *See* Jones, Siseretta
Black physicians
admission to hospital facilities, xv
early twentieth century, 58
to Harlem Hospital, 63–64
black hospital movement and, xiii, 54, 162
economic status of
late nineteenth century, 12
threats to, 42
establishment of hospitals by, late nineteenth century, 11–12
exclusion from hospitals, 28
from Cleveland hospitals, 158
in Cleveland hospitals, 152
professional restrictions of, 176
investment in Tuskegee Veterans Hospital, 71
Kansas City General Hospital, No. 2 and, 9
male, xiv
membership in NHA, 54
opportunites for, Provident Hospital Project and, 149–50
population of, late nineteenth century, 11
practice of, xi
in segregated hospitals, nineteenth century, 8
professional opportunities for, at Frederick Douglass Memorial Hospital and Training School, 23–24
racism and, 12, 21, 29, 30–33, 125, 141, 173–74, 176
response to building of Tuskegee Veterans Hospital, 79
restricted role for, 124
staff appointments
efforts for, early twentieth century, 57–58
at Tuskegee Veterans Hospital, 76–77, 99, 100
support for creation of black hospital in Cleveland, 167
training of, xi
Mercy Hospital Project and, 162
Black-related diseases, African-Americans as experts on, 155
Black Tammany, 67
Black veterans. *See* Veterans, black
Blackwood, Norman D. (Admiral), involvement in Provident Hospital Project, 137, 141, 142
Blossom, Dudley S., 163, 164, 172
Bole, Ben P., 159
Booker T. Washington Community Hospital Association (Newark), 175
Booker T. Washington Sanitarium (New York), 62. *See also* Edgecombe Sanitarium
Boston City Hospital, 59, 60
Boston Lying-In-Hospital, 60
Boston Medical and Surgical Journal, 61
Bousfield, Midian O., 38, 46, 53
as director of Negro Health Division of Rosenwald Fund, 109, 110, 115
Knoxville General Hospital's black unit and, 113–14
observation of black physicians' preparation, 54
professional career of, 40
reorganization of Lincoln Hospital and, 118, 119
views
on NHA, 55
on Provident Hospital Project, 146
visit to Waverly Fraternal Hospital and Good Samaritan Hospital, 120

Bouyer, Harsba, 141
Bowling, W. W., 91
Boyer, Arthyr T., 24
Brandon, William W. (Gov.), 81, 85, 90
Brewster Hospital (Jacksonville, Florida), 54
Brown, E. V. L., 141
Brown, Lucien, 58
Brown, Russell S. (Rev.), 162, 170, 171
Brown v. Topeka Board of Education, 188
Budgets, for black hospitals, 105
Bundy, LeRoy, 171
Burt, Robert T., 13
Burton, Harold (Mayor), Joint Hospital Committee, 178
Butler, Isabelle G., 187
Buttrick, Wallace, 123

Calhoun, John C., 92, 99
Callis, H. A., 127
Campbell, W. W., 94
Cannon, George E., 84, 86
  Tuskegee Veterans Hospital and, 94
    response to Ku Klux Klan march on Tuskegee, 93
Carnegie Foundation for the Advancement of Teaching, 30, 74, 136
Carney, E. R., 54
Carolinas. *See also* North Carolina
  black-controlled institutions in, 121–22
  hospitals in, Duke Endowment Fund aid to, 115–16
Catholics, founding of denominational hospitals by, 13
Charity Hospital (Cleveland), 176
Charlotte, North Carolina, segregation of hospitals in, 188
Chauncey, Herbert, 154
Chicago, Illinois
  African-American community life in, early twentieth century, 18
  African-American population in, early twentieth century, 17
  history of black hospitals in, xvii
  Hospital Planning Committee of, 192
  nursing schools, racially exclusionist policies in, 15
  racism in hospitals, 16
Chicago Defender (newspaper), 139
Chicago Medical College, 16
Chicago Whip, The (newspaper), 91, 130
Chisum, Melvin J., 80, 82, 97
Christian, George B., 82–83
Christian stewardship, 4
Civil rights, 108
  medical, campaign for, 182
Civil Rights Act of 1964, 193
  Title VI, 190
Civil rights activists, 61. *See also* Medical civil rights activists
Civil rights legislation
  elimination of black hospitals and, 193
  of 1960, xv
Civil rights movement
  demise of black hospitals related to, 194
  function of black hospitals and, 191
Civil Service, 81
  eligible list of colored citizens, 83
Civil Service Commission, 84, 86, 92, 100
Civil service examination, for black applicants to Tuskegee Veterans Hospital, 84, 86
Civil War, xii
Clansman, The (Dixon), 21
Cleveland, Ohio, 169
  drive for black hospital, 151–81. *See also* Mercy Hospital; Mercy Hospital Association
    Abraham Lincoln Memorial Hospital, 154
    failed attempts at, 152
    Garvin's efforts for, 154–57
    opposition to, 158–61, 163–64, 166–67
    support for, 157–58, 159, 166–67
    tensions related to, 161
  first black hospital in. *See* Forest City Hospital
  hospitals and health facilities, racial discrimination in, 152–53, 157–58, 159–60, 163, 169, 176–77
  history of black hospitals in, xvii
Cleveland Advocate (newspaper), 152, 154
Cleveland Association of Colored Men, 152
Cleveland Call and Post (newspaper), 180
Cleveland City Hospital
  acceptance of black interns in, 173, 174
  first black physician in, 151
  efforts to integrate, 163–165, 171–76, 178
    compromise efforts in, 169–70
    opposition to, 167
    support for, 171
    view on, 151
  paucity of black appointments in, 152–53
  racist incidences in, 173
Cleveland Gazette (newspaper), 152, 154, 158, 159, 160, 162, 180
Cleveland Hospital Association, 153, 157
  efforts to establish black hospital, 154
Cleveland Hospital Council of the Welfare Federation of Funds, 152, 154

Cleveland Medical, Dental, and Pharmaceutical Association, 154
support for creation of black hospital in Cleveland, 169
Clifford, Edward, 81
Clinical training, 30
early twentieth century, 32
Closed-staff policy, at Douglass Hospital, 26
Cobb, W. Montague, 10, 66, 179, 181
civil rights activism, 182–83
segregation in V.A. hospitals and, 185
"Color Line of Medicine, The" (Pringle & Pringle), 151
Colored Home and Hospital (New York), 31. *See also* Lincoln Hospital
Columbia Hospital (Columbia, South Carolina), 120, 121
Commission on Interracial Cooperation, 108
efforts for black control of Tuskegee Veterans Hospital, 95
Commonwealth Fund, involvement in Provident Hospital Project, 136, 146
Community Chest (Cleveland), 157
Community composition, hospital admissions based on, xv
Community Hospital (Evanston, Illinois), 187
Congress. *See* U.S. Congress
Connors, John Fox, 64
Consultants on Hospitalization
investigation of "negro problem," 74
Tuskegee Veterans Hospital and, 71, 72, 73, 75, 76, 77, 79, 85, 90
efforts for white control of, 94
meeting with National Committee of Negro Veteran Relief related to, 78
Continuing education, of black physicians, 113–14
Cook County Hospital (Chicago), 16, 58, 133
black interns admitted to, 165
Cook County Physicians Association, view of Provident Hospital Project, 143
Coolidge, Calvin (Vice President), 81
Tuskegee Veterans Hospital and, 96
efforts for black control of, 101–2
Cornell University School of Medicine (New York), 31
Corwin, E. H. L., 65
Cotton States and International Exposition (Atlanta, Georgia), 37
Courant, The (newspaper), 27
Crisis (journal), 63, 73, 98
Crossland, J. R. A., 82
Cummings, Hugh S. (Surgeon General), 77, 78
Curtin, Roland G., 24
Curtis, Austin M., 15
Curtis, Nanahyoke Sockum, 15

Dailey Hospital (Chicago), 137
Daily, U. G., 42
Daily Citizen (newspaper), 95
Daily News (newspaper), 94
Dale, Ellis A., 152, 161
Daniels, Sarah, 16
Darrow, Clarence, 156
Davidson, Shelby J., 98
Davis, Benjamin Jefferson, 97
Davis, Jackson, 123
Davis, Michael M., 53, 66, 109, 140
Davison, Wilburt C., 117
Dawson, William L., 186
Dayton, Ohio, segregation in veterans hospitals after W.W.I in, 73–74
Death rate
in black hospitals, 116
surgical, 117
race divergences in, early twentieth century, 47
Deaver, John B., 24
Democratic party, 66
United Colored Democracy (New York), 63
Demographically-determined hospitals, xv
Department of Health, Education and Welfare, 190
Department of Hospitals (New York), 62, 65
Depression
demise of black hospitals related to, 184
Duke Endowment Fund support of black hospitals during, 121
effect on black medical student population, 147
failure of Provident Hospital Project related to, 147, 148–49
Derricotte, Juliette, death of, 46
Desegregation of hospitals, 102. *See also* Integration
efforts in, 182
1960's, 188–89
of veterans hospitals, 185–86
Dibble, J. E., 24
Discrimination. *See* Racial discrimination
Dixie Hospital and Nurse Training School (Hampton Institute, Virginia), 7, 8
Dixon, Thomas, 21
Doane, J. G., view on integration of Philadelphia General Hospital, 166
Douglass, Frederick, 22

Douglass Hospital (Kansas City, Kansas), 9, 24
Douglass Hospital (Philadelphia), xii, 21, 175. *See also* Frederick Douglass Memorial Hospital and Training School; Mercy-Douglass Hospital
  black population view of, 13
  establishment of, 15
  opposition to, 22–23
  white physicians in, 22
Drachman, Virginia C., xiv, xvi
Drakeford, John H., 85
DuBois, W. E. B., 12, 63, 64, 158
  support of black control of Tuskegee Veterans Hospital, 98
Duke, James Buchanan, 115
Duke Endowment, 39, 53
  activities
    at Good Samaritan Hospital (New Bern, North Carolina), 120–21
    at Lincoln Hospital (Durham), 117–20
    at Waverly Fraternal Hospital (Columbia, South Carolina), 120–21
  areas of interest, 115
  development of black units in white hospitals by, 114–15
  education programs for blacks, in medical education, 128
    for internship programs, 128
  financial support of black hospitals by, 105–6, 116–17, 120, 121–22
    collaboration with Rosenwald Fund, 115
  hospital section, 115–16
  interest in Provident Hospital Project, 136
  policy for white supervision of black hospitals, 126
Dumas, M. O., 98

Eaton, Hubert, 189
Eaton v. Grubbs, 189–90
Economics
  General Education Board's support of black education related to, 122–23
  related to philanthropic support of black hospitals, 107
Edgecombe Sanitarium (New York), 62. *See also* Booker T. Washington Sanitarium
Education
  for blacks, General Education Board's interest in, 122–28
  medical. *See* Medical education
  nursing. *See* Nursing education
  Rosenwald Fund's programs for, 109, 110
Educational benefits, of Provident Hospital Project, 147
Educational institutions, for African-Americans, white-run, 7–8
Emancipation, 6
Embree, Edwin R., 67, 109
  involvement in Provident Hospital Project, 136, 138, 139, 146–47
  as president of Rosenwald Fund, 107–8
  professional career of, 108
  response to condemnation of Rosenwald Fund, 130
Episcopal Church, 8
"Equal Opportunity—No More—No Less" (publication), 67
"Essentials of an Approved Internship, The," 30
Ethnic hospitals, 13, 56
Evanston, Illinois, building of black hospital in, 187–88

Fair Haven Infirmary (Atlanta), 14
Federal funds, all hospitals as potential recipients of, 190
Federal hospital system, creation of, 74
Federated Churches, Interracial Committee of (Cleveland), 164
Fellowship programs, created by Rosenwald Fund, 108, 109
Fenger, Christian, 17
Financial problems, of black hospitals, 105
Fisk University (Nashville), 46, 108, 123
Flexner, Abraham, 37, 76
  General Education Board support of black medical education and, 124
  report on medical education. *See* Flexner Report on medical education
  views on black medical education, 124
Flexner Report on medical education, 30, 40–41, 124
Flint-Goodridge Hospital (New Orleans), 127
For-profit hospitals, black, 13
Forbes, Charles F. (Col.), 80
Forest City Hospital (Cleveland), 151
  efforts to integrate, 178, 179
  establishment of, efforts in, 178–79
    opposition to, 179–80
    support for, 180, 181
  opening of, 181
    delay in, 179
Forest City Hospital Association, 177
  fund-raising, challenges faced by, 177–78
Fosdick, Raymond B., 148

Foundation funding, of black medical institutions, 106. *See also* Duke Endowment; General Education Board; Rosenwald Fund
Fourth Circuit Court of Appeals, 189, 190
Franklin County, Virginia, efforts to establish black veterans hospital in, 186
Frederick Douglass Memorial Hospital and Training School (Philadelphia), 11. *See also* Douglass Hospital
  attending physicians at, 24
  closed-staff policy at, 26
  deterioration of, 27
  establishment of, 19–22, 23, 33
  exclusion of black physicians in, 28
  expansion of, 25–26
  fund-raising for, 24–25
  operating room practices at, 26–27, 28
  postgraduate training in, 24
  power struggle at, 27
  relationship with University of Pennsylvania School of Medicine, 32
  state funding for, 33
Free patients, at Provident Hospital, 148–49
Freedlander, Sam, 174
Freedmen's Bureau, xii
  hospitals established by, 6
Freedmen's Hospital (Washington, D.C.), xii, 18, 40, 60, 62, 126
Friedman, Lewis, 64
Fulton County Courthouse (Atlanta), 60
Funding of black medical institutions, 106
Fund-raising, xiv, 105
  for Forest City Hospital, 177–78
  for Frederick Douglass Memorial Hospital and Training school, 24–25
  for Mercy Hospital Project, 162–63
  by NHA, 52–53
  for Provident Hospital Project, 136–37, 138

Gardner, Helen H., 86
Garvin, Charles H., 152, 154, 177
  as advocate of equal rights, 156–57
  family of, harassment of, 156
  personal biography, 155
  professional activities, 155
  support for establishment of black hospital in Cleveland, 157, 163
  view on integration of Cleveland City Hospital, 168
Gaston County Negro Hospital (Gastonia, North Carolina), 122
General Education Board (GEB), 74, 110
  criticism of Provident Hospital Project, 145–46
  education programs for blacks, 122–128
  impact on black hospital movement, 123, 128
    for postgraduate courses, 127
  financial support of black hospitals by, 105–6
  funding for Provident Hospital Project, 132, 134, 137, 142, 148
    termination of contract, 146–48
George, Clayborne, 170, 171
George W. Hamilton Hospital (Dalton, Georgia), 46
George W. Hubbard Hospital of Meharry Medical College (Nashville), 44, 192
Georgetown University Medical School (Washington, D.C.), 166
Georgia, 75
Georgia Infirmary (Savannah, Georgia), 5
Germ theory of disease, effects on health care of African Americans, 7, 109, 124
Giles, Roscoe C., 31–32
Glenton, Mary, 8
Glenville Euclid Hospital (Cleveland), 178
Gonorrhea, 6
Good Samaritan Hospital (Columbia, South Carolina), Duke Endowment Fund activities at, 120–21
Good Shepherd Hospital (New Bern, North Carolina), 122
Government hospitals
  for disabled ex-soldiers, 71
  exclusion of black physicians from, 71
Graduate medical education, General Education Board's interest in, 125
Grady City Hospital (Atlanta), 31, 46
  black ward at, conditions of, early twentieth century, 47
Granady, James W., 58
Gray, Samuel, 189
Greater Cleveland Hospital Fund, 178, 181
Greef, J. G. William, 63
Green, H. (Henry) M., 38, 47, 53, 104, 116, 154
  challenge of accreditation used by American College of Surgeons and American Medical Association, 48
  as executive secretary of NHA, 53
  as president of NHA, 41
  professional career of, 40

Green, H. (Henry) M. (*continued*)
views
on effects of standardization programs, 35–36
on financial support of black hospitals, 105
on Knoxville General Hospital's black unit, 113–14
on northern hospitals, 50
Green, Murray, 56
Green, William R., 154
support for Mercy Hospital Association, 162
Gregg, Alan, involvement in Provident Hospital Project, 139–40, 145
Gregg, E. J., 161
compromise to full integration of Cleveland City Hospital, 168
support for the creation of black hospital in Cleveland, 170–71
Griffin, Charles M. (Major), 99, 101

Hall, George Cleveland, 18, 28, 133, 137, 157
feud with Daniel Hale Williams, 18, 19
Hall, John B., Jr., 59
Hamann, Carl A., 164
Hampton-Brown, Mary K., 9
Hampton Institute, 7, 92
Harding, Warren G. (Pres.), 81
black voters view on, 83–84
death of, 96
staffing of Tuskegee Veterans Hospital with black personnel and, 82–83, 84, 101
departure from commitment to, 86
stance on racial issues, 83–84, 94
Harlem
hospitals of, survey on, 65, 66
medical societies in, 68
need for voluntary black hospital in, views on, 67–68
Harlem Hospital (New York), xv, 61
admission of black physicians and nurses, 57–58, 63–64, 65
black medical school graduates in, 165
nursing school, opportunities for black women in, 166
Harvard Medical School, 63
black medical students at, 164–65
racial discrimination in, 173
Harvard University, 110
admission of black students by, 20
Harvey, B. C. H., 134
Hawkins, Reginald, 188
Hawley, Paul R., (Gen.), 185
Health care
for blacks, in Cleveland, 153
Rosenwald fund programs for, 122
Health departments, integration of, Rosenwald Fund efforts in, 111
Health issues, black, Rosenwald Fund's involvement in, 109
Health status of black Americans, 195
early twentieth century, 47
Heart disease, rate, race differences in, early twentieth century, 47
Heflin, Thomas J. (Sen.), 90, 95
Helsom, Thomas J., 135
Henderson, N. A., 113–14
Hill, Elizabeth, 187
Hill, Lister (Sen.), 187
Hill-Burton Act of 1946
establishment of segregated hospitals and, 186–87
funds from, voluntary hospitals receiving, 188, 189, 190
passage of, 186–87
separate-but-equal clause, challenge of, 188, 189
Hine, Darlene Clark, xiii
Hines, Frant T. (Brigadier General), 84, 85, 86, 94
Tuskegee Veterans Hospital and, 94
efforts for black control of, 90, 91, 92, 96, 99
recruiting of black personnel for, 100, 101–2
Hinson, Eugene Theodore, 27
Hoge, Vane M., 186
Home for Aged and Infirmed Colored Persons (Philadelphia), 23
Home for Colored Persons (Atlantic City), 23
Home for Worthy, Aged, Indigent Colored People (New York), 31. *See also* Lincoln Hospital
Home Infirmary (Clarksville, Tennessee), 11, 13
Hopkins, William R., 159, 168, 171
committee on feasibility of integration of Cleveland hospitals, 164–65
Hospital(s)
black. *See* Black hospitals
function of, late nineteenth century, 11, 12
transformation of, 1870–1920, xiii–xiv
Hospital beds, 122
available to blacks, early twentieth century, 44, 47–48

Hospital reformers. *See* Black hospital reformers
Hospital stay, 122
Hospital Survey and Construction Act of 1946. *See* Hill-Burton Act
Houghton, Henry S., involvement in Provident Hospital Project, 140–41
House Veterans Committee, 186
Howard, Edwin C., 27
Howard, Perry, 84
Howard University (Washington, D.C.), 51
 funding of, 124, 125
 Hospital, xii, 192, 195
 School of Medicine, xi, 9, 36
  General Education Board support of, 125
Hubbard Hospital (Nashville), 125, 126, 128. *See also* George W. Hubbard Hospital
Huey, Samuel B., 22
Hughes, Langston, 131
Hughes Spaulding Pavillion (Atlanta), 193
Hunnicutt, Clara, 92
Hunter, Jane Edna, 153, 154, 158
Hunter, Sara, 8
Hutchins, Robert, 145, 148, 149
Hylan, John, 57

Ijams, George E., 82, 83, 84
Infirmaries, in South, establishment of, 5
Institutions, black-controlled, arguments for, 195
Integrated hospitals
 Rosenwald Fund support of, 114–15
 treatment of black people in, 13
Integration, integrationism, 36, 69, 182
 of black hospitals, support for, 184–185
 of Cleveland City Hospital, 151
  efforts for, 163–65
 effect on black hospital movement, 184–85
 elimination of black hospitals and, 192–93
 medical, Louis W. Wright's efforts in, 59–61
 of municipal hospitals, historical perspective, xvi
 physicians view of, xvi
 of tax-supported hospitals, 58–59
 of veterans hospitals, 186
"Integration Only Practicable Goals," 183
Integrationists, views of
 on black hospital movement, 142
 on Mercy Hospital Project, 158, 159–61
 on Provident Hospital Project, 142–43, 149
 on Rosenwald Fund, 129–30
Intern(s), black
 acceptance to Cleveland City Hospital, 173, 174
 appointments for, 58
 at Cleveland City Hospital, 151, 171–73
International Hospital (New York), 64
"Interne at Provident" (Hughes), 131
Internship, internship programs, 116, 122
 for black medical school graduates
  early twentieth century, 30–31, 42, 43
  support for, 128
 in black hospitals
  accreditation of, 133, 183–84
  early twentieth century, 43
 early twentieth century, 30–31
Inter-State Tattler (newspaper), 104

Jackson, A. L.
 involvement in Provident Hospital Project, 138, 140, 144, 146, 148
 resignation from Provident Hospital Project, 145
Jackson, Algernon B., 44, 127
 study on black hospitals, 51
Jails, black patients housed in, 12, 73
James Walker Memorial Hospital (Wilmington, North Carolina), 189, 190
Jeliffe, Russell, 162
Jersey City Hospital (Jersey City, New Jersey), 166
Jews, founding of denominational hospitals by, 13
Jim Crow institutions, 106
 black hospitals as, 158
 government, 103
 Mercy Hospital as, 160
Jim Crow laws, xvi, 109
Jim Crow plan, 66
Jim Crowism, 88
 Cleveland's drive for black hospitals and, 152
 related to creation of black hospital in Cleveland, 169
 related to Provident Hospital Project, 144, 149
John A. Andrew Clinics, 41
John A. Andrew Memorial Hospital (Tuskegee Institute, Alabama), 79
John and Mary Markle Foundation, 146
John Gaston Hospital (Memphis), black unit of, NAACP endorsement of, 188
Johns, Ethel, 10, 51
 assessment of Provident Hospital, 132–33
 study of black nurse training schools, 43
Johnson, Douglas B., 58

Johnson, Henry Lincoln, 84
Johnston, L. W., 94
Jones, Siseretta ("Black Patti"), 25
Jones, T. E., 86
Josiah Macy, Jr. Foundation, 146
Journal(s), medical, black, 36–37
Journal of Infectious Disease, 61
Journal of the American Medical Association, 61
Journal of the National Medical Association, 10, 29, 37, 41–42, 144, 155, 170, 174
  civil rights and, 182, 183
  NMA and NHA view on black hospital reform and, 55
  Tuskegee Veterans Hospital and, 79
Julius Rosenwald Fund. *See* Rosenwald Fund
Justice Department, 189

Kansas City, Missouri, 8
  establishment of municipal hospitals for African Americans in, 9, 10
Kansas City Colored Hospital. *See* Kansas City (Missouri) General Hospital, No. 2
Kansas City (Missouri) General Hospital, No. 1, 10
Kansas City (Missouri) General Hospital, No. 2, 7, 9–10, 53, 58, 165
Kenney, John A., 38, 54, 56, 79, 86, 91, 187
  black hospital movement and, 183
  personal biography, 41
  professional career of, 41
  Provident Hospital Project and, 144
  as secretary of NHA, 41–42
  Tuskegee Veterans Hospital and, 82, 100
  white philanthropic funding for black hospitals, support of, 129
Kenney Memorial Hospital (New Jersey), 41
Kenzie, W. N. (Major), 76, 77
  endorsement of Tuskegee Veterans Hospital, 77, 80
Kirby, George H., 72, 74
Knoxville General Hospital (Knoxville, Tennessee), Rosenwald Fund support of, 112–14
Knoxville Medical College (Knoxville, Tennessee), 40
Koch, Estelle C., 164
Kohlsaat, Herman, 15, 17
Ku Klux Klan, 21, 84, 97, 159
  march through Tuskegee, Alabama, 70–71, 92–94, 95
Kusmer, Kenneth L., 153, 162

L. Richardson Memorial Hospital (Greensboro, North Carolina), 122, 188
Lakeside Hospital (Chicago), 137
Lakeside Hospital (Cleveland), 152
  racial discrimination in, 157
Lambert, Robert A., 39, 127
  involvement in Provident Hospital Project, 137, 140, 141–42, 145, 147
  study on obstacles to black physicians, 125–26
Lambright, Middleton H., Sr., 154, 157, 177
Lane, J. F., 71
Lane, Roger, 22
Lane College, 71
Lange Hospital (Kansas City, Missouri), 9
Legal action, related to segregation of hospitals, 188–90
Lester, J. A., 79
Lewis, Julian H., 135
Liberty Heights Medical Center (Baltimore), 192
Lincoln Hospital (Durham), 31, 116, 191
  advisory committee, white physicians as, 119
  Duke Endowment Fund activities at, 117–20
  endowments to, 121–22
  mortality rates, 119
  nurse training school, 31
  restructuring of, 118–19
Lincoln University (Oxford, Pennsylvania), 19, 20
Local governments, establishment of segregated hospitals by, 8
Lone Star State Association, 37
Love, John W. (Lt.), 78
Loyola University (Chicago), 18
Lying-in-Hospital (Chicago), 135, 138
Lynk, Miles V., 36–37
  professional activities of, 37
Lyttle, Hulda, 44

MacNeal, A. C., 130
Macon County (Alabama), 95
  Courthouse, 94
MacVicar Hospital (Atlanta), 7, 8
Malaria, 109
Manhattan Medical Society, 67
  criticisms by
    of construction of black veterans hospitals, 103
    of Provident Hospital Project, 144
    of segregated medical system, 66, 67
  formation of, 65
  goals of, 65
  survey of Harlem Hospital and, 66

Mason, Ulysses G., 174, 177
Massachusetts General Hospital (Boston), 60
McBride, David, xiii
McCormick, Cyrus H., 15
McDonald, Roger E., 81
McDougald, J. Q., 24
McLean, Franklin C., 133, 134
  involvement in Provident Hospital Project, 137, 138, 140
McMillan, P. J., 164
McMorries, John H., 164, 168, 174
  appointment to Cleveland City Hospital, 168
Medicaid, 190
  decline of black hospitals related to, 193–94
Medical and Surgical Observer, The (journal), 36–37
Medical care. *See* Health care
Medical civil rights activists
  efforts to desegregate hospitals
    1960's, 188–89
    veterans hospitals, 185–86
  targeting of racial policies of medical societies by, 191
  view on detrimental effects of hospital segregation, 185
Medical College of Georgia, Negro Hospital of, 127
Medical education
  American, reforms in, 30
  black
    General Education Board involvement in, 124–28
    Provident Hospital Project and, 149
  early nineteenth century, 4
  specialty, 42
Medical Education in the United States and Canada (Flexner). *See* Flexner Report on medical education
Medical leaders, black, recognition of limitations of hospital reform movement, 183
Medical schools
  black. *See* Black medical schools
  black enrollment in
    late nineteenth century, 20
    1948–1990's, xii
  integration of, opposition to, 166
Medical societies
  black, 37
  local, exclusion of black physicians in, 29
  racial policies, of challenge to, 190
Medical Society of Virginia, 126
Medical students, black. *See* Black medical students
Medicare, 190
  decline of black hospitals related to, 193–94
Medicine, advances in, late nineteenth century, 11
Medico-Chirurgical Society of the District of Columbia, 37, 185
Meharry Medical College (Nashville), xi, 17, 36, 76, 106, 108
  General Education Board appropriations to, 123
  George W. Hubbard Memorial Hospital, 44, 125, 126, 128, 192
Meier, August, 56
Mellon, Andrew W., 74
  Tuskegee Veterans Hospital and, 71, 72, 79–80
Mental institutions, housing of black veterans in, 73
Mercy-Douglass Hospital (Philadelphia), xi, xii. *See also* Douglass Hospital and Mercy Hospital and Nurse Training School
Mercy Hospital (Chicago), 16
Mercy Hospital and Nurse Training School (Philadelphia), 28, 49, 51, 130
  establishment of, 33
  financial stability of, 33
  financial support for, 50
Mercy Hospital Association (Cleveland)
  efforts for black hospital in Cleveland, 157–58
  collapse of, 163
  division of black community over, 161–62
  fund-raising activities, 162–63
  opposition to, 158–61
  support for, 159, 162
Merrick, John, 116
Messenger, The (magazine), 89
Methodist Episcopal Church
  efforts in support of black control of Tuskegee Veterans Hospital, 95
Metropolitan Nashville General Hospital, 192
Middleton, Charles, 65
Militancy, New Negro, after W.W.I, 86
Ministers, within black community
  opposition to black hospitals in Cleveland, 152
  opposition to Mercy Hospital Project, 160–61
Minton, Henry M., 49
  opposition to creation of black hospital in Cleveland, 167

Minton, Russell, 110
Mississippi, hospital situation for African Americans in, early twentieth century, 48
Mississippi State Hospital (Natchez), 5
Missouri hospitals, black interns admitted to, 165
Modern Hospital (journal), 109
"Modern Hospital: Its Construction, Organization, and Management, The" (Mossell), 27
Montgomery, Alabama, refusal of black veterans hospital in, 75
Montgomery Advertiser (newspaper), 84, 92
Moore, George, 45
Moore, Lillian Atkins, xii, xiii
"More or Less Critical Review of the Hospital Situation Among Negroes in the United States" (Green), 41
Morehouse College, 123
Morgan, Daniel E., 171, 172
Morton, Ferdinand Q., 63, 66, 67
  criticism of segregated medical system, 66
  Manhattan Medical Society and, 66
Morton, Thomas S. K., 24
Moses H. Cone Memorial Hospital (Greensboro, North Carolina), 188
Mosley, Hattie E., 23
Mossell, Charles, 19
Mossell, Gertrude, 22, 25
Mossell, Nathan Francis, 27, 175
  confrontation with University of Pennsylvania School of Medicine, 32
  control of Douglass Hospital by
    criticism of, 26–27
    exclusion of black physicians, 28
  medical education of, 20
  personal biography, 19–21
  professional activities of, 20–21
  support of black hospitals, 176
Moton, Robert Russa (Maj.), Tuskegee Veterans Hospital and, 79, 80, 81, 100
  campaign for, 75–76
  staffing of, 78
  support of black control of, 87, 91, 97–98
  support of black personnel in, 77, 81–82
  support of white control of, 91–92
  threats against, 91
Mt. Zion Temple Congregational Church (Cleveland), 157
Municipal Civil Service Commission (New York), 63
Municipal hospitals
  for African Americans, establishment of, 7–9
  historical perspective, 4
  integration of, historical perspective, xvi
  New York, administration of, 63
  training programs, black medical school graduates admission to, 165
Murray, Peter Marshall, 38, 39, 62, 104
  black hospital reform and, 39
  criticism of Wright, 64
  hospital admission of black physicians by hue and, 59
  integration of Cleveland City Hospital, 167
  personal biography, 39
  professional career, 39
  resignation from Harlem Hospital, 64
  restructuring of Lincoln Hospital and, 118
  Tuskegee Veterans Hospital and, 102
  view of northern hospitals, 50
Myers, George A.
  on integration of Cleveland City Hospital and, 164
  opposition to Mercy Hospital Project, 158, 159

NAACP. *See* National Association for the Advancement of Colored People
NACGN. *See* National Association of Colored Graduate Nurses
Narcisse, Marie J., 23
Nashville, Tennessee, 76
Nation of Islam, 195
Nation, The (journal), 88
National Association for the Advancement of Colored People (NAACP), 18, 21, 57, 61, 69, 70, 185
  assistant secretary, Walter White, 46
  campaign for medical civil rights, 182
  Memphis branch, endorsement of black unit at John Gaston Hospital, 188
  opposition to Forest City Hospital, 179–80
  publication, *Crisis*, 63, 73, 98
  support for integration of black hospitals by, 184–85
  Tuskegee Veterans Hospital and, 78, 93
    response to Ku Klux Klan march on Tuskegee, 93
    stance on staffing with black personnel, 81–82, 83
    support for black control of, 87, 98
    view on Morton's stance on, 98
  view on black hospitals, 63
    nineteen thirties, 61–62
  view on Mercy Hospital Project, 160, 161–62
  Wright's activities in, 61

National Association of Colored Graduate Nurses (NACGN), 185
  disbanding of, 195
National Committee for Mental Hygiene, 72, 74
National Committee of Negro Veteran Relief, Tuskegee Veterans Hospital and, 78, 79
National Conference of Hospital Administrators, 55
National Home for Disabled Volunteer Soldiers, 72
National Hospital Association (NHA), xiii, xvi, 35–69, 113. *See also* Black hospital reformers
  agenda, 38
  aims of, AHA endorsement of, 52
  budget of, 54
  demise of, 55
  effectiveness in black hospital movement, 184
  efforts for establishment of black veterans hospitals, 102
  election of officers, 38
  establishment of, 35
  executive committee, 42, 53–54
  fund-raising by, 52–53
  hospitals belonging to, 38
  impact of, 55
  indifference of black physicians to, 54
  lobbying by, 50–51, 52
  membership in, 54
  nursing education and, 44
  organizational structure, 38
  plans for hospital reform and professional advancement, 55–56
  standardization criteria, 36, 48–49, 50
  support to black hospitals, 184
  view on first-class black hospitals, 56
National Medical Association (NMA), xiii, xvi, 35–69, 70, 74, 113, 118, 185. *See also* black hospital reformers
  annual conventions sponsored by, 37
  campaign for civil rights activism, 182–83
  charter, 37
  civil service examination for black applicants to Tuskegee Veterans Hospital and, 84
  Commission of Medical Education and Hospitals, 48
  effectiveness in black hospital movement, 184
  efforts for desegregation of hospitals, 182, 184–85
  efforts for dismantlement of "Negro medical ghetto," 182
  efforts for establishment of black veterans hospitals, 102
  establishment of, 17, 21
  establishment of black-controlled hospitals and, 11
  establishment of National Hospital Association, 35. *See also* National Hospital Association
  founders of, 59
  indifference of black physicians to, 54
  involvement in opening of Tuskegee Bureau Hospital, No. 91, 35
  journal of. *See Journal of the National Medical Association*
  lobbying by, 50–51
  NHA and, 55
  North Harlem Medical, Dental and Pharmaceutical Association and, 93–94
  Philadelphia Academy of Medical and Allied Sciences and, 21
  plans for hospital reform and professional advancement, 55–56
  position on racism in the North, 29
  presidents
    L. A. West. *See* West, L. A.
    Midian O. Bousfield. *See* Bousfield, Midian O.
    Peter Marshall Murray. *See* Murray, Peter Marshall
  standardization criteria, 36
  support for creation of black hospital in Cleveland, 170, 174
  support to black hospitals, 184
  Tuskegee Veterans Hospital and, 79
    criticism of Moton's view, 98–99
    support for black control of, 87
    view on compromise in black control of, 99
  views
    on first-class black hospitals, 56
    on Manhattan Medical Society's activities, 68
    on need for voluntary black hospital in Harlem, 67–68
    on Provident Hospital Project, 144
    on separatism, 57
  work in hospital field, 38
National Negro Business League, 18
National Negro Press Association, 70, 80, 82, 97
National Tuberculosis Association, 72
Neal, J. Park, 9

"Negro Health and Its Effect Upon the Nation's Health" (Embree), 109
"Negro Hospital Renaissance" (Kenney), 42, 183
Negro Medical Association of Virginia, 126
Negro Professional Man and the Community, The (Woodson), 44
Negro Welfare Association (Cleveland), 161, 163
New England Hospital for Women and Children (Boston), xiv
New Jersey State Republican Committee, 94
New Republic, The (magazine), 88
New York Age (newspaper), 97, 104
New York Amsterdam News (newspaper), 104
New York, New York
  approaches to problems of black physicians and patients, 62–63
  hospitals
    admitting privileges to black physicians in, 63, 64
    exclusion of black interns in, 31
New York City Hospital Information Bureau, 65, 66
New York Medical College for Women, 30
New York State Board of Education, 166
New York Times, The (newspaper), 88
New York University (New York), 113
New York World (newspaper), 97
Newport News, Virginia, 12
Newspapers. *See also* specific newspaper
  black, 22, 23, 27, 70, 91, 104, 139, 144, 152
    opposition to establishment of Forest City Hospital, 180
    support of black control of Tuskegee Veterans Hospital, 88–89
    view on Moton, 97
  white, support for black control of Tuskegee Veterans Hospital, 94
NHA. *See* National Hospital Association
Niagara Movement, 21, 158
Nineteenth century, establishment of black hospitals during, 10–11
NMA. *See* National Medical Association
Norfolk Virginia-Pilot (newspaper), 95
North
  African-American hospital admissions
    early nineteenth century, 5–6
    early twentieth century, 44
  African-American migration to, 83, 109
  cities, black population in, 153
  efforts for black hospitals in, 55
  establishment of black hospitals in, early twentieth century, 28–29
North Carolina, segregation of hospitals in, 188, 189
North Carolina College for Negroes, 118
North Harlem Medical, Dental and Pharmaceutical Association, response to Ku Klux Klan march on Tuskegee, 93–94. *See also* North Harlem Medical Society
North Harlem Medical Society, 57, 64, 65, 66. *See also* North Harlem Medical, Dental and Pharmaceutical Association
  black physicians abandonment of, 65
  survey of Harlem Hospital and, 67
  view of Manhattan Medical Society, 67
Northside Infirmary (Birmingham), 176
Nurse(s)
  black
    in armed forces during World War II, 186
    exclusion from Cleveland hospitals, 158
    staff appointments, efforts for, early twentieth century, 57–58
    on staff at Tuskegee Veterans Hospital, 76–77
    support for creation of black hospital in Cleveland, 167
    training of, Mercy Hospital Project and, 162
  white
    employment in Tuskegee Veterans Hospital, 82
    support for creation of black hospital in Cleveland, 166–67
Nurse maids, black, employment in Tuskegee Veterans Hospital, 82
Nurse training schools
  for black women, 8, 122
    in Cleveland hospitals, 153, 171
    early twentieth century, 43, 51
    establishment of, 11, 21, 22, 58
    Frederick Douglass Memorial Hospital and Training school. *See* Frederick Douglass Memorial Hospital and Training School
    growth of, early twentieth century, 28–29
    Lincoln Hospital, 31
    municipal, 165–66
    NHA interest in, 44
    at Provident Hospital, 143–44
  racially exclusionist policies in, 15, 166
Nursing, role of, late nineteenth century, 12
Nursing education, early twentieth century, 12

Nursing students, black
  admission to Cleveland City Hospital, 164
  exploitation of, 43

O'Neil, Cosmo, 57
Obstetrics, 32, 60
Old North State Medical, Dental and Pharmaceutical Association, 37–38
Operating room practices, at Frederick Douglass Memorial Hospital and Training school, 26–27, 28
Organizations, black, 194–95

Palmer, Henry, 16
Palmetto State Medical Association, 37
Patients
  black
    racism and, 5–6, 8, 9, 10, 12–13, 44–48, 73–74, 133, 142–44, 149, 153, 176–77
  white, racism of, 173
Paying patients, care for, late nineteenth century, 12
Payne, Lawrence O., 171, 172
Pearce, Richard M., 134
Penn, I. Garland, 59
Penn, William Fletcher, 59
Pennsylvania
  Commonwealth of, support of black hospitals by, 50
  State Board of Charities, 25
Pennsylvania Hospital (Philadelphia), 6
Pepper, William, III, 32, 165
Perry, E. B., 54
Perry, John E., 53, 167
Perry Sanitarium (Kansas City, Missouri), 53. *See also* Wheatley-Provident Hospital
Peter Bent Brigham Hospital (Boston), 60
Philadelphia, Pennsylvania, hospitals in
  black hospitals, 27–28
  discriminatory practices of, 33
Philadelphia Academy of Medical and Allied Sciences, 21, 38
Philadelphia County Medical Society, 20
Philadelphia Hospital, 4, 175
  nurse training school of, 22
    admission of black women to, 21
Philadelphia Negro, The (DuBois), 12
Philanthropies. *See* Private philanthropies; White philanthropic community
Phillis Wheatley Association (Cleveland), 154
Phillis Wheatley Club of Nashville, Tennessee, 3
Phillis Wheatley Home (Cleveland), 158
  opposition to, 160
Physician(s)
  black. *See* Black physicians
  education of. *See* Medical education
  support at black hospitals, loss of, 193
  women
    development of, xiv
    integrationism and separatism effects on, xvi
Pinn, Petra, 38
Pittsburgh Courier (newspaper), 97, 104, 129
Pneumonia, 109
Postgraduate training, for black physicians, 41
  difficulty in obtaining, 30
  at Frederick Douglass Memorial Hospital and Training School, 24
  funding for, by General Education Board, 125, 126, 127
Powell, Adam Clayton, Jr., 186
Powell, R. H. (Rep.), 90, 94
  Tuskegee Veterans Hospital and, 85
Pringle, Henry F., 151
Pringle, Katharine, 151
Private hospitals, black, early twentieth century, 13
Private philanthropies, influence on black medical affairs, 64–65
Professional organizations, black, 36
Protestant Orphan Asylum (Chicago), 16
Provident Hospital (Baltimore). *See also* Liberty Heights Medical Center
  closing of, 192
Provident Hospital (Chicago), 3, 11, 110, 126, 127, 131–50, 179
  affiliation with University of Chicago, 133
    advantages of, 133
    black community response to, 135–36
    conditions for, 134–35
    controversy related to, 144
    critics of, 143–44, 145–46
    demise of, 148–49, 150
    educational benefits of, 147
    financial problems related to, 142
    fund-raising for, 136–37, 138, 139
    GEB termination of aid to, 145–48
    improvement in medical services, 141
    officials' view on, 134
    opportunities to black physicians offered by, 149–50
    organizational changes related to, 137–38
    problems related to, 138–42
    racial composition related to, 140

Provident Hospital (Chicago)
affiliation with University of Chicago, (*continued*)
segregation inherent in, 135
white supervisory staff for, 135
closing of, 194
establishment of, 15–19
evolution into black hospital, 17–19
expansion of, 17
financial status of, 132–33, 139
medical services at, 133
reopening of, 194
Provident Hospital (St. Louis), 24
Pryor, Jessie, xii
Psychoneurotic disorders, veterans with, 72
Public health activities, Rosenwald Fund support of, 110
"Public Health and the Negro" (Jackson), 44
Public Health Service. *See* U.S. Public Health Service
Pullman, George M., 15
Purvis, Charles B., 153

Quality of care, at black hospitals
Duke Endowment Fund effects on, 122
early twentieth century, NMA survey on, 38
Quinland, W. S., 110

Rabinowitz, Howard N., 7
Race, xii, xviii
as factor in admissions to medical schools, xii
Race relations
in Chicago, deterioration of, early twentieth century, 17
related to establishment of Tuskegee Veterans Hospital, 77
related to Provident Hospital Project, 147
Rosenwald Fund programs in, 108, 122
Racial customs and mores, restriction of black access to hospitals and, 5–6
Racial discrimination, 3. *See also* racism and segregation
in Cleveland hospitals and health facilities, 152–53, 157–60, 163, 169, 176–77
early twentieth century, 45–46
in Harvard Medical School, 173
Racial diseases, 155
Racial hierarchy, reinforcement, by white control of black hospitals, 129
Racial ideology, related to Provident Hospital Project failure, 150
Racial issues, Harding's stance on, 83
Racial politics
Provident Hospital Project failure and, 149
related to black hospitals, 132
Racial pride, related to black hospitals, 117
Racial tensions, 11
in Tuskegee, related to efforts for black control of Tuskegee Veterans Hospital, 90–92
Racism, xiii, xvi
in American Nurses' Association, 195
in Cleveland City Hospital, 173
related to black medical students, 20, 32–33, 125–26, 134, 142–43, 144–45, 153, 164–67, 173
related to black nurses, 15, 21, 153, 166
related to black patients, 6, 9, 12–13, 44–47, 73–74, 133, 142–44, 149, 153, 176–77, 189
related to black physicians, 12, 21, 29, 30–33, 125, 141, 173–74, 176
responses to, xvii
in southern hospitals, early twentieth century, 47
Rankin, John E. (Rep.), 186
Rankin, Watson Smith, 53, 115
black hospitals and, 116–117
concept of black district hospital, 117
efforts to close Waverly Fraternal Hospital and Good Samaritan Hospital, 120–21
Lincoln Hospital and, 117, 118
Rosenwald Fund support of mixed hospitals and, 114
Reconstruction, 6
Red Cross, tuberculosis hospital program, 72
Reed, David (Sen.), 104
Reformers. *See* Black hospital reformers
Refresher courses, General Education Board funding of, 127
Relief patients, at Provident Hospital, 148–49
Religious hospitals, 13
Republican(s), black, efforts for black control of Tuskegee Veterans Hospital, 94
Republican party, tie with African Americans, 71, 81, 83, 84
Residency programs
in black hospitals, approval of, 183
for black physicians
at Frederick Douglass Memorial Hospital and Training School, 24
at Provident Hospital, 149–50
Reynolds, Emma, 15

Reynolds, Louis H. (Rev.), 15
Rich, William M., as administrator of Lincoln Hospital, 119, 120
Roane, Daniel, 189
Rockefeller Foundation, 43, 74, 108, 123, 132
  Division of Medical Studies of, Provident Hospital Project and, 134
  racist attitudes in, 123
Rogers, L. B., 81, 90
Roosevelt, Franklin D. (Pres.), 61
Rosenberg, Charles E., xiii, 13
Rosenwald, Julius, 106. *See also* Rosenwald Fund
Rosenwald, Lessing H., 139
Rosenwald Fund, 39, 52, 53, 65
  areas of interest, 108–9
  efforts in integration of health departments, 110
  black hospital support by, 50, 105–7, 111, 112, 117, 118, 128, 129
    areas of interest, 106–7
    collaboration with Duke Endowment Fund, 115
    condemnation by integrationists, 129–30
    criteria for, 111–12
    for internship programs, 128
    to Knoxville General Hospital, 112–14
  black social welfare support by, expansion of interests, 107
  interest in Provident Hospital Project, 132, 133, 134, 135, 136, 138, 139, 140, 145, 146, 148
  involvement in black health issues, 109
  involvement in health education, 111
  Manhattan Medical Society criticism of, 67
  mixed hospitals support by, 114–15
  Negro Health Division, 40, 65, 109–10
    function of, 114
  programs in race relations and medical care, 122
  public health activities support by, 110
  reorganization of, 107–8
  restructuring of Lincoln Hospital and, 118
  survey of Harlem hospitals and, 66
Rosner, David, xiii

St. Agnes Hospital (Raleigh), 7, 9
  endowments to, 122
St. Andrews Episcopal Church (Cleveland), 162
St. Augustine School (Raleigh), 7, 8
St. Louis, segregated municipal hospitals in, 10
St. Louis (Missouri) City Hospital, No. 2, 7, 10, 58, 165
St. Luke's Hospital (Chicago), 19
St. Philip Hospital (Richmond), 126
  postgraduate education, General Education Fund support of, 127, 128
Salmon, Thomas W., 74
Sampson, Calvin C., support of black hospitals, 191
Sanger, W. T., 39
Satcher, David, 192
Saturday Evening Post (magazine), 151
Savannah Journal (newspaper), 94
Savitt, Todd L., xiii
Schuyler, George, condemnation of Rosenwald Fund, 129–30
Scientific medicine, rise of, 29
Scott, Frank W., 191
Scott, R. W., 179
Sears, Roebuck, and Company, 106, 130, 139. *See also* Rosenwald Fund
Secondhand products, transfer to blacks, 10
Segregated hospitals
  establishment of, Hill-Burton Act and, 186–87
  nineteenth century, 7–8, 9–10
Segregation
  effect on black Americans, 123
  NHA and NMA and, 55–56
  of hospitals
    detrimental effects of, 185
    legal action related to, 188–90
    of veterans hospitals, 73–74, 186
  related to creation of black hospital in Cleveland, 169
  related to Provident Hospital Project, 135, 143, 144–45
  residential, 7
  self-imposed
    black hospitals as, xvi
    Mercy Hospital Project as, 162
Self-help, black, 11, 18, 194–95
  black hospital as, 42
Separatism, 56–57
  black physicians protest of, 59
  effects of, xvi
Sexism, xvi
Shepherd, C. H., 117, 118, 119
Sibley, Hiram, 192
Simkins, George C., opposition to segregation of North Carolina hospitals, 189
Simkins v. Moses H. Cone Memorial Hospital, 188

Slave(s)
former
hospitals for, xii
medical care for, 6–7. *See also* Freedmen's Bureau
use as experimental subjects, 13
Slave hospitals, creation of, 4–5
Smith, Barry, 146
Smith, Harry C.
opposition to creation of black hospital in Cleveland, 169–70
opposition to Mercy Hospital Project, 158–61
Smith, Robert T., 194
Social institutions, American hospitals as, xiv
Social status, of blacks, improvement of, black hospital movement and, 44
Societies, medical. *See* Medical societies
South
black hospitalization in, early twentieth century, 44–47
black hospitals in, AMA funded survey on, 51
economic reconstruction of, 123
hospitalization of black veterans in, after W.W.I, 73, 79. *See also* Tuskegee Veterans Hospital
segregated hospitals in, early twentieth century, 8–10
slave hospitals in, 4–5
South Carolina. *See* Carolinas
South Side Dispensary (Chicago), 16
Southerners, white, response to black staff at Tuskegee Veterans Hospital, 84–85
Spear, Allan, 18
Specialty boards, development of, 42
Specialty training and practice, 42
Spelman College (Atlanta), 108
Spelman Seminary (Atlanta), 7
Spencer, E. B., 177
Staff appointments, for black physicians and nurses, efforts for, early twentieth century, 57–58
Stafford, Samuel P., 24
Standardization of hospitals
American College of Surgeons, 49–50
of black hospitals
attempts at, early twentieth century, 48
goal of, 49
NHA and NMA, 35–36, 48–49, 50
as threat to black medical profession, 35, 36
Stanley, Robert H. (Col.), 90, 99
as commander of Tuskegee Veterans Hospital, 80–81, 82, 85
view on black control of, 92
transfer to Veterans hospital in Bayard, New Mexico, 99
Star of Zion (newspaper), 97
Steiner, Robert E., 80, 85
Stevens, David H., 123
Stevens, Rosemary A., xii, xiii
Stocklen, J. B., 178
Stubbs, Frederick Douglass, 172, 174
education of, 172
as first black intern at Cleveland City Hospital, 172–73
personal biography, 172
professional success of, 174–75
racist experiences of, 173
refusal of residency at Cleveland City Hospital, 173
view on black hospitals, 175–76
Supreme Court. *See* U.S. Supreme Court
Surgery, 11
Sutton, George C., view on building of Abraham Lincoln Memorial Hospital, 154
Swartz, M. W., 75
Sweet, Ossiah H., 156
Syphilis, 6, 111

Tammany Hall, 63, 64
black Tammany, 67
Tax-supported hospitals, integration of, 58–59
Teaching fellowships, for black professors, 123, 125
Third party payers, decline of black hospitals and, 193–94
Thomas, Joe T., 153–54, 161, 172
Thompkins, William J., 9
Training centers, 117
Truman, Harry S. (Pres.), 186
Tuberculosis, 109, 155
among African Americans, 175
black veterans with, after W.W.I, 72, 73, 74
Tuomey Hospital (Sumter, South Carolina), 114, 115
Tuskegee, Alabama, history of black hospitals in, xvii
Tuskegee Veterans Bureau Hospital, No. 91. *See* Tuskegee Veterans Hospital
Tuskegee Institute, 11, 70, 76, 106
Cadet Corp, 93

donation of land for Tuskegee Veterans Hospital, 77, 78
John A. Andrew Memorial Hospital, 79
Tuskegee Syphilis Study, 111, 220 n. 45
Tuskegee Veterans Hospital, 49, 58, 69, 70–104, 186. *See also* Consultants on Hospitalization and Veterans Bureau
backing of, by white community, 77
dedication of, 81
efforts for black control of, 71, 90
black community response to, 101
compromise in, 96–100
Ku Klux Klan response to, 92–94
racial tension resulting from, 35, 90–92
success in, 101–2
Veterans Bureau support of, 96
efforts to recruit African Americans, 84
white southern response to, 86
efforts for white control of, 76, 77, 80–82, 86, 88–89
African-American response to, 86–88, 89
black newspapers response to, 88–89
NAACP response to, 87, 88
establishment of
black veterans response to, 78–79
events leading to, 70–75
opposition to, 76–77
financial support for, 50
size of, 79–80
staffing of, 76–77, 78
violence, related to efforts for black control, 90–91
Typhoid, 109
Tyson, James, 20, 24

Underwood, Oscar W., 95
United Colored Democracy (New York), 63
U.S. Congress, 71, 73
passage of Hill-Burton Act, 186
U.S. Constitution
Fifth Amendment, 189, 190
Fourteenth Amendment, 189, 190
United States Public Health Service, 71, 72, 76
U.S. Supreme Court, 189
Brown v. Topeka Board of Education, 188
Eaton v. Grubbs, 189–90
Simkins v. Moses H. Cone Memorial Hospital, 188
University of Chicago
Billings Hospital, 133, 136
black medical students enrolled in, 1931–1938, 147
clinics, Provident Hospital attempt at affiliation with. *See* under Provident Hospital
indifference toward Provident Hospital Project, 149
University of Pennsylvania Hospital, 20
nurse training school, 22
University of Pennsylvania Medical School, xii, 20, 24
black students at, 165
relationship with Douglass Hospital, 32
University of West Tennessee College of Medicine and Surgery (Jackson), 37
Unthank, Thomas C., 8
direction of Kansas City General Hospital, No. 2 by, 10
Urban League (New York), 57

Vanderwall, Isabella, 30–31
Vanderbilt University School of Medicine (Nashville), 192
Vare, Edwin, 33
Veterans, black
hospital for. *See* Tuskegee Veterans Hospital
hospitalization of, after W.W.I, policy for, 74
response to establishment of Tuskegee Veterans Hospital, 78
vocational rehabilitation program for, 76
Veterans Administration, hospital system, segregation in, 185
Veterans Bureau
black physicians wanting to work in, 104
Tuskegee Veterans Hospital and, 84
efforts to recruit black personnel, 90
staffing by, 80, 81, 82
support of black control of, 96
support of white staff, 86
Veterans Bureau Hospital. *See* Tuskegee Veterans Hospital
Veterans hospitals
black, establishment of, 102–4
efforts to desegregate, 185–86
white, 75
Vincent, George, 108
Vincent, U. Conrad, 64
Virginia, medical schools in, General Education
Board funding of, 126, 127
Virginia Union University, 126
Vogel, Morris, xiii
Voluntary hospitals, 4
development of, 4

Walcott, William H. (Col.), 93
Walker, William O., support for construction of Forest City Hospital, 180
Walsh, William H., ad hoc Committee on Hospitalization of Colored People, 52
Walz, F. M., 171
Ward, John A., 49
Ward, Joseph H., 38
  professional activities of, 100–101
Warfield, William A., 167
Washington, Booker T., 37, 41, 70, 77, 87, 91, 107
  Atlanta Compromise speech, 37
  political ideology, related to establishment of black hospitals, 14
Washington, D.C., 6, 79
Washington, Margaret Murray, 91
Washington Tribune (newspaper), 97
Watts, Charles D., 191
Waverly Fraternal Hospital (Columbia, South Carolina), Duke Endowment Fund activities at, 120–21
Weekly Tribune, The (newspaper), 22, 23, 26
Weil, Walter, 178
Weiner, Robert E., 75
Welch, S. W., 75
Wesley, Nathaniel, 192
Wesley Long Community Hospital (Greensboro, North Carolina), 188
West, L. A., 42
Western Reserve University School of Medicine (Cleveland)
  involvement in integration of Cleveland City Hospital, 168
  Lakeside Hospital, 152
Wheatley Provident Hospital (Kansas City), 53. *See also* Perry Sanitarium
White, Charles W.
  opposition to creation of black hospital in Cleveland, 169
  support for construction of Forest City Hospital, 180
  view on appointment of Dr. McMorries to Cleveland City Hospital, 168
  view on Mercy Hospital Project, 161–62
White, George, 46, 47
White, Jacob C., Jr., 22
White, Walter F., 46, 92, 156
  criticism of NMA's efforts for establishment of black veterans hospitals, 103
  death of father, 46, 47
  reorganization of Harlem Hospital and, 63, 64
  Tuskegee Veterans Hospital and, 103
    support for black control of, 88, 98
White, William Charles, 72
  Tuskegee Veterans Hospital and, 74–75, 77, 79
    meeting with National Committee of Negro Veteran Relief related to, 78
    staffing of, 78
White Committee, Tuskegee Veterans Hospital and. *See* Consultants on Hospitalization
White community
  establishment of black hospitals by, 5, 7
  support of black hospitals, xv
    of Frederick Douglass Memorial Hospital and Training school, 24–25
    of Mercy Hospital Project, 159
White hospitals
  African-American views of, 13
  black units in, Rosenwald Fund support of, 113–14
White institutions, placement of African Americans in, Rosenwald Fund and, 110
White medical schools, graduates of African-American, 68
White philanthropic community
  control of black hospitals by, 128–29
  financial support for black hospitals, 105–30. *See also* Duke Endowment; General Education Board; Rosenwald Fund
    controversies related to, 129, 142
  industrial, 123
  paternalistic attitudes of, 126
White physicians
  as advisory committee for Lincoln Hospital, 119
  black physicians working under, 29, 113
  cutting of ties with black hospitals, 193
  late nineteenth century, 11–12
  resistance to hiring of black physicians, 113–14
  supervisory roles in black hospitals, 117, 126
    Lincoln Hospital and, 118
    in Provident Hospital, 140, 141–42
  support for creation of black hospital in Cleveland, 166–68
Whittaker Memorial Hospital (Newport News, Virginia), 12

Williams, Daniel Hale, 3, 61, 131, 132, 160, 172, 175
  establishment of Provident Hospital by, 15–16, 17–18
  feud with George Cleveland Hall, 18, 19
  personal biography, 16
  professional activities, 16, 18
  resignation from Provident Hospital, 18–19
  return to Provident Hospital, 18
Williams, Daniel, Jr., 16
Williams, Fannie Barrier, 15
Williams, Sarah, 16
Wilson, James L., 66
Wilson, Mary E., 23
Wilson, Woodrow (Pres.), 60, 71
Within Our Gates (play), 32–33
Wolters, Raymond L., 86
Woman's College (Montgomery, Alabama), 75
Women
  black, xvi
  contributions to black hospital movement, xiv
  physicians. *See* Physicians, women
Women's Medical College (Philadelphia), xii, 22
Woodson, Carter G., 44
Woodward, Frederic, 134
World War II
  black hospital population following, 183
  black nurses in armed forces during, 186
  decline in black hospital movement after, 184–85
Wright, Ceah, 59
Wright, Louis T., 57, 58, 62, 65
  black physicians hostility toward, 68
  civil rights activities, 61–62
  criticism of, 64, 68
  criticism of Provident Hospital Project, 144
  Manhattan Medical Society and, 65
  NAACP activities, 61
  personal biography, 59
  as president of North Harlem Medical Society, 66
  professional career, 59–61
  role in staff changes at Harlem Hospital, 63
  view of black hospitals, 63
Wright, Lulu, 59
Wye, Christopher, 171

Yale University, admission of black students to, 20
YMCAs, 18, 106
Young, Ralph, 58
Younge, Walter, 182

Zion Wesley African Methodist Episcopal Church (Philadelphia), 25